OXFORD STUDIES
IN THE
PRICE MECHANISM

OXFORD STUDIES

IN THE

PRICE MECHANISM

EDITED BY

T. WILSON

FELLOW OF UNIVERSITY COLLEGE, OXFORD

AND

P. W. S. ANDREWS

FELLOW OF NUFFIELD COLLEGE, OXFORD

OXFORD
AT THE CLARENDON PRESS

Oxford University Press, Amen House, London E.C. 4

GLASGOW NEW YORK TORONTO MELBOURNE WELLINGTON
BOMBAY CALCUTTA MADRAS CAPE TOWN

Geoffrey Cumberlege, Publisher to the University

FIRST PUBLISHED, 1951
REPRINTED, 1952

PRINTED IN GREAT BRITAIN

PREFACE

THIS collection of papers on the price-system consists partly of articles originally published in *Oxford Economic Papers* and partly of new essays.

The earlier issues of *Oxford Economic Papers* contained a number of articles which have now been accorded a place of some importance in recent economic literature. Unfortunately, because of war-time and other difficulties, these issues were small, and have been unobtainable for some time. The editors have therefore received suggestions that some of these articles should be reprinted, and the possibility of doing so was first considered when Mr. C. J. Hitch was General Editor. After he had left Oxford, it was finally decided to proceed with the project, and the editorial responsibility was undertaken jointly by us as, respectively, General Editor and Honorary Secretary to the Editorial Board.

It was decided that the best procedure would be to select a number of articles which dealt with important aspects of the price-system and to supplement them with some new essays which would indicate more recent developments in thought and practice. The task of selecting the older articles for reprinting was by no means easy, and we regret that it has been necessary to omit a number of interesting contributions.

We have been greatly assisted in our work as Editors by Professor R. S. Sayers, who advised us on the selection and editing of the older articles on the rate of interest, and by Mr. Herbert W. Robinson, who offered to summarize the pre-war Oxford studies of the mobility of labour which he had originally helped to prepare. Mr. Robinson's summary was read by Miss Helen Makower who made some valuable suggestions.

The important article on 'Price Theory and Business Behaviour' by Mr. R. L. Hall and Mr. C. J. Hitch has been reproduced in its entirety. It is followed by new essays by Mr. B. D. Giles and by Mr. Andrews which, although not directly related to the earlier study, deal with the same broad field. Professor Sayers, Professor A. J. Brown, and Mr. Robinson have contributed new essays on their respective topics, in which they develop and bring up to date the conclusions of the earlier studies. It will be appreciated, however, that the inevitable delays in preparing a book of the present kind make it impossible to keep pace with the accumulation of new material, and Professor Sayers has asked us to record that his fresh appraisal of the functions of the rate of interest was written at the beginning of 1949.

We must express our thanks to all these contributors and to the authors of the older articles who have allowed us to reprint their work. We are also most grateful to the other members of the Editorial Board of *Oxford Economic Papers*, who are not, however, responsible for this publication, and to the staff of the Clarendon Press for their patient co-operation and advice.

T. W.

P. W. S. A.

CONTENTS

INTRODUCTION

As the title of this book indicates, the essays of which it is composed are linked by a unity of interest. Each paper is concerned with some aspect of the price-system, and the topics discussed are relevant to the contemporary controversy about the respective merits of markets and plans. At the same time the title implies that a comprehensive survey has not been attempted, and the book is, in fact, more limited in scope than it would have been if a group of authors had been invited to co-operate in a study of the price-system as such. In compiling the book we have not tried to add yet another volume to the vast literature on the controversial issues of present-day policy; we have sought rather to present a collection of fairly detailed monographs on some of the basic problems which must be solved before a final verdict can be given.

The first chapter is concerned with the price of loans, or the rate of interest. For many years it has been recognized that this price—or, to be more accurate, this group of prices—does not operate with such unerring efficiency as to ensure monetary equilibrium, and it has even been suggested that it is of very little importance at all in influencing the decisions of either savers or borrowers. As far as the borrowers are concerned, this far-reaching scepticism has been greatly strengthened by the results of some research work carried out in the United States and by the outcome of the inquiry conducted by the Oxford Economists' Research Group before the war. (Doubts as to the effect of changes in the rate of interest on decisions to save are, of course, much older than this.)

Unfortunately, the earlier issues of *Oxford Economic Papers*, in which the Oxford inquiry was described, have been unobtainable for some time. Although the results have not, for that reason, been forgotten, the lack of ready access to the original articles has led occasionally either to their being dismissed on inadequate grounds, or—perhaps more often—to their being exaggerated and quoted without reference to the necessary qualifications. These articles have now been reprinted in a slightly abbreviated form and prefaced by a new survey written by Professor Sayers, in which the pre-war inquiry is brought into perspective.

Some commentators have complained that, since the rate of interest is such a weak weapon, the attention devoted to it by economists, including Keynes himself, has been altogether disproportionate. The matter cannot, however, be dismissed as easily as that. Even if it were true that business decisions had been affected to only a minor degree by changes in the price of loans, the effect would obviously have been more marked if the fluctuations in this price had been greater! Two questions must therefore be asked. First, what has prevented the rate of interest from varying to the extent required to preserve equilibrium ? Second, is it possible to remove these obstacles in the future ? These subjects have been studied and debated by economists for a century and a half, and the answers refer to banking policy, to the needs of the Exchequer, and to hoarding and dishoarding (or, in modern terms, 'liquidity preference' and 'speculation'). With these questions the Oxford inquiry was not directly concerned; its object was to discover whether the actual changes in the rate of interest had had much effect. Elsewhere, of course, Oxford economists contributed to the discussion of these wider topics, and, of the articles published in *Oxford Economic Papers*, we have selected an econometrical study by Professor Brown (Chapter I (iv)). (Reference should also be made to the work of Mr. M. Kalecki which is not represented in this volume because it has already been reproduced in book form.)

In his earlier writings Keynes shared the fairly general optimism about the possibility of making interest rates behave in a way in which they had manifestly not behaved in the past and of thus preserving equilibrium. But in *The General Theory of Employment, Interest and Money* he was more doubtful, and there is now a good deal of agreement that monetary measures alone will not suffice. Here, then, is a case where the adjustment of a price may not do the trick, and more direct control, perhaps exercised through the budget, seems to be required.

To say this does not, of course, imply complete scepticism about the usefulness of changes in interest rates; that is a further step and a much more doubtful one. In his new essay Professor Sayers expresses some concern over the recent tendency to extend the argument in this way and seeks to correct the bias by reminding the reader that 'the efficacy of the rate of interest has changed and will go on changing continuously, some forces tending to dull its edge, while others sharpen it'. After all, although the rate of interest may not be capable of doing everything, it may be capable of doing something which cannot be done so well by other means.

The next chapter of the book is concerned with another price of great importance, the rate of exchange. Admittedly this was a price which, in the traditional theory of the price-system, was not supposed to be varied; for that theory usually assumed that a gold standard was in operation, and any necessary adjustments to the balance of payments were to be made in other ways. During the inter-war period, however, ideas began to change, and the rigidity of the gold standard was strongly criticized. There is, of course, no painless method of correcting an unfavourable balance of payments, but it was hoped that the pain might at least be less severe if the rate of exchange were varied; and it was suggested that, in this way, a country might be able to achieve, if not independence, at least rather more autonomy than was possible under the gold standard.

Is it certain, however, that this new price-policy will produce the right results ? A change in price may not always restore equilibrium in a market ; in certain conditions, when the reactions are perverse, the position may even be worsened. In an important article, published in the sixth number of *Oxford Economic Papers* (Old Series) and now reprinted as the first part of Chapter II, Professor Brown describes the conditions with regard to the elasticities of demand and supply which must be satisfied at home and abroad if the outcome of an alteration in the rate of exchange is to be satisfactory. The author also refers to multiplier effects and introduces some discussion of capital movements and of such barriers to trade as import quotas. Towards the end, the article becomes less formal, and Professor Brown makes some suggestions about the possible effects of a change in the value of the pound. If the theoretical analysis is far from easy, the attempt to provide an empirical content must meet further difficulties, and only very tentative conclusions can be reached.

Naturally enough, there has been a difference of opinion as to what can be achieved by changes in the rate of exchange, and there has been some tendency since the war to react against the new philosophy of adjusting the external value of a currency and to favour, not indeed a return to the gold standard with classical freedom of trade, but a policy of fairly rigid exchange rates coupled with the use of import- and exchange-controls of one kind or another. Professor Brown's new article in the second part of this chapter is, therefore, of considerable interest. He sets out to summarize and appraise the factual material which has now been accumulated, and although he is rightly cautious, there is some guarded optimism in his con- clusions. (Of course, it is one thing to argue that an adjustment of exchange rates is likely to foster the achievement of equilibrium, but a very different matter to suggest that this method alone should be used in practice.)

The rate of interest and the rate of exchange are prices which may be expected to affect most of the economy in a greater or lesser degree, and it has become fashionable to describe that part of economics which deals with such topics as 'macrocosmic'. In the next three chapters, however, the analysis is more concerned with the operational units of the economy and relates to the behaviour of the individual firm or industry. A price- economy may have no explicit production plan; the output which it achieves will in any case be the result of decisions taken independently by countless individuals. A coherent pattern can, nevertheless, emerge, and several generations of economists have sought to explain the working of the 'invisible hand' by which this result is achieved. That it does work is undeniable, but there is no guarantee that it will work satisfactorily. Firms may not make the 'right' response to a change in circumstances, and the composition of output may be so distorted by monopolistic imperfections as to impair the efficiency of the whole system. Whereas it was the concern of the earlier economists to trace the pattern underlying the competitive price-system, the economists of the nineteen-thirties laid much more stress on the possible defects. The traditional accounts of a competitive order thus came to be replaced by the new theories of imperfect, or monopolistic, competition—with the emphasis on the adjective rather than the noun.

At the same time, the analysis of business behaviour began to relate much less to industries and larger social units; indeed, it was finally argued that the old analysis of industrial equilibrium should be jettisoned altogether. It was, however, still generally assumed that the behaviour of the individual firm could be explained with reasonable precision by means of the traditional marginal analysis. If competition were imperfect, the equilibrium position might not be satisfactory from the social point of view, but there would, at least, be some such position of rest towards which the firm would tend to move. Gradually, however, these tidy theories of the firm came to be threatened from two sides: on realistic grounds it was objected that the assumptions of 'marginal' analysis were unsatisfactory in themselves; on a more theoretical plane, it was alleged with increasing frequency that oligopolistic conditions could no longer be regarded as so rare as to give rise to no more than a relatively unimportant special case, and such conditions were notoriously difficult to handle in a satisfactory manner with the usual analytical tools.

One of the best-known contributions to this debate was made by Mr. R. L. Hall and Mr. C. J. Hitch in the article on 'Price Theory and Business Behaviour' which has been out of print for years and is now reproduced as Chapter III of the present volume. This article, which was the second major result of the inquiries of the pre-war Oxford Economists' Research Group, should be regarded from two aspects. First, it presents the information accumulated by the Research Group which suggests that business men often base their price-quotations upon 'full cost', with a consequent tendency for the prices so determined to be relatively stable. In the time which has elapsed since the original publication of this article, these results have become widely accepted and have in themselves led to considerably greater realism in economic discussion. Second, there is the economic theory which the authors construct in the light of these facts. By modifying the theory already developed to deal with monopolistic competition, the authors introduce the notion of a 'kinked' demand curve, to explain geometrically the stability of market price under oligopolistic conditions.

The process of revising the theories of the firm and of the industry, in which the article by Mr. Hall and Mr. Hitch played an important part, is still going on, and it is a little early, perhaps, to try to draw conclusions about the outcome of the debate. Partly because of the war, a lot of the discussion is very recent and the issues are still confused. But it is at least of interest to note that the new orthodoxy of the nineteen-thirties has itself come under heavy fire.

Chapter IV is a new essay by Mr. Andrews, whose industrial researches have recently led to relevant conclusions in this field. In it Mr. Andrews reviews the development of business theory since Marshall and goes on to develop his own views. Marshall's industrial analysis tended to be thrown overboard because it appeared to be inconsistent with the theory of the individual firm as it was developed before the war. Mr. Andrews pleads for a restatement of this older orthodoxy and puts alongside it a theory of the firm which seems to him to be consistent both with it and with the results of factual research. The reader is reminded that, although competition may rarely be 'perfect' in the special sense defined in pre-war theory, it may, nevertheless, be a powerful and useful force in determining industrial development.

Whatever difficulties may be encountered in other sectors of the economy, it may appear at first sight that agriculture is an industry to which the theories of the inter-war years can be applied with confidence. In this case, the tiresome complications of oligopoly should not arise, and competition should be sufficiently perfect to provide an example of the price-system operating under the most favourable circumstances. Yet, in practice, agriculture is beset by at least as many difficulties as any other industry. The explanation of this apparent discrepancy is not difficult to find: the theory of the text-books is largely 'static' and when the special assumptions, such as that of perfect foresight, are removed, the discussion must proceed on somewhat different lines.

The economist who is not a specialist in this field has little time to study the voluminous literature on agriculture, most of which is written from a technical rather than an economic point of view. Mr. B. D. Giles has, therefore, performed a useful service by adding to the comparatively small number of economic studies of the subject, and his essay on 'Agriculture and the Price Mechanism' is published below as Chapter V. The large amount of factual material which he has managed to summarize is related as far as possible to the hypotheses of price-theory, and some attention is also devoted to the problems of state intervention.

The last chapter deals with the response of labour to economic incentives. As the author, Mr. Herbert W. Robinson, observes, the 'adjustment of the supply of labour in different occupations and in different areas to correct disequilibria presents, perhaps, the most difficult of all the problems of optimum economic change'. How are such adjustments brought about in a free economy where the movement of labour is not enforced or controlled ? And if liberty is sacrificed, how effective in practice is the alternative policy of state regulation ?

In the years 1936–9, a group of research workers at the Oxford University Institute of Statistics set out 'to reduce mobility of labour to a measurable quantity in order to discover, on a scientific basis, the variations in the response of labour to economic incentives at different times, in different places, and among different people'. The description of this inquiry, which was given in several articles in *Oxford Economic Papers* (Old Series) and in the *Sociological Review*, was too long and too detailed to be reprinted in full, and Mr. Robinson felt it would be more satisfactory to write a summary than to attempt the difficult task of pruning the original material. This summary has been published as the first part of the chapter, and naturally it relates to pre-war conditions. In the second part, Mr. Robinson discusses the lessons of man-power policy during the war and comments on the difficulties of the post-war economy, where direct control is no longer attempted but the pre-war incentives have ceased to operate with their old force.

Enough has been said to indicate the scope and limitations of the book, but some further reference must be made in conclusion to the Oxford Economists' Research Group and the Institute of Statistics. With the exception of Professor Brown's paper which forms the first part of Chapter II, the older papers reprinted here were all based on work carried out or sponsored by one or other of these organizations. The first was an informal body set up in 1935 to promote co-operative research. The second, also established in 1935, was an official body designed as a University centre for statistical and other research in applied economics and equipped with a library and other facilities. Sir Hubert Henderson was the first Chairman of the Research Group and was succeeded by Mr. R. F. Harrod; Professor J. Marschak was Director of the Institute until the outbreak of war. Both bodies were assisted in their early work by a grant from the Rockefeller Foundation.

The two organizations worked in close contact with each other, and it was not surprising that both were mainly interested in the problems of unemployment and the trade cycle which occupied the attention of so many economists at the time. The Institute of Statistics sponsored several projects in this field of which the study of labour mobility (Chapter VI (i)) was one. The Research Group itself sponsored other work which is not represented here; but since this is scarcely the place to attempt a general survey of economic research at Oxford, attention will be confined to the methods employed by the Group itself in carrying out those projects for which it was directly responsible. Unfortunately these methods have not always been fully understood outside Oxford, and there has been some tendency to discount unduly the results obtained.

The Group decided to make a special study of the forces influencing business activity over the trade cycle, and question-papers were prepared to guide and discipline its proceedings. The Group then invited a number of business men to join its meetings and to submit to intensive questioning about their own experiences. The Group did not, therefore, rely simply upon written answers to a questionnaire; that method was used only at a later stage when it was decided to subject to a further test the results reached by the more intensive method. At each meeting the information was obtained by prolonged and detailed discussion, and the implications of question and answer were carefully scrutinized. The conclusions were then embodied in a report which was submitted to the business man concerned for correction or further elucidation. After much discussion of these reports, articles were written by particular members of the Group which described the methods and commented upon the significance of the results.

The difficulties and limitations of this method of research are obvious enough. It was impossible to deal with a large number of cases when the intensive method was used; alternatively, when a bigger sample was obtained by inviting written answers to a questionnaire, there was the danger that the results in each case would be less reliable. Nevertheless, it can, I think, be claimed that the method proved to be a useful one, and provided the qualifications are borne in mind, the conclusions may be deemed valuable and significant. The reader will, however, find an adequate description of the techniques in Chapters I and III, and will be able to form his own opinion about their worth.

T. W.

UNIVERSITY COLLEGE
July, 1950

I

THE RATE OF INTEREST

(i) *The Rate of Interest as a Weapon of Economic Policy*

By R. S. SAYERS

In the second of the inter-war decades Oxford had at least its fair share of the rising generation of English economists, and the outlook and interest of these economists were fairly reflected in the early issues of the *Oxford Economic Papers*. These economists in no sense formed a 'school of thought': they were drawn from surprisingly varied sources and had scarcely had time to do more than understand and explain work originating in the older homes of economic thought. But to suppose that they were content to find illumination in traditional doctrine would be a grave injustice: they were also keenly interested in putting traditional doctrine to the test of practical experience and in arriving at practical maxims for economic policy. It was inevitable, in this atmosphere, that dissatisfaction with the literature on the rate of interest should lead to discussion and factual inquiry: an attempt to provide a sounder basis for economic policy. The five papers here reproduced as subsequent sections of this chapter can be regarded as progress reports on this discussion.[1]

The purpose of the present paper is to explain the setting in the history of thought on the subject of the reprinted papers which follow and to review subsequent developments. I do not pretend here to write a complete history of thought: rather this is a 'sample' review designed to bring out the main turning-points on those problems which formed the particular subject of 'the Oxford inquiry'. Similarly in reviewing the present state of the debate I have not attempted to be exhaustive but only to illustrate by summarizing the position taken by certain outstanding authorities. (Many other writers have made useful contributions and I trust that they will not misunderstand the absence of a comprehensive review.) Then in conclusion I offer a few disjointed comments on aspects which have not yet, I think, received sufficient attention.

The belief that changes in the rate of interest powerfully influence economic activity reached its high-water mark in Keynes's *Treatise on Money* (1930).[2] Looking back now, I am astonished at the confidence and

---

[1] I should perhaps add that I myself was too late an arrival to share in the main inquiry: it was only when all the material was collected that I saw the results for the purpose of writing the review which is reproduced on pp. 67–74 below.

[2] See especially pp. 200–9 in vol. i. My quotations are all taken from these pages.

simplicity of Keynes's argument at the critical points. The argument turned, it will be remembered, on the power of the rate of interest to upset the balance between the value of investment and saving. Both quantities were affected, Keynes argued, though he believed the effect on saving to be often 'quantitatively small in practice, especially over the short period'. The more sensitive quantity, Keynes obviously believed, was the value of investment. The demand price for capital goods depended on two things: 'on the estimated net prospective yield from fixed capital (estimated by the opinion of the market after such allowance as they choose to make for the uncertainty of anticipation, &c.), measured in money, and on the rate of interest at which this future yield is capitalised.' The connexion with bank rate is therefore 'immediate, direct, and obvious'. Keynes went on to show how the organization of the capital market tends to accentuate the effect of interest-rate movements, there being abnormal difficulty (if bank rate has risen) or abnormal ease (if bank rate has fallen) 'for new borrowers to float their wares at a price approximating to the prices quoted in the market for existing loans'.

This clear argument is qualified[1] by phrases which I believe logically cover all the substantial reservations that subsequent writers have developed at length. What distinguishes Keynes's treatment from that of later writers is that his qualifications are so introduced as to leave the reader with the decided view that the qualifications do not upset the conclusions for practical purposes. There will be, he says:

'a decided effect on the rate at which producers of capital goods will be able to find buyers for their products at a satisfactory price, even if the change in the rate is believed to be a short-period fluctuation; and all the more so, for other and more obvious reasons, if the change is expected to last. At least this will be the case unless the rise in the market rate of interest . . . is compensated by a simultaneous rise, for other reasons, in the estimated prospective yield of fixed capital. Only if the higher rate merely offsets market optimism about the prospective yield of new fixed capital, will the change be without direct effect on the output of capital goods. Thus, generally speaking (i.e. unless the change in bank rate happens to be balanced by other contemporary changes), we may expect . . .'

and so on: all valid enough, but certainly calculated—as was the rest of the book—to lead the reader to suppose that the rate of interest was a powerful contra-cyclical weapon.

By 1936, when *The General Theory of Employment, Interest and Money* appeared, Keynes had changed his position substantially. Not that the revolutionary innovations of *The General Theory* entered this particular field. Actually Keynes did not in this book go at all systematically into the effects of changes in the rate of interest. The title of the most relevant chapter is itself symptomatic: 'The State of Long-Term Expectation.' In

---

[1] Particularly on p. 204.

this chapter Keynes let himself go, in his most exhilarating manner, on the way speculators work, given 'the extreme precariousness of the basis of knowledge on which our estimates of prospective yield have to be made'. Against this chapter, in which Keynes writes as one who knows how to make a fortune by speculation (which, after all, he did), the parallel passages of the *Treatise* read almost as the product of the classroom. The conclusion is certainly very different, for practical purposes, from the impression left in the *Treatise*: at the end of the chapter he says[1]

'. . . we are still entitled to return to the latter [the rate of interest] as exercising, at any rate, in normal circumstances, a great, though not a decisive, influence on the rate of investment. Only experience, however, can show how far management of the rate of interest is capable of continuously stimulating the appropriate volume of investment. For my own part I am now somewhat sceptical of a merely monetary policy directed towards influencing the rate of interest.'

In the years which elapsed between the Macmillan Report and the *Treatise on Money* on the one hand and the *General Theory* on the other, this change of position on the part of Keynes himself had been shared by many other economists, at least in Britain. This swing was perhaps the natural reaction from the enthusiasm evoked by the first systematic analysis of the part played by the rate of interest in the trade cycle. A more careful sifting of assumption and argument led to more cautious views on the efficacy of the interest rate as a regulator of economic activity. But the change was also partly due to the seeming slowness of response to the cheap-money policy pursued in Britain from mid-1932 onwards and in America from a slightly later date. 'Cheap money' had been introduced in Britain primarily because it was cheap to the Exchequer: the Treasury had been looking for opportunity to convert the 1929–47 War Loan from its 5 per cent. basis, and lower interest rates for the rentier had an equitable appeal when the policy of the National Government was 'cuts all round'.[2] That it appealed to theorists and business men as an anti-depression stroke was a purely incidental advantage. Then, having been introduced for Exchequer reasons—and pressed home by a Treasury unusually quick to see how the implications of depression might be exploited—the cheap money policy was retained as an anti-slump weapon. Business revival was, however, painfully slow. Although we can now, by inspection of the statistics, perceive that the upturn came about the middle of 1932, and that there was a decided spurt throughout 1933, it was not so easy to be sure at the time that a lasting and general recovery was in progress. Throughout 1934 and even in 1935 the margin of unemployed and under-employed

---

[1] On p. 164.
[2] The logical basis of this policy is to be found in the McKenna–Keynes–Bevin Addendum to the Macmillan Report (pp. 190 et seq. of Cmd. 3897 of 1931).

resources continued to be very wide, and when the revival had, as we can
now see, already gone a long way people in this country were still apt to
think of the depression as something that had been dragging on for years
and was still dragging on. In these circumstances it was natural that, while
the success of more specific remedies—such as import tariffs—might be
descried, the efficacy of so general and imprecise a remedy as cheap money
was widely doubted. Academic economists, already inclining to scepticism,
were particularly strongly infected by these doubts. Their position was
very clearly stated in Sir Hubert Henderson's article, reprinted here practically as it appeared in October 1938 in the first number of the *Oxford
Economic Papers*. In this article he analysed the effects of changes in the
rate of interest, explained how the first 'Oxford inquiry' came about, and
commented on the results of the close questioning of business men. The
results themselves were analysed in the paper by Messrs. J. E. Meade and
P. W. S. Andrews, in the same issue of the *Oxford Economic Papers* (extracts
from which are reprinted below). They were on the whole negative, in the
sense that most of the business men denied that their activities had been,
or were likely to be, directly affected in any way by changes in interest
rates, though it is notable that some of the majority 'witnesses' none the
less 'held the view that the rate of interest is an important factor in the
economic situation for reasons not easy to ascertain'. The availability of
liquid resources appeared, from the business men's answers, to loom larger
than the rate of interest in the making of decisions about investment.[1]
This was also brought out in the econometrical article by A. J. Brown,
published in the second issue of the *Oxford Economic Papers* (May 1939)
and reproduced below (pp. 31–51).

In this first investigation the number of firms covered was very small
and, it was feared, biased in consisting only of prosperous firms in a strong
financial position. The Oxford Economists' Research Group thought that
the results obtained in this first round were sufficiently important to justify
more extensive and more systematic inquiry, and in 1939 some 1,300
firms were asked to reply to a very brief and simple questionnaire. The
procedure adopted is described at the beginning of the article by Mr.
Andrews, which appeared in No. 3 of *Oxford Economic Papers* early in
1939. Mr. Andrews there analysed the replies and gave a summary of the
comments which 209 firms gave in response to an invitation to supplement

---

[1] Looking back after eleven years, Professor Meade comments as follows: 'What seems
to have been overlooked is the extent to which our interviews were confined to risky
manufacturing or commercial business, where one would expect the rate of interest to have
the least effect because the 'risk premium' is everything. Things may be very different in
e.g. housing, railway electrification, &c., &c., and these may account for a very large part
of total investment. Nor, reading through the answers again, does it appear to me to be
reasonable to conclude that the direct and *indirect* (e.g. liquidity) effects of a change in
the rate of interest are negligible even in the field which we did cover.'

their replies to the questionnaire. On pp. 51–67 below there is reproduced the whole of the article by Mr. Andrews with the exception of the summary of comments (which occupied 22 pages of small type). Mr. Andrews's analysis of the comments is included in our reprint (pp. 64–67 below). At the same time (in No. 3 of *Oxford Economic Papers*) I wrote a short article on the upshot of the whole inquiry. This, except a paragraph about war finance, is reproduced below (pp. 67–74). My broad conclusion was that 'the potency of that weapon [the rate of interest] in a constantly changing world must, I think, be described as very low'. I also emphasized that both stages of the inquiry had borne out 'the relevance to a firm's expansion policy of the firm's internal resources', but concluded that the banking system could do little to influence this by varying the amount of 'idle money' in existence. In general, I concluded, 'the evidence warns us not to expect the instruments of banking policy—particularly the rate of interest—to do more than help us in the right direction. Banking policy is not enough.'

Meanwhile publication of the first stage of the Oxford inquiry had prompted a Harvard economist, Mr. J. Franklin Ebersole, to look over the 'business cases' accumulated by the Harvard Graduate School of Business Administration since December 1920, to see what light these cases might throw on the attitude of American business men towards rate of interest changes. Mr. Ebersole's results are given in his article 'The Influence of Interest Rates upon Entrepreneurial Decisions in Business—a Case Study', in the *Harvard Business Review*, autumn 1938 (xvii. 1).

In the Harvard files there were in all 13,119 cases. These had been gathered by trained field-men carrying proper introductions. But none of them had been designed to throw light on the interest problem, nor had the field-men been properly briefed on it. A very large proportion of the cases was therefore of no help at all. Five hundred and ninety-one cases were picked out as most likely to be of use, on the basis of the indexing, and of a further 1,637 less likely cases a sample of one-tenth was picked out. Of the total examined, only 93 'involved entrepreneurial problems of the type in which interest rates might have been a factor': of these, 63 did not mention it, and 30 did. Mr. Ebersole's summary of these thirty cases must be quoted in full: there were

'twenty in which it was not a factor contributing to the decision whether or not to expand or contract, and only ten in which the interest rate, or cost of capital funds, was recognized as a factor in the making of the decision. Of the ten cases in which interest rate was a factor, not one case was found in which it was either the sole or the decisive factor.'

To this investigation Mr. Ebersole added an inquiry as to how much mention of interest rates was made in classes of the Harvard Business

School in 1936–7, since the distribution of time in these classes, conducted by instructors in close touch with business men, should reflect in some measure the thoughts uppermost in the minds of business men. Here again the upshot was almost completely negative; and on the basis of the two inquiries Mr. Ebersole concluded that

'there is a strong presumption, which should be verified by more elaborate tests of fact by the case method, favouring the thesis that: The rate of interest is not viewed as an important problem by business management; the interest rate is seldom considered as a factor in the entrepreneurial decisions of business to expand or contract, and is a controlling factor in a negligible number of instances.'[1]

These empirical studies have, since economists resumed their peace-time interests, been the subject of penetrating comment both in America and in Britain. More strictly, I should say that the comments have been on the 'first stage' of the Oxford inquiry, because the second stage, the results of which were not published until Britain was at war, does not appear to have been noticed much outside Oxford.[2] But I do not think wider knowledge of the second stage would have made a great difference to the subsequent discussions: writers would perhaps have accepted the fact that the more extensive second stage provided confirmation of the earlier results, while the general tenor of their comments would have been unaffected.

This is, I am sure, true of Professor Machlup's article 'Marginal Analysis and Empirical Research' in the *American Economic Review*, September 1946. This article is mainly about the relations between marginal costs, average costs and prices, and between wages and output, and in it Professor Machlup is very critical of the Hall–Hitch researches, reprinted elsewhere in this volume.[3] He does not mention the parallel Oxford inquiry about the rate of interest, but one of his general arguments is highly relevant. He points out that in this uncertain world entrepreneurs are faced by an 'extreme difficulty of calculating' and that their decisions are necessarily based largely on factors not measured—or, indeed, measurable. The *explanation* of a business man's action, he argues, 'must often include steps of reasoning which the acting individual himself does not *consciously* perform (because the action has become routine) and which perhaps he would never be *able* to perform in scientific exactness (because such exactness is

[1] As regards his first inquiry, Mr. Ebersole emphasized that 'there is the inevitable doubt as to the ability of the field-men to discover or interpret, and of the business executives to recognize and describe, the bases of their decisions and actions'.

[2] The third issue of the *Oxford Economic Papers* had an unusually limited circulation. In the American literature references to Henderson's and Meade's and Andrewes's articles in the first issue are common, but I have noticed none at all to the articles in the third issue. I also happen to know that at least some of the contributors (British as well as American) to the post-war discussions were, when they wrote, completely unaware of the second stage of the Oxford inquiry.

[3] See pp. 107 et seq.

not necessary in everyday life)'.[1] Similar doubts have evidently troubled Professor Robertson. In a recent lecture[2] he said:

'Much attention has been attracted in recent years by certain enquiries in which business men professed that the rate of interest had little or no influence on their decisions. I wonder if they *really* meant that, or if they merely meant that sizing up the whole situation, they often decide in a different direction from that in which the rate of interest, if it were the only factor, would point.'

Before I offer any comment, I must refer to the general position adopted in the last few years by four leading authorities. First there is a very important article by Professor F. A. Lutz, on 'The Interest Rate and Investment in a Dynamic Economy' in the *American Economic Review*, December 1945. This refers to the Oxford inquiry (first stage) and seeks a theoretical basis for the broadly negative conclusions of that inquiry. His conclusions[3] are that (1) short rates are unlikely to influence inventories; (2) long rates are unlikely to influence investment decisions in manufacturing industry; (3) 'under certain circumstances, a change in the (long-term) interest rate may affect investment decisions in the area of public utilities (including railroads) and residential construction'; and (4) changes in interest may affect the readiness of financial institutions to grant credit or to float bonds or stocks 'so that the interest rate may influence the volume of investment even without changing the profit calculations of entrepreneurs'. These conclusions are very much those of Sir Hubert Henderson, in his 1938 article, save that the fourth was not made by Henderson: it had, however, been made in a narrower way by Keynes in the *Treatise*.[4] But in the detailed arguments by which he reaches these old conclusions Professor Lutz has many penetrating passages on the relation between business decisions and the availability of capital. For example, in analysing the effects of interest changes on the demand for durable production goods, he argues that in most branches of manufacturing industry a constant stream of inventions causes the obsolescence factor to swamp the interest factor, while in public utilities 'the rate of technical progress, and therefore the importance of inventions, is probably smaller'. Also, many companies 'base their calculations on some "normal" rate of return which is considered appropriate to their industry, a rate which is independent of the movements of the long-term market rate'—though the entrepreneur's 'normal' standard is likely

---

[1] Quotation from his pp. 534–5.

[2] The lecture can be read in *The Three Banks Review*, Mar. 1949 (the passage quoted above appears on p. 20). For Professor Robertson's views on the whole subject the reader should also refer to the 1948 edition of his *Money*, Chapter X, § 6.

[3] See his p. 830.

[4] pp. 203–4 of vol. i. Another useful American discussion of this varying availability of loan capital is in Henry C. Wallich's article 'The Changing Significance of the Interest Rate', in the *American Economic Review*, Dec. 1946. The article refers to 'The Great Disillusionment' of the Oxford inquiry and Ebersole's article, and it is much affected by the Stagnation Thesis.

in course of time to be revised to match an apparently lasting change in market rates. As public utilities depend more closely on the organized capital markets than does the general run of manufacturing industry, one would expect, on this ground alone, that public utilities would be more sensitive to market-rate changes.[1]

Secondly, there is Mr. Harrod's discussion in his lectures, published under the title *Towards a Dynamic Economics*.[2] Mr. Harrod is mainly concerned with the long-term problems of a dynamic economy, but his discussion of contra-cyclical policy begins with 'a negative point of cardinal importance', namely, that 'variations in the rate of interest will not play an important part in our contra-cyclical armoury'.[3] In an earlier passage[4] he examines the relation between the rate of interest and the supply of saving and comes to a conclusion which is indefinite as to direction and depends too much on slow-moving forces to be of any real importance for contra-cyclical policy. As to investment Mr. Harrod rejects the Hawtrey doctrine about the sensitiveness of inventories to the short-term rate, using arguments which have been made familiar by Keynes and many subsequent writers; and he mentions the testimony of 'The chorus of merchants and traders and producers'. Following the elegant article[5] by Mr. G. L. S. Shackle in the *Economic Journal* (March 1946), Mr. Harrod thinks that though the demand for capital may eventually be more responsive than it is immediately to changes in the interest rate, we should not 'expect a very great increase of capital outlay in the period immediately following a change in the long-term rate of interest'. His more important point is that anyway the long-term rate of interest cannot be useful as a contra-cyclical weapon because it cannot be moved 'up and down by substantial amounts within the ambit of the cycle'.[6]

To this point the tide has been running pretty strongly against the old idea that the rate of interest is an important weapon by which a monetary economy might be kept on the rails. But lately two leading economists have expressed favour for a revival of control by the rate of interest. Professor J. E. Meade, in *Planning and the Price Mechanism*,[7] pleads for more

[1] I should emphasize that Professor Lutz's illumination of the subject is not by any means confined to the points referred to in the last three sentences: I have merely picked out as examples two points that struck me as particularly interesting and I believe novel. I am well aware that I have done scant justice to an article one of the merits of which is its systematic coverage of the whole problem.

[2] Macmillan (London), 1948. The lectures were given in the University of London.

[3] Ibid., pp. 117 et seq.   [4] Lecture Two.

[5] 'Interest Rates and the Pace of Investment.' Mr. Shackle's analysis develops on a high level of abstraction, arguments that are fundamentally similar to those of Sir Hubert Henderson's article of 1938 (pp. 16–27 below).

[6] Mr. Shackle concluded (op. cit., p. 17) 'that *historically* the movements of the long-term interest rate in Britain have seldom been rapid or abrupt enough to constitute appreciable changes of circumstance, or to engage the entrepreneurs' conscious attention as such'.

[7] Allen and Unwin, 1948.

use of the price mechanism in controlling the economic system and for revival, as part of the price mechanism, of the rate of interest as an anti-inflation weapon. He argues that a higher rate of interest would influence both sides of the demand-supply equation: it would discourage consumption-spending by property owners and it would ease the problem of restricting investment. In particular, he argues that a high rate of interest would encourage 'Mend-and-make-Do' in industrial equipment until the immediate pressure dies down. He shows awareness[1] of the difficulty of securing very sharp changes in the long-term rate of interest, but does not appear to regard them as insuperable (as does Mr. Harrod).[2] Then lately Professor Robertson,[3] while not making such precise proposals as Professor Meade, has expressed grave doubts about the wisdom of 'putting the rate of interest in chains' and has pleaded 'for some sustained re-thinking in academic circles'. Like Professor Meade, he suggests that both sides of the equation are likely to be sensitive. Referring to the argument of Cassel that the rate of interest is related to the length of human life he argues that decumulation is greatly encouraged by the extraordinarily low interest rates lately prevailing. Secondly, he argues that capital outlay may be reasonably sensitive to changes in the interest rate. Then he adds a third argument which has not, I believe, appeared elsewhere: under earlier monetary arrangements 'it was fairly evident to everybody that if an exorbitant level of wage-rates was demanded, the money would simply not be there to pay the wage-bill', but if monetary authorities are determined to keep the rate of interest down, there is no monetary check to a wage inflation forced by Trade Unions in full-employment conditions, and the monetary authorities 'have in effect abdicated from exercising that sovereignty over the standard of value which we thought we had committed to their charge'.[4]

And so the debate continues. Where angels have so trodden on each others' feet it is not for me to attempt to close the debate—much less to deliver a confident judgement! But I do want, before closing this paper, to make a few comments on certain particular aspects of the problem.

First a small point. The reader will already have noticed that some contemporary authorities lay considerable stress on the sensitiveness of saving to changes in the rate of interest. In formulating the argument, they almost

[1] pp. 31 et seq.
[2] Professor Meade's substitute—variable taxation of capital goods if sufficient variation of the rate of interest is impracticable—would make every hair of the Inland Revenue Commissioners stand on end.
[3] In *The Three Banks Review*, Mar. 1949.
[4] Professor Robertson does not pursue all the broad implications of this, but I imagine that he would agree that an economy in which people ceased to believe in reasonable stability of the standard of value would quickly cease to have any room for private enterprise.

invariably write of the effect of successive interest rate reductions in encouraging people *to live on their capital*. In this they are followed by a great
number of popular writers on economic subjects: it can almost be said that
contemporary writers are obsessed by the phenomenon of personal capital
decumulation. This was not always so. When I was first studying economics, twenty years or so ago, economists, bankers, and their like used
to speak of the effect of interest *in stimulating saving*. The basic arguments
were, of course, the same, but I cannot help thinking that the contrast in
expression is significant. In the nineteen-twenties interest rates were some
2 per cent. higher than they are nowadays, and personal dissaving was
the exception: now it seems rather to be all too common. It is perfectly
true that increase in taxation of property has altered the position almost
beyond recognition, but may it not also be true that the fall in interest
rates has had something to do with the greater readiness with which the
phrase 'decumulation of capital' slips off our tongues and pens?

Secondly, the arguments of the academic economists are all too apt to
overlook the very great imperfections of the capital market. More or less
implicitly they assume that a firm's lending rate of interest is the same—or
almost the same—as its borrowing rate;[1] that the rates at which capital
can be obtained by various borrowers are, if not identical, at least only so
differentiated by (implicitly measurable) uncertainty factors that all rates
can be assumed to move together; and that a change in the availability of
capital shows itself only in changes in interest rates. In a world in which
the disposition of capital is necessarily linked with personal risks these
assumptions are fantastically remote from reality—even in countries whose
capital markets are most highly developed. It is necessary to consider the
implications of removal of each one of these assumptions.

Even for very large firms it cannot be assumed that borrowing rates and
lending rates are identical. Unless it takes business risks alien to its main
business, a firm cannot temporarily 'invest' its liquid resources except at
the relatively low rates obtainable on bank deposits or very short bonds.
Consequently if the firm already has liquid resources, even a very sharp
rise in interest rates will not deter the firm from capital outlay that previously appeared profitable. The smaller the firm, the wider is the gap
between its lending rates and its borrowing rates, and therefore the more
completely will its capital outlay programme be ruled by the liquidity of
its assets rather than by outside movements in interest rates. Hence the
importance which business men attach to their internal liquid assets, when
they are asked about the determination of their capital outlay.[2]

Secondly, it is tempting to assume that interest rates for different bor-

---

[1] This assumption is implicit in, for example, much of Professor Meade's argument.
[2] Cf. above, p. 4.

rowers are, if not the same, at least related to each other in some regular way. I doubt whether the actual range of effective rates is realized. In England at present bank loans are available to large firms at, say, 3 to 4 per cent., and to small firms at, say, 4 to 5 per cent., and in the United States the range is not much wider. Yet there is in both countries a large amount of credit outstanding at altogether higher rates—for example, hire purchase finance at double these rates, and merchants' credits to buyers on very varied, ill-defined, and often very onerous terms. Because loans are necessarily tied to the uncertainties of individual businesses, widely different interest rates can be—and are—charged to particular borrowers. Borrowers do not all go to the banks, because they can offer no satisfactory security, or are already using bank loans up to the bankers' maxima, or are unwilling to let the bankers sufficiently into the firm's secrets. Moreover, the extent to which a firm is willing to *borrow* at all is limited by its reluctance to commit itself to fixed money payments,[1] and beyond this limit (which itself varies according to the state of business expectations) the firm is willing to add to its capital only by the issue of shares. The difficulty of selling shares varies greatly, especially as between large firms and small firms. Paradoxically enough, the growth of organized security markets has increased the discrepancy—because it has become easy for the 'outside' investor to confine his interest to the companies whose names are household words. A dividend prospect may well have to be 'actuarially' three times as good for the small firm as for the giant if it is to have an equal chance of adding to its equity capital.[2] Now these differences—between loan rates and between 'dividend prospect' rates too—would not upset the economists' argument, if it could be assumed that they merely represented risk valuations made by many lenders (including potential share purchasers) whose money was transferable from one borrower to another, and that the risk valuations were not themselves erratic in behaviour. In fact the risk valuations are highly subjective and the business capital market is divided into an infinite number of pockets between which money does not readily 'spill over' in either direction as soon as an established price differential is disturbed.

[1] Cf. a recent authoritative statement made in an entirely independent context: 'To prime the pump for capital expenditure on re-equipment and modernization, it is necessary for the mill-owner to be enabled to make a good start out of earnings. He will not put his neck into a noose by large-scale borrowing. Nor should he be called upon to do so, as borrowing for re-equipment purposes is what the President of the Master Cotton Spinners recently compared to a man mortgaging his house to repair his roof. "And", he added dryly, "we all know where that will lead him"' (p. 118 of 'Machines and Manpower in Spinning', by C. Henniker-Heaton, in *The Banker*, May 1949).

[2] This passage owes much to some unpublished work by Mr. R. F. Henderson of Corpus Christi College, Cambridge, who has made himself expert in this field. For information about the United States (where these conditions equally exist) Mr. Henderson has drawn on published work, e.g. by Saulnier and Jacoby (*Business Finance and Banking*, New York, 1947).

On both these counts the imperfections of the capital market detract
from the notion that interest rate changes induced by the monetary
authorities can counter business fluctuations. But equally they enhance
the effect of an induced change in expectations. There is a good deal of
reason for supposing that changes in 'the interest rate' do in fact
induce changes in expectations.[1] The changes in expectations induced
by a drop in 'the rate of interest' release capital to borrowers (or other
takers) who could not obtain capital at all before. It is not the case that
when 'the rate' goes down from 5 to 3 a firm can get capital at 13 instead
of 15 per cent.; but when 'the rate' goes down from 5 to 3 the firm which
previously could not get capital on any tolerable terms can now get it (on
tolerable terms) at 13. Various writers have, of course, pointed to particular
manifestations of this tendency: both Keynes and Hawtrey, for example,
have referred to the regulation of the flow of new issues (of the Stock Exchange class of securities) by price movements of recent issues; and Lutz
has emphasized the point generally,[2] mentioning by way of example
housing finance, where the 'down-payments' and repayment periods both
vary so that cheap money reaches borrowers who were previously unable
to borrow at any price. All I have to say here is that these are particular
examples of a very common phenomenon, and that the phenomenon is not
one of 'spillover' which keeps rate differentials constant, but of induced
changes in expectations which completely open or shut channels through
which money flows into the markets for real resources.

If this argument is correct, it is possible that, when a fall in 'the rate of
interest' is caused by monetary factors (whether by deliberate manipula-
tion or in automatic reaction to demand conditions), some capital outlay
is stimulated in the way most theorists supposed twenty years ago, while
a great deal more comes about because potential spenders—especially
small firms—get the feeling that they can obtain more capital when they
want it;[3] and the latter change is due, at least in part, to the belief that
in some way cheap money will cause better trade. All this may seem an
unnecessarily elaborate way of saying that cheap money succeeds because
it is expected to succeed; but to me the elaboration has been necessary in
order to reconcile the argument with the facts revealed by empirical research. Whether elaborate or simple, however, the argument is equally open
to the objection that the business world cannot have invented the idea that
the rate of interest matters, and that there must have been in the past
some more rational basis for the business men's behaviour. It is necessary
to suppose that the *modus operandi* has not always been what it is to-day.

[1] See pp. 14–15 below.
[2] Cf. p. 7 above.
[3] I say 'get the feeling' because the process is not necessarily an abrupt one conscious
enough to secure reflection in replies to a theorist's questionnaire.

I personally do not find this at all difficult to swallow. On the contrary I should find it impossible to believe that, in an economic environment changing in most other respects, the effects of changes in interest rates had always come about in precisely the same way. Recent works by economic historians have thrown some light on the possibility that the rate of interest operated in a Keynesian (1930) way long before there was any prevalent doctrine to infect the business men. Professor Ashton's hints[1] on the earlier period are particularly significant, for the events he describes certainly preceded the formulation of any coherent doctrine. Professor Rostow[2] is more guarded: he concludes that 'the monetary factor' was in his period (1790–1914) 'an essentially negative element in the British trade cycles', and though he argues that the liquidity crisis which *succeeded* the peak made the depression much worse, he apparently ascribes this aggravation to the 'hasty liquidations and spreading of panic' rather than to the high interest rates. On the question whether interest rates were decisive before the crisis, he goes no further than to say

'The evidence suggests . . . that rising interest rates, like rising prices, symbolized an approach to an unstable position of full employment, in the major cycles. They made cost conditions different from those which had been expected when various commitments were undertaken, and they carried psychological overtones as well....'

My own acquaintance with nineteenth- and twentieth-century sources is, of course, much narrower than that of either of these two historians, and it is narrower in a biased way—my acquaintance is mainly with writings on financial aspects, and these may well exaggerate the effect of financial measures. With this warning I will venture, for what they are worth, two general impressions I have gained. First, in the earlier decades of the nineteenth century, not only England's prosperity but that of the whole world depended to an altogether abnormal extent on *English* mercantile activity which used short-term credit in very large accounts. The *availability* of this credit even for the soundest merchants varied sharply (because of the primitive banking system), and the rate of interest varied with the availability. A rise in the rate of interest therefore betokened a credit *restriction* in a very literal way, and the volume of speculative activity—especially in the export trade and therefore in the expanding new industries—was in consequence sharply responsive to interest rate changes. Secondly, in the later decades, when the conditions I have just described had been modified, world prosperity and (with it) English prosperity became more clearly related to the rate of England's lending abroad at long-term, while this lending was in turn highly sensitive to temporary movements in interest rates in the London money market. A rise in London rates caused a hold-up

[1] In his *Industrial Revolution* (London, 1948), *passim*.
[2] In his *British Economy in the Nineteenth Century* (Oxford, 1948) (see especially pp. 56–7).

in foreign capital issues in London and a pretty quick dampening of capital outlay in the outside (borrowing) world, with immediate repercussion on England's export industries. Thus in successive phases—and by rather different mechanisms—Englishmen found that a rise in interest rates should be treated as a warning signal[1]—even though they did not all draw in their horns at once.

In some way such as this business men did undoubtedly acquire the rational basis for what may nowadays be in part an irrational view. But whatever the historical process, that the business world has had such beliefs is beyond question. It is true that when in the thirties interest rates were low, business men were inclined to pooh-pooh their significance; but when in the twenties rates were high, the business men were loud in emphasizing (e.g. in the Federation of British Industries) the depressive effects of dear money: indeed, it was partly because such an agitation was going on that the Macmillan Committee was appointed in 1929. I cannot help wondering what answers an 'Oxford inquiry' would have evoked in the twenties. Moreover, there were in the thirties special circumstances tending towards unresponsiveness of business investment to low interest rates. Many of the writers in the controversy[2] have shown how a high risk factor detracts from the interest-elasticity of investment. Now in the economic collapse that heralded the thirties the business world was shocked in a unique way. During the twenties the British business world had been obsessed with the notion of 'getting back to pre-war' normality; the slump of 1921–2 was accepted as part of the process of shaking down to normal; the return to the gold standard in 1925 and the gradual struggle to prosperity in the succeeding years were taken as evidence that we were 'getting back'. Then came the world economic crisis and the realization that there was no 'getting back', that the world would never be the same again for British trade. To a degree that had no parallel, at any rate within living memory,[3] men really did not know what was going to happen next, and this quite extraordinary lack of confidence lasted for years. With this sombre colour in all recent experience, it would have been surprising if business men had shown less scepticism in their answers to the Oxford economists.

Another factor tending to make business investment less interest-elastic during the inter-war period, as contrasted with earlier periods, was the heavier taxation of big incomes, in so far as this denuded firms of 'internal resources' for development. Because of considerations of capital structure, firms are probably most willing to embark on expansion that may involve some borrowing if they can contribute a large part of

---

[1] I think this is probably Rostow's meaning when he speaks of 'psychological overtones'.
[2] Especially Mr. Shackle and Professor Lutz, in the articles cited above.
[3] Apart from war-time.

the cost from ploughed-back profits, and the new structure of taxation therefore probably had cumulative effect in restraining industrial borrowing through the inter-war years. For these reasons I am ready to believe that the insensitiveness revealed by the Oxford inquiry was something quite new in English economic history. Even so, there remains the fact that in that inquiry business men, while denying that their own actions had ever been directly affected, expressed some vague view that the rate of interest *does* affect the situation.[1]

Taking all these arguments into account, I am inclined to the view that changes in the interest rate may have considerable effect on business activity through their effects on both capital outlay and consumption outlay. But I should add that the former effects arise partly because interest rate changes provoke changes in the absolute availability of capital for particular purposes, and that this chain of causation is based partly on the insecure basis of past experience—experience of conditions different from those prevailing to-day. If this is right—if interest rate changes are effective partly because men know that they used to be effective—we must expect their efficacy to diminish as the propitious conditions fade into the more remote past. Men's actions to-day may be based on the theories of their fathers, these theories in turn being based on the conditions of grandfather's time; but with the passage of time the generations change, and we have ourselves seen how the theories change too. The change may indeed come much more rapidly than I have just suggested—if in the last phase of the nineteenth century the interest rate changes most powerfully influenced the world through their effect on the pace of Britain's foreign lending, it was natural enough that men should begin to have their doubts about the usefulness of this weapon in the inter-war period when Britain's foreign lending shrivelled up.

After a time-lag during which the efficacy of this weapon partly depends (irrationally) on historical conditions that have passed away, we must expect the weapon's efficacy to diminish. But other conditions are perhaps operating in the other direction. In America at least we can expect an increasing proportion of consumption to take the form of durable consumption goods, expenditure on which can easily be postponed or accelerated, and it is noticeable that commentators on American monetary affairs to-day give a good deal of attention to variations in consumers' outlay, which can be greatly influenced by the terms of consumer finance. Secondly, 'the new metallurgy' of the inter-war period, producing ships, engines, and machines of much longer life, may eventually lead to some lengthening of the 'writing-off period' of industrial capital beyond the very short periods prevalent to-day; and, as has been demonstrated by many of the writers

[1] See p. 51 below.

referred to above,[1] it is the shortness of these periods that leaves so slender a basis for interest rate policy in relation to industrial capital outlay. Thirdly, the public utility sector tends to become a larger proportion of the whole economy, in each of the major countries, and it is agreed by these same writers that the capital outlay of this sector should be particularly sensitive to the interest rate. It is true that the Oxford inquiry results suggest a question mark here; but this is I suggest due to the complication of public subsidies, public taxes, and so forth which obscure the position to the managers of public utilities. By housing subsidies, for example, the tenant or purchaser is protected from the full blast of high interest rates, but the taxpayer has to make up for it. Recent discussions show that the public is still sensitive to the weight of public expenditure, and higher subsidy costs (due to higher interest rates) might be expected to provoke a pruning of housing programmes. And similarly with railway or electricity development: the capital outlay decision of a public enterprise may be determined proximately by its financial relations with the government, but the government's own attitude will be coloured by the size of the deficit or surplus which reflects among other things the interest charge on new capital outlay.

My impression is that, for such reasons as these, the efficacy of the interest rate has changed and will go on changing continuously, some forces tending to dull its edge while others sharpen it. The debate on the *modus operandi* continues, but while it continues the phenomenon itself is changing. If we are to keep up with ourselves we really must try to run a little faster.

(ii) *The Significance of the Rate of Interest*[2]

By H. D. HENDERSON

FEW economic questions are of greater interest and importance to-day than that of the part played by the rate of interest in the working of the economic system, and the influence exerted by changes in interest rates on trade activity. The maintenance of cheap money has been a central feature of the economic policy pursued by the British Government since 1932; and this has undoubtedly been largely responsible for the marked reduction in the general level of interest rates that has followed. The fall in interest rates has made the government's financial task of balancing the budget materially easier. There is thus a natural and strong predisposition in official circles to believe in the importance of low interest rates and to claim

---

[1] e.g. Shackle (*Economic Journal*, Mar. 1946) and Lutz (*American Economic Review*, Dec. 1945).

[2] Reprinted from *Oxford Economic Papers*, No. 1.

that the lower rates established have been a material factor in promoting general economic recovery.

For different reasons this predisposition is shared by the majority of academic economists. Withdrawn, as he is, from close contact with the details of the economic system, the academic economist is especially interested in those forces which are at work throughout the economic system as a whole, and the importance of which appears to be fundamental. The rate of interest is a force of this character. The movement in gilt-edged interest rates from the level of $4\frac{1}{2}$ per cent. or more which prevailed until 1932 to the level of 3 per cent. or less which was established in 1935 is to the detached student of economic affairs an event of great interest and intrinsic dignity, and his mind is ready to welcome the idea that it may have played an immensely important part in ways not easy perhaps to detect in detail, in the changes that have taken place in economic activity. This inclination is strengthened by the widespread preoccupation of economic analysis in recent years with the relations between savings and investment. While economists have been divided by abstract and complex issues as to the relative importance of the forces by which the rate of interest is determined, there has been little dispute as to the importance of its consequences. That a large part of the prolonged economic malaise of the post-war period might be attributable to a rate of interest markedly in excess of the level required for equilibrium is a doctrine agreeable to the instincts of economists of both orthodox and heretical leanings.

Thus both official circles and academic economists have a bias in favour of propagating the view that lower interest rates have been a major factor in recovery. Nor is the business community predisposed to quarrel with it. To the industrialist or trader, who works with borrowed money, lower interest rates mean a reduction in his costs. The reduction may not strike him as particularly important; none the less he welcomes it. Banks, insurance companies, and others who lend money for interest may be adversely affected, it is true, by lower interest rates, so far as their annual income is concerned; but owing to the consequential rise in security values many of them derive a compensatory benefit in the shape of a stronger balance-sheet position. Thus, up to a point at least, most lenders are not inclined to cavil at cheaper money. The investing public also welcomes the rise in security values. Low interest rates, in short, either are or seem to be to the material advantage of the great majority of the economic community. Add to this the natural tendency of the human mind to accept *post hoc* as *propter hoc*, and it is not surprising that the idea that cheap money has been one of the chief factors in economic recovery should have been accepted by public opinion in general as an established, if somewhat mysterious, truth.

C

Yet beneath this impressive harmony of outward acceptance there lurks a widespread bewilderment and detailed scepticism. If the question is put 'What is the *modus operandi* by which low interest rates stimulate economic activity?' there are few who are ready to offer a coherent answer, and they include hardly any one who is intimately acquainted with the actual working of the economic system. Consider some of the difficulties that arise. Are lower interest rates really effective in inducing business men to undertake operations that they would not otherwise have undertaken? If so, what sort of business men and what sort of operations? Will manufacturers or traders be induced to purchase additional stocks of materials? There are obvious difficulties in supposing an affirmative answer to these questions. By increasing his stocks in excess of his requirements the manufacturer or trader will incur an unnecessary expense. Lower interest rates, it is true, will make this expense less than it would otherwise have been. But there will be an avoidable expense, and the question arises why either the manufacturer or trader should deliberately incur it. He may, of course, calculate that the prices of his materials are likely to rise or that the demand for his products will increase. If so, it is this expectation of higher prices or increased sales rather than the cheaper terms of borrowing that will constitute the real inducement. Moreover, in this event it is difficult to suppose that variations in interest rates will be an important factor in the calculation. No one is ever able to estimate with precision the magnitude and degree of probability attaching to an expected rise of prices. A man may form an opinion that it is more likely than not that prices will rise by anything from 5 to 10 per cent. or more in the next few months. His opinion will seldom be more precise than that. If, on such grounds, he decides that it is wise to purchase now in excess of his normal requirements, one would expect him to come to the same conclusion even if the annual charges for a bank overdraft were 1 or 2 per cent. higher than they are.

It may be, of course, that changes in interest rates constitute one of the reasons why business men expect prices to rise or trade to improve. There is little doubt, indeed, that this is true in some degree; for there is a fairly well-recognized tradition that a low bank rate helps to promote a rise of prices and greater trade activity. A rise in bank rate to a really high figure would undoubtedly be regarded by many business men as a warning signal enjoining a policy of caution, and, conversely, reductions in bank rate to a low figure probably serve as an influence inducing business men in a strong financial position to regard the business outlook more hopefully. It is clear enough, therefore, that changes in bank rate may, and probably do, exert some influence on business activity through the channel of psychology. But two observations suggest themselves. First, it hardly seems reasonable to suppose that this influence can be of major importance.

There have been times when bank rate has remained low for a long period before any recovery in commodity prices has ensued. Most business men are concerned, moreover, not with the general movement of prices but with the prices of certain particular commodities which they buy or sell. It is difficult to suppose that they could give a very prominent place to reductions of bank rate in forming their view of the prospects of the markets in which they are interested. Secondly, whatever may be the practical importance of this influence, it leaves the essential question unanswered. Presumably the expectation that lower bank rate will make for better trade or higher prices rests on some rational foundation; otherwise its influence would be precarious. What, then, is the solid basis for this expectation? The essential link in the chain of cause and effect has still to be discovered.

Let us pass then to another possibility. Is it reasonable to suppose that lower interest rates may stimulate long-term capital expenditure by business men, that manufacturers, for example, may be encouraged to extend their works or introduce new and improved machinery? At first sight an affirmative answer to this question seems more plausible; but when it is closely examined rather similar difficulties arise. We may suppose a manufacturer to be considering the question as to whether he should instal some new labour-saving machine which will entail a certain saving in his wages bill for a given volume of output. The annual saving thus effected may be estimated with some precision. There is no difficulty in supposing that it may be computed so as to represent some definite percentage of the capital cost of the machine. If the machine could be expected to last for ever or for a long period, such as 20 or 30 years, there would also be no difficulty in supposing that a difference of 1 or 2 per cent. in the long-term rate of interest might turn the scales of the calculation as to whether it was worth while to introduce the machine. In fact, however, most modern labour-saving machinery has a comparatively brief period of effective life. The same progress of invention which has given rise to the machine which the manufacturer is considering may, a few years later, produce a still better machine which will effect still larger reductions in the annual wages bill. In calculating, therefore, the profitability of introducing the machine a rapid rate of obsolescence must be assumed. In other words, the machine must be expected to pay for itself over a comparatively few years; not 20 or 30 years, but 7 or perhaps 5 or perhaps 3. This, however, makes it much harder to translate the problem into terms of a calculation of annual gain and loss in which the rate of interest is likely to be a material factor. For if such a calculation is made, the allowance for obsolescence or depreciation will inevitably be a much larger item on the debit side than the charge for interest. Yet the allowance for obsolescence must necessarily be of an arbitrary rough-and-ready character, and the event may diverge from it materially in the one direction or the other. The machine which is assumed to have an effective life of 5 years may actually be retained for 7 or, on the other hand, it may become obsolete in 3. Thus a high degree of uncertainty would necessarily attach to any calculation of annual gain or loss, and it is hard to suppose that a difference in interest rates, which could only represent a small item in the calculation, could play a material part in the decision reached. It is doubtful, indeed, whether many manufacturers calculate the profitability of a new machine along lines which take account of variations in the rate of interest.

A large part of a manufacturer's fixed capital may not, of course, be of a highly obsolescent character. It will represent rather buildings and fixed equipment which will usually have a long period of effective life. But if it is easier in this case to calculate with precision the annual cost represented by the capital, it is much more difficult to calculate with precision the annual return which it is likely to yield. If a manufacturer is considering whether to put up new works which will enlarge his productive capacity, his dominating question, it is natural to suppose, will be whether he is likely to be able to sell profitably the extra output of goods. This is a question which seldom lends itself to precise calculation, and it is again hard, therefore, on general grounds, to suppose that many manufacturers would pay much attention to the prevailing rate of interest in deciding to enlarge their productive capacity. There remains the possibility that a manufacturer may choose a period of low interest rates to execute capital extensions which he has decided on other grounds to undertake before very long. But here again an awkward question suggests itself. Is this consideration likely to weigh for very much in practice as compared, for example, with the level of building costs ?

There are, then, serious difficulties in supposing that a change in interest rates will exert any very important influence of a direct character on the capital expenditure of the ordinary trader or manufacturer, whether upon working capital or fixed capital. There remain other classes of capital goods, in respect of which these difficulties are less formidable. There are those capital goods the demand for which comes not from manufacturers or traders, but from private individuals, i.e. durable consumers' goods, the leading instance of which is a house or other dwelling. It is comparatively easy to see how a change in the rate of interest may affect materially the demand for houses. The utility of a house to its occupier does not depend, as a rule, on any uncertainty as to the profits he can make from living in it; he can therefore estimate directly the annual value to him of a house of a certain size and quality in a particular place. On the other hand, a house lasts for a long period of years and the interest on its capital cost is not, therefore, unimportant as compared with the allowance that must be made for its depreciation. There is no difficulty, therefore, in supposing that a substantial fall in the rate of interest may give a material stimulus to house building.

There are also durable capital goods which are owned neither by manufacturers, traders, nor private consumers but by public authorities, such as the state or municipalities. Capital goods of this character comprise a vast variety of types, and they account in the aggregate for a large proportion of the accumulated capital of the community. Here, as in the case of houses, the normal life of the capital goods is so long as to make the rate of interest a major factor in computing the annual cost. Their utility may be of a type which it is hard to measure in financial terms at all; but in such cases it is usually independent of necessarily doubtful calculations as to future earning capacity. On the other hand, where the capital goods are of a commercial character and represent the capital equipment of trading services such as gas or electricity, it is usually possible to calculate the probable demand for their services with a fair degree of precision. This last consideration applies also to public utility concerns. It is therefore possible that such concerns in considering whether to modernize their plant or enlarge their capacity might measure the expected annual yield against the cost of the capital expenditure in a way that would take account of the prevailing rate of interest. There is thus no fundamental difficulty in supposing that changes in the rate of interest may exert a considerable effect on the amount of capital expenditure undertaken by public authorities and public utility concerns.

The broad effect of the foregoing argument is to suggest that the influence of the rate of interest on capital expenditure is far less general and all-pervasive in character than is commonly assumed in economic discussion. There are only two types of capital goods on which it is plausible to suppose that expenditure might be appreciably stimulated by a lower, or appreciably retarded by a higher, rate of interest, namely (1) durable consumers' goods, and (2) the assets of public bodies and public utilities. These two classes of capital goods are both of very great importance; and over a period of years it is probable that they account between them for a very high proportion of our aggregate capital expenditure. If, therefore, the influence of the rate of interest were limited to these two spheres it might be a factor of great consequence; but it would be less automatic and reliable than is sometimes assumed. So far as the second category is concerned, the decision whether or not to undertake public works expenditure of a non-commercial character will seldom, if ever, be determined solely on financial grounds. Many considerations of policy, both local and national, will be taken into account. There is nowadays, for example, a growing advocacy of the view that public bodies and public utilities should regulate their capital expenditure systematically with the object of steadying the course of trade. In so far as this view is accepted, it appears at first sight as though the influence of the rate of interest would be weakened. As regards the other category, houses and other dwellings represent the only important type of consumers' capital goods likely to be affected materially by changes in the rate of interest. But the demand for dwellings is clearly dependent also on other factors, notably on the rate at which the number of families is growing in different sections of the community. In view of the trend of our vital statistics it seems probable that we are approaching a phase in which the number of families will cease to grow. It is difficult to suppose that under such conditions the demand for new private dwellings can remain at a very high level, however low the rate of interest may fall. This suggests that one of the major classes of capital expenditure which is susceptible to variations in interest rates may in future represent a much smaller part of our aggregate capital expenditure than it has done in the past. So far as the argument has gone the conclusion would appear to be that the influence of the rate of interest on capital expenditure is limited to certain particular directions, and that its continued efficacy in those directions is threatened by modern tendencies.

The argument, however, is not, as yet, complete. Changes in the rate of interest may affect economic activity through a channel different in kind from any that have hitherto been considered. A fall (or rise) in the rate of interest serves to raise (or lower) the Stock Exchange prices of fixed-interest securities, and has a considerable effect on the prices of most ordinary shares. This may affect the willingness of large sections of the public to purchase goods and services in general. When prices are rising on the Stock Exchange, dealers and speculators make profits, whereas as a body they are apt to make losses when Stock Exchange prices are falling. Many of them expect to make profits over an average of years and regard these profits as a part of their spendable income. When, accordingly, the trend of Stock Exchange prices is upwards, dealers and speculators will feel better able to spend money than when times are bad. Under the heading of speculators in this connexion may be included not only professional speculators but a large number of persons who habitually buy and sell shares with a view to capital profits. People who do this are much more numerous nowadays than they used to be, and they probably account for an appreciable fraction of the aggregate purchasing power of the community. Moreover, even people who seldom change their securities are influenced in their state of mind by a rise or fall in their capital value and would be more likely to feel that they can afford a certain piece of expenditure when security prices are rising than when they are falling.

There are grounds for supposing that this particular influence is of con-

siderable and growing importance. It is notorious that a slump or boom on
the Stock Exchange quickly affects the demand for certain luxury goods,
e.g. the more expensive types of motor-cars. It is fairly well established,
again, that the Wall Street crash in 1929 led directly to a substantial cur-
tailment of consumers' purchases. Indeed, this chain of cause and effect
supplies one of the most probable explanations of the fact that trade movements are normally more violent in the United States than in Great Britain;
for the distinction between income and capital still retains in Great Britain
a far greater degree of sanctity than it does in the United States. Thus, in
the influence of the rate of interest on security values, and the influence of
the level of security values on effective purchasing power, we have a channel of connexion which is consistent both with common-sense considerations
and the broad facts of recent experience.

A rise in security values, it should be added, may affect businesses as
well as private individuals. It will improve the balance-sheet position of
a business which holds marketable securities; and it will also make it easier
for companies to raise new capital without incurring prior charges. In these
ways, businesses might be encouraged to undertake extensions to which a
certain risk attached. Conversely, a fall in security values may be an influence making for more cautious business policies.

The minds of many economic students have been feeling their way in
recent years towards the tentative conclusions which have been set out
above. But it has seemed desirable to some of us at Oxford that a more
systematic effort should be made than hitherto to ascertain whether these
conclusions, positive and negative alike, are well founded. There has been
in existence for some years among the tutors engaged in teaching economics
at Oxford a research group which has been investigating the factors affecting the course of economic activity. These investigations cover a considerable range of problems, and the methods include both statistical analysis
and interviews and discussions with business men. One of the questions
examined has been that of the effects of changes in the rate of interest, and
a number of leading business men, representative of different branches of
industry, commerce, and finance, have been closely questioned by us as
to the way in which, as they see it, their activities are affected. The results
are summarized in the paper that follows. Broadly, it will be observed, the
opinions of the business men whom we have examined are in conformity
with the argument developed above. The majority deny that their activities
have been, or are likely to be, directly affected in any way by changes in
interest rates. Of those who take the view that they might sometimes be
affected, few suggest that the influence is an important one. This applies,
it should be observed, with some qualifications, even to the representatives
of the building industry whom we consulted. In at least the majority of

cases the negative character of the answers given cannot be attributed to prejudice. It was common to find witnesses who denied that their activities were in any way affected by changes in interest rates, but who, none the less, held the view that the rate of interest is an important factor in the economic situation for reasons not easy to ascertain. Still less can the nature of the answers be attributed to misunderstanding or confusion of thought. Our questions were closely pressed and reiterated in different terms, and they covered every possible reaction. Frequently, moreover, in response to our questions, the methods of calculation actually employed in weighing projects of capital expenditure were precisely explained; and these were such as to disregard altogether variations in interest rates.

Our investigations in the Oxford Economists' Research Group have been intensive rather than extensive, and the 'sample' of firms consulted is small. Moreover, the sample may be said to be biased in one important respect. The majority of business men we have consulted represent prosperous firms in a strong financial position. It may be that changes in interest rates have a greater influence on the actions of businesses which are in financial difficulties. Certainly on general grounds one would expect that such businesses would be more likely to be affected by changes in the ease or stringency of credit conditions, i.e. in the abundance or scarcity of bank money as distinct from the rate charged for it.

It seems fair, however, to claim that our investigations, though not amounting to a conclusive demonstration, confirm with a high degree of probability the negative conclusions which have been tentatively advanced on grounds of common sense, i.e. that the direct influence of variations in the rate of interest on the actions of the majority of businesses of an ordinary industrial or commercial character, either in purchasing materials or in undertaking capital expenditure, is not likely to be very great. Indeed, they go somewhat further than this, and suggest that the influence exerted indirectly through the change in the level of security values and consequently in balance-sheet positions, though of some importance, is not of great importance so far as the actions of businesses are concerned.

Though these conclusions are essentially negative, we think that their publication may contribute, if only by way of clearing the ground, to the constructive development of economic thought. It is of interest, therefore, to consider some of the corollaries which appear reasonable if these conclusions are accepted.

In the first place it would be very rash to infer that the importance of the rate of interest in the working of the economic system has been exaggerated. The economist's presumption that great importance must attach to a factor so fundamental as the rate of interest remains, and should not be lightly dismissed. What emerges is that the role played by the ordinary business man in the transmission of the effects of interest changes is an essentially passive role. The active agents in the process must be looked for elsewhere ; and the directions in which they may be found have already been indicated. Possibly the suggestions conveyed by the general trend of economic analysis in the past have under-estimated these other effects of interest changes as much as they have over-estimated the direct reactions upon the ordinary business man.

It was suggested above that the growing vogue of the idea of regulating public works with a view to trade stability might seem calculated to weaken the influence of the rate of interest on the volume of this type of capital expenditure. It may well be, however, that this is a superficial view. One important aspect of all projects of public works expenditure is the budgetary aspect. This is an aspect which is apt to receive only slight attention in economic discussion, largely because of the spread in recent years of the idea that unbalanced budgets may be a useful instrument in recovery from depression. But the necessity for governments to balance their budgets over a period of years remains inexorable. Two powerful tendencies are at work to-day which are likely to make this task increasingly difficult. There is first the unprecedentedly heavy expenditure on armaments which is being undertaken in many important countries. Secondly, there is the movement from rapidly growing towards declining populations which is in progress throughout the western world, and which is likely in various ways to aggravate budgetary difficulties. In these circumstances it is to be expected that governments in many countries, including particularly Great Britain, will be increasingly preoccupied in future years with the problem of budgetary equilibrium. It follows that the financial aspect of projects of public works is likely to be of crucial importance. Schemes of public works which would entail substantial charges on the national exchequer or on local funds would encounter formidable resistance on financial grounds.

The rate of interest may, therefore, play an extremely important part in determining the volume of public works expenditure which it proves practicable to undertake. There are many types of public works or public utility expenditure which yield an appreciable financial return, which, however, may be insufficient at the prevailing level of interest rates to cover the service of the loan required. If a materially lower level of interest rates could be established, the range of public works which were commercial propositions would be enlarged, and the range which could be undertaken without imposing serious burdens on the budget would also be enlarged. Moreover, a low rate of interest by facilitating a reduction in the annual charge for the national debt contributes directly to balancing the budget, and thus makes it easier to undertake public works schemes which are not fully remunerative but are desirable on general economic grounds. For these reasons it may well prove that a low rate of interest will be of vital importance in the years that lie ahead. It may represent the only means of reconciling the conflict between considerations of economic activity and considerations of financial solvency, neither of which can be disregarded without disaster.

The influence of the rate of interest on the expenditure of private individuals may prove equally great. It has already been suggested that the direct effect of changes in interest rates on the purchase of consumers' capital goods may prove of diminishing importance in future; but that, on the other hand, the indirect effect on general expenditure exerted through Stock Exchange prices may be of increasing importance. If this conclusion is sound, the problem of securing a reasonable stability in Stock Exchange values becomes of central importance in the working of the economic system, and deserves more systematic attention than it has hitherto received.

But there is another aspect of this question which is of great interest to the analytical economist. A generation ago there was much discussion of the question whether a fall in the rate of interest was likely to increase or decrease the volume of saving. The traditional view was that a lower rate of interest would diminish saving, and vice versa. But, discussing the question exclusively in terms of the ability to save and the incentive to save, economists found it increasingly difficult to reconcile this assumption with common sense and general experience, and the discussion ended in a prevailing agreement that the effect of a change in the rate of interest on the volume of saving was about as likely to be in the one direction as the other, and was not likely to be important in either case. The reactions of the rate of interest on security prices have, however, an important bearing on this question. As we have seen, there are substantial grounds for believing that an important section of the public is induced by an upward movement on the Stock Exchange to spend more freely, and consequently, other things being equal, to save less. Indeed, the importance of the rate of interest in the working of the trade cycle may, perhaps, lie as much in its reactions on saving and consumption as in those on investment.

This, however, is a short-period transitional influence, associated with falling rather than with low interest rates. Is it possible that as a long-period proposition also the old-fashioned assumption that a lower rate of interest will check saving and vice versa is more soundly based than economists in the past generation have felt able to assume? This is a question that is likely to prove of great importance to the economic stability of society. For a period which may be fairly prolonged we have before us the prospect of large and increasing armament expenditure. But it seems inevitable that sooner or later we shall be confronted with the necessity of effecting a transition to a new economic equilibrium in which capital expenditure plays a substantially smaller part than it does to-day. Loan expenditure on rearmament must come to an end eventually. The expenditure of the public on houses cannot be expected to continue at anything like the level of recent years when the number of families has ceased to grow. It is difficult to suppose that expenditure on public works will be undertaken on a scale that will compensate fully for the possible decline in capital expenditure under these two headings. But if the demand for capital goods must be expected to diminish it will be essential, if a prolonged period of economic malaise is to be avoided, to secure a corresponding increase in the demand for ordinary consumers' goods. Indeed, the central economic problem of the next generation may be how this can be effected against the background of difficult budgetary conditions. The problem is formidable in the extreme. The difficulties in the way of an adequate solution are immense. But a solution would become much easier if it could be assumed that the establishment of a materially lower rate of interest would exert an enduring influence on the habits of a large section of the public in regard to expenditure and saving.

(iii) *Summary of Replies to Questions on Effects of Interest Rates*[1]

Prepared by J. E. MEADE *and* P. W. S. ANDREWS

THE following paper summarizes the answers given by business men to the Oxford Economists' Research Group regarding the influence of the rate of interest. The business men consulted numbered 37, and included manufacturers in a wide range of industries (covering both capital and consumers' goods), merchants, and financial institutions. We have also had the benefit of the advice of an accountant and of two American Professors, one of Business Administration and the other of Accounting.

Before each meeting a questionnaire was sent out to give a general idea of the questions to be asked. The questions dealing with the effects of the rate of interest and with related matters were as follows:

1. Is the rate at which you can borrow from the bank an important consideration to you? Has an alteration in the bank rate ever had a material direct influence in inducing you to expand or to contract your activities?

2. Have you ever increased your stocks of raw materials on account of a fall in the bank rate?

[1] Reprinted from *Oxford Economic Papers*, No. 1.

3. Is the long-term rate of interest an important factor in regard to policies of capital extension?

4. Do you ever postpone, or speed up, extensions or renewals of plant because you expect the costs of building or the price of machinery to rise or fall?

5. Does it ever happen that the existence of large undistributed profits induces businesses to embark on capital extensions which they would not have undertaken otherwise? Conversely, does the desire to maintain dividends out of reserve during a depression, or to maintain a liquid position, sometimes act as an influence leading to the postponement of plant renewals or desirable capital extensions?

These questions were supplemented in discussion by many others, and the following matters were thus considered:

1. The effect of short-term interest rates and of the banks' lending policy on investment in fixed plant or in stocks.

2. The effect of long-term interest rates on investment in fixed plant.

3. The effect of expected price changes on investment in stocks.

4. The effect of expected changes in constructional costs on investment in fixed plant.

5. The effect of the state of demand for the product on investment in fixed plant.

6. The effect of abundance or scarcity of liquid resources on investment in fixed plant.[1]

SUMMARY OF REPLIES

The broad effect of the opinions may be summarized as follows:

1. There is almost universal agreement that short-term rates of interest do not directly affect investment either in stocks or in fixed capital. The reason usually given for this is either that the business does not borrow from the bank or else that the effect of changes in the rate is too small in comparison with the profit margin to make any difference. There are three exceptions to this. I. 6 stated that bank rate might affect the decision to purchase machines, but implies that it would not affect stocks. I. 3 says

[1] At this point there followed a section giving the information extracted from each one of the individuals questioned, the information being given under each of the foregoing six heads. In the section which follows (which appeared as the concluding section of the original paper) these six heads are referred to by Arabic numerals, while the Roman numerals refer to the individuals classified thus:

I. Consumption goods industries.	VI. Finance.
II. Textiles.	VII. Building.
III. Capital goods industries.	VIII. Merchants.
IV. Transport.	IX. Accountants.
V. Retail Trade.	X. American Professors.

that bank rate would affect the carrying of stocks, but admits that stocks would not be increased solely because of a fall in bank rate. VIII. 1, whilst denying that the rate had any importance for merchants in general, thought that it might affect the policy of the speculative merchant who is buying stocks for small changes in price, and pointed out that the volume of stocks held by this type is not heavy. On the other hand, several business men took the view that the psychological effects of a change in bank rate are important, arguing that there is a tendency to regard such changes as analogous to a weather report, and as indications of the probable trend of trade. Merchants tended to stress this influence. Some witnesses, moreover, asserted that the willingness of the banks to lend, as distinct from the rate charged, was an important consideration, and that this was liable to vary.

2. The majority deny that the long-term rate of interest affects investment directly, although some indicate that it is of some importance to them. I. 5 stated that it might affect the installation of labour-saving machinery, although the subsequent course of the interview suggests that it had not in fact done so. I. 7 and II. 2 suggest that it is a contributory cause in deciding upon investment. II. 5, IV. 1, V. 2, and VI. 2 suggest that it is of some importance; IV. 1, emphasizing the importance of low rates if they persist for some time, and V. 2 emphasizing the importance of interest rates to retailers to whom rent expenses are peculiarly important. I. 2, while denying that it is of importance to him, suggested that it would be important to firms owning land and buildings. VII. 1 and 2 thought that the rate might have some effect on the demand for dwelling-houses, but tended to deny that it could have an important effect. They both deny that factory building is influenced either by costs or by the rate of interest, and both gave as the reason, that if trade is good increased costs do not matter. The majority who deny its importance give as their reasons either that they do not need to borrow for extensions or that it is too small an element in comparison with depreciation, obsolescence, or the uncertainty of the market for the product.

There is, however, some evidence that a fall in long-term rates would have favourable indirect effects. VI. 3 emphasizes the fact that this, by raising the price of gilt-edged securities, increases the liquidity of a business and that this is very important in affecting the readiness to go ahead. This point should be considered in connexion with the replies analysed under (6) above, from which it will be seen that a large number of entrepreneurs stated that the willingness to go ahead would be affected by the presence of liquid resources. X. 1 emphasizes the importance of a slightly different effect, namely that the conversion of fixed debt to a lower rate of interest increases the willingness to take risks.

We have evidence, then, that in ordinary manufacturing business the long-term rate of interest is of some, though very limited, direct importance in affecting investment. It seems that the indirect effects in increasing the resources of the business readily available for the finance of development may be of considerably greater importance. The builders, also, while admitting that the rate of interest, especially if very high or very low, might have some effect, tended to deny its importance. We have had evidence from VII. 1 and VI. 4 that a fall in interest rates may have some effect in inducing large corporate investors to undertake greater risks, for example, construction of buildings for themselves as investments.

3. A considerable number of businesses seem to relate their purchases of raw materials to expected changes in their price or to expected difficulties in obtaining delivery. Although this is not a universal practice, and is denied by some entrepreneurs, we may at least conclude that it is of considerable importance.

4. There seems to be a great divergence of practice in the matter of considering the price of capital construction in deciding whether to embark on capital construction or not. This difference ranges from denials that it is ever of importance to assertions that it is a very important consideration. A sufficient number, however, state that they do take expected changes in cost of construction into account for us to be able to conclude that this is an important factor when we are considering industrial investment as a whole.

5. There is considerable divergence of practice among the business men as to whether the presence or absence of liquid resources induces or discourages investment and renewals. Those who asserted that the presence of liquid resources induced extensions and renewals were more numerous than those who denied this; and those who asserted that the absence of liquid resources discouraged extensions and renewals were again more numerous than those who denied this. But those two majorities are not composed of the same entrepreneurs. There is certainly sufficient evidence for us to conclude that the presence or absence of liquid resources is a consideration of some importance in this connexion.

It was stated by I. 11 that the presence of large liquid resources gave a rational inducement for extensions, as they could then afford to take more risks, and the answer of X. 1 bears out this contention. It was suggested by IV. 1 that the presence or absence of liquid resources is of more importance in this connexion to small private businesses than to large public companies.

(iv) *Interest, Prices, and the Demand Schedule for Idle Money*[1]

By A. J. BROWN

1. Introduction

THE function of interest rate and its relations with other economic variables seem to be subject to a variety of interpretations at the present time. On the one hand, a controversy rages between the supporters of Mr. Keynes and what is sometimes called the 'Classical' view. On the other, we have, in an article by members of the Oxford Economists' Research Group printed in the first number of this publication, a considerable body of evidence that interest has far less direct importance for entrepreneurs than economists have hitherto thought. The ultimate purposes of this article are to suggest that strong statistical evidence can be brought to support either a Keynesian or a Wicksellian interpretation of the interrelations of interest, money, and prices, that these two bodies of evidence are mutually consistent, and that in view of them it is possible so to amend the theory of the relation between interest and investment as to make it more consistent with the facts.

More immediately, however, it is proposed to show that Mr. Keynes's general liquidity-preference schedule can be made a useful instrument of statistical analysis, and that there is some evidence that it remains fairly stable through time. In a previous article[2] it was seen that the concept, in a rather complicated form, is applicable to the asset-holdings of the London clearing banks. In that case the liquidities of the various types of asset may be assumed, as a first approximation, to remain reasonably steady, and the total resources of the banks may be easily ascertained and used as an independent variable in the schedules. When the economy as a whole is considered, however, the assumption of the constant liquidity of most kinds of assets ceases to be plausible even as a starting-point, since the same asset may serve very different purposes in the hands of different people. Moreover, information about resources becomes inadequate, since distributional changes which are neither negligible nor measurable introduce very formidable complications.

It therefore seems most useful to take Mr. Keynes's own simple definition of the liquidity-preference schedule as the relation between the total of idle funds in the hands of the public and the rate of interest. These terms themselves stand in need of a fuller definition, and it may be best to proceed to

---

[1] Reprinted from *Oxford Economic Papers*, No. 2.

[2] 'The Liquidity-Preference Schedules of the London Clearing Banks', *Oxford Economic Papers*, No. 1.

this by way of the relation between interest and the still simpler concept
of the total money in existence in the economy.

2. Total money and interest

The 'total amount of money' is a heterogeneous mixture of cash and
bank deposits of various kinds. As a first approximation, however, it will
be adequate to take the total volume of deposits of all kinds in the London
clearing banks. The cash which makes up most of the remainder of the
country's 'total money' may be assumed without risk of serious error to
vary in much the same way as these deposits. 'The' rate of interest may
perhaps best be taken for this purpose to be the yield of Consols. To justify
this completely, it is necessary to assume that the other main rates are
either fixed or bear some constant functional relation to the Consol rate,
which latter hypothesis is probably not far from the truth in the fairly long
run.

When the annual averages of these two variables, total deposits and
interest, are examined for the years 1921–36, quite an impressive negative
correlation is found to exist between them. The Pearsonian coefficient is,
in fact, $-0·7682$, where the '1% point' according to R. A. Fisher's tables
is 0·606. The regression equation connecting them is:

$$D = 2394 - 153r,$$

where D (deposits) is regarded as dependent upon r (interest), or:

$$r = 10·97 - 0·00388D,$$

where the opposite relation of dependence is assumed. If the relation is
expressed in the form used by Professor Frisch, which implies no assumption about its causal character, it becomes:

$$D = 2585 - 198r,$$

so that a fall of 1 per cent. in the yield of Consols is associated with a rise
of about two hundred million pounds in the deposits of the clearing banks.
The coefficient of r (198) is the geometric mean of the corresponding coefficients in the two previous equations, and the range of its variation, according as one or other of the variables is regarded as independent, may be
expressed by writing it as '198 multiplied or divided by 0·7682', or, as in
Frisch's notation, '198./.0·7682'.

This relation is largely, however, one between simple trends in the
variables, and, as such, is less certainly indicative of a genuine connexion
than if it were a relation between more complex variations. The partial
correlation between D and r, excluding the linear variation of both with
'time' is only $-0·536$, where 5 per cent. point is 0·497 and 1 per cent.
point is 0·623. The relation between the trend-free variables is therefore

not by any means satisfactorily close, but it is at the same time significant enough to encourage further investigation.

3. The estimation of 'idle money'

The relation between total money and the rate of interest is not, in any case, one which we should expect to be very close, since the schedule of the marginal utility of money must move about from time to time with variations in the amount of work in effecting transactions which money is called upon to perform. Mr. Keynes's recognition of this fact in *The General Theory* leads him (from p. 199 onwards) to divide the total schedule of liquidity-preference into two parts, relating the amount of money held from the 'transactions motive' to the national income and that held from the 'precautionary' and 'speculative' motives to the rate of interest.

The problem is to find out how large the 'transactions deposits' are—to find the amount of money required for the purposes of active trade—in order to be able to eliminate them from total deposits and to see what is the relation between interest rates and those money holdings to which they may be expected to be directly relevant.

The direct method of approach would be by way of multiple regression analysis. We might try to find the relation between total money on the one hand, and interest rate and some measure of the volume of transactions effected with the various kinds of 'transactions deposits' on the other. This may, in fact, be attempted. The total 'transactions deposits' may be divided into two main parts: the 'active business deposits' which probably make up most of the active deposits of the country, and the 'active financial deposits', lodged mostly in the City of London, comparatively small in volume, and circulating with a very high velocity to affect (according to the estimate of Dr. Shackle and Mr. Phelps Brown[1]) some four-fifths of the total transactions of the country. A rough indication of the sizes (and a good indication of the variations) of the business and financial circulation respectively is given by the volumes of 'Metropolitan, Country, and Provincial' bank clearings and of 'Town' clearings.

It is possible to use these clearing figures as the basis of estimates of the *absolute magnitudes* of the non-financial (or business) and the financial circulations, and not simply as *indices* of them. Since 1930 the Bank of England has published in its *Statistical Summary* the total debits to current account in all the London clearing banks, i.e. the total transactions carried out with money as we have chosen to define it here. By a very detailed direct estimate of the total non-financial cheque payments in 1930 Dr.

---

[1] *Statistics of Monetary Circulation in England and Wales, 1919–1937*, by E. H. Phelps Brown and G. L. S. Shackle. London and Cambridge Economic Service, 1938.

Shackle and Mr. Phelps Brown have ascertained that this was about 1·588 times the total MCP clearings of that year, and that the financial circulation was (by difference) some 1·420 times the Town clearings. Using these multipliers, we can make estimates of the financial circulation (F) and the non-financial circulation (B) in any year for which the clearing figures are available.

These estimates of circulation serve as measures of the 'needs of active trade' for money. The residual deposits which remain idle may be supposed to be related to the rate of interest in accordance with Mr. Keynes's second liquidity-preference schedule $M_2 = L_2(r)$, together with another factor—the rate at which the general price-level has lately been changing. This new factor is included as a measure of the expectations of appreciation or depreciation of money which may be supposed to exercise some influence on the propensity to hoard it. It may be represented by the current year's value of the Sauerbeck index *minus* the previous year's value, and will be referred to as P'.

When this multiple regression equation is worked out, it proves to be:

$$D = 1868 + 0·0640B + 0·0045F - 239·7r - 3·333P'.$$

This relation, for what it is worth, indicates that the velocity of circulation of 'active business deposits' is 1/0·064 or 15·6 per annum, while that of 'active financial deposits' is 1/0·0045, or 221·0 per annum. The volume of 'idle money' is given by the terms other than those concerned with the needs of active trade, namely:

$$1868 - 239·7r - 3·333P'.$$

These results are very highly plausible. If it is assumed that financial deposits are negligible in volume as compared with business deposits, and the 'average business velocity' is calculated by dividing total current accounts into estimated business circulation, as Dr. Shackle and Mr. Phelps Brown have done, it is found that the highest velocity attained in the period for which data are available is one of 14·64 reached in March 1920. If at that rather exceptional time there was very little idle money on current account (as seems probable in view both of the high activity and of the high bank rate prevailing), and the proportion of financial to non-financial deposits was low, the average velocity of *active* current accounts would then be a little over 14·64, and might therefore be near our estimate of 15·6. The plausibility of the estimate of active financial velocity is not so easily checked. It is not really surprising that it should prove to be very high, since professional operators in the commodity or foreign exchange markets or on the Stock Exchange will naturally seek to turn their money over frequently, especially if it is borrowed in the first place; and, since their whole income is derived from manipulating their financial resources, they will try to keep the proportion of their capital which is earning no interest, or on which they are paying interest, at a minimum. The expression for idle money also seems plausible, indicating that more idle hoards are held in times when interest is low, and when the value of money has been recently rising.

At the same time, the relation is open to severe objections from the purely statistical point of view. As regards its closeness as a whole, it leaves little to be desired, the coefficient of multiple correlation being 0·9456 (1 per cent. point = 0·821). The ratios of the net regression coefficients to their own standard errors of estimate (the Fisher coefficients 't') are, however, as follows:

Variable	't'	
B	2·036	
F	0·789	5% point = 2·201
r	3·508	1% point = 3·106
P′	3·501	

Thus, the net regression coefficients of deposits on the two components of the circulation (especially the financial one) are 'not significant' by this test, though their net regression coefficients on interest and price-velocity are 'highly significant'. The velocities of active business and financial deposits thus calculated, therefore, plausible though they are, cannot be regarded as deriving any validity from their manner of calculation. The experiment is interesting, however, as suggesting that the quantity of money is more closely connected with interest rate and expectation of price-change than with the volume of transactions which it is required to perform.

In the event, it does not seem to matter very much which reasonable method is used for estimating total idle money. Fairly similar results are obtained by allowing for the needs of active trade on any reasonable supposition. There are, for instance, two simple methods depending respectively on the assumptions that the velocity of active money is homogeneous, and that financial deposits are negligible in volume.

If the first of these is chosen, the procedure is to calculate the average velocity of current accounts in each year, take the highest velocity of this series as the normal velocity of active money, find the amount of active money required in each year to perform all the transactions at this normal velocity, and so arrive at idle current accounts by difference. This quantity is then added to deposit accounts to obtain total idle money. In the period under review we find a series of average velocities ranging from 49·1 in 1933 to 70·2 in 1929. It is therefore assumed that there was no idle money on current account in the latter year, and 70·2 is divided into total debits in

each year to obtain a series for total active money. Hence idle current
accounts and total idle money are estimated.

If the second method is chosen, the procedure is the same except that an
estimate of business circulation is used instead of total debits. The maximum average business velocity, which is taken as the normal velocity of
active current accounts, is in this case 11·20 which was attained in 1925.
The following table shows the series of idle current accounts obtained by
the above two methods, as well as by assuming for active business and
financial deposits the different velocities obtained by the plausible but
unreliable multiple correlation method.

It will be seen from this that the differences between the three series are
in magnitude rather than in pattern. All show the rising trend, the minima
in 1925, 1929, and 1934, the local maxima in 1926 and 1933, and the maximum for the whole period in 1936. There is little room to doubt that the
idle deposits on current account varied over the period in a way corresponding to the common variations of these series.

*Idle Current Accounts (to which Deposit Accounts are added subsequently
to obtain Total Idle Money). (£ millions)*

Year	Assuming normal active vel. 70·2	Assuming normal business vel. 11·2	Assuming vels. 15·6 and 221
1921 . . .	260	111	185
1922 . . .	206	122	155
1923 . . .	185	91	133
1924 . . .	91	46	78
1925 . . .	65	0	32
1926 . . .	81	55	75
1927 . . .	69	19	42
1928 . . .	24	23	35
1929 . . .	0	10	18
1930 . . .	1	53	50
1931 . . .	103	98	120
1932 . . .	169	85	128
1933 . . .	294	175	234
1934 . . .	231	97	143
1935 . . .	277	148	197
1936 . . .	353	208	266

Some additional support is lent to these estimates (particularly the
second one) by the fact that the division of total idle money between
current and deposit accounts which they indicate can be fairly adequately
and plausibly explained by variations in bank rate and in the volume of
business transactions; but to discuss this at present would be too great a
digression. It may now appear justifiable to proceed straight to a consideration of the relation which idle money, estimated in the above ways, bears
to interest rate and other relevant economic quantities.

4. The schedules of 'idle money'

Idle money shows a stronger negative correlation with interest rate than does total money. The series obtained by the first of the methods described in the last section, for instance, has a correlation of $-0\cdot8155$ with interest rate, while that calculated by the second method has one of $-0\cdot8028$. These relations are to some extent matters of trend. In the case of the first estimate of idle money, its correlation with interest when trend is removed from both variables is reduced to $-0\cdot608$ (1 per cent. point $= 0\cdot623$; 5 per cent. point $= 0\cdot497$). The corresponding correlation between total money and interest, trend being eliminated, was $-0\cdot536$. What is perhaps as important as the fact that the correlation is by no means reduced to insignificance by the removal of trends is that the regression coefficient of idle money on interest is not greatly changed by this removal. Thus, a change of 1 per cent. in interest rate is associated, according to the evidence of the crude series, with a change of between £234 and 348 millions in idle hoards; according to that of the trend-free series the corresponding change in idle money is between £225 and 626 millions, the limits being those set by considering first one, then the other, variable to be the independent one. The two estimates thus overlap, the more accurate being entirely within the range of the wider one; and it seems to be not unreasonable to suppose that the relation between the trends is very much the same as that between the deviations from trend, and that nothing is therefore gained, but valuable evidence lost, by removing the trends from the variables.

For the sake of comprehensiveness it will be wise to examine the relations between a number of possibly relevant variables of which idle money (calculated by the first of the above methods) is one. The most relevant variables are probably the following:

(i) the quantity of idle money, M;

(ii) the total deposits of the clearing banks, D;

(iii) the yield of $2\frac{1}{2}$ per cent. Consols, r;

(iv) the change (r') of r over the past year (since expectations of change in interest rate, which may be based on actual recent changes, are likely to affect hoarding);

(v) the change P' in the Sauerbeck index of wholesale prices over the past year, since recent price-trends may also influence hoarding.

The correlation coefficients between these variables are:

	D	r	r'	P'	M
D	1	$-0\cdot7682$	$-0\cdot1524$	$+0\cdot0815$	$+0\cdot9069$
r	..	1	$+0\cdot2496$	$-0\cdot5494$	$-8\cdot8155$
r'	..	..	1	$+0\cdot0916$	$-0\cdot4074$
P'	..	..	..	1	$+0\cdot0267$
M	..	..	..	..	1

The complete examination of the interrelations of the variables, however, can be done only by Professor Frisch's method of 'Confluence Analysis'.[1] The essence of this is the investigation of the relation between all possible pairs of variables in all combinations of the variables containing them. The investigation is performed by means of 'bunch maps' from which it is possible to tell whether the relation between any two variables is made closer or otherwise, or is altered quantitatively, by the introduction of an additional one. The result is a table showing, for each pair of variables, whether the relation between them in any set is 'better' or 'worse' than in the best of the simpler sets in which they occur. The process is laborious (in the present five-variable problem eighty bunch maps have to be drawn), but it affords a very thorough description of the relations subsisting between the quantities concerned. Finally, only those sets of variables are admitted as possessing clear interrelations in which the net relations between all possible pairs are at least as good as those existing between them in all simpler sets. To this test, which shows the absence of 'multicollinearity', we may add another for the total closeness of the relation between all the variables in the set—namely, the test of 'scatterance' (the numerical value of the correlation determinant, which vanishes for a perfect linear relation between the variables). By these means it is possible to select those sets of variables out of all the possible ones within which close and genuine linear relations exist. The table for the present data is as follows:

Set	Dr	Dr'	DP'	DM	rr'	rP'	rM	r'p'	r'M	P'M	Admissibility	Scatterance
Drr'	N	B	..	..	N	..	..	..	..	..	Yes	0·3828
*DrP'	B	..	B	..	..	B	..	..	..	..	Yes	0·1702
DrM	B	..	..	N	..	..	W	..	..	..	No	0·0586
rr'P'	..	..	..	..	B ?	N	..	B	..	..	Yes	0·6023
rr'M	..	..	..	..	B	..	N	..	B	..	Yes	0·2725
r'P'M	..	..	..	..	..	..	..	N	N	W	No	0·8229
Dr'P'	..	N	N	..	..	..	..	N	..	..	Yes	0·9595
*DP'M	..	..	B	N	..	..	..	..	..	N	Yes	0·1741
*rP'M	..	..	..	..	..	B	B	..	..	B	Yes	0·0564
*Dr'M	..	B	..	B ?	..	..	..	..	B	..	Yes	0·1010
*Drr'P'	N	B	B	..	B	N	..	B	..	..	Yes	0·1310
Drr'M	W	B ?	..	N	B	..	W	..	B	..	No	0·0330
DrP'M	W	..	W	W	..	B	N ?	..	..	B	No	0·0097
Dr'P'M	..	N	N	N	..	..	..	W	N	W	No	0·0988
* ?rr'P'M	..	..	..	..	B	B	B	B	N ?	B	Yes ?	0·0458
Drr'P'M	W	B	W	N ?	N	B ?	W	B	N	W	No	0·0055

B here stands for 'better', W for 'worse', and N for 'no important change', the comparison being, of course, with the best relation between the two variables concerned in any simpler set.

[1] *Statistical Confluence Analysis by means of Complete Regression Systems.* Oslo, 1934.

Taking the double standard of admissibility by the test for multi-collinearity, and of closeness of fit by the scatterance test, there are five groups of variables which show definite relations among themselves, and a somewhat doubtful sixth. They are starred in the above table.

It is arguable that r' and P', being measured over periods *before* those for which the corresponding values of the other variables are taken, must necessarily be treated as independent. Apart from this, however, there seems to be no clear presumption about the relations of dependence and independence among the variables, and Frisch's method of writing the regression equations is therefore most appropriate, since it implies no such presumptions. It does not matter, when this method is adopted, which variables are put on the left-hand side of the equation, except, of course, that the range of error attached to each coefficient on the right-hand side refers to the vagueness of that term's contribution to the estimation of the variable on the left. The latter, though it is represented as being estimated from the others, is not thereby stamped as causally dependent upon them.

The six 'satisfactory' relations so expressed, with the range of error allotted to each coefficient, are:

(i) $D = 1477 - 236(./.0.87)r - 4.26(./.0.64)P'$
(ii) $M = -1667 + 1.438(./.0.96)D - 4.23(./.0.36)P'$
(iii) $M = 2280 - 340(./.0.96)r - 5.55(./.0.88)P'$
(iv) $M = -1461 + 1.330(./.0.94)D - 319(./.0.65)r'$
(v) $D = 2706 - 250(./.0.88)r - 276(./.0.33)r' - 4.44(./.0.68)P'$
(vi) $M = 2142 - 333(./.0.95)r - 4.97(./.0.93)P' - 229(./.0.25)r'$

(there being some doubt about the relation of M to r' in the sixth equation).

The equations involving both M and D (ii and iv) have no direct interest, since we know by definition the exact relation between those variables, namely, $M = D$—'active money'. An examination of the equations concerned will show, however, that the net coefficients of P' and r' have at any rate the same *signs* when total money is added to the formula for estimating idle money as they had when it was absent; nor are these coefficients changed too drastically in magnitude. Therefore we have some evidence that recent changes in interest and prices exercise an effect upon idle money which cannot be explained by variations in total money.

The remaining equations, showing the relations between either idle or total money and interest, price-change and interest-change, indicate that, while the forms of the relations are similar for both, those for the idle part of deposits are closer than those for the whole. Thus, the scatterance in the group (M, r, P') is only 0.0564 against 0.1702 for the group (D, r, P'), while the corresponding values for the sets (M, r, r', P') and (D, r, r', P') are

respectively 0·0458 and 0·1310. Moreover, the ranges of error of the individual coefficients are in every case but one (r') smaller for the relations involving M than for those involving D. It seems, therefore, that the primary connexion is between *idle* money (rather than *total* money) and the other variables.

It is a moot point whether the insertion of r' into equation (vi) is justified. It probably does no harm to introduce it, but it is evident from the extremely small difference which it makes to the scatterance of the set that it does very little good. In the *ordinary* multiple regression equation its 't' coefficient is 2·676, where 1 per cent. point is 3·055 and 5 per cent. point 2·179. It therefore remains, at all events, very probable that its sign is right, even if its magnitude is doubtful, i.e. that a rise of interest rate over the past year is systematically associated with a net diminution in the quantity of idle money. This runs contrary to the natural presumption that falling bond prices will be associated with large holdings of idle money, but the regression coefficient of M on r' is negative in all possible combinations of the variables. It may be that the rate of interest is highly stable, so that the movement of the past year is generally expected to be reversed.

The interpretation of the other coefficients in equations (iii) and (vi) is easier. When prices have been falling, large idle bank balances are accumulated in preference to large stocks of commodities, and probably also to industrial equities, which tend to vary in value with commodity prices. The net relation between interest and idle money remains, however, much the closest of those considered.

When this analysis (or rather, the analysis of those relations here found to be most significant) is repeated with the second estimate of idle money made in the previous section, similar results are obtained. The correlation coefficients are:

	r	r'	P'	M
r	1	+0·2496	−0·5494	−0·8028
r'	..	1	−0·0916	−0·3145
P'	..	..	1	+0·0921
M	..	..	..	1

As soon as the standardization net regression coefficients are worked out, it is clear that the variable r' has almost no connexion with M (its coefficient is only −0·0002). In terms of the other two variables, r and P', the equation for M, worked out in the Frisch manner with the ranges of error of the coefficients added, is:

$$M = 1883 - 259(./.0\cdot90)r - 4\cdot367(./.0\cdot72)P'.$$

The multiple correlation coefficient for the whole relation is 0·9052, where the 1 per cent. point is 0·712.

It will be remembered that in the full regression equation used in the last section when attempting to separate the financial and business circulations, an expression for idle money terms of P' and r was isolated, which had highly significant 't' values for both its net regression coefficients. This may be regarded as the ordinary (as opposed to the Frischian) schedule for idle money estimated as in the third column of the table at the end of that section, where separate velocities are assumed for active financial and business deposits. If we take the liberty of making idle money the dependent variable, and r' and P' the independent ones, we can at once write down in their *ordinary* forms the schedules already worked out in the Frischian manner. They can then be compared more suitably with the idle money expression from the full regression equation. It will be seen that the difference between the Frischian and the ordinary forms is slight here, as it is bound to be wherever the relation is very close.

We now have liquidity-preference schedules corresponding to all three of the estimates of idle money made in the last section. They are:

$$\text{Estimate I} \qquad M = 2229 - 327r - 4\cdot84P'$$
$$\text{Estimate II} \qquad M = 1795 - 235r - 3\cdot06P'$$
$$\text{Estimate III} \qquad M = 1868 - 240r - 3\cdot33P'$$

The difference between these schedules, like the difference between the estimates themselves, is clearly one of scale rather than of fundamental pattern. The first and second, which follow from choosing opposite extremes in the matter of assumptions about the total circulation of money, are not widely different except that the former gives a 39 per cent. greater influence to interest changes and a 58 per cent. greater influence to changes in price-velocity in accounting for fluctuations which have a standard deviation some 31 per cent. larger. The relative magnitudes of the coefficients are more nearly equal in the Frischian form of the schedules, the influences of interest and of price-velocity being respectively 31 per cent. and 27 per cent. greater when the first estimate of idle money is used than when the second is employed. The third estimate is, of course, a compromise between the other two, though nearer to the second than to the first, and this is seen also in the schedule based upon it.

It seems that, whatever reasonable method of estimating idle money we use, the resulting series shows a very strong connexion of much the same kind with price-velocity and interest rate. Moreover, this seems to be considerably the closest relation which is to be discerned among the variables total money, idle money, interest, price-velocity, and interest-velocity—a group wide enough to contain the ingredients of many theoretically plausible connexions. If it is a criterion of the importance of a relation that it should emerge clearly in practice, this form of the liquidity-preference schedule would appear to be of very considerable importance.

5. The traditional function of interest

The foregoing appears to suggest that the rate of interest is intimately connected with the quantity of idle money, and thereby to support Mr. Keynes's contention that it is to monetary factors, not to those envisaged by Classical interest theory, that we should look when discussing it. This is not the place for an exhaustive discussion of the relation between Mr. Keynes's theory of interest and the Classical one (whatever the latter label may be supposed to cover), but two remarks may be made to allow of the controversy's being decently laid aside for the remainder of this article. In the first place, there is no reason to quarrel with Mr. Robertson's dictum[1] that interest is the market price of loanable funds. In the second, to say that the price of loanable funds, or wheat, or any other commodity, is governed by the conditions of its supply and consumption *per unit of time* is not to deny that it is also closely related to the visible stocks of that commodity in existence or in the particular market concerned. The 'savings and investment' theory of interest is couched in terms of *flows*, the Keynesian theory in terms of *stocks*, but since the rate of change of the stock is simply the difference between the flows (suitably defined), the alternative approaches to the problem need not be mutually unrelated.

The most systematic expression of the theory that interest is concerned with the equilibrium between the flows of savings and investment is that developed by Wicksell and found in its most mature form in Mr. Keynes's *Treatise on Money*. Its central contention may be expressed in the form of the relation

$$P_1 - P_0 = k(n-r),$$

where n is the natural or equilibrium rate of interest at which savings and investment are equal, r is the rate ruling in the market, and P_0 and P_1 are the wholesale price indices in the year for which the rates are measured and the following one respectively. It is clearly difficult to get any direct statistical verification of this relation, since n is an independent variable not capable of being measured in any obvious way. It is surprising to find, therefore, that there is, for some periods in particular, a significant negative correlation between $P_1 - P_0$ and r; i.e. that there is evidence for the existence of the relation even on the assumption that n is relatively constant. Moreover, it seems to be usually the case that this correlation is higher than that between r and $P_0 - P_{-1}$, the change of prices over the *previous* year, so that interest rate appears to be the cause and price change the effect rather than the reverse. If the data used are annual averages of the yield of $2\frac{1}{2}$ per cent. Consols and the first differences of the annual averages

---

[1] See the *Quarterly Journal of Economics*, Nov. 1936, and the *Economic Journal*, Sept. 1937.

of the Sauerbeck Index, with linear trends removed from both in each of the secular periods taken, the correlation coefficients are as follows:

Period	With previous price change	With subsequent price change
1849–73 . . .	−0·0741	−0·4702
1874–96 . . .	−0·1160	−0·0380
1897–1920 . .	+0·8054	−0·3571
1921–36 . . .	−0·4248	−0·7250
1849–1936 . .	−0·0688	−0·2146

Of the coefficients relating to *subsequent* price-change, the first is well above 5 per cent. point, the second quite insignificant, the third not far below 5 per cent. point, the fourth well above 1 per cent. point, and the last, in view of the large number of data involved, above 5 per cent. point.

There is thus a certain amount of evidence that the Wicksell relation may be traced even with the highly improbable assumption of a constant natural rate. It may, in fact, be shown that this constancy of natural rate is inconsistent with the existence of cyclical fluctuations such as are actually observed in interest and prices. One of the most striking constancies in the whole field of empirical economics is the relation known as the 'Gibson Paradox'. This has been described by Mr. Gibson, after whom it is named, by Mr. Coates, and by Professor Irving Fisher, and there is no need here to quote the evidence for it which these writers give, nor the supplementary evidence which has been collected to support the remarks about it which follow. To summarize the main facts: the long-term rate of interest and the wholesale price-level move together, but with the latter leading the former by about one year, in all their long-term movements. In the trade-cycle movements, which may be isolated, for instance, by eliminating linear trends over the periods distinguished in the above table, a similar relation between the variables persists in the periods 1849–73 and 1897–1920, but not in the other two.

Assuming that the period we are considering is one in which this Gibson relation holds over the course of an eight-year trade cycle, we can easily see that there will be a substantial negative correlation between interest and price-change in the succeeding year, for, owing to the one-year lag of interest behind prices, the former is still low when the latter is well towards its maximum rate, and still at its maximum when the curve of the prices ruling an average time of a year and a half before is falling at nearly its greatest rate. Indeed, it may be ascertained that, with sinusoidal curves of eight years' period, interest lagging a year *and a half* behind prices, the latter would have a perfect negative correlation with the change in the price-level over the succeeding year, since we should be comparing one series with the first derivative of a similar one differing in phase by a quarter of a period. The correlation coefficient between two sinusoidal series being itself a sinusoidal function of the lag between them, it may be deduced that the correlation between r and P_1-P_0, with the actual one-year lag of interest behind prices, where the two series are sine curves, is approximately -0.92. The validity of the Gibson relation in the short period (i.e. in the course of the trade cycle) therefore *implies* the existence of an inverse connexion (though not quite a perfect one) between interest and subsequent price-change. The converse does not seem to be necessarily true, for in the period when the connexion between interest and subsequent price-change is closest (1921–36), the Gibson relation does not hold between the *trend-free* series of interest and prices.

The question may be approached in another way by examining deductively the consequence of a perfect connexion between interest and subsequent price-change combined with the strict application of the Gibson relation. This may be done by combining the equations of the two relations into a single difference equation which is then solved by one of the methods described by Frisch and Holme,[1] and used by Tinbergen. The Gibson relation is written

$$P_0 = a + br_1$$

and the Wicksell relation

$$P_1 - P_0 = k(n - r_0).$$

If r is measured as a deviation from the assumed constant natural rate, then these give

$$r_2 - r_1 + \frac{k}{b} r_0 = 0.$$

The method of solution is to put $r_t = Cx^t$, in which case we get

$$x = \tfrac{1}{2} \pm \sqrt{(\tfrac{1}{4} - k/b)}.$$

This, it is clear, gives complex solutions if k/b is positive and greater than $\tfrac{1}{4}$. Such a complex solution may be transformed into the shape

$$p(\cos\theta \pm i\sin\theta) \text{ where } i \text{ is } \sqrt{(-1)}.$$

The general solution, which is the sum of the two special solutions thus obtained, is clearly a damped cosine wave,

$$r_t = Cx^t = 2Cq^t \cos\theta t$$

(by de Moivre's theorem).

If the solution is real, on the other hand (i.e. if k/b is negative or less than $\tfrac{1}{4}$), the movement of r as a result of the simultaneous operation of the Gibson and Wicksell relations is exponential, i.e. the rate (and prices with it) increases or decreases 'at compound interest' indefinitely.

---

[1] Ragnar Frisch and Harald Holme: 'The Characteristic Solutions of a Mixed Difference and Differential Equation Occurring in Dynamic Economics', *Econometrica*, April 1935. Tinbergen: *Econometrica*, July 1935, pp. 276–7 and *An Econometric Approach to Business Cycle Problems*, Paris, 1938. Also *Business Cycles in the United States of America, 1919–32*, Geneva, 1939, pp. 142–7.

If the solution is periodic, the period is clearly

$$\frac{2\pi}{\tan^{-1}2\sqrt{(k/b-\tfrac{1}{4})}},$$

while the damping factor q is $\tfrac{1}{2}/\cos\theta$. It follows, therefore, that for an eight-year cycle, $\cos\theta$ being $\sqrt{\tfrac{1}{2}}$, q is 0·7071. This means that, in the course of a single cycle, the amplitude of the oscillation would be reduced to one-sixteenth of its initial value. For the cyclical movement to be undamped, θ would have to be $\cos^{-1}\tfrac{1}{2}$, or $\pi/3$, so that the period would then be six years. Any shorter cyclic movement would be anti-damped. As for the exponential solutions, any plausible one must not require a very rapid geometric decrease or increase of interest and prices. A gradual fall is produced if k/b is a very small positive quantity (i.e. if the Wicksell effect operates relatively feebly); a rise requires that k/b shall have a small negative value.

An exponential solution is therefore not very probable, and the only undamped trade-cycle movement of both interest and prices consistent with the assumptions made is a six-year one, the more realistic eight-year cycle being highly damped if our suppositions hold. The conclusion is that, assuming the Wicksell and Gibson relations both to hold over the course of the eight-year cycle, we cannot maintain the assumption of a constant natural rate of interest.

How must the natural rate be supposed to vary in order to make the Gibson and Wicksell relations compatible with an eight-year cycle? Mr. Keynes, in his *Treatise on Money* (vol. ii, pp. 203–5), suggests that the Gibson relation may be due to the 'stickiness' of market rates in the face of a changing natural rate. He points out that, if the natural rate is always a little ahead of market rate in its movements, it will be above it when both are rising, thus causing prices to rise, and below it when both are falling, thus bringing about a continuous fall in the price-level. This may be thought of mostly as a long-run process, but, as the Gibson relation sometimes holds for trade-cycle movements too, it is necessary to see in what circumstances this short-run agreement between interest and price-series may be explained in this way. The above question may therefore be put in the form: what lag between movements of natural and market rates is consistent with the truth of both the Gibson and Wicksell relations, and with an eight-year cycle?

The results of postulating various lags may be investigated by embodying the conditions in difference equations, which are then solved by methods similar to that shown above. It is not necessary to give details here. This investigation was carried out for lags of half a year, a year, a year and a half, two years, and three years. Only in the last case is any cyclic movement of interest and prices compatible with the assumptions. With the three-year lag all the cyclic solutions give undamped oscillations, the period varying with the ratio of the Wicksell to the Gibson coefficient, k/b, as for instance:

k/b	Period
0·333	Infinity
0·400	8·70
0·414	8·00
0·500	6·00
1·000	4·00

The values of k/b compatible with cyclic movements of the variables therefore lie between $\frac{1}{3}$ and 1. There are exponential solutions if k/b falls below $\frac{1}{3}$, but these are extremely sensitive to changes in the value of k/b, which is therefore limited to a very narrow range if the results are to remain realistic, and the probability of there being a three-year lag and an exponential solution is therefore small.

The three-year lag which must be supposed to exist between movements of natural and market rates if Mr. Keynes's explanation of the Gibson relation is to apply over the course of an eight-year cycle in prices and interest may seem too long to be plausible. There are, however, further considerations which render the theory interesting. If natural rate is three years ahead of market rate, then, since market rate is one year behind prices, natural rate must be two years (a quarter period) ahead of prices—i.e. it must move exactly with the rate of change of prices. Professor Irving Fisher has tried to demonstrate, with a degree of success which is seriously questioned, for instance, by F. R. Macaulay,[1] that market rate varies, over long periods, directly with price-velocity, but this, whatever may be the case in the long run, certainly does not hold in the short run. We have seen that the correlation of interest with succeeding price-change, as well as with preceding price-change in most periods, is inverse, not direct. It now appears that, according to our theory, the correspondence which Professor Fisher expects for *market* rate ought to hold in the case of *natural* rate.

The natural rate, as ordinarily understood, is expressed in money terms. Therefore, if the price-level starts changing, and is expected to go on changing over the period of any new contracts entered into at a rate dP/dt, then, for the *real* natural rate to remain what it was before the price-change began, the natural rate expressed in terms of money must change to $n + \dfrac{100}{P}\dfrac{dP}{dt}$. In order that the real equilibrium rate shall remain constant, the money rate corresponding to it must vary directly with the first derivative of prices to an extent depending on the lengths of the contracts for which

---

[1] *The Movements of Interest Rates, Bond Yields, and Stock Prices in the United States since 1856*, Appendix B. National Bureau of Economic Research, N.Y., 1938.

the rate is to maintain equilibrium and on the lengths of time for which the current price-velocities are expected to persist. The beginning of a price-change without any alteration in market rate means, of course, that the natural rate (defined in the simplest manner as the rate which keeps the price-level constant) has changed, but what matters here is the further fact that, as soon as price-change *does* set in, with any likelihood of its continuing, natural rate (in money terms) has to go *beyond* its new long-term equilibrium value for the special purpose of offsetting expectations based upon the current price movement.

If the price-index P stands somewhere near its basic value of 100, the addition which must be made to the old natural rate to allow for an expectation that current price-velocity will continue indefinitely is about equal to dP/dt. The fluctuations of natural rate, in other words, will have, in these circumstances, the same amplitude as those of price-velocity. We have assumed, however, that natural rate foreruns market rate, and thus has its amplitude of oscillation exactly; and from these two pieces of information we can easily calculate the proportion which the allowance for price-change in our idealized cycle bears to that which would be made if the current price-velocity were always expected to continue for ever. Price-movements may be written

$$P_t = P_0 + g \sin \tfrac{1}{4}\pi t,$$

whence $$dP/dt = \tfrac{1}{4}\pi g \cos \tfrac{1}{4}\pi t.$$

The amplitude of price-velocity is therefore $\tfrac{1}{4}\pi g$. That of market rate (and hence of natural rate) is, of course, g/b, where b is the regression coefficient in the Gibson relation. The required ratio, which might loosely be called the probability assigned to continuance of current price-velocity, is therefore $4/\pi b$. If b is about 44, as it seems to be for the period 1849–1936 as a whole, this is 0·029, or 1/34·5. This result may be obtained in another way, using the fact that the Wicksell coefficient k is $b \times (0·414)$, or 18·2.

The assumption that the Wicksell relation holds exactly may therefore be used in developing a very convincing picture of the relations between interest and prices in the eight-year cycle. Interest lags a year behind prices (an observed phenomenon) and three years behind the natural rate, which fluctuates with the rate of change of the price-index, though with less than a thirtieth of the latter's amplitude. All this is consistent with a perfect negative correlation between the excess of natural over market rate and the change in prices in the following year. The picture would be highly plausible were it not for the difficulty of showing in greater detail how interest rate affects enterprise at all. The article by Mr. J. E. Meade and Mr. P. W. S. Andrews in the first number of this publication has shown that, in a not insignificant sample of entrepreneurs, very few were aware that they took account of interest changes either in adjusting their stocks (as Mr. Hawtrey's writings suggest) or in embarking on new capital construction, as the argument of Mr. Keynes's *Treatise* requires. Yet this difficulty in showing any causal connexion does not affect the existence of the empirical connexion which may be traced even on the assumption that natural rate is constant, nor the plausibility (in view of the Gibson relation's existence) of the theoretical scheme of relations suggested above. Any scheme of causal connexions alternative to the Wicksellian one must be capable of explaining the Gibson relation at least as well if it is to be accepted.

6. Liquidity preference and the Gibson relation

Let it be assumed, however, that the rate of interest does in fact have hardly any effect upon the decision to invest, and consequently upon income, but that this decision is affected solely by the level or rate of change (or both) of effective demand for the product, with some secondary regard, perhaps, to the level of costs in which interest charges constitute in most cases an insignificant item. Let interest, which has by this means been reduced to comparative insignificance as a causal factor, be thought of in the Keynesian way as related to the volume of idle money by a schedule of liquidity-preference such as was derived in section 4 above. Is it now possible to explain the close relation between the levels of interest and of prices as satisfactorily as by the Wicksellian assumptions of the last section ?

It will be wise to consider only the business circulation, leaving financial transactions out of account on the assumption that they are financed by separate and comparatively not very large deposits reserved for that purpose. In this case, we may write

$$B = P_0 T,$$

where B is the total of business transactions per annum, P_0 the current price-level, and T the real flow of commodities which change hands.

If D represents total deposits, and M the portion of them remaining idle, the second method of deriving M used in section 3 gives the equation

$$M = D - B/V,$$

where V is the assumed standard velocity of 'active business money', or

$$M = D - P_0 T/V.$$

The liquidity-preference schedule derived in section 4, however, is a relation of the form

$$M = x - yr - z(P_0 - P_{-1})$$

(P_{-1} being the price-level obtaining in the previous year). Thus, equating the two expressions for M and rearranging slightly

$$P_0\!\left(\frac{T}{V}-z\right)+zP_{-1} = D-x+yr.$$

The meaning of this can be seen more clearly if it is assumed tentatively that T and D remain constant at their mean annual values over the period 1921–36 and if the appropriate values of the other coefficients from the second liquidity-preference schedule are also inserted. In this case, the relation may be reduced to

$$P_{-1}+0\!\cdot\!832P_0 = -27\!\cdot\!7+59\!\cdot\!3r.$$

With a constant total quantity of money and a constant real volume of trade, therefore, the liquidity-preference schedule implies a relation between r on the one hand and a weighted average of the current and previous years' price-levels on the other which agrees remarkably well with the Gibson relation, implying in the present case a lag of interest behind prices by about three-fifths of a year. As for the size of the coefficient of r, this may be checked against that obtained in the simple regression between P_{-1} and r by supposing P_0 to be equal to P_{-1}. The coefficient then becomes $59\!\cdot\!3/1\!\cdot\!832$, or about $32\!\cdot\!4$, whereas by direct regression analysis it is $35\!\cdot\!5$. The degree of precision with which the liquidity-preference schedule accounts for the Gibson relation, even on the crude assumptions of constant total money and constant real volume of trade, is thus remarkably high.

If the volume of bank deposits varies in the same way as prices, the chief effect will be to increase the coefficient of r and to modify the lag between interest and prices. The closeness of the indirectly estimated to the directly estimated coefficient demonstrated above seems to indicate, however, that the adjustment required on this ground has not been great in recent times—unless it has been already made by the offsetting variation of some other quantity so far supposed constant, such as T.

The effects of supposing that T varies with the price-level are less easy to see, since the equation then becomes quadratic in P_0. It can be deduced, however, by considering very small variations of the quantities concerned, that the general effect of such a supposition is to *decrease* the coefficient of r. Since the directly determined coefficient is *above* that calculated indirectly without the supposition that T moves with P_0, then either that supposition must be the contrary of the truth, or the effect of varying real turnover must be more than offset by the opposing effect of varying total money. Since real turnover clearly varies *with* prices rather than in the contrary sense, the latter explanation seems to be the correct one.

The liquidity-preference explanation seems to stand so long as the real
turnover of commodities does not vary too much with the trade cycle (or,
more strictly, with prices) relative to the variation of total money, and,
as Mr. Phelps Brown and Dr. Shackle have shown,[1] real turnover has very
little variation from trend. It seems, therefore, that the Gibson relation
may be accounted for as well on the assumption that the rate of interest
is a comparatively unimportant price, related to the quantity of idle money
and to recent trends in the general price-level by the liquidity-preference
schedule, as on the Wicksellian supposition that it is the chief regulator
of new enterprise.

7. Implications

The above considerations show that the relations between money, prices,
and interest may be quite well expressed in either Keynesian or Wicksellian terms. Moreover, the results of the attempts made here to express
them in these two ways for the period 1921–36 are mutually consistent,
as they ought to be if both are at all successful. The explanation of the
relations in terms of a causal mechanism, however, is quite another matter,
and, as we noted at the end of section 5, entrepreneurs themselves seem unaware of the existence of such an effect from interest changes as is required
by the Wicksellian explanation. The authors of the article there referred
to, however, thus summarize the replies to another of their questions:

'There is considerable divergence of practice among the business men as to whether
the presence or absence of liquid resources induces or discourages investment and
renewals. Those who asserted that the presence of liquid resources induced extensions and renewals were more numerous than those who denied this; and those who
asserted that the absence of liquid resources discouraged extensions and renewals
were again more numerous than those who denied this. But those two majorities were
not made up of the same entrepreneurs. There is certainly sufficient evidence for us
to conclude that the presence or absence of liquid resources is a consideration of some
importance in this connexion.'[2]

It would perhaps be presumptuous to assert more than that the entrepreneur's liquidity position is probably of considerably more direct importance to him than is the rate of interest, but so much, at any rate, seems to
be justified by the evidence. If the liquidity of entrepreneurs' positions in
general is to be judged by the total quantity of idle money, calculated in
one of the ways used above, it may be that the causal connexion between
high liquid resources and increased enterprise furnishes the explanation of
the factual connexion between low interest and increased enterprise; low
interest being, not a factor of any causal importance in itself, but merely a
result of abundance of idle funds, which is the real stimulant.

[1] 'An Index of Real Turnover, 1919–36', *Oxford Economic Papers*, No. 1.
[2] Ibid., p. 30.

Mr. Colin Clark has recently developed a similar suggestion. In 'A System of Equations explaining the U.S. Trade Cycle, 1921 to 1941' (*Econometrica*, April 1949) he takes up a point made in discussion by Mr. C. F. Rees, namely, that 'most corporations are strongly influenced by the cash position in deciding whether to accumulate or de-cumulate inventories'. Mr. Clark finds that *total* bank money fits well as one of the independent factors explaining the changes of inventories in the United States. This theory of the dependence of the most sensitive portion of investment on the monetary position is an interesting variant of Professor Hawtrey's view that inventories respond readily to changes in interest rates. Mr. Clark does not attempt to introduce the monetary situation as a factor directly affecting *fixed* investment, to which the above summarized replies of the entrepreneurs refer; it would be interesting to know whether any such effect could be traced—although in principle the monetary factor might no doubt operate with great power through the medium of inventory investment alone.

(v) *A Further Inquiry into the Effects of Rates of Interest* [1]

By P. W. S. ANDREWS

THE first number of *Oxford Economic Papers*, October 1938, contained a summary and discussion of the answers received by the Oxford Economists' Research Group to questions upon the rate of interest and kindred matters during its interviews with business men. It was found that there was practically complete agreement that investment in stocks and in fixed capital was not affected by short-term rates of interest. The majority of the business men also denied that the long-term rate of interest affected investment directly, although some considered that it had, or might have, some importance.[2]

The business men who gave those answers were approached through personal introduction, and mainly represented prosperous firms in a strong financial position. The number questioned, 37, was necessarily limited by the method of intensive personal interview which was adopted. It was felt

---

[1] Reprinted from *Oxford Economic Papers*, No. 3.

[2] I should like to take this opportunity of calling the attention of English readers to J. F. Ebersole, 'The Influence of Interest Rates', *Harvard Business Review*, XVII. i. 1938. This paper reached similar conclusions from different, American, material. Ninety-three cases in the records of the Harvard Graduate School of Business Administration, 'which involved entrepreneurial problems of business of the type in which interest rates might have been a factor' were examined: 30 cases mentioned the rate of interest, but in 20 of them 'the interest rate was not a factor contributing to the decision whether or not to extend or to contract'.

that the nature of the replies which were received might have been affected by the smallness of the sample and by a bias arising from the prosperity and relative importance of the businesses represented. The Oxford Economists' Research Group therefore decided, in view of the interest and importance of the conclusions resulting from its interviews, that it was desirable to make a further inquiry into the effects of the rate of interest, and to send a questionnaire to as large and as representative a sample of British business men as possible.

OXFORD ECONOMISTS' RESEARCH GROUP

Have any of the following

(a) Bank Rate
(b) Rate of Discount on Bills
(c) The level of interest charged on bank overdrafts
(d) The facility with which bank overdrafts can be obtained
(e) Yield on Government securities
(f) The facility with which you can raise new capital from the public

ever affected:

  I Your decision to make, or to defer making, expenditure on plant extensions ? ....

  II Your decision to make, or to defer making, expenditure on maintenance and repairs ? ....

  III The size of your holding of stocks ? ....

Please indicate in the right hand margin opposite each of these which of (a), (b), (c), (d), (e), (f), if any, has affected you. If none of them has affected you, please insert the word 'None'.

NOTE. In the cases of an affirmative answer to any question we should welcome further details, however brief, as to the way in which a particular rate of interest has affected you, with dates. Similarly, in the cases of negative answers we should much appreciate it if you could state a general reason why rates of interest and the cost of borrowing money do not affect you. If you are willing to give this information, space is provided on the next page.

[*Facsimile of the Questionnaire, the answers to which are discussed in this paper*]

The questionnaire which was used is reproduced. It was sent on 22 February 1939 to 1,308 businesses, with a covering letter from the Chairman of the Research Group, Mr. R. F. Harrod, and was addressed to the Managing Director. The principal source of addresses was the Federation of British Industries' *Register of British Manufacturers*, from whom 1,000 names were taken by strict sample. Although this register is fairly representative of British manufacturing industries, some non-manufacturing industries are inadequately represented, if at all. A list of public companies was therefore used to obtain names of companies in the following industries:

Retail Trade, Wholesalers and Merchants, Shipowners, Transport, Public Utilities, Builders and Contractors, Breweries and Distilleries, Hotels and Restaurants, Cinemas and Theatres. Some of these, especially Merchants, and Builders and Contractors, were additions desired because of the general tendency to discuss these as industries that are *a priori* affected by rates of interest. The general aim was to make the field of inquiry more representative of British industry as a whole. Where the number of companies listed in these supplementary industries was large, a sample was taken, but all the companies were included when the number was small. The list of public companies yielded 308 names.

One part of the final sample was thus obtained by random sample; this, as is stated above, gave 1,000 names. The remaining 308 were obtained on a selective basis so far as the industries represented were concerned. The fact that the second part of the sample originated in a list of public companies causes it to be more unified in entrepreneurial type than the first part. The first part, being selected from the F.B.I. *Register*, resulted in replies from firms ranging in size from large public companies to small private partnerships and sole-proprietorships. At the same time, it must be understood that the public companies did include many which were of small or only moderate size. A further point is that the businesses were not all independent. The inclusion of subsidiary or associated firms in the field was permitted if they had separate addresses. The replies received did, in some cases, come from associated firms, but their answers were not always identical.

The form of the questionnaire should be carefully noted. The letters *a, b, c, d, e, f* are used in the following summaries of replies and comments to indicate respectively the factors: bank rate, rate of discount on bills, the level of interest charged on bank overdrafts, the facility with which bank overdrafts can be obtained, yield on government securities, and the facility with which new capital can be raised from the public. The numerals I, II, III are used to refer, according to the context, to the particular decision referred to against them, or to the actual items concerned: expenditure on plant extensions, expenditure on maintenance and repairs, and the size of the holding of stocks, respectively. It is to be regretted that the form of question III is not symmetrical with I and II. This must be the main reason for some businesses unexpectedly giving the absolute size of their holdings of stocks. In six cases these replies, besides giving a negative answer to questions I and II, had placed the word *none* against each of the six factors *a* to *f*. Here a negative answer to question III has been presumed. Question I which, applied in its narrow sense of *plant* extensions would not affect some of the businesses covered, appears to have been interpreted in the wider sense of *extensions*.

It will be noted that the questionnaire gave an opportunity for businesses to make comments upon the answers which they gave. A gratifying number did so, and their comments are summarized and discussed later in this paper.

Eighteen refusals or returned letters were received, and 313 businesses completed, or endeavoured to complete, the questionnaire; 254 of the replies were from businesses in the F.B.I. *Register*, and 59 from businesses in the list of companies. It was not possible to utilize one of the replies, and three others gave general answers without reference to the details of the questionnaire. One of these had apparently been affected by *b* in connexion with bills on goods sent to a certain foreign country, but not by anything else (this should certainly be considered a negative reply); one had apparently not been affected at all, and one company was obviously seriously affected by difficulties in obtaining finance in order to alleviate the effects of its having had to replace a major asset. The remaining 309 replies are indicated below: not all of them were complete, and, in some cases, the categorical answer has been determined from the comments, the questionnaire being not filled up, or not returned.

QUESTION I

The decision to make, or to defer making, expenditure on plant extensions

Two hundred and forty-six said that none of the factors mentioned in the questionnaire had affected their decisions. One said that none had done so except for the period during the last war,[1] when *f* was important. One reply was 'not directly' and the business had not apparently been affected.[2] Two said that the question was not applicable to them.

There were 57 affirmative replies. One said 'No', but stated that *f* would be important; one stated 'scarcely except *cf*'; one replied in the affirmative, but said that none of the mentioned factors weighed strongly, although *d* had done so 30 years ago and might again be important; one said that interest rates were a relatively small factor; one said 'Yes'; and one said 'Yes, certainly'. There remain 51 replies of a categorical nature; these may be tabulated as follows:[3]

> *a* 1. *c* 3. *d* 7. *f* 5. *af* 1. *cd* 4. *df* 4. *abc* 1. *acd* 9. *bcd* 1. *cdf* 4. *acf* 1. *def* 1. *acef* 1. *abcd* 4. *acdf* 3. *abcdf* 1.

It will be observed that 16 mentioned only *d* and/or *f*.

Two businesses did not answer this question.

---

[1] i.e. First World War.   [2] No. 30 in the first part of the summary of comments.
[3] The letters indicate the nature of the replies, and the numerals immediately following each letter or group of letters is the number of businesses which gave that particular answer.

QUESTION II

The decision to make, or to defer making, expenditure on maintenance and repairs

Two hundred and eighty-four said that none of the mentioned factors had affected this. One said that the question was not applicable.

Eighteen affirmative replies were received. These were:

c 1. *f* 2. *cd* 3. *ae* 1. *df* 1. *abc* 1. *acd* 3. *bcd* 1. *acef* 1. *abcd* 2. *acdf* 2.

Three businesses mentioned only *d* and/or *f*.

Four did not answer this question.

QUESTION III

The size of the holding stocks

Two hundred and thirty-nine negative answers were received, and to these must be added 6 answers where the absolute size of the stock held was given but where, as explained above, a negative answer may be presumed (thus making 245 negative answers). One business said that the factors had not directly affected this, and they did not appear to have done so. Two said that the question was not applicable.

Forty-eight replies were of an affirmative nature. One said that the factors mentioned had affected this only to a limited extent; one said that they had to some extent; one said 'Yes'; one 'Yes, but not deciding'; one 'Yes, decidedly'. The remaining 43 are as follows:

c 4. *d* 6. *e* 1. *f* 1. *ac* 3. *ae* 2. *bd* 1. *cd* 8. *df* 1. *abc* 2. *bcd* 1. *acd* 5. *acef* 1. *abcd* 3. *acdf* 3. *bcde* 1.

Eight of these mentioned only *d* and/or *f*.

Thirteen did not answer this question.

Two hundred and seventeen businesses gave a negative answer to each of the three questions; to these may be added 7 businesses which made a negative reply to the first two questions and for whom, as explained earlier, a negative answer may be presumed to the third. This would mean that at the least 70 per cent., and at the most 72 per cent., of the 309 firms whose replies are tabulated said that they were not affected at all by the rates of interest, or facilities for borrowing mentioned. There were also 7 who did not answer one question, but said 'No' to the other two, and 2 who said that one or more questions were not applicable to them, but who said 'No' to the other questions or question. If these 9 answers are added, the upper limit of the percentage not affected by any of the mentioned factors is raised to 75.

There follows an analysis of the replies according to the industries to which the businesses belong. I, II, and III and letters or combinations of letters are used to indicate the questions and the answers respectively, as previously. The following abbreviations are also used:

Total = total of replies coming from the industry.
NO = Number who said No.
Not App. = Number who said that the question was not applicable.
No Ans. = Number who did not answer the question.
(N...) = Total which may be interpreted as negative.
(Y...) = Total which may be interpreted as affirmative.
(NNN) = Number previously tabulated which gave a negative answer to all three questions.
(DF) = Number who said that they were affected *only* by d or f.

(i) General Consumers' and Household Goods
Total 37.

I

NO 33. *d* 1. *df* 1. *acd* 1. *acef* 1.   (N. 33. Y. 4.)

II

NO 34. *f* 1. *acef* 1. No. Ans. 1.   (N. 34. Y. 2.)

III

NO 31. *d* 1. *df* 1. *acef* 1. *acdf* 1. No Ans. 2.   (N. 31. Y. 4.)
(*NNN* 31. DF 2.)

(ii) Textiles[1]
Total 29.

I

NO 23. *c* 1. *cd* 1. *abc* 1. *bcd* 1. *abcd* 2.   (N. 23. Y. 6.)

II

NO 23. *c* 1. *cd* 1. *abc* 1. *bcd* 1. *abcd* 2.   (N. 23. Y. 6.)

III

NO 22. *c* 1. *cd* 1. *abc* 1. *bcd* 1. *abcd* 2. *bcde* 1.   (N. 22. Y. 7.)
(*NNN* 21. DF 0.)

(iii) Clothing[2]
Total 9.

I

NO 6. *cd* 1 (chiefly *d*). *acd* 1. *cdf* 1.   (N. 6. Y. 3.)

II

NO 9.   (N. 9. Y. 0.)

III

NO 7. *cd* 1. *acd* 1.   (N. 7. Y. 2.)
(*NNN* 6. DF 0.)

[1] Three companies (1 *bcd, bcd, bcd*; 2 *abcd, abcd, abcd*) are associated.
[2] Does not include businesses which retail.

(iv) Brewers, Distillers, &c.

Total 7.

I

NO 6. *cdf* 1. (N. 6. Y. 1.)

II

NO 7. (N. 7. Y. 0.)

III

NO 6. *cd* 1. (N. 6. Y. 1.)

(*NNN* 6. DF 0.)

(v) Hotel and Restaurant

Total 4.

I

NO 4.

II

NO 4.

III

NO 4.

(*NNN* 4. DF 0.)

(vi) Retailers

Total 20.

I

NO 11. 'Yes' 1. *a* 1. *d* 1. *f* 2. '*f* would be' 1. *acd* 1. *cdf.* 1.
    acdf 1. (N. 16. Y. 9.)

II

NO 16. 'Yes' 1. *f* 1. No Ans. 2. (N. 16. Y. 2.)

III

NO 13. 'Yes' 1. *c* 1. *d* 1. *f* 1. *ac* 1. No Ans. 2. (N. 13. Y. 5.)

(*NNN.* 8. DF. 5.)

(vii) Amusement

Total 3.

I

NO 2. *acdf* 1. (N. 2. Y. 1.)

II

NO 2. *acdf* 1. (N. 2. Y. 1.)

III

NO 2. *acdf* 1. (N. 2. Y. 1.)

(*NNN* 2. DF 0.)

(viii) Public Utilities

Total 8.

I

NO 6. 'No, except for *f* during War' 1. *af* 1. (N. 7. Y. 1.)

II

NO 8. (N. 8. Y. 0.)

III

NO 5. *c* 1. No Ans. 2. (N. 5. Y. 1.)

(*NNN* 4. DF 0.)

(ix) Merchants and Wholesalers[1]

Total 20.

I

NO 13. *d* 1. *df* 1. *cdf* 1. Not App. 1. No Ans. 2.   (N. 13. Y. 3.)

II

NO 17. Not App. 1. No Ans. 1.   (N. 17. Y. 0.)

III

NO 14. *c* 1. *d* 1. *ac* 1. 'To some extent' 1. No Ans. 1.   (N. 14. Y. 4.)

(*NNN* 9. DF 3.)

(x) Chemicals, Drugs, &c.

Total 16.

I

NO 14. *c* 1. *acf* 1.   (N. 14. Y. 2.)

II

NO 16.   (N. 16. Y. 0.)

III

NO 14. *ac* 1. No Ans. 1.   (N. 14. Y. 1.)

(*NNN* 13. DF 0.)

(xi) Paints, Colours, &c.

Total 10.

I

NO 10.

II

NO 10.

III

NO 10.

(*NNN* 10. DF 0.)

(xii) Leather[2]

Total 8.

I

NO 5. 'Yes, certainly' 1. *cd* 1.   (N. 5. Y. 2.)

II

NO 5. 'Yes' 1. *cd* 1.   (N. 5. Y. 2.)

III

NO 2. *d* 1. *cd* 2. *abc* 1. 'Yes, decidedly' 1.   (N. 2. Y. 5.)

(*NNN* 2. DF 1.)

(xiii) Vehicles

Total 5.

I

NO 3. *c* 1. *acdf* 1.   (N. 3. Y. 2.)

II

NO 4. *acdf* 1.   (N. 4. Y. 1.)

III

NO 1. *acdf* 1. 'Only to limited extent' 1. 'Yes, but not deciding' 1. No Ans. 1.   (N. 1. Y. 3.)

(*NNN* 1. DF 0.)

---

[1] One business is not tabulated but was obviously affected by *df*.
[2] One answer is not tabulated.

(xiv) General Engineering, &c.

Total 54.

I

NO 45. 'Scarcely, except possibly *cf*' 1. 'Yes, but none
weighs strongly, except possibly *d*' 1. *d* 2. *f* 1. *acd* 3.
Not App. 1.   (N. 45. Y. 8.)

II

NO 54.   (N. 54. Y. 0.)

III

NO 48. *d* ('a little') 1. *acd* 2. No Ans. 3.   (N. 48. Y. 3.)
(*NNN* 45. DF 3.)

(xv) Constructional and Structural Engineering

Total 11.

I

NO 9. 'Not directly' 1. *abcd* 1.   (N. 10. Y. 1.)

II

NO 11.   (N. 11. Y. 0.)

III

NO 9. 'Not directly' 1. *cd* 1.   (N. 10. Y. 1.)
(*NNN* 10. DF 0.)

(xvi) Metals

Total 16.

I

NO 12. *d* 1. *f* 2. *def* 1.   (N. 12. Y. 4.)

II

NO 15. *ae* 1.   (N. 15. Y. 1.)

III

NO 13. *d* 1. *ae* 1. *bd* 1.   (N. 13. Y. 3.)
(*NNN* 11. DF 2.)

(xvii) Miscellaneous Producers' and Intermediate Goods[1]

Total 38.

I

NO 31. *d* 1. *cd* 1. *acd* 1. *abcd* 1.   (N. 31. Y. 5.)

II

NO 33. *cd* 1. *acd* 2.   (N. 33. Y. 3.)

III

NO 30. *e* 1. *ae* 1. *cd* 2. *acd* 1. *abcd* 1.   (N. 30. Y. 6.)
(*NNN* 28. DF 1.)

(xviii) Builders and Contractors

Total 1.

I

acd 1.   (Y. 1.)

II

acd 1.   (Y. 1.)

III

acd 1.   (Y. 1.)

[1] Two replies not tabulated; one was apparently not affected, one was affected by *b*.

(xix) Shipowners

Total 3.

I

NO 2. *df* 1.   (N. 2. Y. 1.)

II

NO 3.   (N. 3. Y. 0.)

III

NO 3.   (N. 3. Y. 0.)

(*NNN* 2. DF 1.)

(xx) Miscellaneous

Total 14.

I

NO 12. *df* 1. *abcdf* 1.   (N. 12. Y. 2.)

II

NO 13. *df* 1.   (N. 13. Y. 1.)

III

NO 11. Not App. 2. No Ans. 1.   (N. 11. Y. 0.)

(*NNN* 11. DF 1.)

The businesses which have answered this inquiry vary more greatly in their size and cover a wider range of industry than did those questioned in the earlier interviews of the Oxford Economists' Research Group. This inquiry has of course been more narrow in its scope. The questions were restricted to those contained in the questionnaire. One feature whose absence is to be regretted is the detailed probing and testing of the answers supplied, which is a normal feature of the interviews conducted by the Research Group. We have here to accept the answers as they are given. We have depended upon the initiative of the business man who filled up the questionnaire for an amplification or explanation that might be necessary. It was very pleasing that 209 of the questionnaires returned did carry comments, some of them in fair detail, in answer to the note at the foot of the questionnaire. Fifty-seven comments were from businesses who said that they had been affected in one or more of the cases mentioned by one or more of the factors listed in the questionnaire, and 152 comments came from those who returned entirely negative answers. These are summarized at the end of this paper.

This inquiry does broadly confirm the conclusions reached in the earlier papers.[1] As has already been noted on p. 55, 217 businesses gave a negative answer to all three questions. This means that at least 70 per cent. of the businesses whose replies are tabulated had not been affected at all, in the cases mentioned, by any of the factors, rates of interest, and costs of borrowing, listed in the questionnaire. Seventy-seven businesses stated that they had been affected by one or more of the factors mentioned. This is 25 per cent.

---

[1] *Oxford Economic Papers*, No. 1, H. D. Henderson, 'The Significance of the Rate of Interest'; J. E. Meade and P. W. S. Andrews, 'Summary of Replies to Questions'.

of the tabulated replies. If the 7 businesses which did not answer one question but who said 'No' to the other two, and the 6 for whom a negative answer to the stocks question is presumed (see p. 55), are added to this total, the percentage affected by rates of interest would be raised to 29. It is certain that so large an addition would not be justified, and most of the 13 businesses concerned can safely be presumed not to be affected. However, taking these results as they stand, this means that 70–75 per cent. have not been affected by the factors mentioned, and 25–29 per cent. have been affected by the rates of interest and facilities for borrowing mentioned in the questionnaire.

Nineteen of the 77 businesses who said that they had been affected by one or more of the factors mentioned only d or f or d and f in any answer. These have not said that they have been affected by anything other than the facility with which bank overdrafts can be obtained or the facility with which capital can be raised from the public. Deducting these, we see that only 18 per cent. of the firms whose replies are tabulated said that they were affected by any of the rates of interest mentioned. The conclusion is therefore that 18 per cent. said that their decisions to make, or to defer making, expenditure upon extensions or repairs and maintenance, or their holding of stocks, had been affected by rates of interest. This percentage cannot be higher than 22, adding the 13 replies referred to above.

It will have been noticed that the decision to make expenditure upon maintenance and repairs is least affected by financial considerations. The decision to make plant extensions (apparently interpreted generally, as previously noted, in a wider sense as covering all extensions) is most affected. The following table is an attempt to assess the relative importance of the factors a to f in an indirect manner. It is not possible to do so more

TABLE I

Table showing the number of times each Factor is mentioned in the Categorical Replies

Factor	Number of times which it is mentioned in the answers to		
	Question I*	Question II	Question III
a	22	10	19
b	7	4	8
c	33	14	31
d	38	12	29
e	2	2	5
f	23	6	6
Total 'Mentions' . .	125	48	98

* These include the two businesses mentioned on page 54, viz.
'No, but f would be important.' 1.　　　　'Scarcely except cf.' 1.

directly. In this table each factor is credited with the number of firms who mention it either by itself or in association with other factors.

It will be seen that a accounts for 18 per cent. in Question I, for 21 per cent. in Question II, and for 19 per cent. in Question III. It should be noted, however, that the number of times which it is mentioned independently of c is only 5. It has been pointed out that a (bank rate) may well be regarded as important only because it affects c (level of interest charged on bank overdrafts), and this low degree of non-association with c is probably significant. The factors c, d, and f are most important in the table above. In the affirmative answers to Question I d is most important with 30 per cent. of the total mentions, c is next with 26 per cent., and f has 18 per cent. In the answers to Question II, the 'score' is: c, 29 per cent., d, 25 per cent., and f, 12·5 per cent. In Question III, c is 32 per cent., d is 30 per cent., and f is 6 per cent. of the total number of mentions. The facility with which capital can be raised from the public appears therefore to be important in connexion with decisions to make or to defer making expenditure upon extensions. The rate of interest charged upon bank overdrafts and the facility with which bank overdrafts can be obtained are the chief of the factors affecting all three cases, investment in extensions, in repairs and maintenance, and in stocks; the facility with which overdrafts can be obtained being most important in the answer to I, but yielding place to the interest charged upon overdrafts in the other answers, and its appearance there may probably be due, in some replies, to a wish that banks would change their established practice and grant overdrafts more readily for investment in fixed assets.

Table 2 (page 64) provides a summary indication of the extent to which the proportion of negative answers received varied between industries. It will be seen that the four industries which gave the lowest proportions of negative answers[1] were (the industry with the lowest proportion is placed first and the others are in ascending order):

Question I. Retailers, Vehicles, Leather, Merchants.
Question II. Leather, Textiles, Retailers, Vehicles.
Question III. Vehicles, Leather, Public Utilities, Retailers.

The four industries with the highest proportions are (also in ascending order):

Question I. Public Utilities, General Consumers' Goods, Constructional Engineering, Paints.
Question II. (Brewers, Clothing, Public Utilities, Chemicals, Paints, General Engineering, and Constructional Engineering all give a complete negative.)
Question III. Chemicals, Brewers, Constructional Engineering, Paints.

[1] Answers stating that the businesses concerned had not been affected by any of the factors mentioned in the questionnaire.

The four industries with the highest and lowest percentages of replies which were negative or which mentioned only d or f (that is, which were not affected by rates of interest) were as follows (each list is in ascending order):

Question I. Lowest: Vehicles, Leather, Clothing, Retailers and Merchants (equal).
Highest: Constructional Engineering, General Consumers' Goods, Metals, Paints.
Question II. Lowest: Leather, Textiles, Vehicles, Retailers.
Highest: No change in order from the first list.
Question III. Lowest: Vehicles, Leather, Public Utilities, Retailers.
Highest: General Consumers' Goods, General Engineering, Constructional Engineering, Paints.

Table 2 also states the percentage of the replies from each industry which were negative to all three questions, and which therefore came from businesses which were not at all affected by the enumerated factors. In addition, it shows the percentage of businesses in each industry which were not affected by rates of interest in any of the three cases mentioned.

In view of the positive answer of the one builder who did reply, it is a great pity that the industry is not better represented in the replies. The questionnaire was sent to at least eleven builders and contractors. In view of this answer, and of the fact that the two witnesses from the building industry interviewed previously had thought it possible that rates of interest might affect the demand side at least (but said that their supply side had not been affected), it was decided to try again. A new questionnaire was drawn up, designed especially for this industry and covering the points raised by this questionnaire, but with a section devoted to the demand side of the industry.[1] This was sent out as a trial to fifteen firms, and it was hoped to have the answers in time for discussion in this paper. No answer was received. The reason may be that the summer holidays were imminent, that the international situation was disturbed, or that the questionnaire was too detailed. It is to be hoped that, at a future date, this industry will be investigated again.

[1] Before it was circulated the special questionnaire was taken to an interview with a building firm normally engaged on institutional building but which had built domestic houses from 1931–2 until 1937. Their supply side had not been affected by changes in the rate of interest or in financial facilities, for they financed themselves out of cash reserves which they maintained as a matter of policy. In their house-building operations they found that the demand for houses was so great during the building boom that the deposits of purchasers, paid before building commenced, greatly facilitated the finance of the actual building.

As regards the industry in general, they considered that the invention of the builders' pool was the chief factor that enabled builders to finance speculative building in the early years of the recent building boom, but, no doubt, the fall in the building societies' rate of interest from 5 per cent. to $4\frac{1}{2}$ per cent. gave an added impetus to the expansion a little later, especially about 1933. They also thought that trade credits in materials had been an important factor for firms which were purely speculative house-builders.

Analysis of comments[1]

TABLE 2

Table showing the Replies of those Businesses who said that their Decisions had not been affected by the Factors mentioned as a Percentage of the Total Replies from Each Industry giving Five or more Replies

Industry	Total replies	Questions							
		I		II		III		ALL	
		N	Na	N	Na	N	Na	NNN	NNN plus DF
General Consumers . .	37	89	95	92	95	84	89	84	89
Textiles	29	79	..	79	..	76	..	72	..
Clothing	9	67	..	100	..	78	..	67	..
Brewers, &c. . . .	7	86	..	100	..	86	..	86	..
Retailers	20	55	75	80	85	65	75	40	65
Public Utilities . . .	8	88	..	100	..	63	..	50	..
Merchants, &c. . . .	20	65	75	85	..	70	75	45	60
Chemicals, &c. . . .	16	88	..	100	..	88	..	81	..
Paints, &c. . . .	10	100	..	100	..	100	..	100	..
Leather	8	63	..	63	..	25	38	25	38
Vehicles	5	60	..	80	..	20	..	20	..
General Engineering . .	54	83	89	100	..	89	91	83	89
Construct. Engineering, &c. .	11	92	..	100	..	92	..	92	..
Metals	16	75	94	94	..	81	88	69	81
Miscellaneous Producers' Goods, &c. . . .	38	82	84	87	..	79	..	74	76

In the above table:

> N indicates the percentage of negative replies to the particular question indicated.
>
> Na indicates the percentage of replies which were negative or which mentioned only d or f or d and f to the particular question.[2]
>
> NNN indicates the percentage of replies which were negative for all three questions.
>
> NNN plus DF indicates the percentage of replies which were negative or which mentioned only d or f or d and f in answer to all three questions.[2]

The comments of businesses who gave completely negative answers are dominated by those who gave the fact that they had always had sufficient resources for the investments which they made as their main reason for not having been affected by the factors mentioned. Forty-two out of the 152

---

[1] In the original version of this article (in *Oxford Economic Papers*, No. 3) this Part contained summaries of the individual replies received, as, for example,

'23. *acd*, *N*, *N*. The low bank rate and low interest generally caused witness to extend his buildings and plant in 1937–8. Maintenance and repairs are carried out when required, interest rates having no effect on decision. Due to varied lines of manufacture, he stocks according to requirements and does not increase his stocks when interest rates are favourable. Firm is his private property. Owing to banks' lending rates having been low for a substantial period, and being of the opinion that drastic national disturbance would have to take place to cause the bank rate to rise, he has not hesitated to use bank's borrowing facilities for plant and works extensions as conditions warranted.'

The concluding pages, now reproduced, originally contained detailed reference to these summaries of the answers.

[2] When the replies did not include any which were only d and/or f, the second percentage is identical with the first under each question and is not repeated.

businesses concerned stated that their own resources had always been sufficient or ample. Fourteen others (possibly with one other) also appear to belong to this class. In addition, 10 businesses do not borrow, or do not do so to an appreciable extent; 3 are associated or subsidiary businesses and get finance, if needed, without difficulty from other businesses; and 14 appear generally to have adequate resources, or to have no difficulty with banks, &c., if these need supplementing. Some answers give the impression that borrowing is regarded as an evil in itself.

Thirteen businesses stated that interest rates would be, or were, negligible by comparison with the profit expected from any investment (two others appear to take the same view). Nine replies indicate that demand conditions outweigh other considerations—one of them giving equal importance to its bank balance.

Some of the answers contain qualifications. One business thought that a rate above 6 per cent. might deter, unless they could carry out their own finance. Two considered that interest rates below normal levels might affect them, one other stated that it might be affected by catastrophic changes in rates of interest, and one thought that it would be affected by extreme fluctuations coupled with decreased spending by the public. Two businesses, although their decisions had not been affected, indicated that they might use changes in the rates as a general index of business conditions. One business stated that it always considered the rate of interest, but that this had not affected these decisions owing to the financial resources of the business. One thought that, given better facilities for a company of its size to get capital from the public, it would have expanded and gone into a different or allied trade. Six comments contain qualifications and statements of the ways in which rates of interest are considered to have affected them; their reasons range from the statement that interest rates are considered generally to opinions that rates of interest affect their conjuncture.

The comments of businesses which had been affected by the factors mentioned are mixed, but, corresponding to the importance which we have seen ascribed to the possession of liquid funds by many of the businesses with negative answers, there seems to be a strong tendency to be affected by the facilities for raising capital or for borrowing money, as distinct from the actual cost of that finance. It would be important for our purpose to be able to divide the replies into those whose decisions had actually been affected by variations in the facilities offered by banks, for example, and those who mention d because they have always used bank accommodation, or because they could never get enough bank accommodation generally or for certain purposes (the latter would thus hold that, if only banks were more accommodating than they ever are, the business would have expanded more). The essential point of theoretical interest is whether *variations* in facilities have ever affected the decision to expand. Only four businesses state specifically that they have been affected by such variations in bank accommodation, or that such variations have occurred. The comments do not allow of useful generalization on the point at present under consideration. There is an impression, however, that in many cases where *d* or *f* is mentioned the businesses concerned do not mean that they were affected in their decisions by facilities in this sense but merely that they are grateful to their banks for having been so accommodating, or that they wish that their banks were generally more accommodating.

It will be noticed that some of the comments are in abstract form, giving general opinions that interest rates are important for business, without being specifically related to the firms concerned. Some businesses do appear to make comparisons of the rate of interest with the profitability to be expected from a given investment. Five refer to the effects of interest rates on the costs of holding stocks, and two refer to the possibility that cheap rates may affect stocks through slackening the incentive to control, without specific decisions being apparently affected. Three businesses give instances of investments being postponed because rates of interest were high, while four give instances of investments being made which were directly influenced by favourable rates.

It is not, however, possible to give a general reason why the businesses making these comments are affected, whilst the businesses in the first part of this section are not affected in the cases mentioned by rates of interest and facilities for borrowing. The main reason may well be that most of the businesses in list B habitually use overdrafts. Some comments in both lists do appear to regard the fact of having an overdraft as unwelcome in itself, those in the first list being thankful that they are not afflicted. We have also seen that some of the businesses who returned completely negative answers did state that they are always on good terms with their banks. If one could precisely determine the extent of the banks' favours in their case, they would probably counterbalance many of the complaints that the banks are generally niggardly with their accommodation. Those who are adversely affected by a bank's attitude to a desired overdraft will naturally remember that fact. Those who have always found their bank to be obliging, because of the general good state of their business or for other reasons, may not realize its importance.

On the pure rate of interest issue, the apparent predominant importance of the question whether a firm has free resources in determining whether or not its answer is negative, appears to be of great significance. It has been pointed out that in pure theory we do not take cognizance of this distinction. It is there assumed that the earnings of such free resources in open-market investments will be reckoned as the cost of using those resources in the productive assets of the business. A major reason may well be that the profit level at which the businesses work, or which they demand on new investment, is much higher than any such rates of investment earnings. There does, however, also seem to be a tendency to regard the rate of interest when using borrowed funds but not to regard it when using resources originating in the business. It may be that more attention is paid to the rate of interest when the money has actually to be paid out of the business, than when the rate is merely an accounting charge on the assets, if it is not ignored altogether. It must also be noted that, if this interpretation is correct, businesses who mentioned rates of interest in their replies may have meant, in some cases, that the fact that a particular investment would mean borrowing, and hence the payment of interest, may have caused a more pessimistic view to be taken of the matter, to some extent independently of the actual rate of interest.

In question II most businesses agree that it is not the practice to let repairs and maintenance be influenced by financial factors, this item being so important for the carrying on of business. Apart from this, one can sum up by saying that the dominant reason for negative answers appears to be that the business has ample resources or has no difficulty in borrowing. Many businesses also are apparently so profitable, or demand such a high probable return upon new investment, that the cost of borrowed capital is not important. There also appears a tendency for the fact of needing outside resources to be important in itself as acting as a deterrent.

This paper has greatly benefited from the comments and suggestions made by members of the Oxford Economists' Research Group.

I must conclude with giving public acknowledgement of the debt which the Oxford Economists' Research Group owes to the business men who so kindly answered the questionnaire, and especially to those who gave comments explaining their attitudes to the matters which it raised.

(vi) *Business Men and the Terms of Borrowing*[1]

By R. S. SAYERS

SINCE the stabilization of business activity became an important objective of monetary control, the influence of the rate of interest has been a subject of crucial importance in the field of monetary theory. Not all writers, however, have made their analysis depend upon the rate of interest charged to borrowers. Some—Mr. Hawtrey and lately Professor Hicks, for example —have also stressed other means by which variations in willingness to lend to business men may be expressed. The large-scale questionnaire recently

---

[1] Reprinted from *Oxford Economic Papers*, No. 3.

circulated by Oxford economists was therefore designed to secure information not only on the effect of interest variations, but also on the
influence on investment of changes in the willingness of bankers and the
investing public to lend on any terms.

The answers given, and the extremely useful comments which many of
the business men added, are fully analysed in the previous article. Here my
purpose is to discuss the broad inferences which may be drawn from the
answers, and very round figures will suffice. About 25 per cent. of the business men gave some answer to the questionnaire. Of those who replied,
three-quarters stated that the terms (in the broad sense) on which loans
could be obtained had not affected their decisions to add to or maintain
either fixed or working capital. One-quarter of those replying (about 6 per
cent. of those asked) gave some kind of affirmative answer.

In assessing the significance of these results it is necessary to consider,
firstly, whether the 25 per cent. who replied constituted a fair sample, for
our purpose, of the whole. Why, in fact, did the other 75 per cent. throw
the questionnaire into the waste-paper basket? There are, I think, four
probable answers: (1) that the firm just couldn't be bothered with more
forms than the government compels it to complete; (2) that the answers
might be used for some ulterior purpose; (3) that the whole business was
just a toy of 'word-spinning theorists'; and (4) that the terms of borrowing
had never affected the firm. The covering letter was, of course, designed to
overcome such objections as these, in spite of which three-quarters of the
firms declined to act as though the inquiry was important enough to justify
the completion of the very brief form. One can only guess at the solution
to the problem. My own guess is that most of the firms were, as a result of
their own experience, not convinced that borrowing terms make much
difference to their decisions. If this guess is the right one, we must obviously
work on the assumption that the proportion of business-men conscious of
the effectiveness of borrowing terms must be much lower than one-quarter
(the proportion of positive to total replies in our sample), though it may be
rather more than 6 per cent. (the proportion of positive replies to total
forms sent out).

Let us turn now to the positive answers. There were about 70 of these,
and the use which we can make of them is much increased by the fact that
57 added some comment. In the belief that the simpler the questionnaire
the greater would be the number of replies forthcoming, the form was made
extremely brief. The questions were in fact so brief that a mere 'Yes' or
'No' might be consistent with an opposite reply had our questions been
more fully explained (as was possible in the smaller sample inquiry).
Difficulties of this kind are most likely to arise in connexion with the question, 'Has the facility with which bank overdrafts can be obtained ever

affected your decision to make, or to defer making, expenditure on plant-extensions?' and the two associated questions dealing with other branches of investment policy. When the business man answers 'Yes' to this question he may mean any one of four things. He may mean (1) that the bank has, as a result of change in its liquid assets, become more anxious to expand or contract its Advances, and has accordingly altered its willingness to help in financing a particular project; or (2) that the bank has, as a result of its own manager changing his views about the general prospects of the trade in question, altered its willingness to help in financing a particular project; or (3) that the bank has, as a result of fuller knowledge of the firm's creditworthiness, changed its attitude; or (4) that if the bank's collateral rules were something quite different from what they ever have been, the firm would have expanded operations more freely with the aid of its banker. Only the first meaning is relevant to our purpose of testing the efficacy of certain weapons of the monetary authorities.

In the light of considerations such as this, I have felt it necessary to examine each case in the light of the comments offered. Having done this, and exercising the utmost scepticism, I have been able to find only about twenty clearly convincing cases of positive answers to any of our questions. About thirty other cases seem to me worth considering as 'possibles'. Among these more likely cases the rate of interest appears to be slightly more influential than borrowing facilities. Of the three kinds of investment —new fixed, maintenance of fixed, and net investment in stocks—the first appears to have been affected most, the third almost as much, and the second hardly at all. Among the firms giving any kind of positive reply, far more appear to have been affected by the banks' overdraft charges and by the attitude of the banks than by any of the other factors mentioned in the questionnaire.

Thus far the answers appear to verify in a small degree the conclusion of what I have elsewhere called the Keynesian line of thought (that long investment is responsive to changes in capital market conditions), and to verify also in a small degree the Hawtrey line of thought (that short investment is responsive to changes in capital market conditions). But in both cases the degree of confirmation is very small. The significance of the verification dwindles yet further when it is remembered that firms almost invariably insist on the presence of a number of other determinant factors, some of them far more influential than lenders' terms. For this must mean that, of the firms which are conscious of having been at any time marginal in respect of lenders' terms, few are likely to have been marginal borrowers (and investors) in any given short period of time. The efficacy of a weapon of monetary policy depends upon the proportion by which it can change total spending in a given period. If its only effect is to cause one firm in every two or three hundred to make its investments different from what it otherwise would have been, the potency of that weapon in a constantly changing world must, I think, be described as very low.

But, it is sometimes argued, we need not worry about the slightness of the direct effects to an initial stimulus to business. The direct effects—in this case expansion of capital outlay—will itself have further effects because it leads to a chain of expanding demand. The business men's comments in answer to this questionnaire insist again and again that the most powerful stimulus to an extension of plant is provided by a rise in the demand for the product. Accordingly the initial expansion of investment prompted by easier conditions of supply of capital will be followed by a further—and probably much greater—increase in capital outlay as business men in one industry after another find that the market demand for their products is increasing. On these lines it is argued that the slightness of the initial response of business to monetary operations need not discourage our monetary managers: the indirect effects will come to the rescue. This argument is, I believe, unsound. While it is true that an initial change in investment due to a change in monetary conditions will cause a greater eventual change in investment as market demands begin to rise, the same is true also of an initial change of investment due to any other cause. In times of trade boom—and the argument applies equally to the opposite case—there are likely to be several exogenous factors continually entering the situation, some making for continued upswing and some for a downward turn in trade. Every one of these factors is by itself likely to be small, but its effect will be magnified by the initial disturbances causing changes in the demand for products of other entrepreneurs. Unless it can be shown that the change in monetary conditions exerts far more general pressure, at the outset, than does a change in other factors (crop yields or the political situation, for example), there can be no presumption that the monetary weapon in use is the potent weapon which we often want. The doctrine of the multiplier is sound enough: the trouble is rather that *everything* is multiplied!

Bearing in mind these arguments, what are the broad implications, for economic theory and policy, of the results of our own inquiry? The most important purposes for which we want to use monetary weapons may be summarized as control of the trade cycle and the maintenance of an international standard. It is therefore in relation to these two problems that I wish to consider the inferences to be drawn from the business men's answers.

In dealing with cyclical fluctuations the monetary authorities have a choice between three main courses. They can pursue their course unchanged

—meeting the 'needs of trade' and therefore increasing the supply of money to a sufficient extent to enable interest rates and security standards to be maintained unchanged. Or they can be passive in another sense, holding the supply of money unchanged and therefore contributing to the stabilizing forces at work in so far as the cyclical movement itself causes the strain of increased demand to force interest rates and/or borrowing standards up. Or they can consciously pursue a contra-cyclical policy, forcing up interest rates, &c., by reducing the supply of the ideally-liquid asset, money. If the trade cycle were 'a purely monetary phenomenon', in a narrow sense, the first course would be absolutely indefensible. The less extreme argument against it (and therefore in favour of one of the other courses) must be based on the view that interest rates and/or willingness to lend can have an important stabilizing influence. Unfortunately we have to recognize that, while boom and slump generate their own acceleration, the impulses which can be set up by banking policy are likely (in the light of our results) to be no greater than those set up by many other extraneous factors, some of which will be working one way, some another. Our positive results do not appear to encourage the hope that the banking impulses can seriously modify the upward or downward swing, except when it helps the balance of extraneous factors to overcome merely incipient or wellnigh exhausted cyclical forces. A boom or slump may occasionally be ended by banking policy, but I think our results point to the conclusion that the boom or slump is at least as likely to be ended by a budget statement, a dictator's brainstorm, or a trade treaty. Or it may very likely be ended by the temporary glutting (or exhaustion) of important sections of the capital goods markets—i.e. by the boom (or slump) 'wearing itself out'.[1]

Banking policy would thus appear to be a weaker stabilizer than has frequently been hoped. But in one important respect we can be more optimistic than the arguments given in my book *Modern Banking* suggest.[2] It is quite clear from our inquiry that in so far as their investment policy

---

[1] Allyn Young's *Analysis of Banking Statistics under the National Banking Act* led him to the conclusion (p. 28) '. . . An increase of prices and of retail trade draws money from New York, through the outside banks, into circulation. Just how far these different movements could go before reversing themselves appears to have depended upon a general conjuncture of circumstances. I see no basis for the belief that these cyclical savings, once under way, were never halted until the resources of the banks have been exhausted. Monetary factors undoubtedly have much to do with cyclical fluctuations of business activities. Moreover, they set limits beyond which such fluctuations cannot go. But only in cycles of exceptional magnitude do such limits become effective. The greater number of cyclical fluctuations keep well within limits. Crises are incidents, not of all cycles, but only of those which reach or approach their possible limits.' My own view (which refers to Britain between the wars) is more extreme than Allyn Young's (which refers to the U.S.A., 1863–1913), but is along the same lines. Cf. also W. W. Rostow, *British Economy in the Nineteenth Century*, *passim*.

[2] The reference is to the First Edition (1938). In later impressions and in the Second Edition (1947) the relevant passages were amended in the light of the above.

is affected by capital market conditions (in a broad sense) at all, firms are more affected directly by the policies of the banks than they are affected indirectly through the long-term securities markets. What slight power the banks have, to damp down cyclical fluctuations, is based on weapons which they have in their own hands, and is not to any serious degree dependent upon the influence of banking policy on the securities markets.

Now let us turn to the contribution which banking policy has to make to the working of an international standard. Stability of foreign exchange rates in the face of changes in the underlying international trading conditions depends upon three sets of factors. Firstly, there is the magnitude of the strains imposed by the underlying changes—the greater the strains, the less chance there is of the international standard surviving. Secondly, there is the power of the correctives which are at work to pull national price and money income structures into line—the more powerful the correctives, the more chance of surviving has the international standard. Thirdly, there is the temporary elasticity of the system—the ease with which short loans or gold can be moved from centre to centre, pending the operation of the correctives. The great attraction of the interest rate in helping a gold standard to work is that it ideally acts both as a corrective and as a factor which controls international short-loan movements and therefore leaves a slighter temporary strain to be borne by gold reserves.[1] Its disadvantage is that it may encourage the growth (or, as after 1923, the maintenance) of the 'international short loan fund', the volatility of which in the face of international disturbances (political or economic) may put such strains on gold reserves as they cannot stand. Given the existence of this disadvantage, it becomes important to consider whether the value of interest-rate policy as a corrective is sufficient to justify running the risks inherent in its use. If our inquiries lead us to the conclusion that interest-rate policy can do little to pull price and money income structures up or down, then a gold standard system had better be managed without any extensive use of it.

It is true, on the other hand, that international price disequilibria may only arise slowly, and may therefore be usefully corrected by a weapon which exerts continuous new force as time goes on, as does the rate of interest when it affects first one firm's investment policy and then another's. But as a slow-working corrective there is as much to be said for the automatic corrective of the impulse given, through the Multiplier, by a favourable balance of trade to raise prices (and vice versa). Unless the rate of interest can be claimed as a quick-working corrective of international price disequilibria, it and its incidental dangers had better be avoided.

The same cannot be said about alterations in the banks' willingness to

[1] Cf. the celebrated passage in the Macmillan Report.

lend at a given rate of interest. For, access to foreign short loans being barred to the ordinary business man, there is no question of exercise of this weapon bringing the disadvantages of the growth of an international short-loan fund. As therefore this weapon has some power, it is worth retaining. The fact that its influence appears to be slight merely means that we cannot, in this country at least,[1] expect it to contribute much to the feasibility of an international standard.

One matter on which the large-scale inquiry has clearly borne out the tentative conclusions drawn from the small-scale inquiry which preceded it[2] is the relevance to a firm's expansion policy of the firm's internal resources. Many of the firms which gave negative answers to the questions, and many also of those who gave some sort of positive answer, stressed the fact that they usually expected to be able to meet expenditure on new investment out of their own resources. Mr. A. J. Brown has also analysed the statistical interrelations of idle money, interest rates, and price movements during the period 1921–36.[3] He there suggests that the real stimulant to increased trade may be not low interest but the abundance of idle funds which is itself the cause of low interest.[4] It may be thought that our results, stressing the entrepreneurs' dependence on their own resources, reinforce Mr. Brown's argument and suggest that the banking system might exercise much influence by adding to the volume of idle money during the slump, and reducing it during the boom. Unfortunately this conclusion follows only if we assume that somehow or other the idle funds can be pumped into the ownership of the firms. I cannot see how this can be done. The only way in which firms can add to their resources in the relevant sense is by reserving profits and/or reducing expenditure on plant maintenance, &c. To the extent that individual entrepreneurs do this (as they often do when prospects are poor), they are of course merely reducing the profits of other entrepreneurs. Entrepreneurs as a class cannot increase their liquid resources until consumers spend more freely, no matter what the banks have been doing.[5] Particular entrepreneurs whose industries do not suffer in the general depression are likely to increase their liquid resources, and as these accumulate the firms will no doubt become more willing to venture on expansionist policies, so helping us out of the slump. But there will be

[1] I suspect that its potency may be very considerable in some of the great primary producer countries.
[2] See above, p. 4.
[3] *Oxford Economic Papers*, No. 2, pp. 46–69, reprinted above, pp. 31–51.
[4] Above, p. 31. This is not the only interpretation which his statistical results bear; but that is another story.
[5] They can, of course, increase the liquidity of their resources, by selling securities to the public or to the banks, but when a firm talks about expanding out of its own liquid resources, it is already including marketable securities among its liquid resources.

other entrepreneurs who feel their position to be increasingly tight as the depression goes on. I conclude that the evidence in our possession does not allow us to hope that the banking system can give substantial direct help by varying the amount of 'idle money' in existence.

It is perhaps worth mentioning one 'non-monetary' aspect of this preference of entrepreneurs for their own rather than borrowed resources, as a means of financing investment. Greater and greater taxation of profits, particularly undistributed profits, by diverting resources away from the ownership of successful firms, is likely to hinder the process of real investment. The appropriate remedy would be further development of that part of the capital market which is trying to fill 'the Macmillan gap'. But unless entrepreneurs become more willing to do with borrowed resources what they would do with their own resources the problem may be an obstinate one.

The general tenor of this article has, I am afraid, been negative. This being so, I ought perhaps to emphasize the fact that I have not argued that banking policy is useless in dealing with the trade cycle and other economic problems. The evidence which is accumulating, and to which this questionnaire made an important addition, could not by any stretch of the imagination be reconciled with such a stark negative. What I have argued is simply that the evidence warns us not to expect the instruments of banking policy —particularly the rate of interest—to do more than help us in the right direction. Banking policy alone is not enough.

II

THE RATE OF EXCHANGE

(i) *Trade Balances and Exchange Stability*[1]

By A. J. BROWN

THE main purpose of this article is to examine theoretically the condition, as to elasticities of demand and supply, &c., which must be fulfilled if there is to be exchange stability between two countries under a free system. It has long been appreciated[2] that, in some circumstances, the lowering of the external value of a country's currency which is a consequence of a passive balance of payments may lead to an increase in the value of its imports in relation to the value of its exports, thus making its balance of payments still more passive. In these circumstances, it is virtually impossible to maintain free exchanges, since the equilibrium of trade under a free system is unstable, but, as far as I am aware, the exact conditions which are necessary to ensure stability have not been worked out before.[3] In working it out, equations have to be developed which give the relation between, for example, the depreciation of a country's currency from equilibrium and the corresponding surplus of its exports over its imports.

The secondary purpose is, by assigning reasonable values to the relevant elasticities, &c., in the special case of Britain, to make some tentative estimates of the relation between the percentage depreciation of sterling from its equilibrium value relatively to all other currencies simultaneously and the consequent surplus in value of exports (visible and invisible) over imports.

The Demand and Supply Functions

Let us begin by considering two hypothetical countries, which we will call 'Britain' and 'America'. Since no third parties will be taken into account, and since the main interest is in the problems of 'Britain', the model may be made realistic by taking 'America' to represent the whole of the rest of the world. Let us start with an equilibrium situation in which movements of goods and services between the two countries balance, the equilibrium rate of exchange being r_0 dollars to the £. Particular assumptions must, of course, be made about the form of each country's demand-

---

[1] Reprinted from *Oxford Economic Papers*, No. 6.

[2] See, for example, Mr. Keynes, 'The German Transfer Problem', *Economic Journal*, 1929.

[3] The subject is discussed by Mrs. Robinson—*Essays in the Theory of Employment*, pp. 188–94, which I had not seen when this article was written, but her treatment is of a somewhat less general character than that attempted here.

curve for the other country's goods, and it is convenient to assume curves of constant elasticity, since the solution of the problem is then obtained in terms of (among other things) elasticities of demand. It is also simplest, as a starting-point, to assume that total money incomes and the levels of prices in general, and of prices of goods for export in particular, remain constant in both countries, in spite of alterations in the rates of exchange between their currencies. The goods of American origin can be measured in dollars' worth, and goods of British origin may be measured in the same way (i.e. in £'s worth multiplied by r_0).

On these assumptions, the American demand for British goods so measured may be represented by:

$$I_a = k\left(\frac{r}{r_0}\right)^a$$

where r is the rate of exchange actually ruling, and a is the American elasticity of demand for British goods. Similarly, the British demand for American goods (also measured in 'equilibrium dollars'' worth) may be represented by:

$$I_b = k\left(\frac{r}{r_0}\right)^{-b}$$

The constant k, it will be seen, measures the flow of trade in either direction in equilibrium. The coefficients a and b are price-elasticities of demand, defined with respect to a situation in which all prices but those of imports and all money incomes remain constant except in so far as they are altered as a direct consequence of the change in import prices. Their numerical values will, in all ordinary circumstances, be negative.

The export costs in the two countries, however, cannot be expected to remain constant in spite of alterations in the rate of exchange. In the first place, the elasticity of supply of goods for export cannot be assumed to be perfect (though in practice it is probably often fairly high owing to the possibility of diverting goods from home consumption to the export markets). In the second place, the costs of imported factors of production (and the costs of domestic factors also, to some extent) must be expected to rise when the external value of the currency falls. Once the possibility of variation in the British price of British exports is admitted, the American demand-function for imports must be written:

$$I_a = k\left(\frac{p}{p_0}\frac{r}{r_0}\right)^a$$

where p is the actual British price of exports and p_0 the price when the exchanges are in equilibrium. The supply-function of British exports, ignoring for the moment the effect of prices of imports on their cost of production, may be written:

$$E_b(= I_a) = k\left(\frac{p}{p_0}\right)^f$$

where f is the elasticity of supply of the goods in question. Hence,

$$\frac{p}{p_0} = \left(\frac{I_a}{k}\right)^{1/f}.$$

If the effect of the lowering of the external value of the £ from r_0 to r is to raise the marginal cost curve of export goods in the proportion $(r/r_0)^{-u}$, where u is a positive proper fraction, then:

$$\frac{p}{p_0} = \left(\frac{I_a}{k}\right)^{1/f}\left(\frac{r}{r_0}\right)^{-u}.$$

Substituting this value for p/p_0 in the American demand-function, we get:

$$I_a = k\left(\frac{r}{r_0}\right)^{\frac{af(1-u)}{f-a}}.$$

Similarly, it may be shown that the British demand-function for American goods (still measuring the goods in dollars' worth at equilibrium prices and at the equilibrium exchange rate) is:

$$I_b = k\left(\frac{r}{r_0}\right)^{\frac{bg(v-1)}{g-b}}.$$

The imports of the two countries have been measured so far in 'equilibrium dollars' worth'. To get them into terms of current dollars, it is necessary to multiply I_b by the ratio in which American export prices have changed due directly and indirectly to the alteration in the exchange rate from r_0 to r, i.e. by:

$$\left(\frac{r}{r_0}\right)^{\frac{b(v-1)}{g-b}+v}.$$

American imports, I_a, similarly, must be first converted to the British price-level corresponding to the exchange rate r, and then multiplied by r/r_0 to get them into terms of dollars at this rate as opposed to the old rate r_0. Hence, in terms of current dollars,

$$I_b = k\left(\frac{r}{r_0}\right)^{\frac{b(g+1)(v-1)}{g-b}+v}$$

while

$$I_a = k\left(\frac{r}{r_0}\right)^{\frac{a(f+1)(1-u)}{f-a}-u+1}.$$

For convenience, the index of r/r_0 in the expression for I_b will be referred to as B, and the corresponding index in the expression for I_a as A.

The Conditions of Stability

The surplus S of British exports over British imports in current dollars, when the rate of exchange is r, is therefore:

$$k\left[\left(\frac{r}{r_0}\right)^A - \left(\frac{r}{r_0}\right)^B\right]. \qquad (\mathrm{i})$$

Differentiating with respect to r, we get:

$$\frac{dS}{dr} = k(Ar_0^{-A}r^{A-1} - Br_0^{-B}r^{B-1}).$$

If this is positive, the surplus of British exports over British imports is increased by raising the external value of the £ and the exchanges are unstable, but if it is negative, then a rise in the external value of sterling means a fall in the British export surplus (or a rise in the import surplus), and the exchanges are stable. To find under what conditions the equilibrium exchange rate is stable, we have simply to put $r = r_0$ in the above expression for dS/dr, and to see under what conditions the resulting expression is negative. This resulting expression is:

$$\frac{k}{r_0}(A-B).$$

Hence, the equilibrium rate of exchange is stable so long as $(A-B)$ is negative, i.e. so long as:

$$\frac{a(f+1)(1-u)}{f-a} - u + 1 - \frac{b(g+1)(v-1)}{g-b} - v \text{ is negative.}$$

The main facts implicit in this are as follows:

(a) If the elasticities of supply of exports, f and g, are zero, the expression is equal to -1, so that equilibrium is stable for all values of a, b, u, and v.

So long as elasticity of demand for exports is numerically greater than unity, an increase in their elasticity of supply is a stabilizing influence, but if the demand elasticity is less than unity, the reverse is the case.

(b) If demand for exports is elastic (elasticity numerically greater than unity), then a higher import-content of exports diminishes the efficacy of depreciation as a producer of a credit balance—it is destabilizing. With an inelastic demand for exports, the reverse is the case.

(c) In the special case where the two countries are similar in their economic behaviour, so that $b = a$, $g = f$, $v = u$, the maximum value of a consistent with stability is always algebraically greater than $-\frac{1}{2}$, i.e. the minimum elasticity of demand for imports in both countries consistent with stability is numerically less than $\frac{1}{2}$.

The general impression left by this conclusion is that the stability conditions are fairly likely to be fulfilled in practice. Most of the actual measurements which have been made of price-elasticities of demand relate to commodities of very low elasticity—frequently the result has been less than $\frac{1}{2}$. Even the imports of a country like Britain, however, do not consist by any means entirely of goods of such low demand elasticity: there are always other more elastic items, such as foreign manufactures with only a narrow margin of comparative advantage over the home product, foreign substitutes for home-grown foodstuffs, and, most elastic of all, services rendered to British tourists abroad. These more elastic items are likely to form a higher proportion of the total the more prosperous Britain is, and the less restrictions there are upon imports in the widest sense. Even if the elasticity of British demand for imports is very low, however, the foreign elasticity of demand for the exports of Britain, or, indeed, of almost any single country, especially an industrial one, is likely to be fairly high. The danger of instability is likely to become acute only if there is some quantitative limitation of trade in one direction or in both.

Let it be supposed, for instance, that 'Britain' in our example imposes quota restrictions upon all imports, whether of goods or services, limiting the imports of them (by quantity) to the level ruling in the existing equilibrium. The coefficient b then becomes zero so far as any possibility of increase in imports is concerned, but retains its old value in the event of circumstances bringing about a fall in imports. Any slight accidental fall in the external value of sterling below the equilibrium level will then bring into play forces which make for a return to equilibrium if the stability conditions investigated above are fulfilled. Any slight rise of the external value of sterling above equilibrium, however, will bring stabilizing forces into play only if these conditions are fulfilled with b equal to zero, a requirement considerably less likely to be realized in practice. All will still be well, of course, if the British elasticity of supply of exports is zero (a very unlikely circumstance). Otherwise, stability requires a much higher price-elasticity of demand for British exports than is needed to maintain stability when imports are free to increase. If, for instance, $u = v = 0$, and f is infinitely large, the least American elasticity of demand for British imports consistent with stability is 1. If the demand is not as elastic as this in these circumstances, the rise in the external value of the £ will become cumulative, and force America to apply exchange control or otherwise limit the dollar value of its imports.

If American imports are also limited by quota to their equilibrium quantity, then either a fall or a rise in the rate of exchange from equilibrium will be much more likely than under a free system to lead to a cumulative movement in the same direction.

In practice, the effect of quotas will not be as drastic as suggested above, since such restrictions do not extend to all imports, invisible as well as visible, and some of the items which they do not limit are those which have the greatest elasticity (such as services) and therefore the greatest effect in bringing about equilibrium.

Assuming that exchange equilibrium is stable, however, what will happen if the depreciation of sterling is continued? Will the export surplus, measured in dollars, continue to grow indefinitely, or rather, up to the point where it is limited by sharply falling elasticities of supply of exportable goods?

It will be remembered (see p. 60) that

$$\frac{dS}{dr} = k(Ar_0^{-A}r^{A-1} - Br_0^{-B}r^{B-1}).$$

If reduction of r does not cause S to increase indefinitely, but brings it to some maximum value which cannot be exceeded, then there must be some real value for r which makes $dS/dr = 0$, d^2S/dr^2 being at the same time negative. It will be seen that if $dS/dr = 0$, then:

$$\frac{r}{r_0} = \left(\frac{B}{A}\right)^{1/(A-B)}.$$

Real values of r fulfil this condition, in general, only if A and B are of the same algebraic sign, so that A/B is positive. It is easily shown that, when $dS/dr = 0$,

$$\frac{d^2S}{dr^2} = k\frac{r^{B-2}}{r_0^B} B(A-B) \quad \text{or} \quad k\frac{r^{A-2}}{r_0^A} A(A-B).$$

We are concerned in practice only with cases where r is positive, and where $A-B$ is negative (the condition for exchange stability), so that the above expression is negative provided that B (or A) is positive. Hence, it is clear that there is some positive value of r corresponding to a maximum value of S so long as both A and B are positive, that if both are negative there is some positive value of r giving a minimum (i.e. maximum negative) value of S, and that, if one is positive and the other negative, S may be increased indefinitely in either the positive or the negative sense by lowering or raising r.

Under what conditions would the possible British export surplus, measured in dollars, be limited? So long as b is negative and v a positive proper fraction, the expression B cannot be negative unless g is negative (i.e. unless the supply-curve of American export-goods is downward-sloping), and then only if $g > -1$ but $< b$ or if $g < -1$ but $> b$ (these are necessary, though not quite sufficient conditions: this point, however, is not perhaps worth pursuing here). These conditions are possible, but hardly probable, and B is likely in general to be positive.

The expression A can be put into the form:

$$\frac{f(1-u)(a+1)}{f-a}$$

which, so long as a is negative and u a positive proper fraction, must be negative unless $a > -1$ (f being positive or numerically less than a) *or* unless (a being < -1), $f < 0$ and $> a$ (this latter implies a downward-sloping and rather inelastic British supply-curve of exports, which is not very probable).

As long as the supply-curves of exports in both countries are upward-sloping (the most likely case), B will be positive, while A will be positive or negative according as the American price-elasticity of demand for British goods is numerically less or greater than unity. If it is less, then there is a limit to the net amount of dollars that Britain can earn on current account by depreciating her currency; if it is greater, there is no such limit, so long as the postulated elasticities hold good.

The Effect of the Multiplier

It has been assumed in the above discussion that the level of economic activity in both the countries concerned is constant, in spite of changes in the balance of payments. It is equally interesting, and perhaps more realistic, however, to consider the case where there is full employment in neither country in equilibrium, and where real home investment in both countries is constant, so that changes in the trade balance, causing, as they will, equal changes in the total amounts of investment in the two countries, will be the sole factors causing alterations in the levels of employment. It would be desirable to allow for some change in the general price-level in each country as the level of activity changes, i.e. for imperfection in the elasticity of supply of factors of production, but to do so leads to great difficulty in the solution of the problem, and it is therefore proposed to deal systematically only with the case where the elasticities of supply of all goods and services (including f and g, the elasticities of supply of goods for export) are infinite. For present purposes, too, very little error will be introduced by taking real income to be proportional to level of activity, i.e. by assuming that average real labour costs of production are constant over the relevant range, and that changes in the terms of trade affect the national income only to a small extent. The effects of changes in the terms of trade upon demand for foreign goods (acting through changes in real income) are allowed for in the demand elasticities a and b (see their definition on page 76 above).

If the British national income in equilibrium (measured in dollars) is i_0'', then, at any moment when, measured still in dollars at the equilibrium rate of exchange and at equilibrium prices, it stands at i' (the exchanges not being in equilibrium), the British demand for foreign goods will be:

$$I_b = k\left(\frac{i'}{i_0''}\right)^y\left(\frac{r}{r_0}\right)^B,$$

where y is the income-elasticity of demand in Britain for foreign goods. It is supposed that income has been changed from i_0'' to i' entirely by the action of the trade balance (valued at S in current dollars) acting through the multiplier. Now, the British trade balance, measured not in current dollars, but in equilibrium dollars at the equilibrium British price-level (when $f = $ infinity) is:

$$S_b = S\left(\frac{r}{r_0}\right)^{u-1},$$

and, if Q is the real income multiplier in Britain, $i'-i_0'' = QS_b$, so that:

$$\frac{i'}{i_0''} = 1 - \frac{Q}{i_0''}S_b.$$

Similarly, for the rest of the world ('America'),

$$I_a = k\left(\frac{i}{i_0}\right)^x\left(\frac{r}{r_0}\right)^A,$$

and:

$$\frac{i}{i_0} = 1 - \frac{P}{i_0}S_a,$$

where i and i_0 are the American real incomes in some disequilibrium situation and in equilibrium respectively, P is the real income multiplier in America, and where S_a, the American export surplus measured at equilibrium prices, is $S(r/r_0)^{-v}$.

Writing p for P/i_0 and q for Q/i_0'', we have:

$$S = k\left[(1-pS_a)^x\left(\frac{r}{r_0}\right)^A - (1+qS_b)^v\left(\frac{r}{r_0}\right)^B\right]. \tag{2}$$

It can easily be shown that, at the point of equilibrium, where

$$S = S_a = S_b = 0,$$

and where $r = r_0$,

$$\frac{dS}{dr} = \frac{k}{r_0}\frac{A-B}{1+kpx+kqy}.$$

This confirms (since the denominator of the fraction is always positive in all its terms) that the condition of equilibrium in the exchanges is the same as when the level of activity (or real income) is fixed—namely that $A-B$ should be negative. It also confirms the fact, obvious on general grounds, that the operation of the trade-balance upon real incomes through the multiplier decreases the sensitivity of the trade balance to alterations in the exchange rate, or, to put the matter the other way round, increases the change in the rate of exchange which is necessary to bring about any given change in the balance of trade. The sensitivity of trade-balances to exchange rates is clearly diminished in the ratio $1/(1+kpx+kqy)$, so that it is diminished more the greater are the ratios k/i_0 and k_0/i' of reciprocal trade to national income in the two countries, and the greater are the multipliers P and Q and the income-elasticities of demand for foreign goods, x and y.

Investment Income and Capital Movements

The results arrived at can clearly be applied to the investigation of two very important practical questions: What adjustment is necessary to restore equilibrium when Britain loses a certain amount of her overseas investment and shipping income? and: What adjustment is necessary if there is an outflow of capital from Britain to America?

The loss of overseas income may be interpreted as a fall in the American demand for British invisible exports—a shift of the demand-curve for them to the left. In the simple case where real incomes, both in Britain and in America, remain unaffected by the change, the condition for the new equilibrium, after L dollars of income have been lost as compared with the old equilibrium situation, is:

$$k\left(\frac{r}{r_0}\right)^A - L - k\left(\frac{r}{r_0}\right)^B = 0$$

from which it is immediately evident that the relation between the loss of income and the alteration in the external value of sterling necessary to restore equilibrium is that given by solving equation (1) above, putting $S = L$.

If the real incomes of Britain and America are, however, not fixed, but are acted upon by the trade balance, working through the multiplier, the situation demands further consideration. Britain's invisible exports are decreased, so are America's invisible imports; British incomes fall, American incomes rise; British imports are therefore decreased and American imports increased, quite apart from the further effects produced in the same direction by the change in the rate of exchange. In other words, if rates of exchange do not alter, the change in the trade balance caused by the elimination of a particular source of British overseas income is smaller than the income lost, because of the accompanying changes in national incomes and in imports. On the other hand, it has been seen that the multiplier increases the depreciation which is necessary in order to achieve any given alteration in the trade balance. These two tendencies actually balance each other, for, when equilibrium is restored by alteration of the exchange rate, there is, by definition, no excess of imports over exports or the reverse, and the real incomes of both countries are therefore the same as before, but for the alterations brought about by the change in the terms of trade—alterations which are, however, already allowed for in the definition of the price-elasticities a and b, and may therefore be ignored at this stage. Hence, the relation between the amount of overseas income lost and the depreciation necessary to re-establish equilibrium remains in all circumstances that given by Equation (1).

It remains to consider the effect of international capital movements upon the equilibrium rate of exchange between two countries. Here, two different kinds of case may be discussed. First, suppose that America has large sterling balances in Britain, which are being withdrawn at the rate of L dollars per year, and, further, that monetary policies in the two countries are such that this movement of capital does not have any directly inflationary or deflationary effect. It is clear that equilibrium will be re-established only when Britain develops a surplus of exports (of goods and services) over imports equal to L. If, therefore, activity in the two countries is unaffected by alterations in import and export surpluses, the relation between the capital flight and the necessary adjustment of the exchange rate will be the same as that between S and r/r_0 given by Equation (1). If, however, employment is affected by trade balances through the multiplier, the relation between L and the proportionate adjustment necessary in the exchange rate will be the same as that between S and r/r_0 given by the solution of Equation (2). It may be, of course, that the capital flight brings about, through the banking system, a fall in home investment and economic activity in Britain and a rise in activity in America, in which case a British export surplus will result quite apart from any alteration in the exchange rate. If the tightening of the British credit position and the corresponding expansion in America are functions of the reduction in the amount of foreign capital in Britain and the increase in the funds held in America respectively (i.e. if they are relatively permanent) then the effect will be to reduce the amount of adjustment necessary in the exchange rate. If, however, the alterations in credit conditions depend purely upon the current rates of outflow and inflow of funds, the exchange adjustments required will not be affected, since, in the new equilibrium position, the capital movement will be offset by payments on current account, and the credit positions in the two 'countries' will therefore presumably be restored to their previous conditions.

The second kind of capital movement to be discussed may be exemplified by British residents cutting down their home long-term investment by L dollars in order to invest that sum in America, where the total of home investment is thereby increased by this amount. It is not hard to see that the adjustment required here, too, is that given by Equation (1) for,

when the new exchange equilibrium is reached, the fall of internal investment in Britain is compensated by an export surplus of the same magnitude
as the rate of investment, while in America the increase in total home investment is compensated by the development of an equivalent import surplus,
so that economic activity in the two countries is finally the same as before.
This assumes that Britain's lending is not partially offset by the accumulation of sterling balances by some Americans into whose hands the proceeds
of the loan eventually fall, in which case the net lending would, of course,
be less than L, and the required adjustment less than is indicated above.
It also assumes that, in so far as the process of transferring the loan involves a loss of gold or foreign exchange by Britain, this does not have an
enduring effect upon the British or American internal credit situations,
and hence upon the internal activity in the two countries. If it does so,
then, again, the adjustment in the exchange rates which is required to
restore equilibrium will be less than is indicated by Equation (1).

An Application to the British Case:

(a) *Assuming constant activity.* It is perhaps worth while applying the
results obtained above to the special case of Britain, assuming that sterling
changes in value relatively to all other currencies simultaneously. It will
first be assumed, also, that the levels of economic activity in Britain and
in the rest of the world are not affected by the change in the value of
sterling, i.e. an attempt will be made to find the relation between S and
r/r_0 given by Equation (1).

In order to do this, it is first essential to have some idea of the magnitudes of elasticities of demand for imports, and this is difficult to obtain,
on account of the complications which arise in practice from alterations
in trade barriers, and from variations in national incomes. Tariff changes,
in particular, tend to invalidate the results of a straightforward multiple
correlation analysis, which would appear at first sight to offer the best
prospects of a reliable estimate. It is not impossible, however, to obtain a
certain amount of evidence on the matter. In the United Kingdom, for
instance, between 1924 and 1929, the volume of imports (at 1924 prices)
rose by 14 per cent., while their average price fell by 14·3 per cent. and
the money value of the national income rose by 9 per cent. Between 1934
and 1937 (another period in which changes in British trade barriers were
not very important), the volume of imports rose by 13·5 per cent. while
their average price rose by 25·3 per cent. and the value of the national
income rose by 20·6 per cent. These data may be put into the form of two
simultaneous equations, the solution of which gives a value of about one-
third for the price-elasticity and a value of about one for the income-
elasticity of demand for imports. Similar calculations for different pairs of

periods, each period being reasonably free from changes in British trade
barriers, give values for the price-elasticity between 0·1 and 0·5 and for
the income-elasticity between 0·6 and rather over 1·0. It therefore seems
reasonable to take the values obtained for 1924–9 and 1934–7 as the basis
of further discussion. Incidentally, it is worth noting that similar calculations for the United States give an income-elasticity of demand for imports
somewhat greater than the British (between 1·1 and 1·4), but a price-
elasticity very much greater—between 0·8 and 1·4. The elasticities so obtained do not correspond precisely in definition to those required for the
present purpose, but the discrepancy is probably not important.

The foreign elasticity of demand for British exports is extremely
difficult to calculate from empirical data. It can be presumed, however,
that it is relatively high. The elasticity of demand for many goods which
Britain exports is considerable—probably greater than unity—even on the
assumption that every change in their price is matched by a similar change
in the price of competing goods from elsewhere, and, even if retaliation by
Britain's competitors in the form of price-cutting or the erection of barriers
against 'exchange dumping' is to be expected, some competitive advantage
in many parts of the export market is certain to be gained as a result of
depreciation of the pound. It would therefore probably be highly conservative to put the price-elasticity of foreign demand for British exports as
low as $1\frac{1}{2}$.

As to the other magnitudes involved, it is reasonable (or, at any rate,
conservative) to assume that costs of production of export goods in the rest
of the world are virtually unaffected by the external value of the £, i.e.
that $v = 0$, and that the elasticity of supply of exports to Britain (g) is
infinite. The elasticity of supply of British exports (f) cannot be so easily
disposed of. Mr. Colin Clark (see *National Income and Outlay*, pp. 257–9),
calculated that the marginal real labour cost curve in mining and manufacturing in Britain is a falling one, but it will be seen from his data and
his diagram that he has omitted to remove the trend due to the steady improvement in efficiency over the period (1928–36) from which his data are
drawn. If this is done by a rough and ready method, a comparison of the
periods 1932–4 and 1934–6 shows a tendency for the marginal cost curve
to rise, the elasticity being somewhat under $1\frac{1}{2}$. When the imperfection of
the elasticity of supply of labour is taken into account, this elasticity is
presumably lowered, but the elasticity of supply of exports is no doubt
raised considerably by the possibility of diverting goods and factors from
the home market. On the whole, a value of 2 would appear to be as low as
could reasonably be assigned to this elasticity (f). The coefficient u, which
relates changes in British export costs for any given output to the change
in the sterling value of foreign currencies, is harder to determine empirically.

It may, however, be plausibly put at $\frac{1}{5}$, which is approximately the proportion of the costs of manufacturing industry represented by imported materials.

The way is now prepared for the calculation from Equation (1) above of the export surplus, measured as a proportion of the total dollar value of British exports in equilibrium, which should follow from the depreciation of sterling by any given percentage from its equilibrium value. It must be emphasized that the values allotted to the coefficients are claimed to be reasonable rather than accurate, and that they are intended in all cases to be conservative, i.e. to be such as will lead to an under-estimate rather than an over-estimate of the response actually likely to follow from depreciation. The following results are obtained, assuming $a = -1\frac{1}{2}$, $b = -\frac{1}{3}$, $f = 2$, $g = \text{infinity}$, $u = \frac{1}{5}$, $v = 0$.

TABLE I

Percentage Depreciation of Sterling from Equilibrium	Consequent Surplus of Exports over Imports (per cent. of dollar exports in Equilibrium)
10	5·9
25	15·9
50	37·7

(b) *Taking account of variations in activity caused by the trade balance, but assuming elasticities of supply infinite.* The special case of Britain may now be investigated under the conditions assumed in obtaining Equation (2). To solve this equation for S is clearly a difficult matter in general, however, for it would involve expanding $(1-pS_a)^x$ and $(1-qS_b)^y$ and approximating by the omission of all but the first few terms. On page 86 above, however, it was argued from the available evidence that x and y are, in the cases of Britain and the United States, at all events, not far different from unity. It seems, therefore, that relatively little error will be involved in making them equal to unity in general, and, if this is done, we get:

$$S = \frac{k[(r/r_0)^A - (r/r_0)^B]}{1 + kp(r/r_0)^{A-v} + kq(r/r_0)^{B+u-1}}. \tag{3}$$

From this equation, it is possible to work out the trade balance which would result, upon the assumptions discussed above, and for any given values of the relevant coefficients, from any given degree of depreciation of the £ from equilibrium. For this purpose, f and g (as explained above) are taken as infinite, a, b, u, and v are given the values assigned to them as reasonable in view of the available evidence (see above), the ratio of equilibrium trade to national income in Britain (k/i_0') is taken as $\frac{1}{5}$, and the ratio of equilibrium trade with Britain to total income in the rest of the world is taken as $\frac{1}{60}$ (it is clearly a small fraction, and the precise value given to it matters very little).

As to the multipliers, it should be explained that, for the present purpose, they have to be defined as $1/(1-c)$, where c is not, as is usually taken to be the case, the proportion of an increment in income which is spent upon home-produced consumption-goods, but is the proportion of such an increment which is spent upon home-produced consumption-goods *and imports*. Mr. Colin Clark (see the *Economic Journal*, September 1938) has made it clear that this is the definition which must be taken if the whole of the balance of payments, and not merely that part of the balance which would still exist if imports did not vary systematically with national income, is to be treated as what he calls a 'determinant'. Mr. Clark has estimated that the multiplier, on this definition, was just over 2 in Great Britain in the slump 1929–33, and somewhat over 3 in the recovery period 1934–7. It seems reasonable, therefore, to take the multiplier as $2\frac{1}{2}$ for both of the countries concerned.

Using these coefficients, we get the following results:

TABLE II

Percentage Depreciation of Sterling from Equilibrium	Consequent Surplus of Exports over Imports (per cent. of dollar exports in Equilibrium)
10	5·3
25	13·8
50	32·2

The surpluses of exports over imports are somewhat smaller than those shown in Table I for the case where levels of activity are constant, notwithstanding that the elasticity of supply of British goods for export is here assumed perfect, whereas it was before assumed to be no greater than 2.

(c) *As in* (b), *but assuming elasticity of supply of British export goods finite, while other elasticities of supply are infinite.* It is arbitrary in the extreme to assume that a rising supply of British exports can be obtained only at rising marginal costs, while a rise in the level of activity in non-exporting industries involves, in itself, no rise in costs there, but, as mentioned above, it is difficult to take account of cost-changes associated with changes in activity throughout the economy as a whole. On these arbitrary assumptions, it may be calculated that (with the elasticity of supply of British exports equal to 2), depreciations of sterling by 10, 25, and 50 per cent. respectively from equilibrium would result in export surpluses amounting in dollar value to about 4·0, 10·4, and 23·1 per cent. of the trade in either direction in equilibrium.

What kind of difference would be made to these results if changes in costs in non-exporting industries due to changes in the level of activity could be taken into account ? In so far as, for example, the general rise in prices consequent upon expansion of activity raises costs in the exporting industries by raising their factor-prices, the effect is clearly similar to that of a rise in the coefficients u and v, which is set out under (b) on page 78. On the other hand, a low elasticity of supply of factors of production reduces the variability of real income and so of demand for imports, thus increasing that sensitiveness to some extent. In spite of this off-setting factor, however, my impression is that the general variability of costs with the level of activity makes the sensitivity of the trade-balance to variations in the exchange-rate less than it is when only export goods show an imperfect elasticity of supply.

Conclusion

The theoretical conclusions of this article, in their simplest form, may be summed up thus:

(i) The equilibrium rate of exchange between two countries will be stable so long as their elasticities of demand for each other's goods and services (assuming them to be the same for both countries) are numerically greater than a certain critical value, which in most cases is probably somewhat less than $\frac{1}{2}$.

(ii) If these two countries each limit their imports of all goods and services by quantity (i.e. by a quota system) to the levels ruling when there is equilibrium under the existing exchange-rate, the critical value of the elasticities of demand for foreign goods, which must be attained if the equilibrium is to be stable, is raised from something not far below $\frac{1}{2}$ to not far below 1.

(iii) Provided that levels of activity are not appreciably affected by trade balances, the amount, measured in terms of the receiving country's currency, which one country can transfer to another by depreciation of the paying country's currency, is unlimited, up to the point where the elasticity of supply of goods for export becomes zero, so long as the elasticity of demand in both countries for foreign goods is greater than some value slightly above unity. If the elasticities are below this value but large enough to be consistent with stability, there will, in general, be some maximum amount which can be transferred, and depreciation beyond the point necessary to effect this transfer will reduce the paying country's export surplus in terms of the receiving country's currency.

(iv) If the trade balance, acting through the multiplier, affects the levels of activity in the two countries, the critical values of the elasticities necessary to make equilibrium stable are not affected, but the trade balance is made less sensitive to changes in the rate of exchange from equilibrium than when levels of activity are fixed.

(v) If a country loses a source of income from abroad (e.g. foreign investments), the depreciation of its currency necessary to restore equilibrium is
(whether levels of activity are fixed or are influenced by the trade balance)
always that which would be necessary to achieve an export surplus equal
to the income lost under conditions of invariable economic activity. In
order to effect the transfer of an international loan, on the other hand, that
depreciation is necessary which will secure an actual export-surplus equal
to the amount transferred, and the necessary depreciation will therefore
be affected by the relative change brought about in the levels of activity
in the two countries by virtue of any change caused in their rates of total
investment either directly or through alterations in credit conditions.

As to the more empirical conclusions reached in this article, it must be
admitted that they rest upon very slender foundations. The impression left
is that the British exchange equilibrium is likely to be stable in practically
any imaginable circumstances, but that the extent of depreciation of sterling necessary to make up for any given loss of (say) foreign investment
income, or to make possible the transfer of any given loan is highly pro-
blematic. The values assigned to the various coefficients are such as to give
the highest probable rather than the most probable estimate of the necessary depreciation, and the result, for what it is worth, may be stated in the
form that, to fill a gap in our balance of current items equal to, say, X per
cent. of our equilibrium imports (or exports) of goods and services, a
depreciation of sterling by probably a good deal less than $2X$ per cent.
would suffice: to render possible the transfer abroad of a flow of capital
equal to X per cent. of equilibrium trade, it might be necessary to depre-
ciate sterling (against all other currencies) by considerably more than $2X$
per cent.—the necessary depreciation depending very much upon the
response of levels of activity here and in the outside world.

Only one certain conclusion can be drawn from this empirical study;
namely that further empirical work upon the elasticities of demand and
supply and related coefficients in foreign trade, though exceedingly
difficult, would be abundantly worth while if it achieved any results at all.

(ii) *The Fundamental Elasticities in International Trade*

By A. J. BROWN

SINCE the preceding section was first written a considerable amount of work has been done in attempting to measure the fundamental elasticities which characterize the response of trade and trade balances to changes in prices and rates of exchange. Indeed, the work had begun earlier, though most of it has appeared only since 1945.[1] It may be useful to appraise the results of this work in order to see what practical conclusions it suggests.

The Price-elasticity of Demand for Exports

The actual measurement of the price-elasticity of demand for a country's exports presents enormous difficulties. In the first place, the measurement of their price is difficult; secondly, the prices of competing foreign goods have to be taken into account; thirdly, effects of price-changes have to be sorted out from those of income changes; fourthly, trade barriers of all kinds, and, still more, changes in them, introduce innumerable disturbances; and fifthly, full adjustment to price-changes takes place only after a time-lag which it is difficult to allow for in empirical investigations.

As in all systems of many variables, however, it is always possible that the effects of some may not be large enough to obscure those of others; one can but look and see if there is any sort of regularity. One has then still to face the task of interpreting the regularity perceived, remembering that inter-correlation between 'independent' variables may make this impossible.

This last difficulty is a particularly formidable one, since the prices of both exports and imports tend to follow much the same cyclical pattern as world income, or as almost any importing country's income. In most attempts which the present writer has made, or seen, to separate the effects of income on volume of exports or imports from those of price, confluence analysis clearly demonstrates the inherent unreliability of the result. This casts doubt upon many of the calculations of Mr. Tse Chun Chang, who does not apply confluence analysis. Indeed, in only one case (in the first

[1] The main published works are: Derksen and Rombouts, 'Influence of Prices on Exports', *De Nederlandsche Conjunktuur, Special Memo*, No. 1, 1939; Adler, J. H., 'Import Demand during the Interwar Period', *Review of Economic Statistics*, 1945; id., 'The Postwar Demand for U.S. Exports', *Review of Economic Statistics*, 1946; Tinbergen, 'Some Measurements of Elasticities of Substitution', *Review of Economic Statistics*, Aug. 1946; Tse Chun Chang, 'The British Demand for Imports in the Inter War Period', *Economic Journal*, June 1946; id., 'International Comparison of Demand for Imports', *Review of Economic Studies*, vol. xiii (2); id., 'The British Balance of Payments 1924–38', *Economic Journal*, Dec. 1947; id., 'A Statistical Note on World Demand for Exports', *Review of Economics and Statistics*, May 1948; *Research Project on International Trade at Various Levels of Economic Activity*, under the direction of Hans Neisser (Institute of World Affairs—New School for Social Research); 'The Propensity of Industrial Countries to Import Food' (June 1948) and 'The Propensity of Industrial Countries to Import Manufactured Goods' (Nov. 1948).

of the articles in the *Economic Journal* referred to above) does he give all the correlation coefficients between the three variables (imports, price, and income); but in this case it can be shown that the correlation between price and income is too high for any reliable conclusion to be reached as to their respective influences on the volume of imports. Little faith can, therefore, be placed in the results of this straightforward multiple regression analysis.

On the other hand, the effects of general income-variations and trade barriers can be partially eliminated by transferring one's attention from the price-elasticity of demand for exports to the elasticity of substitution between (say) British exports of a certain class and those of other countries. In so far as British and competing foreign exports of the class concerned are similar, go to the same markets (or markets which experience similar income changes and make similar changes in import restrictions), and are similarly affected by the changes in restrictions which are made in all important markets, all is well, provided that one can measure changes in the relative prices and relative physical quantities of the British and foreign exports concerned. This elasticity of substitution is the chief component of the price-elasticity of demand for British exports which should be derivable from it as explained below.

These elasticities of substitution between the products of different countries have been measured by various workers for quite a large number of particular commodities entering particular markets. Messrs. Derksen and Rombouts were apparently the first in this field, measuring the elasticities of substitution between certain Dutch products and the products of all other countries (taken together). In the Netherlands East Indies market they found an elasticity of $-2 \cdot 0$ for shoes and of $-4 \cdot 8$ for cotton manufactures; in the Belgian market an elasticity of $-2 \cdot 0$ for coal. Professor Tinbergen later measured a number of similar elasticities, finding some much higher values (as might be expected) for particular grades of wheat and a few other raw materials and foodstuffs for which well-organized world markets exist. Mr. Chang, likewise, measured some elasticities of substitution between products from various sources entering the British market, obtaining values between $-1 \cdot 1$ and $-1 \cdot 35$, except in the case of Australian and New Zealand wool (which, of course, are of very dissimilar average qualities) for which the result was $-0 \cdot 69$.

The largest investigation of particular products entering a particular market (in this case the United Kingdom market in the years 1921–38) has, however, been undertaken by Mr. Kubinski of the University of Leeds. His work is still in progress, but some preliminary results may be quoted.[1]

Mr. Kubinski's commodities were selected from the British import list

---

[1] For a fuller and slightly later summary of this work, see the *Yorkshire Bulletin of Economic and Social Research*, Vol. 2, No. 1 (January, 1950).

at random, except that the selection is necessarily confined to those cases where a fairly reliable measure of physical quantities coming from each of the main sources is given in the statistics. It is usually the elasticity of substitution between the two largest sources of supply which has been calculated, the method being the straightforward one of calculating the regression of the ratio of the quantities from the two sources (measured logarithmically) on the ratio of the average prices per physical unit from the two sources, similarly measured. In cases where it appeared from the scatter-diagrams or time-series that the correlation would be increased thereby, the effect of eliminating a linear trend or of introducing a distributed lag (of quantities behind prices) was tried.

Up to the time of writing, Mr. Kubinski has investigated 243 commodities, but in certain cases the period studied divides naturally into two parts, so that the number of regressions is increased to 280. Of these, 256 showed a negative correlation between the price-ratio and the quantity ratio and 24 a positive correlation; 133 of the negative correlation coefficients and 13 of the positive ones possessed a statistical significance above the 5 per cent. point. The evidence of a time-lag in the working of the price-mechanism seems to be conclusive in 89 (or nearly a third) of the 280 cases investigated. In most of these instances, a 3 or 4 years' distributed lag appeared to be most effective, but a shorter one was sometimes indicated. It does not seem possible to generalize at this stage of Mr. Kubinski's work, about the nature of these commodities with regard to which there is clear evidence of a time-lag.

Mr. Kubinski has calculated the regression coefficient of the quantity ratio on the price-ratio (both measured logarithmically) for all 280 of the cases so far investigated, whether the correlation is positive or negative, significant or non-significant, and obtains the following frequency distribution:

Range of Regression Coefficients (elasticities of substitution)	Number of Instances
More than +6 . .	4
+4 to +6 . . .	3
+2 to +4 . . .	8
0 to +2 . . .	9
2 to 0 . . .	107
−4 to −2 . . .	67
−6 to −4 . . .	19
−8 to −6 . . .	17
−10 to −8 . . .	10
−12 to −10 . .	4
−14 to −12 . .	6
−16 to −14 . .	11
−18 to −16 . .	2
Less than −18 . .	13
Total	280

It is clear that this is a distribution with a very high degree of negative skewness, and with a clearly-defined mode in the region of an elasticity of −1. The unweighted arithmetic mean of all the elasticities is actually −4·55, and their median value is −2·21. If attention is confined to the 146 coefficients of regression (elasticities of substitution) which are statistically significant, as being above 5 per cent. point, the unweighted arithmetic mean is found to be −5·47. For the 69 cases of commodities in the food, drink, and tobacco class which were investigated, the arithmetic mean elasticity was −6·05; for the 58 raw materials and semi-manufactures, −2·60; and for the 153 cases of articles mainly manufactured, −4·64. The dispersion of the elasticities within each class was such that the differences between these values may be regarded as significant.

Attempts to measure directly the elasticities of substitution between more broadly defined classes of goods flowing into the world market from different sources have also been made by a number of writers. For instance, Professor Tinbergen used the statistics of export prices and volumes from 1924 to 1938, published in the League of Nations' *Review of World Trade, 1938*, to calculate elasticities of substitution between the entire exports of certain countries and those of the rest of the world as a whole. Values mainly in the neighbourhood of −2 were obtained. Mr. Chang, however, has pointed out that much of the apparent price-substitution concerned is, in fact, simply a rise in the volume of the exports of agricultural countries relatively to those of manufacturing countries in the depression, when the prices of agricultural commodities suffered the greater fall. The maintenance of the volume of agricultural exports in these circumstances was due only partly to the fall in their relative price, being partly an income effect.[1]

Indeed, one would expect only a very low elasticity of substitution between (say) British exports, three-quarters of which were finished manufactures, and all other countries' exports, two-thirds of which were goods of other classes. If, for instance, there were only a negligible amount of price-substitution between manufactured goods and goods of other classes, one would expect the 'over-all' elasticity of substitution between British manufactures and the exports of *all* kinds from other countries to work out at something like one-third of the elasticity of substitution between those British goods and *manufactured* products from elsewhere. Mr. Chang's rough estimate that Professor Tinbergen's results suggest a true 'over-all'

[1] This point has been elaborated by Dr. Polak ('A Note on the Measurement of Elasticity of Substitution in International Trade', *Review of Economics and Statistics*, Feb. 1950), in which it is shown that highly deceptive results are possible if income-elasticities of demand for the products of the two countries compared are different, and if world income is highly correlated with the ratio of the prices of those goods.

elasticity in the region of -1 is therefore not inconsistent with elasticities of much higher numerical value between the *comparable* goods of different countries.

In the light of this, it may appear surprising that Mr. Chang's estimate, from the same statistical source, of the elasticity of substitution between British and United States *manufactured* exports is as low as $-0\cdot30$, that his estimate of the elasticity of substitution between British and Swedish exports is only $-0\cdot87$, or that the corresponding elasticities between the entire exports of agricultural countries (Eire, Australia, New Zealand, and Denmark) were estimated at various values between $-0\cdot25$ and $-0\cdot76$. On closer inspection, however, it is seen that the blocks of exports thus compared differ more from one another in composition than might at first be thought. It is not surprising that the highly specialized industrial exports of Sweden, for instance, do not appear very highly substitutable for the much more varied industrial exports of the United Kingdom, considered as a whole. Nor are the exports of the agricultural countries concerned very similar in composition; Australia relies very heavily on wool; New Zealand combines wool with dairy produce; Denmark combines dairy produce with pig products; Eire relies more heavily on meat, and so on. All these countries competed with each other, but the members of any pair compete directly only over a limited portion of their total range of exports.

Even the United States and the United Kingdom did not compete very actively over the whole range of their manufactured exports, but one would, nevertheless, expect the degree of competitiveness between them to be fairly high. Unfortunately, the data for the inter-war period do not enable a reliable measurement to be made. United States exports are more income-sensitive than those of other industrial countries (including the United Kingdom) and the changes in the ratio of United States to United Kingdom exports are partly due to an income effect. The real difficulty of measurement arises, however, from the fact that world income was very highly correlated, in the period concerned, both with the ratio of American to British export prices and with the ratio of their export volumes (for the years 1929–38, the coefficients were: income and price-ratio, $-0\cdot7728$; income and volume ratio $+0\cdot6013$; volume ratio and price-ratio, $-0\cdot5547$). The result is that the introduction of income as a third variable completely disrupts the estimate of the net relation between relative price and relative quantity, while the introduction of relative price as a variable similarly destroys the closeness of the estimated net relation between income and relative quantities exported.

The same inter-correlation between variables whose effects one wished to separate forbids any reliable measurement of the price-elasticity of substitution between United States and *all* other manufactured exports in the inter-war years. This, however, is fortunately not the case with the United Kingdom. The League of Nations has provided indexes of the British share of world manufactured exports and of the corresponding British export prices, measured relatively to world prices from 1929 to 1938. It is plain from a scrutiny of the data that there is a substantial income effect here too—that British manufactured exports were somewhat more sensitive than those of the industrial countries generally to changes in world income (here measured by the League of Nations world index of industrial production). Confluence analysis shows that the three variables, price-ratio, export ratio, and income are in this case free from such inter-correlation as would prevent their relations from being disentangled. The correlation coefficients are: price-ratio and income, $+0.6222$; volume ratio and income, $+0.0691$, and price-ratio and volume ratio, $+0.6602$; the relations between all three pairs of variants are 'improved' (according to the criteria of confluence analysis) by the introduction of the third variant. The equation works out at:

$$\log Q = 5.13 - 1.96 \log P + 0.35 \log Y$$

where Q, P, and Y are the quantity ratio and the price-ratio (U.K./world total, 1929 = 100) and world industrial production (1913 = 100). The price-elasticity of substitution between United Kingdom and other exports of manufactures thus appears to have been -1.96. The ratio of the standardized net regression coefficient of quantity ratio on price-ratio to its own standard error of estimate is 4.825, the 1 per cent. point, according to R. A. Fisher's tables, being 3.499. The multiple correlation coefficient for the whole relation is 0.885, the 1 per cent. point being 0.855.

An alternative method of eliminating the effects of income variation (or, at least, most of them) would be to consider only the short-term movements of the price-ratio and the quantity ratio—for example, their deviations from their respective three-year moving averages. If this is done, a correlation coefficient of -0.913 is obtained, and a regression coefficient of quantity ratio on price-ratio of -1.99. Although the numbers of data are very small, significant correlations (of -0.943 and -0.972 respectively) are obtained for the two sub-periods 1929–32 and 1933–8, the corresponding regression coefficients (price-elasticities of substitution) being -2.01 and -3.50 respectively, so that it is plain that a short-run quantity-price relation was observable not merely in the years 1931–2, when currency devaluations produced violent disturbances, but at other times as well.

There is a slight sign of a time-lag between the short-term movements of relative quantities and those of relative prices, but with annual data which show such irregular movements it is hard to measure it. If, however, one examines their longer-term movements—the movements of their three-year moving averages—one at once finds clearer traces of a lag of quantity-movements behind those of prices. It is therefore interesting to re-work the relation between quantity-ratio, price-ratio, and income, introducing a lag of the first-named behind the other two. Best results are obtained with a one-year distributed lag—the quantity ratio of 1930, for instance, is related to a price-ratio and an income which are the averages for 1930 and 1929. When this is done, the multiple correlation coefficient is raised a little (from 0·885 to 0·910), and the ratio of the standardized net regression coefficient of quantity-ratio on price-ratio to its standard error of estimate is increased more significantly from 4·82 to 5·34. The new equation of regression is:

$$\log Q = 6 \cdot 40 - 2 \cdot 54 \log P_1 + 0 \cdot 30 \log Y_1$$

where P_1 is the average index of price-ratio for the year in question and the previous one, and Y_1 is the corresponding figure for world industrial production. The introduction of a lag thus raises the estimate of price-elasticity of substitution between British-manufactured exports and those of the world at large to 2·54.

It would be satisfactory if elasticities of substitution between the similarly described products of different countries could be measured in ways which avoided some, at least, of the pitfalls with which the way of the investigator of time series is strewn. One such method would be to correlate the average prices at which the commodity concerned is imported into a market from different sources during some chosen year, with the quantities taken from those sources. It may be worth mentioning a simple calculation which the present writer has performed, arising out of a device developed by Mr. G. D. A. MacDougall for illustrating the elementary theory of international trade. This device consists in comparing the relative volumes of British and United States exports of a number of commodities with their relative direct labour costs of production as measured in man-hours by Mr. Rostas. If these two sets of ratios, measured logarithmically, are plotted for thirteen commodities for which the requisite data are readily accessible in what seem reasonably comparable forms (radios, motor vehicles, paper, footwear, cotton goods, woollen and worsted goods, rayon yarn, rubber tyres, soap, pig iron, steelworks' products, cement, linoleum, and oilcloth), a correlation of −0·811 is obtained (1 per cent. point being 0·661). Perfect correlation is, of course, prevented in this case, not only by imperfections in the market and differences in quality between the products of the two countries, but also by differences in their wage structures and in the relations which average direct labour costs of production bear to the selling prices of exports in the British and American industries compared. Since a fairly good correlation is obtained, however, the corresponding regression coefficient (which is a kind

5211   H

of mean 'static' elasticity of substitution between British and American manufactures) is of some interest. Its value, on the basis of this, is −4·26.

Another method of calculation, which does not exclude changes over time, but has the merit of comparing them for a number of countries at once, is to relate the changes in the volumes of exports (preferably of sharply defined kinds) from various countries between some chosen pair of years to the corresponding changes in their prices. In order to try out this method in the most interesting (and unfavourable!) case, the present writer has applied it to the total exports of such countries as published the necessary indices of volume, between the year 1937 and the third quarter of 1948. The sixteen countries considered exhibit little correlation when taken all together; they are, of course, a mixed bag, and the exports of some are almost entirely non-competitive with those of others. The industrial countries among them which sell widely in the world market, however—United States, United Kingdom, Switzerland, France, Sweden, and the Netherlands—lie on a very good line, with a correlation of −0·87 (half-way between the 5 per cent. and 1 per cent. points), and a slope of −1·98. The inclusion of the United States is perhaps hardly permissible, since, on the one hand, exports include goods shipped under E.R.P., while, on the other, the under-valuation of the dollar means that the export price is not the only factor limiting exports. If that country is excluded, however, the correlation exhibited by the five European industrial exporters is still −0·85 (about 5 per cent. point), and the elasticity −1·86. It is noteworthy that the points representing Norway and Czechoslovakia lie near to the line of the other industrial countries. The circumstances of the former of these two are so peculiar, and the exports of the latter so specialized, that it seemed hardly justifiable to include them in the general correlation; but if this was done, the significance of the correlation would be somewhat increased without the slope of the regression line being appreciably altered. The only four countries, indeed, which give points far from the line are easily accounted for—Turkey, Austria, and Hungary, all of which are exporting only 30 or 40 per cent. of the quantities which their prices would suggest because of their former dependence on the German market and, (in two cases) the circumstances attending occupation, and Finland (with export prices some 60 per cent. higher than seems appropriate to her volume of exports) because mainly of the special nature of those exports. Of the agricultural exporters included, Australia and the Argentine both show price-rises (for a given volume of exports) about 15 per cent. greater than the industrial countries, while Eire and Denmark lie a little on the opposite side of the industrial countries' regression line.

The following facts about elasticities of substitution between goods from different countries therefore emerge:

1. Wherever measurements have been made for goods of the same narrow classes entering a single market, results have been obtained which, while they vary greatly, are, on the average, quite high— certainly well above unity. The number of measurements of this kind is such as to give a reasonable basis for generalization.

2. Where elasticities of substitution between more broadly defined groups of exports, or total exports to the world market from different countries have been measured, lower results have been obtained. This is readily reconcilable with point (1) above, since

   (a) the goods coming from different countries, even where they fall under the same very broad headings (e.g. 'manufactures') are frequently not close substitutes for each other,

   (b) in some cases there are income-effects which cannot be separated out from the price-effect.

   Where these two difficulties do not arise, or can be overcome, e.g. in comparing the United Kingdom's exports of manufactures (which are in composition not unlike total world trade in manufactures) with total exports of this class, one obtains a result which is not so low as to conflict strongly with the evidence from more narrowly defined commodities in particular national markets.

3. The above evidence in which sources are taken two at a time and commodity-groups one at a time receives some confirmation from investigations in which a number of commodities or changes in the exports of several countries are all compared together, thus eliminating disturbances due to changes in total world income over time. Even the changes in the exports of the main industrial countries between 1937 and 1948 show a surprising degree of correlation with, and sensitiveness to, changes in their prices.

The elasticity of substitution between (for instance) British exports and other countries' exports is, however, less interesting than the price-elasticity of foreign demand for British goods. What is the difference between the two? It can hardly be great. If British exports were substitutable only against other countries' exports of manufactures (not against their domestic output in the home market) then the price-elasticity of demand for them would probably be appreciably (though not very greatly) below the elasticity of substitution. British exports contributed before the war as much as a fifth of the manufactures entering into international trade, and the one-fifth thus lopped off the substitution effect cannot have been restored by the income-effect because British-manufactured exports constituted only some 1 per cent. of total world income. British-manufactured exports were, on the other hand, substitutable against

foreign manufactures in their domestic markets, though to what extent it
is hard to say. In the unlikely event of their being equally substitutable
against *all* foreign manufactures, whether entering into international trade
or not, the price-elasticity of demand would be practically the same as the
elasticity of substitution, for British exports of manufactured goods
constituted only about 2 per cent. of total world output of goods thus
classified. Hence, while the price-elasticity of demand for a country's goods
might lie somewhat below the average elasticity of substitution between its
exports and other countries' exports of similar goods, the difference cannot
be great.

In contrast with this conclusion, Mr. Chang has, for twenty-two countries,
obtained mostly low values for price-elasticities of demand by a direct
method—namely, by correlating the volume of the country's exports from
1924 to 1938 with their price measured relatively to that of exports from
the main competing countries, and with world real income. His results are
as follows:

	Income Elasticity	Relative Price Elasticity
U.S.A.	2·91	−0·43
Germany	2·00	−0·58
U.K.	1·81	−0·40
Sweden	1·50	−0·36
France	1·23	−0·77
Switzerland	1·36	−0·44
Japan	1·08	−0·60
Italy	0·95	−0·81
Chile	3·38	−0·17
Canada	1·52	−0·35
Malaya	1·52	−0·18
S. Africa	1·17	−0·31
Estonia	0·89	−1·29
Argentina	0·88	−0·46
Latvia	0·84	−1·84
N.Z.	0·72	−0·52
Finland	0·72	−1·23
Norway	0·62	−0·62
Hungary	0·61	−1·10
Eire	0·55	−0·65
Denmark	0·35	−0·45
Australia	0·22	−0·66

The discrepancy between these results and the foregoing conclusions can
be explained only in so far as:

(a) there is, again, no evidence that inter-correlation between Mr.
Chang's 'independent' variables (which is, on the face of it, likely
to exist in many cases) is not such as to render his results unreliable;

(b) the high correlation which exists between almost any country's real
exports (indeed between world trade as a whole) and world real

income tends to 'swamp' the subsidiary relation between exports and the price-factor, and reduces the significance of the regression coefficient of exports on relative price—it would probably have been better to work with the country's exports *measured relatively to those of its competitors* as the dependent variable;

(c) the exports of a country *considered as a whole* are in many cases not very direct substitutes for those of any other country or group of countries taken as a whole—one gets a true picture of the extent of price-substitutability only by considering particular classes of the country's exports in relation to foreign exports of the same class; and

(d) price-substitution is effective with some commodities only after a time-lag (this was true of nearly a third of the commodities in Mr. Kubinski's sample), so that the net regression of quantity on relative price is blurred.[1]

The whole field clearly demands more attention before the conflicts between results obtained by different workers can be fully resolved, but in the present writer's view the indications given by the work on single commodities are the most reliable yet available.

It must be remembered that all the estimates made refer to the conditions prevailing in a particular period—usually the late 1920s and the 1930s. The elasticities concerned are much affected by commercial policy. Take, for instance, the United Kingdom's position before the war. At least an eighth of our export trade in 1938 seems to have been subject to quantitative import restrictions which must have reduced severely the sensitivity of that portion of it to price-changes. Moreover, on our export trade as a whole, the average incidence of overseas customs duties was probably about 10 per cent. (excluding purely revenue duties), and probably more than half of these duties were specific. Thus, it may be that quantitative restrictions and those specific duties over which some of our goods managed to climb reduced the price-elasticity of demand for our exports by something between 10 and 20 per cent. What cannot be estimated even with this low degree of confidence—but may nevertheless be important—is the effect of reductions in duties (either specific or *ad valorem*) which were prohibitive to British goods before the war. Only a detailed study of our trade (and our potential trade), item by item, could help much in suggesting how important this might be.

It must be remembered also that all this refers only to our exports of merchandise; it would be harder to make estimates relating to the whole

---

[1] The reasons for differences between the statistically measured 'elasticities' and true elasticities have been more fully discussed by Mr. Orcutt ('Measurement of Price Elasticities in International Trade', *Review of Economics and Statistics*, May, 1950).

mass of invisible exports, which before the war were so important for the United Kingdom in particular. Interest on British foreign investments is not responsive to changes in British prices; it constitutes, so to speak, an invisible export the price-elasticity of demand for which is unity. The effect of changes in the external value of the pound in this field is to change correspondingly the external purchasing power of sterling due from our overseas debtors and the foreign-exchange equivalent of our sterling liabilities. Income from shipping and tourist expenditure, on the other hand, is certainly price-sensitive. It might be possible to estimate the elasticity of substitution between British and foreign shipping on some selected routes on which there has been a marked change-over, and for which freights are known. It might also be possible to shed some light on the responsiveness of tourist traffic to prices and exchange rates from French, German, Swiss, and Italian experience though various complicating factors such as travel concessions would have to be watched.

The Elasticities of Demand for Imports

The chief measurements in this field are due to Mr. Chang (see his *Review of Economic Studies* article referred to above) and Dr. Hans Neisser. While Mr. Chang again gives no evidence of the absence of harmful intercorrelation between price and income—which appears to arise, for instance, in the United States data, according to preliminary investigations made by Mr. E. J. M. Buckatzsch some years ago—there is a certain plausibility about the results which suggests that their value is not entirely destroyed by this. The income-elasticities, for instance, rise from a little above unity for the industrial countries, which import mainly food-stuffs and raw materials, to as much as 3, 4, or 5 for countries whose imports are largely of durable manufactured goods. This agrees quite well with estimates of income-elasticities which have been made both from family budget data and from time-series of incomes, prices, and consumption of various types of goods. The income-elasticity of demand for total factory products (other than food) in the United States seems from family budget data to be rather over unity; that for clothing seems (from family budget data from several countries) to lie between 1 and $1\frac{1}{2}$; Mr. Stone has estimated the income-elasticities of demand for durable household equipment and automobiles in the United States (from time-series) at about 2 and 2·9–3·9 respectively. On the other hand, the income-elasticity of demand for food in the United States is, naturally, much lower—Mr. Stone estimates it at about one-half. It is harder to assign reasons for the variations of the price-elasticities between countries, but in some of the most important instances they carry conviction—the value is highest, for instance, (0·97) for the United States, which is clearly the country best able to produce substitutes for many of the commodities it imports, while it is lowest (under 0·3) for those countries which, like the United Kingdom, Switzerland, Czechoslovakia, and Finland, are least in a position to do so. Equally plausible are Mr. Chang's estimates of the British and American elasticities of demand for particular classes of import. The price-elasticity is here shown to be over unity for imports of finished manufactures into the United States, and of manufactures into the United Kingdom—a result fairly well in accordance with the same author's estimates of elasticities of substitution in the United Kingdom between imported and home-produced manufactures of certain kinds.

Dr. Neisser's published results have been limited to those cases where the estimate of price-elasticity of demand, as well as that of income-elasticity of demand, could be shown to be statistically significant, though evidence of the absence of harmful inter-correlation between price-ratios and incomes is again lacking. The price-elasticity of substitution was calculated only for those imports into the United Kingdom and the United States which were held to be substitutable for home products—for the United Kingdom, all manufactured goods, except wood and timber, oils and fats, resins, paper, and cardboard, and for the United States, all manufactures except burlap and newsprint. The results obtained are:

	Relative Price Elasticity	Income Elasticity
U.K., 1924–31 .	−1·63	1·79
,, 1932–8 . .	−1·17	2·24
U.S.A. 1932–8 .	−1·67	0·73

These estimates are somewhat higher than the most nearly comparable ones of Mr. Chang, but the degree of agreement is fairly high.

Dr. Neisser's estimates of elasticities of demand for food imports similarly show low values—for the United Kingdom both income- and price-elasticities appear to have been about one-fifth, while for the United States the former was about two-thirds and the latter one-seventh.

Thanks to these two workers, therefore, it may be said that, although the inter-correlation of price and income data renders estimates of the corresponding elasticities of demand for imports somewhat unreliable, there is unlikely to be any serious dispute about their general orders of magnitude.

Elasticities of Supply of Internationally Traded Goods

The direct computation of these is extremely difficult; hardly any numerical data are readily available which would enable it to be done. In any case, both the elasticity of supply of (for instance) British goods for export and that of overseas goods for importation into the United Kingdom must vary a great deal with the states of economic activity here and abroad respectively. At present, for instance, it is clear that the short-term elasticity of supply of many things is relatively low, as is even their elasticity of supply *for export*. If an effective full-employment policy for this country is to be assumed, then the supply of our exports will presumably be less elastic than in the past, while the supply of our imports will similarly be less elastic than hitherto in proportion as the outside world succeeds in keeping its total output of goods in general nearer to full capacity.

These generalities help very little towards assigning numerical values. It is, perhaps, more helpful to reflect that since only a fraction of manufactured output is exported, the elasticity of supply for export is presumably higher than the elasticity of supply for manufactures in general. If 'manufactures' were a homogeneous commodity, the elasticity of supply of which was S and the *home* price-elasticity of demand for which was d, the proportion going to export being a, then it can be shown that the elasticity of supply for export revealed by a small change in the price offered (assuming the market perfect, so that this price-change applies to the whole output) would be:

$$\frac{S+(1-a)d}{a}.$$

Thus, even if the elasticity of supply of manufactures in general is zero (as might be the case in the short run with full employment) their elasticity of supply for export is still likely to be considerable, for the coefficient a—the proportion of manufactures which goes to export—was before the war only about $1/7$, and d, the home price-elasticity of demand, was probably of the order $\frac{1}{2}$–$1\frac{1}{2}$. On these assumptions, therefore, the elasticity of supply of British goods for export could hardly be less than (say) 3, and would probably be very much higher. In fact, of course, it is not justifiable to regard 'finished manufactures' in this way as a homogeneous commodity divided between home and export uses in a perfect market. Many British exports are specialities with little or no home market, while some other manufactures are (in normal times) virtually unexportable. If S refers to the elasticity of supply of *exportable* manufactures and a to the proportion of them which is actually exported, S is unlikely to be as low as zero and a will be larger than $1/7$. Thus, it is hard to say in which direction the estimate of elasticity of supply of exports will be moved by taking account of the non-homogeneity of manufactures.

There are certain qualifications to this. Price elasticities are defined subject to the condition of constant money income. If, however, the price-level of all British manufactures is raised, money incomes are automatically raised, unless the prices of non-manufactured domestic goods are correspondingly reduced. If they are raised, say by a percentage bearing a ratio g to that in which the prices of manufactures are raised, then the home market will absorb more; the appropriate formula is then:

$$\frac{S+(1-a)d-(1-a)ge}{a}$$

where e is the home country's income-elasticity of demand for manufactures. If $S = 0$, then the elasticity of supply for export will actually be *negative* if $ge > d$. Suppose, on the other hand (to pick out another possibility), that a policy of stabilizing the internal average price-level is pursued. In that case: (*a*) since changes in the prices of manufactures must be offset by contrary changes in those of non-manufactures, some substitution between the latter and the former will take place, and the elasticity of supply of manufactures for export will be somewhat raised; (*b*) since any increase in exports at the expense of home consumption will have to be accompanied by a reduction in the total home purchasing power, there will be an income effect which still further increases the apparent price-elasticity of supply of manufactures for export.

The elasticity of supply of imports into the United Kingdom can similarly be discussed only in general terms. British imports of foodstuffs before the war were only about 5 or 6 per cent. of world output, but much of that output was, of course, subject, for reasons of national policy or of transport difficulty, to price-régimes on which changes in British demand price would make no impact. Our demand price, however, might impinge upon considerably more of the output than actually entered into international trade (an amount equal to about three times our imports). Thus, if world price-elasticity of demand for foodstuffs is, say, one-quarter (a not-improbable figure to which Schultz's work lends some support) and the world elasticity of supply of those foodstuffs which our demand price affects is zero (as it may be in the short run), the elasticity of supply to us may be as low as (say) unity, though this is rather improbable. In the somewhat longer run, in which the total supply of foodstuffs affected by a small change in our demand price is expansible, the elasticity of supply to us is doubtless much higher.

Our imports of raw and semi-manufactured materials were probably about an eighth of the rest of the world's output and a fifth of its exports. It is improbable that the elasticity of the total supply affected by a small change in our demand price would ever be down to zero, even in the short run, over this field as a whole (though it might be for materials of agricultural origin). Thus, even assuming a very low world price-elasticity of demand for these goods, as was done above for foodstuffs, it seems that the elasticity of supply to the United Kingdom is likely to be considerably higher than in that case. Certainly it seems likely that the elasticity will be higher still for the relatively small portion of United Kingdom imports which consists of finished manufactures, even though many of them are specialities.

Thus, taking a weighted average over the whole range of British imports, it seems reasonable to suppose that the lowest elasticity of supply we might encounter on the short run could hardly be less than, say, 3, and that in the longer run—anything longer than a year or two—the appropriate figure is likely to be so large that no very great error (by the rough standards applicable to such calculations) is likely to be made in assuming it infinite. This latter supposition is, of course, intended to apply only over the relatively small ranges of variation which are probable in the volume of British imports. For other countries, less important in world markets than the United Kingdom, elasticities of supply of imports would doubtless be higher still.

Conclusion

The above discussion may serve to show, at least, how great is the amount of attention which, in recent years, has been given to the evaluation of some of the fundamental elasticities in international trade, and how little has been given to others—especially to elasticities of supply. At the time of writing, the results of statistical work on the most discussed elasticity (the price-elasticity of demand for exports) were still highly inconclusive, and the months which elapsed between then and the correcting of the proofs added considerably to the volume of published discussion without making possible anything like a satisfying summing-up. Meanwhile, if history was unwilling to pay the econometricious the compliment of waiting for their results, it has at all events provided them with a set of adjustments in currency-values and relative prices, delightfully uncorrelated with changes in income. Not long after this book is published, it should be possible to begin to use these to carry the argument further.

III

PRICE THEORY AND BUSINESS BEHAVIOUR

By R. L. HALL *and* C. J. HITCH[1]

FOR several years a group of economists in Oxford have been studying problems connected with the trade cycle. Among the methods adopted is that of discussion with business men, a number of whom have been kind enough to submit to questioning on their procedure in various circumstances: and among other matters in the questionnaire were inquiries about the policy adopted in fixing the prices and the output of products. Mr. Harrod and Mr. Hall have given some of the results of these questions in papers read to the British Association, Section F, in 1937 and 1938. Neither of these papers was published, and the present paper includes the evidence on which they were based as well as what has been collected since: it also extends and modifies the theoretical structure which has been emerging from the facts. The data which it contains have been collected by various members of the group, and the results have been discussed at its meetings. The authors are responsible only for the form of their presentation and for the speculative part of the paper.

The purpose of the paper is to examine, in the light of the interviews, the way in which business men decide what price to charge for their products and what output to produce. It casts doubt on the general applicability of the conventional analysis of price and output policy in terms of marginal cost and marginal revenue, and suggests a mode of entrepreneurial behaviour which current economic doctrine tends to ignore. This is the basing of price upon what we shall call the 'full cost' principle, to be explained in detail below.

1. Significance and limitations of the evidence

The method followed has been to submit the questionnaire to business men who were willing to answer it, and to discuss the questions and answers at length in an interview. The authors are acutely conscious of the shortcomings of an inquiry of this kind. We considered the evidence of only 38 of the entrepreneurs interviewed, which is far too small a sample to warrant any final conclusions. Of these, 33 were manufacturers of a wide variety of products, 3 were retailers, and 2 builders. The sample is thus strongly biased in favour of manufacturers, and any conclusions relate particularly to this type of entrepreneur. It is also biased by the fact that most firms were approached through personal introductions, and it is

---

[1] Reprinted from *Oxford Economic Papers*, No. 2.

probable that the entrepreneurs interviewed were more successful and more intelligent than the average business man. In the light of the smallness and the biased character of the sample, no significance can be attached to the precise percentages of firms behaving in particular ways. But on some questions the replies are so nearly unanimous that it is impossible to ignore their implications; and in general the answers fall sufficiently clearly into patterns to leave no doubt in the minds of the authors that current economic theory tends to regard behaviour that is of small practical importance as typical, and what is a well-marked mode as unusual.

In the body of the paper only the summary results of the evidence will be given. This evidence has been taken in large part from the specific answers to the relevant questions, but it has been necessary, in some cases, to supplement the information in the light of subsequent discussion and subsidiary questions. The answers of the entrepreneurs have been paraphrased, under appropriate headings, in the Appendix, pp. 126–36: these should be regarded as an integral part of the present paper, some sections of which will be much clearer when illustrated by the actual expressions on which the argument has been based.

2. Current doctrine on price and output policy

The basis of current doctrine on the price and output policy of the entrepreneur is that he expands production to the point where marginal revenue and marginal cost are equal. In the special case of perfect (or 'pure') competition in the market for the product, marginal revenue is equal to price, to which marginal cost is equated. In the special case of pure competition in the market for the factors, marginal cost is equal to the cost of additional factors necessary to expand output by one unit, and this is equated to marginal revenue. In all other cases (except where discriminating prices may be charged) marginal revenue is less than price, and marginal cost is greater than the cost of additional factors, and the only rule of equilibrium within the firm is that marginal revenue and marginal cost are equated.

The equation of average cost and average revenue, if it occurs at all, is assumed to take place as the result of the entry of new firms where average revenue exceeds average cost, and by the dropping out of old ones where the reverse is the case (i.e. under the stimulus of profit or loss). It is not an equation which any particular entrepreneur attempts to bring about, or indeed one which he desires. It is customary to distinguish, somewhat unsatisfactorily, between industries in which 'free entry' is possible, in which there is a long-run tendency for average revenue and average cost to be equated; and others in which there are obstacles to free entry, where this tendency does not exist.

The precise content of the terms 'marginal and average revenue' and 'marginal and average cost' is usually left in obscurity.[1] Most writers, including Professor Chamberlin, have concentrated on long-run equilibrium, where the difficulties of finding the appropriate content for the curves is least. Even here, however, there are the extremely important questions: on the cost side, of the allocation of selling costs; on the demand side, of the functional relation between selling costs and the demand curve, and of the nature of the demand curve. Is the relevant demand curve 'real', i.e. does it show what actually happens when price is changed; is it hypothetical, in the sense of being based, like Marshallian demand curves, on some particular assumption regarding the behaviour of other firms; or is it imaginary, i.e. does it merely show what the entrepreneur believes will happen when price is altered? Professor Chamberlin is the only writer who has attempted a systematic solution of these difficulties, and it cannot be claimed that his treatment is definitive.

In the short run, which has been relatively neglected, the same difficulties of interpretation remain and others appear. Here the only rule of equilibrium is the equation of marginal cost and marginal revenue. But are the relevant marginal curves those drawn from the short- or the long-run average curves? Probably most economists would say that it was short-run marginal cost which the entrepreneur would consider in deciding how much to produce with given plant, and that long-run marginal cost would be relevant only when he was considering the desirability of expanding or contracting the plant. Probably they would ignore altogether the very important distinction between short- and long-run demand curves, because it has long been customary to assume in analysis that demand conditions, in some sense, remain constant over time. The fact that demand in the future depends upon present as well as future prices, which makes it impossible to derive marginal revenue from any single demand curve, is usually dismissed, if it is considered at all, with a brief reference to 'maintaining goodwill' or 'spoiling the market'.

It has become customary in recent years to distinguish various 'conditions' in which firms produce on the basis of the nature of the markets in which they sell. The following classification, which is

[1] Compare, for example, Joan Robinson, *Economics of Imperfect Competition*, p. 21: 'Complications are introduced into the problem of the individual demand curve by the existence of advertising, but these have been ignored'; and, on the same page: 'In an industry which is conducted in conditions of imperfect competition a certain difficulty arises from the fact that the individual demand curve for the product of each of the firms comprising it will depend to some extent upon the price policy of the others. . . . In drawing up the demand curve for any one firm, however, it is possible to take this effect into account. The demand curve for the individual firm may be conceived to show the full effect upon the sales of that firm which results from any change in the price which it charges, whether it causes a change in the prices charged by the others or not. It is not to our purpose to consider this question in detail.'

chiefly based on Professor Chamberlin's, appears to the authors to be exhaustive.[1]

(1) Pure competition, in which no single producer can significantly affect the market price by varying his output.

(2) Pure monopoly, in which the demand curve of the firm is negatively inclined, and in which, because there are no close substitutes, the entrepreneur assumes that a change in his price or output will cause no other producer to change his.

(3) Monopolistic competition, or 'polypoly', in which the demand curve of the firm is also negatively inclined, because its product is differentiated from others, and in which the entrepreneur assumes that his demand curve is independent of the reactions of other producers, not, as in the case of monopoly, because there are no close substitutes, but because there are so many competitors within his 'group' that no *one* is affected to a significant extent by a change in his price or output.

(4) Oligopoly (including, as a special case, duopoly), in which a few firms produce an identical product, and each realizes that a change in its price or output may induce a change in the price or output of one or more competitors.

(5) 'Monopolistic competition with oligopoly', or 'monopolistic competition in the small group', which is like polypoly in that the product is differentiated, but like oligopoly in that the producer does not assume that his competitors' price policy is independent of his own.

In technical terms a monopolist (or a monopolistic competitor) is distinguished from an oligopolist by the fact that the cross elasticity of demand between his product and the product of any other one firm is negligible, and his own demand curve therefore 'determinate'. If any cross elasticities between his and other firms' products were not negligible, he ought to take into account the possible reactions of these other firms to any change in his own price, and the situation would thus be oligopolistic.

There are two factors which, if present, tend to make these cross elasticities small. One is the smallness of the proportion of consumers[2] (or potential consumers) for whom the elasticity of substitution is high between the firm's product and *any* other, a condition which will tend to make the firm's demand curve inelastic. For the smaller the number of consumers who transfer their allegiance after any change in price, the less

---

[1] The definition of monopoly does not correspond to Professor Chamberlin's (see Table 9, p. 123, in which the firms interviewed have been arranged according to our classification).

[2] Properly weighted, of course, by the number of purchases each makes.

likely is any one other firm to find its demand significantly affected. The
second factor is the range and evenness of 'scatter' of the affected consumers among the products of other firms. There are two cases in which
the range of scatter would be great and the distribution even:

(a) That of monopoly. Here there is only one firm in the 'group' or
'industry'. If its price is raised it will lose some customers, but, there being
no close substitutes (in the ordinary sense), the customers who desert are
likely to choose such varying alternative ways of spending their income
that no single firm's demand will be affected to a significant extent.

(b) That of monopolistic competition. Here there are many competitors
in the 'group', and in general the elasticities of substitution between any
firm's product and those of some other firms in the group are high for a
significant proportion of that firm's consumers. If it raises its price, the
customers it loses will, for the most part, choose alternative products within
the group. But because there are many such products, and because the
preferences of consumers are fairly evenly divided among them, the number gained by any particular firm is likely to be negligible.

With these definitions it is clear that there can be border-line cases
between monopoly and monopolistic competition with determinate demand curves. The 'group' is a vague and unsatisfactory division, and can
only be defined in terms of the high elasticities of substitution among products of 'many' or 'typical' consumers. In general, the smaller the proportion of consumers for whom elasticities of substitution are high
between products of firms operating in the 'group', the smaller can be the
number of firms within the group consistent with determinate demand
curves. The evidence of the interviews suggests that in the case of certain
luxury and fashion goods it is possible for cross elasticities to be negligible,
and competitors' reactions to be ignored, despite the fact that only a
very few firms are operating within the 'group' or industry as ordinarily
conceived.[1]

The 'current doctrine' of the equilibrium of the firm, which runs in
terms of marginal cost and marginal revenue, is held to apply in its simpler
form only to the first three of the categories in our classification, i.e. to
pure competition, pure monopoly, and monopolistic competition. It breaks
down in the remaining two, i.e. oligopoly and monopolistic competition
with oligopoly; these, as special cases, are relegated to footnotes or left
to mathematicians, because the demand curve for the product of the individual firm, and therefore marginal revenue, is indeterminate where the
price and output policies of the firms are interdependent. Attempts have
been made to solve the problem of equilibrium in these last two cases by

---

[1] The authors intend to develop the implications of the classification in a subsequent
article.

complicated variations of the simpler rule, but no one attempt has met with sufficient approval to be considered a part of current doctrine.

Subconsciously, when dealing with other problems and when teaching, most economists probably consider the case of oligopoly to be exceptional, and assume the general relevance of the simple analysis in terms of marginal cost and marginal revenue. They assume that the elasticity of demand for the product of the firm is a good measure of the 'degree of monopoly', that production is carried to the point where this elasticity is equal to the ratio[1] $\dfrac{price}{price-marginal\ cost}$, that if the elasticity is less than this ratio, price is raised, if more than this ratio, price is reduced.[2] They assume that each factor is hired up to the point where its marginal product is equal to its wage or, more generally, where its marginal cost (dependent on its elasticity of supply) is equal to its marginal revenue (dependent on the elasticity of demand for its product).[3]

For the above analysis to be applicable it is necessary that entrepreneurs should in fact: (a) make some estimate (even if implicitly) of the elasticity and position of their demand curves, and (b) attempt to equate estimated marginal revenue and estimated marginal cost. We tried, with very little success, to get from the entrepreneurs whom we saw, information about elasticity of demand and about the relation between price and marginal cost. Most of our informants were vague about anything so precise as elasticity, and since most of them produce a wide variety of products we did not know how much to rely on illustrative figures of cost. In addition, many, perhaps most, apparently make no effort, even implicitly, to estimate elasticities of demand or marginal (as opposed to average prime) cost; and of those who do, the majority considered the information of little or no relevance to the pricing process save perhaps in very exceptional conditions.

3. The 'full cost' policy

The most striking feature of the answers was the number of firms which apparently do not aim, in their pricing policy, at what appeared to us to be the maximization of profits by the equation of marginal revenue and marginal cost. In a few cases this can be explained by the fact that the entrepreneurs are thinking of long-run profits, and in terms of long-run demand and cost curves, even in the short run, rather than of immediate

[1] Since this will be the point where marginal cost will equal marginal revenue.
[2] See, for example, Joan Robinson, *Economics of Imperfect Competition*, passim; R. F. Harrod, *The Trade Cycle*, chaps. i and ii; and A. P. Lerner, 'Monopoly and the Measurement of Monopoly Power', *The Review of Economic Studies*, vol. i, no. 3.
[3] See, for example, J. M. Keynes, *The General Theory of Employment, Interest and Money*, p. 5 and passim; A. C. Pigou, *The Economics of Welfare* and *The Theory of Unemployment*; and J. E. Meade, *Introduction to Economic Analysis and Policy*.

profits. This is expressed to some extent by the phrase commonly used in describing their policy—'taking goodwill into account'. But the larger part of the explanation, we think, is that they are thinking in altogether different terms; that in pricing they try to apply a rule of thumb which we shall call 'full cost', and that maximum profits, if they result at all from the application of this rule, do so as an accidental (or possibly evolutionary) by-product.

An overwhelming majority of the entrepreneurs thought that a price based on full average cost (including a conventional allowance for profit) was the 'right' price, the one which 'ought' to be charged.[1] In some cases this meant computing the full cost of a 'given' commodity, and charging a price equal to cost. In others it meant working from some traditional or convenient price, which had been proved acceptable to consumers, and adjusting the quality of the article until its full cost equalled the 'given' price. A large majority of the entrepreneurs explained that they did actually charge the 'full cost' price, a few admitting that they might charge more in periods of exceptionally high demand, and a greater number that they might charge less in periods of exceptionally depressed demand. What, then, was the effect of 'competition'? In the main it seemed to be to induce firms to modify the margin for profits which could be added to direct costs and overheads so that approximately the same prices for similar products would rule within the 'group' of competing producers. One common procedure was the setting of a price by a strong firm at its own full cost level, and the acceptance of this price by other firms in the 'group'; another was the reaching of a price by what was in effect an agreement, though an unconscious one, in which all the firms in the group, acting on the same principle of 'full cost', sought independently to reach a similar result.[2]

The formula used by the different firms in computing 'full cost' differs in detail, as will be seen by referring to the information in column B in the chart of evidence; but the procedure can be not unfairly generalized as follows: prime (or 'direct') cost per unit is taken as the base, a percentage addition is made to cover overheads (or 'oncost', or 'indirect' cost), and a further conventional addition (frequently 10 per cent.) is made for profit. Selling costs commonly and interest on capital rarely are included in overheads; when not so included they are allowed for in the addition for profits.

It would be useful for economic analysis if the magnitude of 'full cost' in any case could be deduced from the technical conditions of production

---

[1] For a classification of firms according to the strictness with which they adhered to the 'full cost' policy see Tables 6, 7, and 8, pp. 119 and 121.

[2] In several cases trade associations published 'standard' figures of costs in an attempt to secure equal prices; firms in the industry were urged to use the 'standard' costs in applying the full cost principle.

I

and the supply prices of the factors. This is in fact impossible, for four reasons. The first is that the firm is not necessarily of 'optimum' or of any other size, so that the extent to which internal economies or diseconomies are reflected in the figures depends upon historical accident.[1] The second is that the addition for overheads varies according to the policy adopted for calculating the output over which total overheads will be distributed. As Table 1 shows, somewhat more than half the firms used figures of actual or estimated output, the others (including, in general, the more competitive firms) full or conventionally 'full' output. The third is that the conventional addition for profit varies from firm to firm and even within firms for different products.[2] The fourth is that selling costs, which depend upon the demand, are included.[3]

TABLE 1

Output assumed for Distribution of Overheads

(Firms classified according to strictness of adherence to full cost principle.)

	Conventional or full	*Actual or forecast*	*Ambiguous or no information*
Not adhering . . .	..	..	8
Rigidly adhering . . .	4	7	1
Normally adhering . . .	5	6	4
Adhering in principle . .	1	2	..
Total	10	15	13

Why do entrepreneurs base price on 'full cost', as defined, rather than attempt to equate marginal cost and marginal revenue? The information relevant to this question given by the thirty entrepreneurs adhering to the full-cost policy is paraphrased in column C in the Appendix and is tabulated in Tables 2–5.

A study of the replies confirms the existence of a strong tradition, already referred to, that price 'ought' to equal full cost. This tradition is accounted for to some extent by an idea of fairness to competitors and is undoubtedly one of the reasons for the adherence to the full cost policy. The other factors which seem to be most important in inducing entrepreneurs to follow this policy may be summarized under six heads.

(i) Producers cannot know their demand or marginal revenue curves, and this for two reasons: (*a*) they do not know consumers' preferences;

---

[1] The information on the slope of the cost curve at the point of equilibrium will be found in column E in the Appendix. In many cases it is inadequate because the question was frequently not asked. Thirteen firms were apparently operating under conditions of decreasing costs and four under conditions of constant cost. Two firms stated that costs were increasing because labour became more expensive as output was expanded; but it was not clear whether the diseconomy in question was an internal or an external one.

[2] This allowance, when given, is stated in column B in the Appendix.

[3] Information about the magnitude of selling costs, when given, will be found in column E in the Appendix.

REASONS FOR ADHERING TO FULL-COST PRINCIPLE[1]

TABLE 2
General

Belief that this is the 'right' price	5[2]
Loyalty to Association	2
Experience proved its advisability	2

TABLE 3
Reasons for not charging more than Full Cost

Fear of competitors or potential competitors (including belief that others would not follow an increase)	11 plus 6 of the 7 textile firms.
They do not go in for a high profit	2
They prefer a large turnover	2
Buyers technically informed regarding costs	3

TABLE 4
Reasons for not charging less than Full Cost

Demand unresponsive to price	9
Competitors would follow cuts	11
Difficult to raise prices once lowered	2
Trade Association minimum prices	3
Convention with competitors	1
Quasi-moral objections to selling below cost	8
Price cuts not passed on by retailers	1

TABLE 5
Reasons for not changing Prices (however fixed) once settled

Conventional price in minds of buyers	5
Price changes disliked by buyers	4
Disinclination to disturb stability of market prices	3

(b) most producers are oligopolists, and do not know what the reactions of their competitors would be to a change in price.

(ii) Although producers do not know what their competitors would do if they cut prices, they fear that they would also cut.

(iii) Although they do not know what competitors would do if they raised prices, they fear that they would not raise them at all or as much.

(iv) Prices are not lowered by actual or tacit agreement among producers

[1] Little significance can be attached to the actual numbers in each category, since in most cases only those reasons volunteered by the entrepreneurs are included. Thus the fact that only three mentioned the technical information of buyers as a reason for not charging more than cost does not mean that in the other twenty-seven cases this reason was not operative.

[2] This is exclusive of the two in Table 3 who 'do not go in for a high profit', the eight in Table 4 who had quasi-moral objections to selling below cost, and the three in Table 5 who are disinclined to disturb stability.

because of the conviction that the elasticity of demand for the group of products is insufficient to make this course pay.[1]

(v) If prices are in the neighbourhood of full cost, they are not raised by actual or tacit agreement because it is thought that, while this would pay in the short run, it would lead to an undermining of the firms by new entrants in the long run.[2]

(vi) Changes in price are frequently very costly, a nuisance to salesmen, and are disliked by merchants and consumers. Several entrepreneurs referred explicitly to the fact that there are conventional prices to which customers are attached, and that these have to be charged, which means that in these cases only large changes in price which are clearly unprofitable are possible.

All these reasons militate against changing price from the conventional level. In addition, (i) is a reason for not adopting the alternative price policy of equating marginal cost to marginal revenue; (vi) makes it undesirable and almost impossible to equate short-run marginal cost and marginal revenue; and (v) is a reason for the conventional price level being no higher than 'full cost' including a 'reasonable' addition for profit—a tendency reinforced by tradition.

If it is desired to illustrate the position of equilibrium geometrically, this may be done for the typical case where oligopoly elements are present by the use of a kinked demand curve, the kink occurring at the point where the price, fixed on the 'full-cost' principle, actually stands. Above this point the curve is elastic, because an increase in price will not be followed (or so it is feared) by competitors, who will be glad to take any extra sales. Below the point the demand is much less elastic because a reduction in the price charged will be followed eventually by competitors who would otherwise lose business. If this is the character of the demand curve it follows that over a wide range of marginal costs the existing price is the most profitable. It also follows that, with given costs, this price is most profitable over a wide range of possible fluctuations of the demand curve, since wherever the demand curve may be the kink will occur at the same price.

The two diagrams (Figs. 1 and 2) are intended to help the reader to grasp one point in the argument; like all diagrams, they are much more precise than the circumstances they purport to explain.

In Fig. 1 *AA* represents the demand curve for the product of one firm of the 'group' if all other firms maintain their prices at *P*: *BB* represents the demand for the product of the firm if all other firms vary their prices as it does, this being a proportionate share of the market demand.

---

[1] In this they are, in most cases, certainly right, since the elasticity of demand for the products of the group as a whole is less than that for the product of any one firm.

[2] If prices are below what entrepreneurs consider the full cost level they will be raised by agreement provided that it is possible to secure one.

If competitors are forced to cut prices below P when any firm begins such a movement, but do not raise their prices above this point if only one firm does so, then it is very likely to pay any firm to maintain price at P. For its own demand curve will have the shape of the heavy line, kinked at P. If MR_a is the marginal revenue curve to the curve AP, and MR_b the marginal revenue curve to the curve PB, then the marginal revenue to

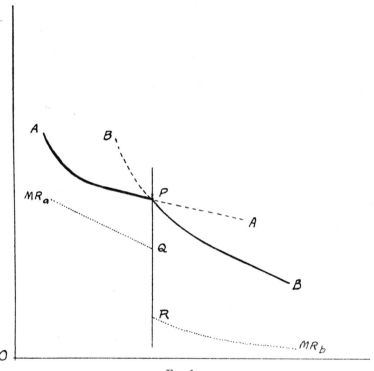

Fig. 1.

any firm is discontinuous below the point P. And as long as the marginal cost of the firm intersects the line PQR at any point between Q and R, P must be the most profitable point and price therefore stable.

If the demand curves shift, but the kink remains at the same price, there will still be a range between the two marginal revenue curves on the perpendicular below the actual position of P: and price will be stable for a wide range of marginal costs.

In Fig. 2 let AC represent a section of the short-run average cost curve for a firm, excluding profits. If the firm assumes that it will sell an output OA, and adds 10 per cent. of its average cost at that point for profit, it will set the price at OB, and be willing to sell, in the first instance, whatever is demanded at that price. If other firms act in the same way, the price

will be stable for the reason explained in connexion with Fig. 1. The curves
$d'd'$, $d\,d$, and $d''d''$ represent various positions which may be actually taken
by the demand curve: only at P are the profits which are made those which
were expected, but the price will not be changed for the other positions.
Any circumstance which lowers or raises the average cost curves of all
firms by similar amounts, on the other hand, e.g. a change in factor prices,
is likely to lead to a re-evaluation of the 'full cost' price OB.

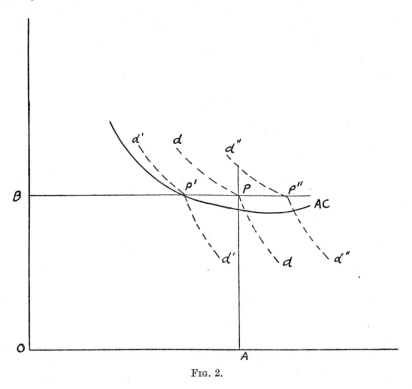

Fig. 2.

If the demand curve shifts much to the left of $d'd'$ and remains there for
some time, the price is likely to be cut in the hope of maintaining output.
The reason for this cannot be explained geometrically except in the special
circumstances where the lower part of the demand curve becomes much
more elastic when it moves to the left or where marginal costs fall considerably as output is reduced. Usually one entrepreneur is overcome by
panic: 'there is always one fool who cuts'; and the rest must follow. If the
demand curve shifts much to the right of $d''d''$ the price is likely to be
reduced in the long run, because the long-run average cost curve is likely
to be falling and entrepreneurs fear that the high profits will induce competition. (In Fig. 2 the long-run average cost curve would lie below the
short-run curve AC on either side of the point below P.)

4. Extent and strictness of adherence to 'full cost' policy

From so small a sample it is difficult to generalize concerning the strictness with which firms adhere to the full cost policy, but an examination of the answers summarized in the Appendix, pp. 126–36, and of Tables 6, 7, and 8, indicates that it is the rule rather than the exception to attempt to do so.

TABLE 6

Degree of Adherence to Full Cost Principle (Classified according to Types of Market)

	Not adhering	Adhering rigidly	Adhering normally	Adhering in principle
Monopoly	1	2	1	..
Oligopoly	1	..	3	..
Monopolistic competition	3	5	2	1
Monopolistic competition with oligopoly	3	5	9	2
Total	8	12	15	3

TABLE 7

Adherence to Full Cost Principle (Classified according to Types of Product)

	Not adhering	Adhering rigidly	Adhering normally	Adhering in principle
Consumers' goods	4	4	7	..
Textiles	1	2	1	3
Intermediate goods	1	3	..	..
Capital goods	1	3	3	..
Retailers	1	..	2	..
Builders	..	..	2	..
Total	8	12	15	3

Of the 38 firms which we investigated, 12 maintained that they adhered to the 'full cost' policy, with negligible exceptions,[1] at all times and in all circumstances. Of the remainder, 15 adhered to it in normal times, most times being 'normal' in this sense. In addition 3 firms (all in textiles) professed to adhere 'in principle', but not in fact because of the severe and chronic depression in the trade. Of these 18 firms adhering normally or 'in principle', 12 said that if business were very depressed they would cut prices below full cost, and 6 of these expressed a reluctant willingness to

[1] Selling below cost on 'loss leaders', shading prices on one line and making it up on another, and cutting slightly on large orders have not been considered inconsistent with 'rigid' adherence.

cut all the way to prime cost if that proved necessary to 'keep going'.[1]
Only 2 of the 30 firms adhering said that they would charge more than full
cost in exceptionally prosperous times when they were having difficulty
in filling orders, and it is doubtful whether even these two would charge
in such circumstances as much as the market would bear in the short run :
rationing by refusing to take orders or to fill them promptly was preferred
to 'excessive' prices.

The behaviour of a certain number of firms is clearly not explicable in
terms of full cost, and in the Appendix these have been omitted from the
table and discussed separately on pp. 137–8. One seems to be a monopolist
who behaves more or less in the text-book manner. Four had deliberately
cut prices in fairly normal times because they estimated (explicitly in three
cases) that the demand was elastic enough to make this course pay.[2]

5. Stability and instability

We may distinguish two main cases, which we shall call those of price
stability and instability, since the terms equilibrium and disequilibrium
have a connotation too precise to be warranted here. The distinction corre-
sponds fairly closely to that made by some economists recently between
non-aggressive and aggressive price policies.[3]

(i) In cases of relative stability each firm adheres as closely as it is able
to its own formula. Where costs do not differ widely within an industry all
firms will charge similar prices, and the consumers will be distributed
among them according to the factors which make the market imperfect,
such as the proximity or attachment of customers to particular firms. The
price may be set by the strongest firm, or by a process of trial and error
with all firms making some adjustments; in any case it is unlikely to pay
small or new firms to make such departures from it as to call attention to
themselves. We cannot say precisely what this price will be, for reasons
already explained; if it is set anywhere over a fairly wide range it will have
a tendency to stay there. The nearest that we can get to an exact statement is that the price ruling where these conditions obtain is likely to
approximate to the full cost of the representative firm; and that this price
is reached directly through the community of outlook of business men,
rather than indirectly through each firm working at what its most profit-

---

[1] These cases of cutting to prime cost present a difficulty for the analysis in terms of
marginal cost and marginal revenue as well as for that in terms of full cost, since none of
the firms had a perfectly elastic demand curve. The explanation in all six cases is that the
producers are working to contract—most are contractors and capital goods manufacturers—
which means that each unit produced is unique. This allows price discrimination and makes
price and marginal revenue identical.

[2] Two firms in the 'full cost' group said that they would cut prices in the (rare) cases
in which they thought demand sufficiently elastic.

[3] See, for example, J. M. Cassels, 'Excess Capacity and Monopolistic Competition',
Quarterly Journal of Economics, May 1937.

able output would be if competitors' reactions are neglected, and if the play of competition then varied the number of firms.[1]

The occasions on which prices stabilized at the full cost level will be changed have been summarized in column D of the table in the Appendix and in Table 8. A change in price may or may not upset 'stability' in our sense. The price is likely to be changed without a departure from price stability if there is a change in costs which will affect all firms together, such as a change in wages or the price of materials, or if a new process is generally adopted; in these cases the idea of the right price will change and with it the price itself. From this point of view there may be something to be said for business men who assert that income tax is added to price, since if all competitors in any trade regarded it as a cost it would tend to become one.

TABLE 8

Occasions on which a Departure from Full Cost Principle might be made

(a) *Price reductions:*

Depressed trade	6
Cyclically on competitive lines	2
When necessary to 'keep going'	4
Necessity to follow a competitive price	8
If competitor broke agreement	1
Loss leaders	2
Attempt to capture new markets	2
To obtain a large contract	3
Seasonally to stimulate sales	2
To clear old stock	1
Cases where demand was elastic	2

(b) *Price increases:*

In specialities	1
To maintain unemployment	1
More work not wanted	1
Need for funds for expansion	1
On expensive lines, to cover concessions on cheap ones	1

If demand shifts, prices may be allowed to deviate from full cost without disturbing stability. As trade conditions deteriorate, for example in a slump, full cost, where this is computed by distributing overheads over actual or estimated output, will often be allowed to rise above price. This tendency is strengthened by the anxiety to keep plant running as full as possible, giving rise to a general feeling in favour of price concessions. This may pass into a condition of price cutting, and the industry is then in a position of 'instability'.

(ii) Prices in an industry become 'unstable' as soon as any of the competitors form an idea of a profitable price which is markedly different from

[1] The variation in the number of firms may still serve the purpose of tending to equate the rate of profits on capital to the normal level. Thus, if a 'normal rate' of profits of 10 per cent. on turnover represents an abnormally high rate on capital, the entry of new firms may reduce it, without affecting price, by increasing 'excess capacity'.

the existing prices. From our inquiries this seems most likely to happen
when a trade becomes really depressed, and is a potent factor making for
an agreement which will substitute a formal arrangement for what was
previously only a sense of fitness. Conversely, it may happen when orders
increase to the point where existing firms have difficulty in filling them.[1]
Otherwise, it seems most likely to happen when there is a new entrant who
is determined to establish himself on a large scale, perhaps because of
the cupidity or inefficiency of the existing producers; or when one competitor thinks he has a method in advance of those of his competitors; or
(more rarely) when one of the participants begins to act on the assumptions
of competition in text-books. The price then becomes 'what the market will
bear', and the size and number of units in the industry and its methods of
production are likely to be changed.

6. Comparison of full cost analysis with current doctrine

The modification of conventional theory which the answers require may
be discussed under two heads: (i) modifications in long-run analysis; (ii)
modifications in short-run analysis.

(i) In general: the answers as summarized in Table 9 suggest that pure
competition, pure oligopoly, and pure monopoly (in the sense defined
above) are rarely found in the real business world. Monopolistic competition is more common, but the typical case is that of monopolistic
competition with an admixture, which is usually large, of oligopoly. The
answers indicate, moreover, that while Professor Chamberlin's analysis of
price determination in this typical case is correct in the sense that he has
probably defined the limits within which price must lie, the process of its
determination within these limits is more straightforward and the resulting
price more stable than he implies.[2] These limits may be described as (1) the
polypoly price (i.e. the one which would be established if entrepreneurs
assumed that no other firm would change prices in response to an original
change), and (2) the price which would be established if the industry as a
whole acted as a monopolist. Average cost (including normal profits) will
be equal to price in the long run where there is 'free entry', a condition
unlikely to be fulfilled if the oligopoly element is at all important.

But in the actual cases here examined the precise method by which this
result is attained, and by which price is fixed between the limits, is not
what a reader of Professor Chamberlin's book would infer. In most cases
no attempt is made to estimate marginal revenue from either short period
or long period demand curves, nor to estimate marginal costs. The height

---

[1] This circumstance will remove the kink in the demand curve and make its elasticity
above the old price similar to its elasticity below it.

[2] E. H. Chamberlin, *The Theory of Monopolistic Competition*, pp. 100–4. Professor
Chamberlin's *DD'* and *dd'* demand curves (see, for example, pp. 90–1) are drawn on the
same assumptions as our illustrative curves *BB* and *AA* on Fig. 1, p. 117.

TABLE 9

	Monopoly	Oligopoly	Monopolistic competition[1]	Monopolistic competition with oligopoly
Consumers' goods .	1	..	6	8
Textiles . . .	..	..	3	4
Intermediate products	..	..	1	3
Capital goods . .	3	2	..	2
Retailers . . .	..	..	1	2
Builders . . .	..	2	..	..
Totals . .	4	4	11	19

of price (between the two limits) is determined on the 'full cost' principle, conditioned by such historical accidents as (a) the size and efficiency of the firms in the industry at the time price stability was achieved, and (b) the extent of their optimism and of their fear of potential competitors as measured by the percentage addition for profits. Once this price has been fixed price competition, except in highly abnormal circumstances, ceases. Profits are reduced to normal, if at all, by an influx of firms which raises costs by reducing output per firm (increasing 'excess capacity') or by competition in quality and marketing.

The answers also suggest that the distinction between monopoly and monopolistic competition on the one hand and monopolistic competition with an admixture of oligopoly elements on the other is not of very great importance. Only where oligopoly elements are present is the demand curve 'indeterminate' in the economist's sense, but in the other cases it is unknown to the entrepreneur, and this seems to be the essential point. It is true that in the case of monopoly or monopolistic competition the possibility of finding his demand curve by experimenting is open to the entrepreneur; but there are objections to experimentation, and the prospect of a quiet life seems in many cases to have the greater appeal. Entrepreneurs seem to be somewhat less likely to fix prices on the full cost principle where the demand curve is determinate, but there are some who do so.

It proved to be extremely difficult in practice to distinguish between oligopolistic firms and others. The distinction seems to be almost entirely one of degree, for all firms were conscious to some extent of the presence of competitors and the possibility of reactions to changes in their price and output policy. In some cases the distinction seems to rest upon the size of the price or output charge under consideration. While a small change, which stole few customers from others, would be overlooked, a large change would lead to retaliation of some sort. In other cases the

[1] Some of the firms listed as monopolistically competitive were on the border-line between monopolistic competition and monopoly. See p. 111.

distinction seems to depend upon the size of the firm considered. In the same market some firms—normally the smaller ones—would apparently not attach much weight to possible retaliation by competitors whereas others—the larger ones—would. In the classification of firms in the Appendix those which seemed to be little influenced by the possible reactions of competitors to small changes in prices have been included as monopolistic or monopolistically competitive. The test applied is whether the firm is sufficiently independent for a Marshallian demand curve to be drawn which, in the neighbourhood of the actual price, would, in conjunction with the cost curves, form a reasonably accurate guide to the most profitable price policy.

(ii) The answers do not confirm the common analysis of short-run equilibrium in terms of marginal cost and marginal revenue. It seems to be much more nearly true (in the case of manufactured, and particularly of finished products) that, save in very exceptional conditions when the attachment of producers to the conventional price breaks down, the long-run analysis of price, as given above, applies in the short run. This does not mean that there will be no tendency for the prices of these goods to fall in depressions and rise in booms, but simply that there will be no tendency for them to fall or rise more than the wage and raw material costs.

These considerations seem to vitiate any attempts to analyse normal entrepreneurial behaviour in the short period in terms of marginal curves. They also make it impossible to assume that wages in the short run will bear any close relation to the marginal product (or marginal revenue) of the labour employed.[1] Perhaps the most important consequences are for the analysis of the trade cycle[2] and especially of the effects of changes in money wage-rates, in which the assumption is ordinarily made that employment is carried either to the point where the marginal product is equal to the wage-rate, or 'if conditions of imperfect competition prevail', to the point where the marginal revenue (computed from the elasticity of the demand curve) is equal to the wage-rate. Certainly great doubt is cast on the general applicability of a theory which places any weight on changes in the elasticity of demand in the short run as a factor influencing the price policy of entrepreneurs.[3]

[1] The 'Principle of Substitution' is, of course, not invalidated. The ratio
$$\frac{\text{marginal cost of factor}}{\text{marginal product of factor}}$$
will tend to be the same for all factors.

[2] The authors suggest that the price policy here outlined partly explains J. T. Dunlop's statistics in the *Economic Journal*, Sept. 1938, which indicate that real wages tend to vary directly with output during the course of the trade cycle.

[3] The 'law of diminishing elasticity of demand' may be a partial explanation of the price-cutting in some depressions which leads to conditions of 'instability'. Several entrepreneurs testified that depressed markets tended to be 'price markets'; i.e. markets in which buyers are particularly sensitive to price changes.

7. Recapitulation

If our sample is at all representative of business conditions, we suggest that the following conclusions may be drawn:

(i) A large proportion of businesses make no attempt to equate marginal revenue and marginal cost in the sense in which economists have asserted that this is typical behaviour.

(ii) An element of oligopoly is extremely common in markets for manufactured products; most businesses take into account in their pricing the probable reaction of competitors and potential competitors to their prices.

(iii) Where this element of oligopoly is present, and in many cases where it is absent, there is a strong tendency among business men to fix prices directly at a level which they regard as their 'full cost'.

(iv) Prices so fixed have a tendency to be stable. They will be changed if there is a significant change in wage or raw material costs, but not in response to moderate or temporary shifts in demand.

(v) There is usually some element in the prices ruling at any time which can only be explained in the light of the history of the industry.

APPENDIX

Analysis of Replies to Questionnaire on Costs and Prices

In the following pages is summarized the information on which the tables in the text are based. This is sometimes rather vague, either because the replies were vague or because, in the case of firms seen in the early stages of the inquiry, the technique of questioning had not been mastered. We began by expecting that the answers would lie along lines different from those which they actually followed, and we did not always press for information which later we should have found of great importance.

The firms have been classed into monopolies, oligopolies, those working in conditions of monopolistic competition, and those working in these conditions with an admixture of oligopoly. The classification has been made by the authors on the basis of all the information available. In the first part of the Appendix the firms which followed what we have called the 'full cost' principle are listed, including those firms which considered that this was the right policy but had difficulty in adhering to it. In the second part the information obtained from the firms which did not adhere to this policy is summarized.

The letter before the number[1] of a firm indicates the type of product:

a = Consumer's goods.	d = Capital goods.
b = Textiles.	e = Retailers.
c = Intermediate products.	f = Builders.

[1] The numbers do not correspond to those used by J. E. Meade and P. W. S. Andrews in 'Summary of Replies to Questions on Effects of Interest Rates', *Oxford Economic Papers*, No. 1.

MONOPOLIES

Firm	A *Price policy*	B *Method of calculating cost*	C *Reasons for adhering to the full cost policy, or to the modification actually employed*	D *Circumstances in which this policy would be departed from*	E *Selling costs; and any information about whether costs to the firm were increasing, constant, or decreasing*
d 2	Price policy defined as 'endeavour to secure a reasonable remuneration'.	No information about cost formula. Overheads proportionate to direct labour.	Cutting prices in periods of depressed trade leads to bankruptcy, so self-preservation supports full cost principle.		
d 4	Minimum list prices. Trade Association.	These are controlled by costs (? of representative firm). Last year's overheads assumed to be this year's, and divided by current output.	Outside control keeps prices from moving up, association keeps them from going down.	Would keep to list unless evidence of disloyalty.	Selling costs negligible. Costs decrease up to full capacity.
d 8	Prices fixed by cost analysis. Standard reductions for quantity. Trade Association.	Total overheads, excluding selling costs, distributed in proportion to direct labour. Output assumed from current experience. Selling costs spread in proportion to departmental sales.	Association 'genuinely vigilant to guard against exploitation of the consumer'. No advantage taken of inelastic demand.	(Before association was formed.) Though most business men reluctant to start a price war 'always one fool who cuts': then cutting severe in depression.	Selling costs about 20% of total overhead.

OLIGOPOLIES

d 3	Cost is the most important factor. All orders by contract.	Net cost of labour and materials + overhead proportionate to direct labour + 10% for profit, if possible.	Demand not responsive to low prices. Buyers too well informed to pay more than full cost + 10%, and also danger of foreign competition.	Competition acute in depression, but it is usually hoped to cover overheads. Might go nearly to prime costs to get a special (e.g. introductory) order.	Selling costs negligible. Costs increase, because quality of extra labour is worse.
	Usually full cost. Mostly contract work.	Total cost + 6 to 10%. Overheads small.	Nearly all costs direct: no explanation why prices not raised, but apparently competition.	Price cutting not important. Big contractors might cut in slack times to keep staff. Possibly some price agreements in such periods.	
f 2	Usually full cost. Mostly contract work.	Total cost + 10%. Overheads very small.	Nearly all costs direct: no explanation of why prices not raised.	Big contractors might make concessions in slack times to keep key men, but most firms close down if they cannot get expected price.	

FIRMS IN CONDITIONS OF MONOPOLISTIC COMPETITION

a 2	'The price is determined by (average) cost of production.' Occasionally quality is adjusted to price, to keep to formula.	(Direct costs + overheads) + 5% for profits. Overheads based on estimated turnover.	They do not charge more because 'they do not go in for a high profit: they could earn a much higher profit if they chose'. No temptation to cut, as industry expanding.	Price may be reduced seasonally to stimulate sales, or to clear old models. Lower limit is direct costs + overheads.

Firm	A *Price policy*	B *Method of calculating cost*	C *Reasons for adhering to the full cost policy, or to the modification actually employed*	D *Circumstances in which this policy would be departed from*	E *Selling costs; and any information about whether costs to the firm were increasing, constant, or decreasing*
a 4	Full cost. ('Where demand price is less we do not supply.')	Average overheads computed on basis of a conventional output, assuming normal or fairly good trading conditions. 'The margin added for profit is naturally smaller on competitive lines and higher on specialities and novelties resulting from research in design and technique.'	They are disinclined to cut below full cost because full cost experience has shown that it does not pay. Demand inelastic except on a few lines. The margin added for profit is naturally smaller on competitive lines and higher on specialities and novelties resulting from research in design and technique. A trade association sets minimum prices on a few lines. Price changes a nuisance to agents, and disliked by market.	Depression shifts demand to more popular, competitive, lines. It is their experience that timely reductions in these alone have been successful in increasing revenue.	Salesmen's salaries about 6 to 10%, advertising about 5% of sales.
a 7	Full cost of representative firm. The proper price is equal to full cost, but they cannot get this at present because they are new and small with high costs: they expect to in future. Price agreements in some lines.	Must charge a conventional price, and would equate cost to full cost if they were normal age and size. Their price a bit higher and quality a bit better than 'the competitive'. General rule (where agreements) is: price to retailer = direct cost × 3. They cannot get this at present.	They could not charge more without losing too many orders. They prefer reducing sales to reducing price, and are bound by agreements and conventional prices. Price cuts, in any case, are not passed on by retailers.	Sometimes the conventional price is less than full cost, but must be charged. They charge less now because their costs are too high. They would not cut to direct cost in any circumstances.	Selling expenses about 30%. In trade as a whole about 11–15%. Theirs are high because they are young. Costs decreasing (it was not clear whether this was solely due to selling costs decreasing).

b 1	Full cost ought to be charged, but they could not get the business if they did.	Material cost + weaver's wage + a percentage of this wage to cover overheads, &c. Overheads on basis of past six months.	They believe that while one firm can increase its sales by cuts, it simply steals from others. 'The price element as a determinant of sales has been much exaggerated; merchants do not like to buy in a weak market.'	They have to sell at less than full cost because others are doing so.	Selling costs very small. Greater diversity of cloths produced by each firm has raised costs.
b 5	Full cost.	They start from a conventional price, and produce an article whose full cost equals this price. Overheads taken on basis of full working. The selling department then adds 'something' for selling costs, risk, and profit. Allowance for risk varies from line to line.	They do not charge more because they aim at high long-run turnover. They never change a price unless there is a very large change in costs. Retailers dislike changes, particularly reductions, which reduce their margins. In any case, there are conventional prices, and it would rarely pay to move to next lower or higher. They do not follow cuts by competitors because they sell against market in general.	They sometimes improve quality when costs (e.g. raw material) fall. They cut in depression on non-proprietary lines because 'competition makes it necessary'. Difficult to estimate elasticity of demand, but not great on most lines.	(Refused information.)

Firm	A Price policy	B Method of calculating cost	C Reasons for adhering to the full cost policy, or to the modification actually employed	D Circumstances in which this policy would be departed from	E Selling costs; and any information about whether costs to the firm were increasing, constant, or decreasing
b 7	Full cost (nominal).	Price of material + weaver's wage + a percentage of this wage to cover overheads, &c. Fraction varies with cloth, but as a rule $\frac{1}{2}$ to $\frac{5}{8}$. Experience of past 2 or 3 years is basis for output assumed for overheads.	They have a strong belief, which is gaining ground in the industry, that selling below cost does not pay. Can always get business by cutting low enough, but this is too low.	They might accept a little less, but very little and very rarely, where order was large, or merchant's credit very good, or order part of a larger one which showed profit elsewhere. They have had to revise their ideas of what full cost is, and cut their margins.	Selling costs certainly less than 10%. Do not advertise.
d 5	Full cost. Formula changed once in depression, since then new formula practically adhered to.	Old formula: Price = works cost × 2. New formula: Price = works cost × 1.8. Works cost includes overheads in works; these spread evenly.	Experience shows that this formula gives satisfactory results for probable turnover, and increased profits if sales improve. They lead their competitors.	Formula was deliberately reduced in depression in the hope of extending sales, which in fact happened. Slight increase in price as consumers' income improved.	Selling costs 'fairly high'. Costs probably decreasing.
e 2	Cost is initial guide to price.	Manufacturing cost + transport cost + 'reasonable profit' gives wholesale price. This usually doubled to get retail price.	No experience of severe fall in turnover. Long-period policy appeared to be to continue expansion.	Price might be reduced if it were thought that demand was elastic enough to make it worth while. Sometimes the price of one article was raised to cover increase in cost of many.	

FIRMS WITH MONOPOLISTIC COMPETITION WITH ADMIXTURE OF OLIGOPOLY

a 6	Full cost.	Overheads (about 65% of total cost) distributed on the basis of forecast output. There was a range of about 40% between the highest and lowest prices on an article, depending on the size of the order.	Would not raise prices just because he thought market would stand it: would want to 'stand in with rest of trade' in making an advance. When sales fall off, better to go for designers and salesmen than to cut prices. Business community has 'a kind of group instinct leading the business man to aim at covering cost rather than at increasing turnover: the feeling that if you can't get a price that covers cost you would sooner burn the stuff'.	Would cut even below works cost to get a very large contract. There is an instinct to put prices up in a boom because some unemployment is necessary to maintain discipline.	Costs increase in boom (see D). Costs of selling and designing a large proportion of high overheads mentioned.
a 8	Full cost the normal and usual price.	Overheads computed on basis of forecast output, mainly in light of recent experience. Overheads vary from 60 to 400% of works cost in different lines. Distribution expenses taken as a percentage of selling price.	Frequent changes of price would alienate customers. They look on price-cutting as a 'slippery slope'.	They would cut prices if they thought demand sufficiently elastic. This depended on what competitors did; if they followed, it made demand less elastic. The chief reason for price-cutting in depression is the	Selling costs 10–20% of selling price (advertising 1–5%).

necessity of following the small man, whose greatest sales weapon is price.

Firm	*A* *Price policy*	*B* *Method of calculating cost*	*C* *Reasons for adhering to the full cost policy, or to the modification actually employed*	*D* *Circumstances in which this policy would be departed from*	*E* *Selling costs; and any information about whether costs to the firm were increasing, constant, or decreasing*
a 9	They produce at prices consumers want and reduce costs to make this possible.	Overhead costs 'calculated precisely'.	They regard themselves as market leaders, and fix prices independently of competitors.	Price policy to some extent based on estimate of consumers' purchasing power. In depression they would make a special effort to reduce prices, but they would hope to get their costs down in the same proportion. This was not considered to be price-cutting.	Selling costs, including retail margin, about 33% of retail prices. Advertising cost about 6% of selling cost. It appeared from discussion that short-period costs rose and this was a factor limiting rate of expansion.
a 10	In staples, price related to what market will bear. In fancy lines, cost is the basis of price.	Total cost, assuming standard figure of output, mainly based on anticipated sales. Overheads distributed specifically.	Disinclination to sell below full cost universally operative. Reactions of other firms definitely considered: price and profit could be increased if competitors would follow.	No information. Firm assumed that demand was inelastic.	Selling costs 7% of total. Costs decreasing.
a 11	Agreement in some lines. Cost the principal factor.	Works cost + average selling cost + about 5%. Output assumed to be normal. Overheads distributed specifically.	Disinclination to sell below cost, and competitors would follow cuts. Foreign competition limits price where agreement, home competition where no agreement.	There is a temptation to reduce prices in early stages of depression, to maintain turnover. In acute depression, any price contributing to overheads would be worth while.	Selling costs about 9%. Plant about technical optimum.

a 13	Full cost.	$[(\text{Raw material}+\text{wages}) \times \frac{\text{factory overheads}}{\text{last year's wages}} + \text{wage cost of article}] \times 3/2.$	Religious conviction plus successful tradition. Demand not responsive to price changes except in low price ranges.	Might occasionally shade prices on cheap lines and add something on more expensive ones to compensate.	Selling costs about 10% of receipts and rising.
a 14	In normal conditions and when trade is expanding price is based on average cost. Firm is a price leader.	Direct cost + overheads + a variable percentage (depending on whether the line is standard or ephemeral) for profits. Overheads distributed on actual output, except that where expansion of sales is expected, estimated output may be taken.	They do not charge more 'because experience teaches that if they do, the ground is likely to be cut under their feet by competitors'. They do not charge less because competitors would cut if they did. When trade expanding, wise to charge no more than cost to take advantage of expansion and not attract newcomers.	Price might be less in the case of loss leaders, supported for reasons of prestige. In depression they might cut to (direct cost + full overheads) −8%. They charge less than full cost when attempting to capture certain foreign markets.	Selling costs 'very high' on proprietary lines: low on bulk lines.
a 15	'By weighing the competitive position and the cost sheet.' In case of branded goods they must charge same price as the dominant firm (which bases price on full cost). With non-branded goods consumer has no index of quality, and a cost formula can be applied.	Overheads distributed on basis of forecast outputs each year.	Competition prevents him from charging more than rivals on branded lines. Important to discourage other people from coming in. Competitors would react with cuts if any firm made them.	See C. Competition may also force him to charge less than computed costs on bulk lines.	In a typical case, 17½% for advertising and selling, another 4-7% for delivery.

Firm	A\n\nPrice policy	B\n\nMethod of calculating cost	C\n\nReasons for adhering to the full cost policy, or to the modification actually employed	D\n\nCircumstances in which this policy would be departed from	E\n\nSelling costs; and any information about whether costs to the firm were increasing, constant, or decreasing
b 2	In specialities, full cost. In bulk lines depression made it impossible to get orders at cost. (b 2's addiction to full cost illustrated by his 'proof' that new machines should be installed. Full cost with new machines was much more than *prime* cost with old, but *full* cost with old slightly more.)	A conventional capacity assumed for overheads. Never ran a mill at less than 90% capacity.	Although any producer can increase operations to capacity by undercutting, the enormous difference to net profits per unit made by a small cut restrains this tendency. At the time of interview, an agreement reinforced this restraint.	See under A.	Decline of specialization an important factor in increasing cost. They tried one mill on a single count: efficiency increased from 84 to 96% of estimated capacity.
b 3	'In a good market a firm can determine its costs and fix its prices accordingly. In a weak market it is necessary to quote a price which will get the order.' Theirs is now a weak market.	An addition to direct costs made for works overheads and selling costs in turn. Overheads based on forecast output.	They deplore price-cuts, because they do not stimulate sales. Others cut as any one firm does, and no elasticity in demand for whole output.	If they charged full cost in the present depressed state of trade they would have to close half their mills in a fortnight. Agreements have existed, but they break down as soon as depression becomes severe.	Selling costs, including designing and office costs, never quite 50% of works costs.
b 6	Full cost. Start with a conventional price and determine what	Actual output used in assessing overheads, except that when	They have a very strong disinclination to selling below cost.	They accept some large orders (e.g. from government) at less	

article they can produce at that cost.	trade is depressed competition makes it impossible as a rule to raise allocation per unit.	'Price-cutting a miserable way of doing business', and extra sales would not compensate for loss of revenue. Their rule is to change price as little as possible, because this usually means changes in size or quality, which means loss on stocks and is a nuisance on production side. Upper limit to price set by competition.	than cost to keep plant running near capacity. In case of semi-finished goods, the market is nearly perfect, and market price, which fluctuates daily, must be accepted.	Selling costs about 11% of price. Costs decrease slightly.
c 1 Cost the principal factor in price.	(Works cost + selling cost) + 6–10% for raw materials. (Works cost + selling cost) + 20–25% for manufactured goods. Overheads distributed evenly on previous year's output.	Competition is keen, and though products are differentiated it would prevent a higher price. Disinclination to sell below cost, but cuts if made would be followed.	Prices reduced if material gets cheaper (i.e. by formula). Apparently not in other circumstances.	
c 2 Cost is three times as important as what the market will bear.	Materials + labour + overheads + intended profit. Overheads split to departments, then spread 'evenly'.	Prices not raised because this would lose the market. Strong disinclination to sell below cost, and expected that competitors would counter with cuts.	Prices sometimes cut to maintain turnover. Never go below full cost (? excluding profit).	Selling costs small.

Firm	A Price policy	B Method of calculating cost	C Reasons for adhering to the full cost policy, or to the modification actually employed	D Circumstances in which this policy would be departed from	E Selling costs; and any information about whether costs to the firm were increasing, constant, or decreasing
d 6	Normally full cost. Agreement in one line. All business is contract.	Works cost + 20% for selling, &c., + 10% for profit. Overheads usually on past year or two, but not if these years had been very bad ones.	Prices not cut to extend sales because competitors would immediately follow with similar cuts.	Full cost might be exceeded with their special lines. A tendency to cut in periods of depressed trade, and perhaps in order to get a particular order.	Costs decreasing.
d 7	Full cost between narrow limits.	Labour and materials × 2.2 to 2.3; i.e. *assumes* that overheads will be covered by this. Actually this gives 10 to 15% profit.	Does not go above this (15%) maximum profit because a wide margin would tempt competitors. Has low costs, and rarely needs to go below 10%.	With a new model, he would go down to prime cost in the knowledge that he would soon get his costs to his formula. Choice of profit depends on current pressure of work.	Advertisement negligible, no information on selling costs. In short-period, expansion limited by plant. Long-period costs probably decreasing.
e 1	Full cost between limits. Strong traditional ideas as to what price ought to be in some lines.	Material cost + a margin between maximum and minimum limits. Probable turnover assumed for each department. The margin added may vary by about 8% according to speed of turnover and labour costs involved.	They know their price is about the economic minimum, and do not need to go below it. Their long-period policy is to sell at low prices and expand business. But expectation of counter cuts by competitors is always a factor.	Would cut to keep staff together, increase price if he was short of capital for expansion. Competition makes it necessary to continue to reduce prices and give better quality (i.e. conditions not static). Prices once set would not be changed unless costs changed, except possibly to clear lines not going.	

The information under each firm is given in the following order:

A. Price policy.
B. Method of calculating cost.
C. Reasons for adhering to the full cost policy, or to the modification actually employed.
D. Circumstances in which this policy would be departed from.
E. Selling costs: and any information about whether costs to the firm were increasing, constant, or decreasing.

The following gives an account of the policies followed by the firms which did not price their products according to any form of the cost principle.

Firm a 1. This firm produced fashion goods, and though broadly affected by competition, had almost a monopoly[1] in its own range. The demand for its goods was a peculiar one, the price itself being regarded as one of the properties of the commodity, and sales being often higher at a high price than at a low one. Thus it was necessary to discover the 'right' price, which might not be related to cost at all: cost was the bottom limit of price. Price might be cut in depression, but this must be concealed from the customers. On certain staple, more competitive lines, price might be less than would cover full overheads, partly to maintain full employment, partly because these goods were made to train learners. Overheads about equal to works costs. No agreement in this trade, but firms were all anxious to know what their rivals were doing.

Firm a 3. This firm supplies mainly to multiple stores and 'has to take the price as fixed within limits' and work to it. But there is some play of price, and this is very important as affecting sales. Overheads taken as 150 per cent. of direct labour, this being added to material and direct labour charges to get full costs. Their selling firm takes their costs, adds $12\frac{1}{2}$ per cent. for its (selling) costs, and what profit it can get. They will go down to direct costs to keep the business going, but it is difficult to raise prices which have been once reduced. They discriminate in prices according to the season, and for such reasons as bulk orders.

Price reductions stimulate sales, and they produce as cheaply as possible for this reason. There are no agreements, and bad trade leads to a tendency to reduce prices.

Costs fall as turnover increases: it is surprising even to themselves how much.

Firm a 5. Described as almost a monopoly, but has to think about the possibility of new entrants to the industry. What the market will bear is the only consideration *any* business takes into account: bottom limit is prime costs. Costing is carefully done, and overheads are distributed on basis of 80 per cent. operation; but in any case, so long as overheads are covered somewhere, it does not matter which line carries them. Prices are liable to vary at short notice with cost of material and with the competitive position. Demand for most of their products is inelastic: with a competitive line, response to cuts is immediate. But a cut may reduce sales if it leads consumer to suspect quality.

Agreements are the most important factor against competitive cutting and include 'expectation that competitor will counter with cuts'. Even when an agreement has been broken (as tends to happen with any sharp change in trading conditions) you try to keep in touch: you telephone to your competitor and inquire, and if he is cutting you say, 'You get the order, old man, but do let's get together on the price'. (Apparent discrepancy between these paragraphs: informant may have had different lines in mind.)

Selling costs, including wholesalers' margins, which are considered a selling cost, are about 20 per cent. of works cost.

---

[1] Though this firm has been classified as a monopoly, the fact that the evaluation of its product by consumers was not independent of its price makes the analysis on which the classification was based inapplicable.

Firm a 12. This firm is a member of a highly competitive industry to which entry is very easy. What the market will bear is much the most important factor in determining price. Any price which will make some contribution towards overheads is better than nothing. Demand is very inelastic for the industry as a whole, and the sales of any particular line depend mainly on whether the style becomes fashionable or not. To *raise* prices has been disastrous.

Agreements with competitors are no good, and though you expect your cuts to be countered, you do not pay much attention to this. The only factors restraining the tendency to cut prices are belief in the inelasticity of demand, and a strong disinclination to cut below direct costs.

Selling expenses about 16 per cent., profit about 4 per cent. of price to wholesalers. Industry working short time, so that costs would fall owing to spreading of overheads.

Firm b 4. Until 1929 slump this firm had rarely sold anything below full cost. Since then a more aggressive policy has been followed, both to bring in new lines and to expand old ones. Prices are normally got by adding overheads on a 'full' basis to direct costs, and then adding margins depending on the state of the market, which depends mainly on the degree of differentiation of product which they have achieved. Lower limit of price is direct cost plus 50 per cent. overheads, upper limit is fixed by fear of competition, so that it is higher where they have a specially good article. Competitors always counter with cuts. 'The disinclination to sell below cost is all a matter of how much you must do to keep running on full time.'

Selling and warehousing costs about 10 per cent. of price. Cost falls with increase of output, even when they go into overtime.

Firm c 3. 'Price depends mainly on what the market will stand.' Each line is expected to earn a certain margin over prime cost: if it will not do this it is not produced, because resources could be used more profitably elsewhere. Once a price has been fixed, it is changed as rarely as possible. They regard themselves as market leaders: 'If we feel ourselves compelled to increase or reduce prices, we are fairly certain that our competitors will do likewise. Unless they are prepared to accept a sacrifice in their profit rates they will have to follow our procedure.' Reasons against raising prices are that it disheartens salesmen, and probably damages long-run competitive position. Competitors would probably follow any cuts, but doubtful if they would follow increases (made apart from changes of cost).

About half their costs are distributional. They think that costs could be reduced if there were a considerably larger demand.

Firm d 1. All orders by contract. Agreement in one line. In this line the firm sets the prices at total cost plus per cent. This is its upper limit of price: output is estimated and total overheads allocated in proportion to direct labour. The lower limit is direct costs, which include that part of overheads which varies with output. Price not raised above upper limit because this is found to be unwise with permanent business: buyers technically informed. The price reductions in depression do not have much effect on sales, but have to be made to retain share of what business there is. Selling costs about 10 per cent. of price.

Firm e 3. Market highly competitive. Close attention has to be paid to what competitors do, and they must either be led or followed in price-movements. Thus very little attention can be paid to costs. No rigid formula is used for computing these: if competitive price is too low, the line is discontinued. Two departments run at a small loss because of advertisement value. There are really no restraining tendencies against price-reductions (but as the firm is a retailer, the conditions are those of monopolistic competition).

INDUSTRIAL ANALYSIS IN ECONOMICS
—WITH ESPECIAL REFERENCE TO MARSHALLIAN DOCTRINE

By P. W. S. ANDREWS

1. Introductory

UNTIL very recently, the theories of monopolistic or imperfect competition
which were evolved in the nineteen-thirties appeared to have swept all
before them. It is true that distinguished economists have expressed dis-
agreement or dissatisfaction with these doctrines, especially in recent
years.[1] It is equally true that a remarkably long period has passed without
any counter-theory being proposed, or without any restatement of the
older theories as an alternative body of doctrine, apart from the now
almost ignored contributions made by Robertson and Shove in the controversies in which the modern theories originated.[2]

The principal 'victim', of course, has been the Marshallian analysis of
price determination in the 'ordinary run' of manufacturing industries. The
consequences, however, have been much wider than the simple attainment
of Sraffa's objective—that Marshall's theory 'should be abandoned'.[3] A
whole department of economic analysis has disappeared into the gulf that he
opened up. Industrial analysis has been virtually abandoned as a meaningful occupation in theoretical economics, and the only solid legacy has been
a revised version of the theory of the individual business with which the
whole revolt started, together with some use of that theory in the analysis
of social aggregates. Modern analytical economics finds no firm ground anywhere between the individual business and society as a whole. The theory
of inter-business relationships has acquired all the indeterminacy of the
old duopoly analysis, which has shown a great capacity for spreading like
a fog over any theoretical attempts at group analysis, and has recently
begun to blur the edges even of the theory of the individual business itself.

The result has been a greater gulf between theoretical analysis and
practical thought than can have existed during any other period since

[1] Shove, 'The Place of Marshall's Principles in the Development of Economic Theory',
Economic Journal, December 1942; Robbins, 'The Economist in the Twentieth Century';
Economica, May 1949; Stigler, *Five Lectures on Economic Problems*, Longmans, 1949;
Macgregor, *Economic Thought and Policy*, O.U.P., 1949. (This contains an important re-
statement of Professor Macgregor's position and a very critical examination of post-
Marshallian theory, largely in terms of its own concepts.)

[2] Robertson, 'The Trees of the Forest', in 'Symposium', *Economic Journal*, 1930; Shove,
'The Representative Firm and Increasing Returns', ibid. The other reference to Shove above
shows that, at the most, he would in 1942 have given the newer theories a not-proven
verdict, and I hope that Professor Robertson will not mind my adding, on the basis of
private correspondence, that, like Professor Macgregor, he still seems to stand where he did.

[3] Sraffa, Rejoinder to Robertson in 'Symposium', ibid.

before Mill. Practical thought continues to show that an industry is a meaningful concept for its purposes: governments insist on administering in terms of industries, business men persist in thinking against an industrial background, and our official statistics continue to be collected on the basis of definitions of industries which, although they vary from source to source, nevertheless agree in significant details. If it is to have any 'bite', theoretical analysis needs to be capable of statement in industrial terms.

'Old Marshall' at least supplied an analytical framework within which everyday life seemed to take on an intelligible shape. In this sense, his industrial analysis 'works' for the purposes for which it is constructed. Marshall's analysis has certainly not been pushed aside because it fitted its subject-matter worse than the newer analyses, or because it was less reliable as a basis from which to predict the behaviour of actual industrial groupings of businesses; the world of competing monopolies has no industrial syntax. The case is, rather, that Marshallian theory has, it is thought, been convicted of internal inconsistencies. His analysis of industrial equilibrium was proved to be inconsistent with a theory of the equilibrium of the individual business which evolved from the 'Marshallian tradition' and which was believed to be basic to Marshall's own concept of competition. The difficulty has been resolved by dropping industrial analysis and retaining the static equilibrium theory of the individual business. It would have been equally legitimate to have abandoned the latter.

My empirical studies during the last 12 years have forced me to reconsider the whole position of business economics. Naturally enough, my first approach to the individual business was in terms of the modern theories of monopolistic competition. It was soon obvious that the business man made no explicit reference to marginalist concepts, but it was a long step from that to rejecting a theory which had become so strongly established. It was much easier to assume the implicit validity of the theories in terms of which one was trained to think, indefensibly weak though that procedure seems in retrospect. With increasing familiarity with business behaviour, this way of thinking became progressively less tolerable. On several points one became aware of explicit differences in conduct and outlook, which produced an increasing sense of strain and an awareness of the danger of twisting facts so that they might conform to the theoretical approach to which my generation had been brought up. I was therefore forced to work out a theory of the individual business which did satisfy me as far as I could take it.[1] This lent itself quite naturally to thinking about industrial groupings and thus satisfied both requirements of practical research as I saw them. On returning to empirical work, I was aware how Marshallian my broad analysis was becoming, with the

---

[1] *Manufacturing Business*, by P. W. S. Andrews, Macmillan, 1949.

advantage, as it seemed to me, that it was now possible to think consistently in terms of the individual business, whereas Marshall did not push individual analysis beyond a few limited generalizations. The theory of the equilibrium of a competitive industry as presented by Marshall seemed meanwhile to take on the firmness which it must have had for him.

In this paper, therefore, I shall plead for a reconsideration of Marshall's theory of competitive industry, which is, in fact, not inconsistent with what Marshall says about the individual business; he stopped himself from going too far in a theory of the equilibrium of the firm. At the same time, I shall urge that it is now possible to construct a theory of the behaviour of an individual business which is consistent both with the phenomena which it purports to describe, and with Marshallian analysis.

In general, the argument will be restricted to long-run conditions— sufficient time being presumed to allow the entry into an 'industry' of any businesses whose founders consider this likely to be profitable.[1] To save tedious differentiation of cases, the analysis will formally be restricted to manufacturing industry. This restriction of the argument is justified since the modern rejection of Marshall's theory originated in a dilemma (first posed by Marshall himself) in the theory for the individual business in this class of industry. Subject, however, to what I regard as minor changes, the analysis will be applicable to commerce and to retail trade as well.[2]

2. Marshall's Industrial Analysis

Marshall distinguished two classes of industry—competitive industries and monopolies. When we study his competitive markets it appears that the basis of the distinction is whether or not it would be possible for other businesses to produce a commodity with the same technical specifications as the product of any particular firm, and to offer it for sale to that firm's customers. This is a much wider concept than the purely competitive market of later theory with its assumed absence of all buyers' preferences and its stress on homogeneity of actual products.

It is significant that Marshall's principal example of a monopoly is that of a public utility with statutory privileges. A monopoly exists when technical, legal, or other reasons make it impossible for other businesses to offer the same type of commodity to a business's customers.[3] In such a

[1] Whatever the case 60 years ago, it is now unrealistic to imagine that new entrants consist only of brand-new businesses undertaken with all the uncertainties involved. As I have pointed out, we must allow for the new enterprise which in favourable conditions will always be available from businesses established in other lines of industry.

[2] Cf. 'Some Aspects of Competition in Retail Trade', *Oxford Economic Papers*, Vol. 2, No. 2, June 1950.

[3] Marshall also recognized the case of a 'partial monopoly' where a business's wares are better known than 'others which are really equally good' (p. 60 footnote). (All page references so given are to *Principles*.) But for the class of industries with which we are concerned, these cases cannot be analysed on quasi-monopoly lines.

case, the business will have a determinate demand curve of its own, of the kind analysed by Marshall in Book III of *Principles*; granted, of course, that no technically distinct commodity is a sufficiently close substitute for the monopolist to have to take it into account when he is framing his own policy, and given the usual Marshallian assumption that the total receipts of the business will not form a large proportion of its customers' total expenditure.

In so far as the monopolist followed strictly the motive of maximizing his net profits, his output and price policy would be affected as much by his demand curve as by his cost curve. Marshall's analysis of this case (p. 480) is formally equivalent to the modern doctrine that marginal revenue will equal marginal cost and that the latter will be less than price by an amount which will vary inversely with the elasticity of the demand curve. There will be no *a priori* connexion between the price on which the monopolist will settle and the average cost of the output which he will sell at that price.

Marshall thought the case to be completely different for the ordinary run of industry, and he draws no fine distinction here, such as is drawn by later theory, between purely competitive and imperfectly or monopolistically competitive industries. So long as entry into the industry is possible, it will be competitive in Marshall's sense; his analysis now refers to agriculture and now to particular manufacturing industries, without any sign that he is uneasy about putting them in the same fundamental class.[1]

In such competitive industries, Marshall thought that the possibility of entry of other producers would ensure that long-run price would be equal to the normal average cost of production. This is in striking contrast to the theory of monopoly. The contrast is equally strong with the modern theories of the determination of price in 'normally competitive' manufacturing industries.

Where an industry is normally competitive, in this sense of being open to the entry of new producers, Marshall's analysis runs in terms of industrial demand and supply schedules. On the demand side, later theorists have persisted in interpreting the analysis in terms of a perfectly competitive market, on the lines of the simple markets discussed by Marshall at the beginning of Book V. This seems to me to be a mistake. It is quite true that Marshall does start his analysis of the markets for competitive industry

---

[1] Marshall was worried about the case of an industry which had come to be in the hands of a few giant businesses (p. 805). He suggested that this should be treated analogously to monopoly, but he goes on to admit that 'even in such cases competition has a much greater force, and the use of the term "normal" is less inappropriate than seemed probable *a priori*'. The Cournot type of analysis of this case is, of course, unrealistic so far as manufacturing industry is concerned.

by an examination of the type of market which has provided the model for post-Marshallian analyses of pure competition—the great primary markets of the world, the large stock exchanges, &c. In these, with their completely undifferentiated products, not only is there but one price at any one time, but each seller provides so small a part of the total supply that he may be presumed to meet an infinitely elastic demand at the prevailing level of price.

It seems, however, quite clear from Marshall's subsequent discussion of manufacturing industries that the only characteristic of those purely competitive markets that we should take as required by Marshallian analysis is that which has reference to price: i.e. in the long run, at least, no business would be able to get a higher price than any other business would take for an identical product as delivered to the particular customer. It would be as unrealistic as it would be inappropriate, in view of Marshall's later analyses, to require that an individual business should be able to sell any amount at the ruling price. In fact, such businesses will not commonly be able to sell all that they would like to sell at that price. Accordingly, I suggest that we should presume Marshall's competitive analysis for manufacturing industry to imply identical prices for identical commodities, but not individual demands of infinitely large extent at those prices.

The previous paragraph has referred to identical prices for identical commodities; this calls our attention to an important abstraction of Marshall's. He analysed ordinary manufacturing industries as if an identical commodity were produced throughout the industry. He must have known this for the abstraction it was; otherwise, with his knowledge of the world, he could not have referred, for example, to *the* boot and shoe industry, or to *the* woollen industry. A number of realistic asides would justify our assuming him to have known that the typical products of individual producers would quite frequently differ in their technical specifications, their producers thus specializing to meet the demands in different sections of the broad 'market' with which Marshall was concerned. Similarly, it would be common knowledge that, on a strict analysis, the individual business itself would be multi-product, producing a 'range' of products with differing technical specifications, even though it was a specialist within, or on, that range.

I cannot recall that this abstraction of Marshall's has been discussed at all, and, so far as I am aware, Marshall did not call attention to it himself. Once it has been stated for what it is, however, the probable Marshallian justification appears obvious enough. The Marshallian industry will consist of businesses with a sufficiently common technical equipment, knowledge, experience, &c., for them to be able to turn over to making any 'range' of the given commodity or any of the particular commodities within the 'range'. Further, the business men can be assumed to be sufficiently 'in' the general market to be aware of the prices secured by producers of other types of commodities within the market. In this sense, the producers of electric motors would constitute a clearly defined industry, and in an only slightly more diffuse sense the producers of light electrical engineering products might also be analysed as belonging to the same industry.

Granted this, the analysis which Marshall provides for the larger aggregates that he chooses to call industries would apply with even greater strength to the firms producing in any sub-market *within* the industry, for that would be even more readily open to new entry than the broad market for the 'industry' as a whole, of which it forms a part. The gross earnings of management would tend to be equalized over the whole industry when analysed into its separate elements—payment for the capital employed, and for the work of the managers (p. 313). For each sub-market we could therefore take Marshall as imagining a 'representative firm' (this concept will be further examined later; meanwhile it may be accepted without comment). The proportion of long-run price which would be taken by the gross earnings of management of a representative firm would vary with differences in the normal intensities of management between the sub-markets, but subject to that, the relationship between the normal prices for the different 'grades' or types of the industrial product would be strictly determined by differences in the normal average costs of production (i.e. the costs of the relevant representative firms).

Given these assumptions, the complex of commodities produced by an actual industry could be imagined as reducible to a cost-equivalent standard commodity, and Marshall could use the concept of a demand schedule for this 'product' of the industry, giving the corresponding hypothetical demand curve the negative slope of the demand curves proper of Book III, where the analysis is formally in terms of simple uniform commodities.

Marshall's supply schedule is the analytical counterpart of the demand schedule. It relates various amounts of total output to the prices which would have to be paid if these amounts were to be forthcoming in a stable fashion over an indefinitely long period (pp. 343, 345). 'This is the price the expectation of which will just suffice to maintain the existing aggregate amount of production; some firms meanwhile rising and increasing their output, and others falling and diminishing theirs; but the aggregate production remaining unchanged.' Supply price being defined so as to imply a stable supply, the Marshallian concept of long-run equilibrium price follows. At that price the amount taken from the market will equal the amount supplied and the equilibrium will be stable whether the supply curve rises or falls with expansion of the industry's long-run output, so long as, in the latter case, the demand curve has a steeper slope.

In order to understand the inter-war rejection of Marshall, it will be necessary to consider his concept of a supply schedule in a more detailed fashion. Given Marshall's assumptions of the uniformity of market price and of free entry, his conclusion that market price cannot be higher than the level which will bring new businesses into the industry seems a familiar result of modern theory as well. It has, however, a different significance in Marshall. He defines the long run in terms of the stability of industrial output and not in terms of the stability of individual businesses. He therefore does not require that all firms in a given industry should be covering their costs, and thus have their survival assured, even in a position of long-run equilibrium.

For one thing, Marshall refuses to take as 'given' the level of efficiency of the businesses assumed already to be operating in an industry. Of course, Marshall recognizes, as must any realistic thinker, that there would be unsystematic changes in their relative positions; for example, those resulting from the constant pitting of one business man's wits against another's so that one business may make an innovation and go ahead at one time, but others will catch up later and the initiative will pass to a different business man. Theoretical analysis, however, might well smooth this out as a 'random' factor, even though to do so would be to miss an important practical manifestation of competition—in fact, its essence on any dynamic view. But Marshall also thought of the relative efficiency of business men as varying systematically over their lifetime. With his eye on the private business rather than on the great public company, he states this primarily in terms of the contrast between a new business and an old and settled one. It is, however, a more general position that he takes up— that an individual business man will have increasing vigour and grasp of the situation as he matures in his industrial experience.

Over its early years, then, Marshall thought that a business's costs of production would tend to decline for this reason alone. With increasing age, the efficiency of a business man will tend to slow down, will become stationary, or even decline. This generalization is not weakened by the case of a large public company, and Marshall's statements on this are not so tinged with doubt as some of his inter-war interpreters suggested. He thought that such businesses were less likely to be forced to the point of actual death, and recognized that they had one relative advantage, in so far as they provided opportunities for organizing ability not associated with the ownership of capital. On the other hand, of course, they would suffer from a weaker association between ownership and control than in the smaller business. Quite apart from this, however, although the survival of the business will not be so dependent upon the efficiency of a particular business man, the management group in control can surely be imagined as having a similar life-history to Marshall's independent business man; their efficiency waxing and waning, and the tides of fortune accordingly flowing to them or ebbing from them. When we are engaged on the realistic study of actual industries, and see how important over a period is the cumulative effect of quite minor changes, this general view of Marshall's becomes very important. It is easy to overlook this in any static survey of an industry which will concentrate attention on the advantages of the powerful positions of existing businesses at any one time. There can be tremendous changes in the position of individual businesses without actual failure.

Accepting this view of Marshall's, it follows that, at any time, even the stable long-run output which is being presupposed for the industry may well include a declining proportion from established businesses which are slipping back, and even making actual losses. This factor may be compensated by the output coming from new entrants; Marshall's definition of long-run supply price requires such a compensation if the increasing output from the more successful existing businesses is not sufficient. It would not be realistic to require that, on entry, they should be able to get normal profits. They will expect higher costs in the beginning than they will achieve later as they get experience, and will hope for increasing goodwill to enlarge their share of the market. Their entry into the industry will be decided on the basis of estimates of what they can hope to achieve at some relatively more mature stage. Their ideas of this will be derived from what seems to be happening to existing businesses. New businesses will come in so long as they can reasonably expect to cover their running costs in the short period before they have exhausted any spare liquid resources, provided that it seems likely that they will get established at a later stage, achieve a sufficient level of output, and get their average costs down to a sufficiently low level to be able to make satisfactory profits then.

Marshall's analysis is therefore conducted in terms of a representative business whose size and opportunities might thus be taken as the target which attracts the efforts of new-comers. The price which would give this firm a sufficient level of profits to call in the output from new businesses which is required by Marshall's stability assumptions is his long-run supply price for the industry. It seems quite legitimate to follow Robertson in refusing to interpret the situation for the new business in terms of any actual level of normal reward for the particular levels of efficiency which their founders have.[1] Prospective new entrants will not know their actual efficiency until they are in the industry, and they may make optimistic

---

[1] Robertson, 'The Trees of the Forest', loc. cit.

estimates both of the size of the market which will accrue to them and of the level of costs at which they could produce that output. In the event, a large proportion of new enterprise may not make the normal level of profits whose prospect attracted them, and a fair proportion may do so badly as to fail in the long run. Market price, accordingly, will not be determined by this factor but by the 'representative' costs on the basis of which new entry takes place.

Marshall therefore interprets long-term price in terms of the normal costs of a representative firm. This might be thought of as having a real existence at any given point of time. In so far as such actual firms are taken as representative by newcomers, new entry will keep market price at such a level that the representative firm will only make the normal level of profits in terms of which the Marshallian new businesses act. The supply schedule, accordingly, traces out the normal costs of the representative firm for the various levels of output. The supply curve may fall, rise, or, alternatively, remain constant with increasing long-run outputs from a given industry, and an increased demand could therefore be met by a decreased, an increased, or an unchanged price in the long run. We shall argue later that Marshall would ordinarily expect a *falling* supply curve for a manufacturing industry.

Early in this section we referred to Marshall's contrast between a competitive industry which is open to new entry and a monopoly. This is clearly justified on his analysis. The monopolist's price would have no necessary connexion with his average costs. Long-run price for an industry with free entry which behaved in a Marshallian manner would have a determinate relationship with costs. The force of this contrast is strengthened if we make the assumption that the relative efficiencies of businesses remain constant, which has become usual in post-Marshallian attempts to give a Marshallian analysis in terms of the behaviour of individual businesses.[1] On that assumption, there will be a determinate relationship between price and average costs for each individual business, the relationship, of course, varying with the business. If these relative efficiencies are thought of as remaining stable between points of long-run equilibrium, market price will be a determinate function of the costs of any individual business.

It is this assumption of modern theory which gives analytic determinacy to the concept of the marginal firm, and when we reason in terms of the full equilibria of individual businesses, long-run price is easily analysed in terms of the normal costs of such a firm. The long-run supply curve will then be derivable from a particular expenses curve, suitably modified to

---

[1] Shove, *Economic Journal*, 1930, op. cit.; Viner, 'Cost Curves and Supply Curves', *Zeitschrift für National Ökonomie*, 1931–2.

take account of the effect of external economies.[1] Marshall refused to take the initial step, and warns us against any confusion of particular expenses curves with supply curves. Although his objection relates formally to an increasing returns industry, the reasoning is of general application; this is not the only instance where the blunt facts of increasing returns saved Marshall from the use of constructions which would otherwise appear admissible, yet—if the reasoning is general in its application—would have led to misleading conclusions. In Marshallian analysis, the marginal firm, in the sense of a business which is only just managing to hold on in the industry, is not to be seen as the firm whose costs determine total supply and hence prices.[2]

3. Marshall and the Individual Business

Marshall's treatment of the individual business in a competitive industry is much more confused than his treatment of the industry and of the 'representative' business. This is because his analysis of the firm is overshadowed by the concept of static equilibrium, which he was anxious to accept, but which he was, in fact, forced to reject at every decisive point in his analysis where a manufacturing business had to be integrated with its industry. Marshall's very evident desire to ground his analysis on this concept is easily understood. Partial equilibrium analysis was one of his most useful weapons, and continual use made it very difficult to prevent his thoughts from flowing into that mould. (To later theorists, of course, an analysis based upon atomistic equilibrium within the industry had pedagogic attractions, since it made possible an elegantly generalized view of the whole social mechanism.) There is the related point that a static theory of the distribution of income had proved possible only on the basis of such a concept, and Marshall's theories in that field required it for their full validity.[3]

Lastly, the adoption of this concept would have given the supply schedule a meaning by which it would have become the full complement of the demand schedule. The demand schedule resulted from the decisions of individual consumers as to the amounts that they would purchase at the given price; the concept of full equilibrium for the individual business would have enabled the supply schedule to be interpreted as resulting from similar atomistic decisions to supply the commodity. Marshall's supply schedule has generally been so interpreted, but that is an error.

[1] Ref. Marshall, p. 810, n. 2. The particular expenses curve for an industry producing a given output with given economies of production ranges the existing producers' outputs in order of their particular expenses of production.

[2] Ref. Macgregor, *Economic Thought and Policy*, p. 44.

[3] If this concept is rejected, the theory of distribution will need a complete overhaul. The theory of wages and of employment, in particular, needs to be freed from formal dependence on theories of marginal productivity. Ref. *Manufacturing Business*, pp. 215 ff.

Marshall would certainly have liked to have constructed a supply schedule which would be explained formally as the integration of determinate supplies from each individual business. He was, however, compelled to define his supply schedule in such a way as to make it refer only to the terms on which the market could get varying amounts from the industry as a whole. In manufacturing industry, his individual businesses are obviously often quite willing to supply more at the existing market price than the market will take from them at that price. That Marshall does not put the matter in this way is due to his shadow-preoccupation with particular equilibrium analysis, but the conclusion comes out clearly enough when he is talking about realistic industrial situations.

In the event, the principle of substitution was the one general guide to the conduct of the individual business, whether in the short or in the long run, that Marshall insisted on. He thus retains the concept of an equilibrium in the distribution of a business's resources between possible alternative expenditures; but in the text, as distinct from the Appendix, he gives no clear view of an equilibrium determination even of short-run output, and, despite obvious heart-burnings, his analysis leads to no determination of long-run equilibrium *size* of the individual business. In the Mathematical Appendix, as elsewhere when the concept does momentarily emerge, he stresses the danger of pushing mathematical analysis farther than the economic logic warrants, and this is but a further denial of the concept itself, however much he may be tempted to affirm it. His equilibrium analysis for the industry runs, as we have seen, in terms of an individual business whose size and opportunities are taken as representative by new entrants, so that their profits would be satisfactory if they achieved the same; there is, however, no sense in which this gives an equilibrium of output for individual firms, so that more or less would not yield the same or a greater level of profits.

When Marshall was considering a wheat farmer in Book IV he could make his analysis run in terms of the equilibrium of the individual business, whether or not its ability was representative. Subject to the requirements of rotation, he could imagine the production of the crop as being subject to decreasing returns in both the short and the long run. In view of the nature of the market, he could, and did, go on to describe a full state of equilibrium (p. 153, &c.); but it was the peculiarity of the market which enabled him to take this step quite as much as the assumption of diminishing returns. The analytical method was attractive, and he found it difficult to explain why he could not use it as a general rule. But, although he might explicitly reject this view of a firm when it conflicted with the realistic analysis later in *Principles*, at the back of his mind there was always the concept of an individual business taking all decisions and deciding its whole position—including its output and scale—in such a way as to maximize its profits.

His ultimate refusal to persist with this view arose from difficulties which he encountered when trying to apply it to manufacturing industries. The initial difficulty as it arises in Marshall is a long-run matter—resulting from the fact that such industries tend to be in a state of increasing returns. But, once it had been recognized, this fact led him on to make other observations concerning such industries, and especially concerning their markets, which would themselves be inconsistent with the equilibrium theory that he would otherwise have erected. It is misleading simply to accept his view that mathematical complexities stand in the way of the generalizations which he seems to have thought that his readers would expect (ref., *inter alia*, Mathematical Note XIV)—it was much more a question of logical difficulties that could not be settled at all by partial equilibrium analysis of the individual business.

In formal terms, Marshall analysed short-run conditions as though decreasing returns were universal. In my view, this is a major error of Marshall's analysis—and of post-Marshallian analysis of pure competition —for short-run average total costs in a manufacturing business always decrease up to the limit of their short-run capacity. Even apart from this point, for Marshallian theory to apply it would be necessary for the markets of manufacturing businesses to be of the primary product character in the short run, although Marshall refuses them this quality in his long-run analysis when he has to face the problem of increasing returns.

Where Marshall faces the problem of short-run equilibrium of the individual business and its relation to long-run analysis he argues rather loosely in terms of the fishing industry, whose market can be taken as resembling the market for wheat. I have argued elsewhere that these primary markets necessarily differ significantly from industrial markets, and that the differences result from the nature of the market rather than from the degree to which any level of competition exists. I shall also argue later on that such significant differences must also be taken to be presumed by Marshall's analysis, if we argue backwards from his methodology and his conclusions to the implicit rather than the explicit premises (or the premises which are traditionally taken as having been stated explicitly). With a theorist of Marshall's calibre, I do not see it as false piety to refuse to convict him of errors of reasoning which do not get carried over into his final conclusions. The view put forward is accordingly that Marshall was prevented both in his short- and in his long-run analysis from achieving a clear statement of the matter because his vision of the equilibrium of the individual firm constantly got in the way.

In the case of his short-run analysis, however, his conclusions are so vaguely worded that the defects of the reasoning almost amount to error. His main analysis is in terms of markets for primary products, where the buyers can have no reason for preferring one source of supply to another, at the same price. Further, the market organization for such undifferentiated products is such that there is no room for personal contact between the producer and his customers—and little point in it if there were. Such producers sell to the market as a whole, and a single producer need feel no limitation on his market, but can dispose of his whole output without affecting price.

The essence of the market for a manufacturing industry is otherwise. Marshall analysed such industries as if they were producing a uniform product. We have already presumed him to have known which way the truth lay, and have suggested an analytical justification for such a procedure (p. 143 above). In fact, the total output will consist of a mass of more or less specialized products, catering for the orders of particular customers or classes of customers. On my view, even Marshall's theory should be seen simply as insisting that such customers will not willingly pay more for a particular product than they need pay elsewhere. At any given price, they will usually have goodwill towards particular suppliers, and personal contact and familiarity with conditions and requirements on both sides of the bargain will produce the individual business's 'share' of the market. It must be admitted that this view of Marshall did not occur to me until after I had produced my own theory of the firm, but when I became aware how Marshallian a view of industry I was favouring, it seemed to me impossible to make sense of Marshall's analysis on other terms. This might be taken as reading a theory into Marshall in other than the literal sense, but I am glad that I can now cite the high authority of Professor Macgregor as indicating that Marshall's views were consistent with my interpretation, and that he may be presumed to have reached at least a closely similar conclusion:

Marshall 'was fond of emphasizing to his pupils that efficient (or representative) business has always some element of monopoly; that is the "custom" or trade connexion of the business. But this by itself is not a power to raise prices; it is nothing but the fact that the demand can be split up in various ways, one of which is to add to the parts of the demand supplied by each supplier.' (*Economic Thought and Policy*, pp. 39–40.)

This view—that 'goodwill' limits the market available to the individual business at a given level of price—will, accordingly, be taken as fully Marshallian. Marshall did not state it in *Principles*, but it is certainly consistent with the general position into which he was forced when he recognized the fact of increasing returns in manufacturing. Marshall's theories will, therefore, generally be interpreted with its help. It seems worth stressing that, once this is accepted, there can be no use for the concept of static equilibrium for the individual business, in manufacturing, whatever the state of returns in the particular industry which is under discussion. Even if the business were producing at increasing costs, it could be only a matter of accident that the output that it produced would be such that marginal cost equalled market price.

It is not, therefore, very surprising that Marshall's realistic sense prevents him from finalizing the issue, even in the short run, where he does argue that we may rely upon increasing costs to the firm and implies that static equilibrium analysis is applicable ; he never quite perpetrates the explicit nonsense with which later interpretation would credit him. As already stated, the general case is given in terms of a primary industry—fishing— and the analysis uses the concept of marginal supplies to the industry rather than that of the equilibrium of the individual fishing business. Here it makes sense to analyse, as Marshall does, in terms of the costs of the marginal short-run supply to the industry as a whole.

When Marshall turns to manufacturing industry, and wishes to make use of the notions of prime and supplementary costs, whose importance in practical thinking he stresses, he does not, in fact, proceed to a rigorous analysis of the situation in terms of price and the marginal prime costs of the firm. He is clearly aware that, in reality, short-run prime costs, average or marginal, are frequently a good deal below price (p. 375). At several points he also appears to be aware that, excepting at rare boom periods when the whole industry might be extended, and the total output might be less than the market would take, it would be normal for manufacturing businesses to be able to produce additional output at decreasing costs even in the short run. It must surely have been rare, even in Marshall's day, for all the businesses in a competitive manufacturing market to have such pressure on their total resources as he represented as normal in the fishing industry.

To take care of these difficulties of actual cases, Marshall could not use the notion of a representative firm,[1] but something very like representative marginal costs makes a shadowy appearance (pp. 372, 376, &c.). It is surprising that this analysis of Marshall's received so little critical attention later. This is probably due to the apparent cogency of his reasons for decreasing returns in the short run in the stationary state, in terms of which most of Marshall's critics have preferred to argue, and for which they wished to use similar constructions in their own generalizations about the shapes of the cost curves for individual businesses. It is an interesting feature of the history of this branch of economic thought that generalizations which later theorists used as the basis for their cost curves of the firm were originally required in order to make workable a theory which it was their own concern to attack on allegedly realistic grounds.

---

[1] Since he was concerned with short-run analysis.

When it came to long-run analysis, Marshall *had* to face up to the issue of increasing returns. In the famous Chapter 12 of Book V he tried to state his theories in such a way as to meet the requirements of himself and other analysts, and made an effort to achieve the theory of the equilibrium of the firm which the general analysis of the pricing system and the neo-classical theory of distribution required. This chapter has, of course, to be read with Appendix H. Both are still imbued with the notion of the individual business as, in some sense, able to determine its own output, but we should ignore any particular manifestations of this idea which are inconsistent with the rest of Marshall's analysis. In the end we are left, as already foretold, with no theory of the static equilibrium of the individual business. The market for the individual firm is certainly limited; Marshall's reference to the fact that its growth will take time is to be taken as referring to the dynamic process of establishing and enhancing 'goodwill'; the limitation of the market makes Marshall's references to a firm's particular demand curve only formally correct and that 'curve' becomes analytically useless. Further, the type of demand curve which is consistent with Marshall in long-run analysis must certainly be 'kinked', for we have the overriding Marshallian rule that price cannot be higher than that charged by any other business.

It must be admitted that all this is a *reading* of Marshall, but it does make sense. It perhaps remains a puzzle why he did not state it formally. On the negative side the cogent reasons seem to be that he would have liked to make a formal statement of individual equilibrium, and the generalizations which he gives are not inconsistent with a formal marginal statement, even if they render it meaningless. Marshall saw that clearly enough, and when pressed to describe the situation in terms of the marginal costs which determine price, he falls back finally on the representative firm (p. 460). This, however, is unconvincing. The representative market must share the characteristics of the atomistic markets which it represents; it, peculiarly, cannot be given infinite expansibility at the given market price.

The positive reason why Marshall did not go farther is that in his historical studies he was more concerned with industrial development, and he had achieved a firm enough theory of the industry with the help of the concept of the representative business. It is not recorded that Marshall ever worked empirically on the problems of individual businesses as such. If he had, his interesting references to the average-cost-plus-standard-net-profit basis for fixing a reward in an arbitration case (p. 617 and note 1) would surely have leapt to life in his hands instead of its being dismissed because of inconsistency with notions of equilibrium rates of profits. These latter, again, are adhered to because of the fascination of the marginalist theory of the firm which Marshall had assumed elsewhere and wanted to justify in his industrial theory, but had in the end to reject, because it came into conflict with reality and the phenomenon of increasing returns.

Accordingly, it is submitted that a careful reading of Marshall, whilst leaving us with no clear statement of the theory of the firm which would be consistent with his industrial analysis, must lead us to reject any notion of the equilibrium of the firm as an integral part of his analysis. All that we can carry over as clearly Marshallian into the theory of the individual business in a competitive manufacturing industry are his generalizations about the behaviour of its costs if, in fact, its output increases. In this connexion, although Marshall formally argues in terms of rising short-run costs, there is at least a strong suspicion that we should assume that even short-run costs may normally be falling—this would be required by realistic analysis, as I have argued elsewhere.[1] There is no doubt that the long-run costs of the individual business in the Marshallian manufacturing industry *should* normally be taken as falling. Quite apart from the effect of external economies and the final balance which they make with external diseconomies (i.e. making the usual assumption that the prices of the factors be taken as given), its cost curve will be falling with any sustained increase in its output. Coming to the industry as a whole, Marshall thought that for industries of the normal kind where the original costs of primary materials are not a high proportion of the firm's manufacturing costs (p. 318) the net effects of decreasing returns on account of rises in factor prices would be negligible. Accordingly, when we are considering the growth of the whole of such an industry (in response, for example, to an increase in demand) the levels of costs would certainly fall as output increased.

First, any growth will tend to widen the market for all businesses, each obtaining its share of the enlarged output, which is why the representative firm is assumed to grow. Accordingly, the firms making up the industry will reap the consequent internal economies and, at the same time, there will probably be further external economies. For this reason, the growth of an industry will enable the individual firms to produce at a lower cost than if each had merely made the expansion on its own, and the representative firm's costs will always fall faster than would those of an equivalent business growing in isolation. Marshall therefore expected the supply price of an industry, such as those with which we are concerned, to fall with increases in industrial demand.

---

[1] See p. 152. For some increases in output I have suggested that short-run costs should be imagined as lying below the appropriate long-run costs, whilst both would be falling; however, this is another matter, not relevant to Marshall, but inconsistent with a good deal of post-Marshallian analyses and, no doubt, productive of mathematical complexities in the Marshallian sense.

The upshot of this paper so far is that Marshall's theory of price-determination in a manufacturing industry runs in terms of *industrial* equilibria, long-run price in such an industry being analytically tied to average costs of production in the representative business postulated by the analysis. As already noted, if we make the assumption which has become usual in later theory (because necessary for the static theory of the individual business) that the relative efficiencies of the firms in an industry remain constant and given, which Marshall himself would not make, then, of course, the relationship between long-run market price and average costs in each individual firm will similarly be determinate.

In the next section of this paper it will be useful to examine briefly what has happened to the theory of the individual business since Marshall. Its development was initially related to a particular view of Marshallian industrial equilibrium which we have already rejected, but it has led to an alternative body of doctrine, and it is desirable that we should reconsider this before returning to the concept of industrial analysis which these recent theories rendered suspect.

4. Business Theory after Marshall

It would be interesting to know precisely what happened to business theory at Cambridge between the date of Marshall's *Principles* and the attack by Sraffa in 1926 upon Marshallian theory. In the interval, economics had grown up as an academic subject, and this fact alone seems sufficient to account for most of the details that may be inferred. So long as each set of problems was dealt with as fully as possible in its own right, any inconsistencies between the various hypotheses would be of no great consequence. For all Marshall's desire for consistency of vision, his sense of reality, when confronted with a problem, set limits to how far he would go to achieve it in his analyses. A teacher, on the other hand, has to have regard to conceptual difficulties and tends to develop generalized syntheses in which the maximum of apparent reference is made with the minimum of tools. It would be natural from a teaching point of view that Marshall's distinction between monopoly and competition should become a clear division in analysis, and that this should start with a correspondingly general dichotomy of markets. Pedagogic reasons would also make it desirable to argue in terms of the behaviour of individuals, so that the full contrast could be drawn between the two hypothetical states.

The theory of competitive business could most elegantly derive from the theory of the primary markets, which Marshall himself states as examples from which the chief characteristics of competitive behaviour could be grasped most readily. It was unfortunate for the subsequent development of business theory that the demand in such a competitive market as a whole was interpreted simply in terms of the consumers' demand curves of Book III. Marshall had himself analysed markets as if the price of the relevant commodities were those at which they reached the final consumer (pp. 341–2). This led to some confusion in his analysis, but the consequences were to be worse in an academic treatment which, I think, is prone to argue from diagrams, which are too readily taken as both established and understood.[1] The demand curves for all commodities in theoretical economics have been given the general attributes of consumers' demand curves, making it a natural step to argue as if all markets were simply consumers' markets.

Given the total supply to the 'market', demand would determine the 'equilibrium price'. The demand for the products of the individual business can be very simply treated: variations in the amounts put by it on the market will not have any significant effect upon market price; it may, therefore, be considered to have an infinitely elastic demand at any given level of market price. The Marshallian concept of equilibrium in the market as a whole then came to be 'mirrored' by a general concept of the equilibrium of the individual business. Since he can sell what he will, the producer's problem is to determine how much he will produce. Given constant price, the condition for a determinate equilibrium, whether short run or long, is that marginal costs should be rising. Granted the assumed nature of the market and also the concept of individual equilibrium, it could too easily be assumed that such a condition *had* to apply, with the result, perhaps, that it became impossible to examine critically the reasons that traditional theory adduced for the existence of increasing costs.

No difficulty seems ever to have been suspected in postulating increasing costs in the short run for all types of industries; the simple use of the concept of fixed factors of production, analogous to the 'field' in theoretical agriculture, plus the law of 'non-proportional returns' seemed to yield increasing costs as an irrefutable consequence. It followed, of course, that when economists had to recognize the existence of decreasing short-run costs, this could too easily be analysed as the consequence of imperfections of competition rather than as a necessary characteristic of many manufacturing industries in normal times. In long-run analysis, the *dynamic* difficulties which Marshall had adduced as besetting the management of a growing business, when once it got beyond a certain size-stage, made it possible to call in a factor which '*must*' eventually cause the static cost curve of the individual business to turn up, whatever the technical economies which were otherwise available. Accordingly, both in short-run and in long-run analysis, the problem of the behaviour of the individual business, given its efficiency, &c., could formally be solved in terms of

---

[1] See Macgregor, *Economic Thought and Policy*, p. 35.

its supply curve—traced out by the relevant rising curve of marginal costs.

In the analysis of the firm, the ability of the producer would naturally be taken as given, and his cost curve would necessarily be drawn on the assumption of given prices for the factors of production. It was easy enough to take care of any effect of external economies or diseconomies, as the whole output of an industry grew, by letting this affect the supply curve for the industry and imagining the individual cost curves as shifting accordingly. In the long run, full equilibrium was reached when market price equalled the marginal costs of the supply from each individual firm and from the industry as a whole. It would also be equal to the average costs of the firms when all rents were included. All this is so familiar an interpretation of Marshall's theory of competitive equilibrium that it is understandably difficult to turn one's mind round to criticizing it in its own terms; and it was this construction which served as a basis for the attack upon Marshall, for thinking that increasing returns, and especially decreasing costs for the firm, could be present in any market which could properly be analysed as competitive.

Space will not permit of our making the detailed review of the development of the inter-war controversies, which would otherwise be interesting. They started with a statement of the dilemma which faced a teacher when he confronted the logic of the pseudo-Marshallian theory of competition with the cases which Marshall analysed. In so far as increasing returns in an allegedly competitive industry resulted from decreasing costs in the firm, they were incompatible with equilibrium of the kind normally envisaged by the theory. Why did not the individual business just go on growing, until either it ran into a stretch of increasing costs or the competition in its industry had disappeared into a monopoly situation? This dilemma might be evaded by appealing to external economies, but these would militate against the partial analysis of the industry, unless they were of the internal–external type which seemed only doubtfully capable of real content. The restatements of Marshall's theory which were attempted by Pigou, by Shove, and by Sraffa appeared unsatisfactory in so far as they did not challenge the theory of the market for the competitive manufacturing business, which lay at the heart of the dilemma. Robertson's contribution remained most close to Marshall's original formulation, but, because he did not bring this issue out as one which the critics themselves had to face, he was too easily regarded by the inter-war generation as 'downed' by Sraffa's skilful pricking of his analogies.

The solution upon which economists eventually agreed, and practically everything else which was subsequently written on the theory of the equilibrium of the individual business in imperfect competition, was contained in the original article by Sraffa, but it took a good deal of discussion before it was worked out fully. It was eventually accepted that decreasing costs, in both the short- and the long-run senses, were a normal feature of many manufacturing industries analysed by Marshallians as competitive. It was rightly discovered that Marshall's uniform market was, in fact, not uniform, and that producers normally produced differentiated commodities. It was here that the phenomena of *consumers'* preferences were so easily invoked. We have already commented on the weakness of this solution, but the reason for it seems clear: it was essential for the analysis that was to be developed that the buyers' preferences to be invoked should not be related to inherent qualities, for the latter would be reflected in costs, and it was analytically desirable to counter falling costs in the firm by some independent penalty to expansion. Stresses upon the role of advertising and other selling costs made it possible to credit the consumer with irrational differentiation of the market into more or less distinct 'commodities'. It was now possible to bring in the theory of monopoly.

This was done in the contributions made by Harrod and by Mrs. Robinson in the *Economic Journal* controversy.[1] Let the fact of consumers' preferences be taken as conferring upon the business its own demand curve, with consequently falling marginal revenue. (Similar demand—and cost—curves would yield similar prices which would be stable with falling costs.) It was now understandable that it was possible for the firm to stop short at an output or scale with falling costs.[2]

Chamberlin, who had been working independently at the problem, developed similar conclusions, and his large-group analysis had formal relevance to industries where businesses were numerous and where the products were sufficiently comparable technically for them to be produced under similar cost conditions. In such an industry, free entry in the Marshallian sense (new businesses coming in so long as they can get normal profits) plus the necessity of existing businesses covering average costs in order to survive in the long run, gave a Marshallian equilibrium, with businesses earning normal profits but with decreasing costs.

Chamberlin also provided the outlines of a theory for the case where the firms were not so numerous that cross-elasticities of demand could be

---

[1] R. F. Harrod: 'Notes on Supply', *Economic Journal*, 1930; 'The Law of Decreasing Costs', ibid. 1931. J. Robinson: 'Imperfect Competition and Falling Supply Price', ibid. 1932.

[2] Further, as Harrod showed, if conditions in an industry, with this differentiation of the product, were such that the businesses got only normal profits, they would necessarily be producing at decreasing costs in both the short run and the long. For, by definition, the price which they got for their product would equal their average cost, and the tangency of the curves that was thus postulated would mean that costs were falling. In such a situation price would exceed marginal cost, and *excess* capacity—which the economists of the thirties had experienced as a real phenomenon—emerged as the normal condition of such an industry in such a position.

neglected by them. In an ingenious piece of analysis he provided what should now be recognized as a general background to the theory of the 'kinked' demand curve. Starting from any given position of price and demand for an individual business, he imagined two demand curves:[1] the one tracing out its share of the market, if all businesses followed its price policy; the other, tracing out its demand, if it varied its price but the other businesses with whom it was competing held theirs stable. With the aid of these tools Chamberlin analysed the various possible solutions to what was essentially a parallel to the old oligopoly problem, but in which the solutions could be seen in terms of the differentiated market which the newer theories were assuming.

The large-group analysis of Chamberlin did seem to provide a formal solution for the Marshallian dilemma where numerous businesses were competing with one another without serious apparent disparities in their profits and where decreasing costs occurred for the individual businesses. It had, however, involved assumptions which Chamberlin himself called 'heroic' and which did not seem particularly to fit many of the industries to which the analysis should apply. Both this and his small-group analysis came under fire from the theorists of the Walrasian school. Triffin, in particular, launched a critical attack upon the whole concept of an industry, which Chamberlin had preserved with such strenuous efforts. Even in the hands of its founder, the analysis seemed to be wilting under this criticism when the late war broke out, and it began to appear that Triffin's cry of triumph had been justified,[2] and that the old concept of an 'industry' had disappeared for ever from economic theory, although it might be possible to tolerate the empirical worker using such an admittedly vague idea. The theorist was delivered over to a Walrasian world where everything is determinate but nothing can ever be determined.

At the same time, however, a new attack on the problem developed from quite a different angle. Realistic inquiries at Oxford had elucidated the facts that business men, when quoting prices, did not think explicitly in terms of marginal revenues and costs, and that a general method of pricing was to add a margin as for net profit to average short-run costs. Further, business men appeared to adhere firmly to this method of pricing and to be reluctant to cut or increase their prices for the sake of short-term advantages. The important article by Hall and Hitch reporting this research gives a fair summary of the comments of the business men concerned, but the speculative part of the article devotes more attention to the stability of prices than to possible theoretical explanations of the

---

[1] I have found it useful to call these the 'share-of-the-market' demand curve and 'particular' demand curve respectively.

[2] Triffin, *Monopolistic Competition and Equilibrium Theory*, p. 52.

pricing practices disclosed. Businesses were taken as fixing their prices on the 'full-cost' basis, their reluctance to alter them was explained by a very ingenious use of a demand curve of the kinked kind incorporating a segment from each of the demand curves which Chamberlin devised for his small-group analysis. Here, within wide limits, any existing price would be justified; within a possibly large range, marginal revenue would be indeterminate. A rise in price would not be followed by competitors, and sales would shrink along the appropriate elastic 'particular-demand' curve; a cut in price would be countered by other businesses, and output would increase only along the inelastic 'share-of-the-market' curve.

The reason why the 'kink' should occur at the full-cost (better termed 'normal-cost') level of price was not adduced, and the rationale of the costing rules that produced that price were left unanalysed. If anything, the determination of prices appeared even less rational than before, even though, for the first time since the doubts of the inter-war period, economic theory seemed at last to be taking a stand upon what people actually did. Theoretical attention concentrated upon the apparent fact of the kinked demand curve, price appeared to be determinate neither upon a competitive nor on a monopoly basis, but to be a matter of strategy, or of various excursions into actual warfare, if the strategies of the individual businesses diverged. The concept of the price-leader had emerged from the basic empirical research, but otherwise the net result was to bring in the theory of oligopoly as a general method of analysis.

The analytical merit of the approach made by Hall and Hitch was that it preserved intact the old approach via the static equilibrium of the firm. It was still possible to think in terms of marginal revenues and costs, only the indeterminacy of their point of intersection accounted for the vagueness of the resulting theory and the paucity of empirical data. For the teacher, the approach was attractive since it lent itself to the systematic development of the theory of business behaviour from the Marshallian cases of perfect or pure competition and monopoly, through the concepts of monopolistic competition, to a theory which had apparent reference to real procedures whilst retaining at least the forms of marginal analysis.

Harrod, when introducing the results of the Research Group of which he had been Chairman, which were discussed by Hall and Hitch, suggested that the full-cost principle must have its rationale since it was so firmly established. Unfortunately, the fact of the 'kink' appeared to provide a negative sort of reason—the principle gave prices which normally did not provoke the serious competition of other businesses, and the kink explained why such prices were maintained once fixed. Nevertheless, Harrod was right in his wider plea. In fact, a careful examination of the original Hall and Hitch paper will show that the business men who had given evidence themselves offer some of the major elements of a theory which yields a determinate analysis of the normal-cost price, when once the theory of costs is put on a better empirical basis. As has already been said, my empirical studies have forced me to construct such a theory of the firm, and it is in the light of that theory that we shall now reconsider the concept of an industry in the Marshallian sense.

5. The 'Industry' reappears[1]

After the post-Marshallian revolution it is desirable that business analysis should start from and be centred upon the theory of the individual business; the concept of an 'industry' will be acceptable only if it should emerge as a natural extension of the theory of the firm. It is the contention of this paper that it does so, when the basis of price-determination in manufacturing businesses is clearly understood.

It is convenient to commence with the static analysis of a business which is producing a given range of products—only, for simplicity's sake, it will be imagined to produce a single product. At any given time the business will be organized in a definite manner, i.e. it will possess a given equipment and overhead organization run by a management with a given level of ability, energy, &c.; its output will be obtained by the use of amounts of the variable factors of production (including materials) which will vary with the size of that output, and it will be supposed to obtain these at given prices.

Other things being equal, the average direct costs of such a business will be constant over a fairly wide range of actual output, and its average total costs per unit of output will therefore fall as output increases, due to the reduced weight of the fixed indirect costs. There will be a definite limit to the output that the business can produce, given its fixed factors, but as a purely temporary measure it will be able to produce a larger output than it could maintain indefinitely, for it can temporarily 'overwork' its overhead factors of production—especially its personnel. A business man will, however, normally plan to operate within this limit, and, in this sense, a business which is running at its full planned capacity will normally have some reserve capacity available for short-run increases of output. If its

---

[1] It will be understood that the elements of the theory of the firm can be stated much more baldly when we are concerned with the analysis of industrial groupings of firms than would be appropriate when our attention is more narrowly concentrated upon the individual business. In the same way, when we are examining an actual business our thought-pattern has to be much more complex than would be appropriate for a theoretical discussion even of individual businesses. Further, since the aim of this paper is to discuss a normal pattern of analysis for manufacturing industry, even the industrial analysis can be presented in stark outline without bothering overmuch about the differences between one industry and another which concern us in empirical work. Some aspects of each of these more complex questions have been discussed in *Manufacturing Business*, and a more detailed discussion of them will be provided in a later book which will be concerned with empirical studies as such.

output increases so that it can normally produce a larger output than is desirable with its present organization, then the business will reorganize to produce these larger outputs. It is assumed that the average costs for larger outputs will be less than for smaller outputs, the business being appropriately organized in each case.

The individual business will, therefore, produce at decreasing costs per unit, both short and long run. But whereas short-run average costs will decline relatively sharply as output increases over the relevant range of production, the long-run costs will decrease relatively more gently in the case of an established business. It would normally take a substantial increase of output to enable it to run at substantially reduced long-run average costs.

We shall see that, in fact, market conditions are not likely to permit such large relative increases in output to result from factors which are within the control of the business, such as price cutting. But, even if this were not so, it would be wrong in a realistic theory of price-determination to let long-run cost changes have the full force that abstract theory might suggest that they possessed. In actual conditions costs will always be liable to chance fluctuations, and the uncertainty within which the business man plans is such that his estimates will be tentatively used. More important, perhaps, is the consideration that it will always take time for a business to consolidate itself at a significantly enlarged scale, and some time must elapse before actual costs can be got down to the level which the business man may have estimated as possible in the end. Meanwhile he could not postulate that the other factors in his calculations would remain unchanged.

It will, therefore, be very reasonable for a business man to take his present costs as a good guide to his probable costs of production for most increases in output that appear likely. If his output does increase, and he maintains it, then he can count on reductions in costs improving his position, other things being equal.

What about the marketing side of the picture ? First, let us assume that at given prices an individual firm will have a definite clientèle, given that it retains its 'goodwill'. Other things being equal, its customers will prefer to deal with it rather than with other businesses; a brand-new business, similarly, may be imagined as building up its clientèle out of the custom that it gets at seasonal or other times of pressure of demand for its type of products. The *ceteris paribus* clause, however, reminds us that all this is subject to the condition that in the long run no business will be able to charge a higher price than another business would for a product which is technically identical with its own, as delivered to a particular customer. In the long run, therefore, all businesses producing the same product will have to charge the same price, and a business which is producing a speciality will not be able to charge a higher price than another business would charge to produce it, provided that the business has not got a monopoly in the strict original Marshallian sense. In the short run, a business may be getting a higher price, but as the knowledge of this circumstance spreads it will face a decreasing demand for its products, the lower-pricing businesses gaining, until in the long run its demand would disappear altogether—but it will revise its pricing policy long before that happens.[1]

In practice, a business man knows this and reasons accordingly. He will, therefore, try to avoid quoting a price which he could not maintain in the long run. It should be remembered that he is assumed to be a manufacturer who has sunk a good deal in investment which will take some time to justify itself. Goodwill is too precious a commodity, and takes too long to build up, for it to be thrown away on a wrong pricing policy. And on the other side of the picture, the fact of decreasing costs will mean that all businesses will gladly accept extra orders at a price which is no lower than they are getting already. Price-regulating competition does not, therefore, in normal times, involve so long a run as might naïvely be imagined on the old notion of existing businesses all working to capacity, when new competition could come only from the slow development of absolutely new firms.

What determines the competition which a business man will thus have to meet, and the price at which he will meet it? It will pay any existing business, with suitable production facilities, to quote against him, if a lower price would enable it to cover its estimated average costs of production plus a fair profit.[2] Similarly, it will be attractive to set up a new business, if its founder calculates that, in the long run, he may hope to get a total output which would suffice to leave him in a favourable position at the given price.

The experience of a business man in an established business will give him a fair idea of what level of price is likely to be dangerous; and any mistake, if he should be mistaken, will soon show itself in a relatively shrinking demand. But we must not regard him simply as thinking about the right price; it is rather that he adopts a costing-up policy which on his experience will yield him the right price, or, at least, no higher price. This

[1] One reason why this theory here differs so substantially from generally received doctrine is, as I have pointed out, that the typical customer of a manufacturing business is another business.

[2] It will be noticed that here and elsewhere I refer to the business as quoting a price; this recognizes the fact that different businesses frequently produce different products; and, in any case, it is quite usual for the precise nature of the product to be specified by the customer. In practice, then, a manufacturing business is more often in the position that it formally quotes a price than that it sells at a price which is impersonally quoted on a market. That does not prevent businesses from being in competition with one another.

pricing policy will enable him at once to quote a price for a new product at which he can feel reasonably safe against the competition of other businesses.

An established business in a stable or growing market will normally fix its price quotations on the basis of a detailed estimate of its actual costs of production, direct and indirect separately, adding to these a margin as for net profit. Alternatively, quoted price may be reached on the basis of a much more explicitly rule-of-thumb basis of average direct costs plus an allowance for gross profit. I say 'explicitly', for, of course, any allowance as for net profit in the more detailed costings will be no less on a rule-of-thumb basis. In either case the business can be presumed to have an idea of the level of net profits which it is safe for it to take in its line of manufacture, and this has special significance in any dynamic view of profits; but the significant elements (from the static point of view generally assumed for this section of the paper) in the analysis of price-determination, are average direct costs and the gross profit margin which makes up the balance of the quoted price. In price-equilibrium, each business will find that it is able to charge safely only on the basis of a definite level of gross profit, since it will have a definite normal level of average direct costs. And the gross profit margin that it can get will seem to be limited by the competition which is actually or potentially present in its market.

At this point it will be convenient to break off for a discussion of the effect upon quoted prices of changes in a business's costs of production, although it will not be possible to avoid straying a little from our static assumptions strictly interpreted. A manufacturing business will normally be quick to lower price if its costs fall by reason of reductions in the prices of raw materials or in the wages of labour. These will affect other businesses as well, and to neglect to make consequent adjustments in prices will be to invite successful competition in one's market. Moreover, the buyers will normally be fairly well acquainted with the fact and extent of such changes, and will expect a reduction whose size they will often be able to estimate—in fact, where a business is selling to expert buyers, they will frequently have as shrewd an idea as it of the 'right' price, at which they could get such a thing made elsewhere. Similarly, it will generally be fairly easy to revise prices upwards in the event of increases in the prices of such factors; in general, they will occur only during a rising market for such factors, buyers will expect them, they will not affect the strength of the final market, and the competitive normal price will be similarly affected.[1]

---

[1] In practice, a business may not be able to make minor changes in price, which sometimes can be changed only by conventional amounts; it is also generally true that buyers will not like too sensitive a price policy leading to too frequent relatively minor changes in price. It is, therefore, frequently the custom for businesses to delay price rises until they have

It remains to consider the effects of autonomous changes in a business's costs—those due to changes in its output or to changes in its efficiency. An increase in average costs due simply to a reduction in output will, of course, have no upward effect upon price. Whether it is due to a weakening of the business's relative hold over its market, or to a general decline in the demand for its sort of products, to raise price will make matters worse and present its goodwill to other businesses who will be only too anxious to enlarge their sales at the ruling price. The same will be true of a rise of costs due to a decrease in the productive efficiency of the business.

Weak businesses which are only just holding on, or making very low profits relatively to the rest of their industry, will not reduce prices on account of any autonomous decline of costs. Their long-run position will be in danger, and they will both need and be seeking such cost changes in order to ensure that they have the means of continuing in being. The position is very different with the relatively stronger businesses: those which at the given level of price are selling a sufficiently large output and working at such a level of efficiency that they already get satisfactory profits. They will reduce prices fairly promptly if their cost levels fall because their market has expanded and enabled them to produce at lower costs, or if their level of costs for the same output falls because of improved efficiency. It will be borne in mind that the shape of the long-period cost curve will normally require a substantial increase in output before costs are substantially affected. In the latter case, the way that costings are drawn up will generally ensure a fairly prompt reduction if average direct costs fall; a fall in overheads may take a little time to make its presence known, or at least for it to be taken as likely to continue, but once it shows itself in the costings, it will tend to lead to price reductions.[1] It is in this way that a growing efficient business will be one of the chief forces of competition in its market, determining what we have called equilibrium price in its market.[2]

become increasingly justified over a period; and if a rising trend in factor prices is expected to continue it may be allowed for to some extent in the rise of price that is made. There will be a stronger inducement to do something quickly about a fall of costs, but minor changes may be allowed simply to have the effect of improving the quality of the product, or of associated services, or be ignored.

[1] All this, of course, is presuming rather more normal times than we have known recently, in the sense that it must be possible for an efficient business quickly to get the additional equipment, &c., that it will need in order to extend its output; it must also be free to extend in the most appropriate way. The position is very different when an industry is held tightly controlled by outside factors.

[2] When an industry is loosely defined, as it is in most official statistics, it is too easy to be impressed by the large size of the largest business and easy to invoke the modern jargon of oligopolistic price-leadership. When we study the matter from the inside, we find frequently that it is not here that leadership is to be found; the level of prices is much more often determined by the vigorous, medium-sized or small, relatively specialist, business which is bent on growing.

The inducement to reduce price will not only be that it may be able to retain some of any short-period increase in relative sales that it gets from the initial price cut, but that it will certainly increase its long-run hold on its market, continuing to get satisfactory profits which will enable it to have the wherewithal for growth and for innovation, whilst the long-run hold of its rivals will be weakened, if their efficiency remains relatively unimproved. A failure to make such a reduction will carry corresponding dangers and, as has been said, the normal costing rules will tend to cause such a downward reduction to take place.

To return to the static analysis with which we are mainly concerned at present, the upshot so far is that the price quoted by a manufacturing business is to be seen as competitively determined; at that price, at any given time, it will be able to sell only what the market will take. This statement, in itself, means the implied abandonment of any definition of equilibrium output for the individual business, in the sense of the achievement of a balance between marginal revenue and marginal cost. This concept of a deliberately planned (restriction of) output is, it may be observed, one of the major intellectual difficulties in the way of a trained theoretical economist when he turns to empirical studies. We shall return to this aspect of static theory later, for, to some extent, the static method in general has similar disadvantages, although I do not think them so grave as those that flow from this particular static concept. Meanwhile it will be noted that the analysis given here is in terms of an equilibrium of *price*, and not of individual *outputs*.

An existing business will continue in production at the given level of price so long as it can cover all the outgoings that have currently to be met. In the short run, it may be prepared to run at a loss, so long as it is covering at least its direct costs—and the pricing rules will evidently tend to ensure this for businesses which are not surprisingly inefficient or unlucky in the matter of organizing their direct factors of production. In the longer run it will not be able to carry on at all unless it covers all its paying-out costs, for continued production will otherwise imply steadily depleted cash balances. These paying-out costs will in the long run include the costs of the maintenance and replacement of its capital assets as well as the wages of management and other overhead personnel, which will have to be met more continuously. Provided that the business does cover its paying-out costs, it will be able to carry on, even if it is not earning anything by way of interest on its capital; if they are not covered, it will become less efficient, have rising levels of costs, and in the end will be forced out of business.

A new business, of course, will not start up unless it is thought to have a reasonable chance that in the long run it will get a sufficient output to enable it not merely to survive but also to earn satisfactory profits. It would be misleading, however, to make the usual full-static-equilibrium assumption that all businesses which are producing a given product must cover their costs and get normal profits. This would be unrealistic even if additional capacity for the production of a particular product could come only from the starting of a new business. A new business will start too small from the long-run point of view, and will usually 'get by' initially only in the favourable circumstances of a trade boom or with extraordinarily hard work on the part of its management. It will allow for these difficulties by taking as its target some idea of what it may reasonably hope to achieve when it gets established. It will get this idea by guessing or estimating what is happening to established businesses making similar products and, thence, what its own fortune is likely to be. Looked at from the point of view of their actual results, new businesses will, therefore, often have taken an optimistic view. Accordingly, where capital requirements make it relatively easy for new businesses to produce a particular type of product, it is understandable that a substantial part of the output of such types of products should be produced at a loss, when all costs are allowed for.

In the world as it is, however, competition from new businesses is often not the most important source of competition. Granted the limitation of their primary markets, established businesses will normally be looking around for related products which they can take on. Here again, the decision to do so will be related to the chance of the experiments justifying themselves ultimately, rather than upon immediate results. The more narrowly we define a product, in fact, the more normal it will be to find that a proportion of the output is being produced at a loss; but if we considered the *businesses* possessing the appropriate type of production facilities, the proportion of these making losses would be smaller, many businesses will be sufficiently established with their main products to cover the costs of their output as a whole, but will be making current losses on the products where they are trying the market, or tentatively establishing themselves.

Although no formal warning has been given, it will no doubt have already been realized that we have slipped away from the strict analysis of the individual business into talking about groupings of businesses which are apparently playing the same analytical role as the old Marshallian 'industry'. (In the same way, the previous two paragraphs will have suggested the shadowy reappearance of something very much like a 'representative firm'; but it has not, in fact, appeared, and its usefulness will be discussed below.) In fact, we cannot erect the concepts which are needed to understand the behaviour of the individual manufacturing business without at the same time conceiving of the relevant grouping of competing and potentially competing businesses—the 'industry'—through which the forces of the economic environment of the business act and react upon it. From now on, we explicitly define an 'industry' as any grouping of individual manufacturing businesses which is relevant when we study the behaviour of any one such business. The discussion of this paper, however, will formally be restricted to the consideration of product markets; we cannot consider the analogous, but not necessarily coterminous, groupings of businesses which come into view when the markets for their factors of production are analysed.

In the product markets, what is the chief characteristic of an industry? It is largely a matter of technique and processes; an individual business must be conceived as operating within an 'industry' which consists of all businesses which operate processes of a sufficiently similar kind (which implies the possession of substantially similar technical resources) and possessing sufficiently similar backgrounds of experience and knowledge so that each of them could produce the particular commodity under consideration, and would do so if it were sufficiently attractive.

The scope of such a definition will widen as we increase our understanding of the economics of the production of the particular commodity. At first, attention will be concentrated upon all commodities with very similar technical specifications, sold in circumstances entailing that similar services are rendered to the customer. Thus we may consider the producers of fractional horse-power motors or the producers of fitting shoes. Within such narrow groupings our price-equilibrium analysis applies most simply: Technically similar products must have identical normal prices, or normal prices whose differences will be explicable on the basis of a difference in normal costs of production.[1] This narrower definition of an industry will include all the businesses which are in most active competition with one another on any short-run analysis. But, studying the way in which competition actually emerges, we become aware of the significance of a much more widely drawn boundary to the industry—to include all those who possess such facilities, &c., that they could well turn over to the production of our narrowly defined product in a rather longer run, since they will take more time to enter its particular market. Our analysis then runs in very broad terms: 'the boot and shoe industry'; 'electrical engineering'; even, on occasion, 'the leather and footwear industry'; or 'engineering'.

These wider definitions of the industry which are relevant to longer-run analyses will, as already argued, normally be separable into sub-industries each producing its relatively narrow grade or type of product. The typical

---

[1] Compare Mr. Leyland's note on prices in the lightweight bicycle industry: 'A Note on Price and Quality', *Oxford Economic Papers*, June 1949.

gross margins, and net profit margins, of these will differ between them-selves[1]—but normal differences in such margins will tend to be established; for example, as between different 'ends' of the boot and shoe industry; and these will be found to differ with differences in the costs that are normally involved. Even these wide definitions of industries thus take on a sense of reality for economic analysis.

When we are teaching the principles of economic analysis as they are applicable to manufacturing industries, it will, therefore, seem appropriate to do as Marshall did, to use the concept of 'an industry', and to analyse it as if it, in fact, involved producing an identical commodity. In empirical analysis we shall have to break down such a general concept and obtain realistic definitions of the industry which will vary both with the type of commodity with which we are concerned and with the purpose of the analysis; even the same inquiry may therefore use a definition which shifts in its scope as between different parts of the analysis. For general analysis, and for teaching purposes, however, the matter can be left very much in Marshallian terms.

For the hypothetical commodity which will be the subject of such analyses we can postulate a Marshallian demand curve—which should perhaps be given with the realistic warning that it should generally be taken as inelastic in the neighbourhood of existing price (except perhaps after a really long period has elapsed after a change of price, so that the full indirect effects may have been realized). This analytical concept of 'the' demand curve for the industry will have some empirical validity even for an industry which, in fact, produces a great variety of actual products, because they will often be subject to the same broad historical influences (their demands, for example, broadly rising and contracting together). Such a combination will have some meaning from the point of view of producers, because the individual commodities will be alternative products in the long run; it will also frequently be the case that they are all in some sort of competition as substitutes for one another.

At a given level of price the total demand will be analysable, at any one time, into definite amounts demanded from individual businesses and not available to others, unless the favoured business cannot in fact supply all that is demanded of it—which should not be presumed in a long-run analysis starting with some situation of equilibrium. The market will be in equilibrium as long as the total demand at the given price is within the capacity of the industry and of the individual businesses, and as long as the price is equal to the normal cost of producing the commodity, so that on balance any loss of capacity due to businesses being driven from production

[1] And within such sub-industries gross margins will differ between businesses according to the levels of their average direct costs.

is made up by extensions to existing capacity or by the entry of new capacity.

If demand increases at the given price, there will be a general increase in the amounts demanded from the individual businesses. In normal conditions they will meet these up to the full extent of their short-run capacity, price remaining unchanged, and they will extend if their limited capacity makes it desirable to do so. Short-run increases in demand will generally be met at normal price, on our assumptions. (It will be understood that we are maintaining the assumption that factor prices will not have changed; this will not be valid, say, for an increase in demand which is part of a general cyclical increase of trade.) In the long run, however, such an expansion of existing businesses will enable them to reorganize and get the benefit of lower costs. Normal price will, therefore, fall in the long run. An increased demand for manufacturing products will therefore be met eventually at a lower equilibrium price.

In any full analysis of such a change we should have to allow for any effects upon costs which may be due to causes outside the organization of the individual business but due less directly to such a change in demand. These will be any dis-economy to the industry due to the prices of primary factors of production rising with the increased pressure of the demand for them, and also any economies which the larger-scale production may produce in other industries. These will have their effect upon the normal cost price which will be established in the particular industry which we are analysing, and may cause the trend of normal price for the industry to differ from what we should infer from a knowledge of the behaviour of costs in an individual business considered in isolation. It will be recognized that this parallels familiar points in Marshallian analysis, but these are simply other instances of the way in which the theory of the firm which has been discussed here may be used to provide a very fair parallel to the Marshallian description of long-run equilibrium in a manufacturing industry, on static assumptions.

In the process of making the analysis, however, the supply curve concept has dissolved in the same way as we have earlier suggested occurred on a strict interpretation of Marshall's own analysis. We are left with the concept of a given stable demand being supplied at a normal-cost price, of an extension to that demand being met in the short run by increased supplies at the same price, and in the long run at a decreased price. The number of businesses in an industry will adjust themselves to demand in the long run.

One ingredient from Marshall has been prominently absent so far in this section—that is, the representative firm. It has been represented to me that it may usefully be accommodated in the analysis as a concept summarizing the factors which are relevant to long-run competition. Others may like to use it; I myself find it difficult to handle in conditions where we must assume that a good deal of the latent competition will be from businesses which are already in existence, even if not producing the particular product. It owed its origin to the necessity of relating the supply curve to the behaviour of individual firms, when the general tenor of the analysis was in conflict with fundamental notions of individual businesses as tending to be in marginalist equilibrium. It seems to me possible to do without it.[1]

The foregoing analysis has generally been made upon static assumptions, but to an economist who has experience of empirical studies of businesses there is bound to be some sense of strain in the use of such analysis, and this should be recognized here. Static theory is quite adequate for the purposes of general economic analysis, and is useful in training pupils to get the general view of industrial behaviour which will give the broad conceptual basis for empirical work. For an industrial economist as such, however, there is something much more seriously wrong with static analysis of industries than with that of the individual firm from which the wider analysis is built up.

In the case of a given business it seems a natural procedure to take things as they are and work out the implications in terms of the business's long-run capacity to compete and to survive, assuming other relevant factors to remain unchanged. But it is impossible to do this without being well aware just how dangerous it is to take for granted the relative level of efficiency which exists at a particular time. Businesses which are in a very strong position often lose it through becoming complacent, losing such firm control over overhead costs, &c., and losing the drive to be 'just that step ahead' which is necessary in a world where it will be rare for a business to be able to go on making just that particular product in such-and-such a particular way. Equally, a business which is doing badly has so much incentive to do something about it. As has been said before, it is out of the constant passing to and fro of industrial leadership that the essence of actual competition arises.

When we are studying actual businesses we break the bounds of static assumptions fairly easily. The histories of actual individual businesses and their competitors soon make us aware that an important factor in competition is the cost-reducing enterprise of individual business men. It

---

[1] Although I do not advocate the use of the concept of the representative firm in teaching industrial analysis, it should be noted that representativeness is a real enough quality when we are concerned with empirical work. When studying an 'industry' it is useful to get preliminary ideas of the types of business situations, with regard to technique, to marketing, to labour supply, &c., that are to be met with in practice, and then to select for study businesses which seem likely to provide good case-studies from these points of view.

is easy to lose sight of this in static industrial analyses; the concept of an industry is abstract anyway, the static analysis enables us to grasp certain essential elements of a right view, but it is difficult to realize that the theory may be seriously misleading. We may try to remove static assumptions which get explicitly in the way, but the broad picture of a static competition still clogs thinking.[1]

Life does not run with the smoothness that economic theory can legitimately assume for general analysis or for teaching purposes. The very ups and downs of the trade cycle contribute their own element making for the increased efficiency of business over time, but the individual business will also get its share of minor setbacks. Something always remains from the enforced ideas of economy and novelty to which business men are driven by such forces. Innovation and the rest of such factors will mean that the forces of competition, apparently so easily impounded in static analysis, will cause the level of normal-cost price always to fall. It sometimes seems that the whole clue to the history of economic civilization is missing from static analysis.

The abandonment of the concept of static equilibrium for the individual business, which has been urged in this paper, would mean some improvement since it is certainly one of the major elements in his thought-pattern which prevents an academic economist from understanding what is happening in business life.[2] Even so, granted that its disappearance will leave our static theory on a better basis, it will still not be good enough. We need some different patterns of analysis. But these will have to be built up out of empirical studies, just as Marshallian concepts were largely informed by their founder's studies of historical processes. No amount of spinning-out of logical chains of analysis based upon static concepts will help in this task. The need is for more empirical studies, and for the co-operation of business men and academics in their making. Before such co-operation can be fruitful, however, economic theory must not be positively wrong in its approach, and I would conclude this paper by suggesting that that was the negative effect of the inter-war rejection of Marshall.

[1] See Hayek's stimulating essay 'The Meaning of Competition' in his book *Individualism and Economic Order*.

[2] I cannot resist telling the story of a cohort of undergraduates at the last stages of their training who were invited to spend a period in a Midlands works. They spent the whole time not in seeing what did go on, and then trying to interpret it for themselves, but in the much more interesting pursuit of trying to 'prove' that the business man must be mistaken, or at least unaware of the implications of some procedure which their persistent questioning would bring out, when he said that he did not price with any calculations of marginal revenue, marginal cost, or of the right output which would maximize his net profits. They were unconvinced at the end of their stay, and were probably wondering exactly what had been hidden from them. Abstractions in economics sound very much like descriptions!

V

AGRICULTURE AND THE PRICE MECHANISM

By B. D. GILES

I

THE purpose of this paper is to consider critically the operation of the price mechanism in relation to agriculture.[1] Both theoretical and empirical studies will be drawn upon. No claim to originality is made, but, in view of the current interest in agricultural problems and the scattered location of the sources, a brief survey of some of the chief questions may be of interest to those economists whose special field is elsewhere.

The basic assumption of this essay is that agricultural economics is not a special kind of economics; we shall attempt to apply the ordinary rules of economic analysis to agriculture. The equilibrium towards which the hypothetical farm moves is defined in precisely the same terms as that of the firm.[2] Factors are assumed to be employed up to the point where their marginal cost equals their marginal revenue product; output is adjusted to the point where marginal cost equals marginal revenue; the marginal yield of £1 is the same in all possible lines of investment; and so on.

Admittedly, there is some doubt whether a model of agriculture based on a hypothesis of profit maximization is applicable. As Dr. C. S. Orwin has pointed out,[3] the disappointing response of British farmers to price incentives since 1945 may be due to the fact that farming is a 'way of life'. Given an income which he regards as adequate the farmer may take his ease; conversely, a slump in farm prices may not persuade farmers to move into other occupations until bankruptcy drives them from their farms.

It is indeed true that the profit motive does not explain this kind of immobility, but when we observe that the term 'agriculture' covers a diversity of activities almost as wide as that covered by the term 'manufacturing', ordinary analysis appears, nevertheless, to have some application, because farmers have some choice of occupation without abandoning

---

[1] In its final revision this essay has had the benefit of the generous criticisms and suggestions of Dr. K. A. H. Murray, Rector of Lincoln College. I have also profited from discussions on a number of points with Mr. A. Loveday, Warden of Nuffield College, Mr. P. W. S. Andrews of Nuffield College, Dr. T. Wilson of University College, Mr. L. Richenberg of Jesus College, and Mr. A. W. Ashby of the Institute of Agricultural Economics Research. The faults that remain are, of course, my own responsibility. The paper has been prepared and written during the tenure of a Studentship at Nuffield College, Oxford.

[2] Cf. T. W. Schultz, 'Firm and Farm Management Research', *Journal of Farm Economics*, 1939.

[3] Letter to *The Times*, 24 Oct. 1949.

their 'way of life'. There is not a little evidence to show that, of the outputs which are technically possible, the farmer will produce a collection very like that which would yield the greatest profit, although, in fact, he may never operate at the point of equilibrium. For many purposes we can regard the agricultural industries as a non-competing group in relation to the remainder of the economy, and we shall sometimes speak of the terms of trade between agriculture and manufacturing, and on occasions we shall consider agricultural output as a whole.

The title of this essay implies that it will be concerned almost entirely with those sections of agriculture in which the price-system exerts an influence. This excludes the problems of the very large number of the world's farmers whose activities are governed by subsistence needs or social customs. Even more serious, perhaps, is the omission of a consideration of the special problems of those areas which, because of peculiarities of climate or soil, or for other reasons such as transport difficulties, are practically confined to the production for sale of a single crop, but a discussion of these in terms of responses to price-movements would be more than a little forced.

With these limitations borne in mind, the main topics are examined in the following order. We begin with a list of the main characteristics of agriculture which are relevant to economic analysis, we pass on to a consideration of the nature of the supply and demand schedules for farm products, and we use these schedules to elucidate the cyclical problem in agriculture. Then we consider the allocation of resources, firstly within agriculture and secondly between agriculture and the rest of the economy. A section on estimating the future terms of trade for agriculture follows, and we conclude with a short section on agricultural policies. Clearly the treatment of this range of subjects cannot be exhaustive, but the footnotes refer to more adequate discussions of some of the questions raised.

II

To the economist, the most important special features of agriculture are as follows:

(a) One of the text-book conditions of perfect competition exists: there are numerous firms, none of them large enough to influence prices significantly by its own actions.[1] Even if there is a movement towards larger scale production due to recent technical advances, it will be a long time before the concepts of imperfect competition or oligopoly become impor-

[1] Recently there were 290,600 holdings of 5 acres and over in England and Wales, 86 per cent. of which were occupied by full- or part-time farmers. The average size for full-time farmers was 99 acres. (*National Farm Survey of England and Wales (1941–3), A Summary Report.* H.M.S.O., 1946, p. 13.) In the United States there were over six million farms in 1940. (U.S. Dept. of Agriculture, *Agricultural Statistics, 1942*, p. 615.)

tant in considering the relationship between farmers. Because the number of producers is large, the demand schedule facing each of them is perfectly elastic although total market demand may, of course, be inelastic. Hence one of the pre-requisites for the ideal operation of the price-system is fulfilled, and because the cost curve for agriculture, constructed on static assumptions, is probably rising[1] the farmer can maximize profits by adjusting output to the point where marginal cost equals price without incurring losses from adherence to the rule of the welfare economists.

(b) The text-book advantages of perfect competition require perfect foresight on the part of the entrepreneur, and this is even more completely absent from agriculture than from many other occupations. The farmer not only faces 'economic' uncertainty as to the price he will receive for his product; there is also 'technical' uncertainty about yield, because the relationship between inputs and outputs is not known before harvest. Variations in yield might be expected to be offset by compensating variations in price, but since the revolution in ocean transport at the end of the last century, low yields in a single country have not always been offset by high prices within that country, because imported supplies often diminish any price-raising scarcity. The appended table of yields (taken at random from a convenient source) shows year to year variations of up to 30 per cent. for particular crops in single countries taken as a whole.[2] Clearly, some individual farmers would have experienced much wider variations. Hence the problem of stabilizing farm incomes is both seasonal and cyclical and schemes to remedy both types will be discussed later.

(c) In spite of the relative ease with which some farmers can switch from one crop to another, these changes usually take at least a season; the lag between the stimulus of a change in price and the response of supply extends over an appreciable period of calendar time because production is not usually a flow. A series of inputs often precedes an output occurring at a point in time, the size and nature of which is determined by the inputs of a very early stage. This means that a price-change must persist for

---

[1] Cf. Dr. J. R. Raeburn (*Journal of the Proceedings of the Agricultural Economics Society*, vol. vii, No. 1, June 1946, p. 41), discussing Mr. Kirk's paper on 'The Output of British Agriculture during the War', has made a rough calculation indicating that 'the total extra "cost" in 1943–4, at pre-war price and wage levels, was ... £136 million, for an increase in net output of, say, 30 per cent., £62 million'.

[2] Index Nos. of Yields per hectare (1939 = 100):

Crop	Country	1939	1940	1941	1942	1943	1944	1945
Wheat	U.K.	100	98	96	110	107	105	103
Wheat	U.S.A.	100	108	120	140	118	128	120
Wheat (sown area)	Canada	100	96	74	132	87	92	69
Sugar Beet .	U.K.	100	94	90	90	88	74	91
Potatoes	U.K.	100	104	96	97	95	87	95

Sources: *International Yearbook of Agricultural Statistics, 1941–6*, vol. i, Tables 1, 11, 9.

a long time before there is a significant change in supplies reaching the market; there is, so to speak, a period of continuing change in the amount of work in progress without any corresponding change in price, unless there are stocks which can be released. By the time supplies on the market have altered appreciably it may be found that farmers have made an excessive response, but the movement cannot be reversed without another time-lag. Hence such phenomena as the 'hog cycle', or more generally the sequence of events described in the cobweb theorem.[1]

(d) The ratio of prime cost to total cost of many farm products is very low, even if we look several years ahead.

In the first place, if we define prime costs as the difference between the costs incurred in producing something, and those incurred in producing nothing while remaining in the business (i.e. maintaining equipment so that production can be resumed)[2] we find that some costs which at first sight appear to be prime should really be charged to maintenance; many of the operations required to produce a crop are required to maintain fertility, and the prime costs of a crop may be less than the cost of the operations performed during the course of its production. Because farming is a 'way of life' these maintenance costs will probably be regarded as inescapable, and the escapable element in operating costs is correspondingly reduced. Agriculture is not unique in this respect, but it is probable that this kind of difficulty in allocating costs between operation and maintenance is more intractable on farms than in factories.

Secondly, in most businesses, labour costs would be an item in variable costs. In farming, to an even greater extent than in other small-scale business, an important part of the labour force consists of the entrepreneur and his family. The opportunity cost of this labour is very low because a change of occupation would involve the sacrifice of special skill and possibly a loss of social prestige as well. Hence, even if we classify all labour costs as variable it is probable that the price of family labour will fall to a very low level before it seeks employment elsewhere. This immobility reduces neither the national product nor the farmer's income if the marginal value product of farmers in farming is greater than their marginal value product elsewhere, but both the national product and the farmer's income may be increased if, through a course of training, the marginal product of some farmers in other occupations could be raised above their marginal product in agriculture by an amount sufficient to

---

[1] K. A. H. Murray and R. Cohen, *Scottish Journal of Agriculture* (H.M.S.O.), Oct. 1935, p. 357, find the lag for wheat in the United Kingdom is at least a year. R. Cohen in 'Research and Price Control', *Agricultural Economics, Miscellaneous Papers 1935–8* (Oxford), finds a lag for pigs of 21 months, and for potatoes of one or two years. See G. S. Shepherd, *Agricultural Price Policy*, p. 14, for a graph of the 'corn-hog' cycle, 1901–47.

[2] Cf. G. D. A. MacDougall, 'Prime and Supplementary Costs', *E.J.*, 1936.

cover interest and amortization over their working life on the investment in training.[1] But even if transfer appears to be worth while on this basis, there may be other reasons for refusing to encourage it; for example, it may be thought that a sturdy peasantry is a healthy feature in national life. In this paper these borderline economic problems will usually be neglected because they would carry us too far afield, although this omission entails that many of the points raised will not be of the first importance for problems of agricultural policy.

Not only does the cost of family labour appear to behave like an overhead cost in anything but the very long period in which all costs are variable, but the cost of hired labour may be inflexible because each man represents a significant indivisibility in a very small firm. Thus the proportion of labour used cannot be varied marginally unless casual labour is available, and in rural areas this kind of labour is normally used only for seasonal work; to rely on it more frequently would involve the risk that none might be available at a critical period. Reducing his labour force is, for the farmer, a desperate method of cutting costs, and his wage bill is apt to look more like an overhead than a variable cost.

We may sum up this section by saying that, on the supply side, farming is characterized by atomistic competition, uncertainties about yield, lack of short-period control over output, appreciable time-lags and low short-period prime costs. These are the features which lead to such a remarkable steadiness in the volume of farm output, apparently without regard for price; it is not due to obtuseness on the part of farmers.

III

Empirical supply analysis was first undertaken on a large scale in order to provide farmers with forecasts of future supplies and prices on which their plans could be based. In Germany, for example, estimates of future supplies were made with a view to damping down the pig cycle.[2] The United States Department of Agriculture has also undertaken a good deal of this sort of work. More recently, the advent of control schemes and administered prices has given administrators a very direct interest in the relationship between prices and supplies.

[1] See G. W. Barr, Hon. Mention Paper submitted in an essay competition, on 'A Price Policy for Agriculture', *J.F.E.*, 1945. Mr. Barr, apparently a practising farmer, wants more information about prospective prices and about alternative employments.

The age composition of the employed population in an industry would be an important consideration if we were considering whether labour should be encouraged to transfer to other occupations. Because the migrants from agriculture probably consist of the younger men, we should expect to find a high proportion of the farm population in the upper age groups. Thus, even without further migration, a temporary decline in the number of farm workers may occur.

[2] K. A. H. Murray and V. Cornea, 'The Study of Agricultural Prices in Germany', *Journal of the Ministry of Agriculture*, 1934–5, p. 171.

For these and other reasons, numerous attempts have been made to analyse supply conditions for a variety of farm products. Two approaches are conceivable. Ideally, the marginal cost curve of every producer might be constructed and these might be linked to give a Marshallian supply curve. Two facts make this solution impracticable. Firstly, the number of producers is very large; secondly, the expansion of one type of output involves the contraction of other types, and detailed cost accounts would be required for each crop.[1]

The usual practice is to correlate prices with subsequent supplies. Three important complications arise. Firstly, the farmer often has little control over yield, and the mere fact that a change in output follows a change in price may not be of interest if it is desired to measure farmers' intended production; therefore it is customary to correlate prices with subsequent acreages, over which the farmer has more complete control than he possesses over output. Thus, because figures for land inputs are readily available, changes in supply are often measured by changes in a single input, land, and changes in the intensity of cultivation are not taken into account. In so far as farming methods are slow to change, land inputs may provide a good index of farmers' intentions over short periods.

Secondly, the theoretical supply curve is drawn on the assumption that all other prices remain unchanged; this seems to be the least that we can read into the *ceteris paribus* clause. Because other prices do not remain unchanged, to correlate only the crude market price with the subsequent acreage of the commodity being studied is pointless. The price of, say, wheat might remain unchanged while acreage was reduced because the price of some other commodity, which could be produced with the same resources, had increased. Attempts to meet this difficulty have been made by dividing the price index of the commodity under consideration by the price index of competing commodities, to give a relative price index with which subsequent supplies can be correlated.

Third, and most serious, is the difficulty of identifying the prices which are causally related to output. If rotations have to be changed, relative prices two or three seasons previously may be relevant, and the duration of a price relationship may be important. It is also necessary to decide which price relationships influence farmers' plans; for example, the British wheat grower finds the wheat–barley price-ratio more important than the wheat–hops price-ratio. For these reasons, it is not possible to draw up a satisfactory Marshallian supply schedule; if more than one price-ratio is important in the determination of output, and all the ratios do not change together, we cannot put them along a single price-axis in the usual type of diagram.

[1] Cf. J. D. Black, 'Elasticity of Supply of Farm Products', *J.F.E.*, 1924.

Finally, some of the changes in a given period may influence both prices and supplies. For example, if credit conditions become easier, prices may rise even if supplies remain constant, and supplies may increase even if prices remain unchanged. If, in these circumstances, both prices and supplies increase, it is clearly inadmissible to attribute the whole change in supply to the change in price.

For these reasons we cannot hope to derive an ordinary supply schedule from statistical data. Nevertheless, many attempts to relate prices and

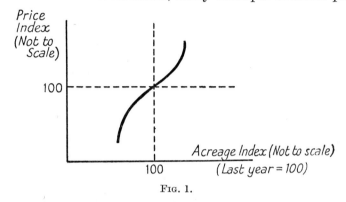

FIG. 1.

supplies have been made. The work of Dr. Murray, Miss Cohen, and Mr. Cornea has been referred to, and in the United States Dr. L. H. Bean has constructed some interesting curves, for several farm products of the general shape of the curve shown in Fig. 1.[1]

This is not the supply schedule of pure theory, although it seems to be related to it. On the Y axis the price index of 100 is a 'stability price'; at this price 100 per cent. of a current year's acreage would be planted in the following year. At prices below 100 a smaller acreage, and at prices above 100 a larger acreage would be planted. If a price is below 100, a rise in price insufficient to reach 100 will produce a further reduction in acreage, although it will be a smaller reduction than would have occurred had prices remained even lower. Similarly, a fall in the price which does not bring it below 100 will result in an increase in acreage, but acreage will be less than it would have been had the price remained at a higher level.

If this model can be applied fairly generally—and in view of the period which may be required to change a crop rotation it has some plausibility—it means that fairly small adjustments to acreage will be made in a single year in response to quite small changes in price, but, after a point, greater price changes have relatively little immediate effect on output. On the other hand, if the price remains constant for a number of years at a level slightly higher or lower than the stability price there will be a

[1] 'The Farmers' Response to Price', *J.F.E.*, 1929.

continuing expansion or contraction of acreage. Thus the curve shown appears to be connected with both short-period and long-period supply schedules in the Marshallian sense.

The foregoing discussion refers to supply schedules for particular products. These are almost certainly more elastic than the supply schedule for agricultural output as a whole. (In spite of our inability to derive a Marshallian supply schedule, the concept is not useless, and we shall

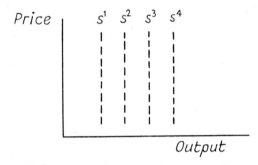

Fig. 2. ($s^1, s^2 \ldots$ are supply curves during successive periods.)

retain it here.) An interesting attempt has been made by Mr. W. W. Cochrane to construct a farm-supply schedule for food in the United States over the period 1912–46.[1] He points out that in order to derive a supply schedule from historical price and quantity data the schedule sought must be assumed to remain stationary during the period considered, so that the realized points on the price–quantity diagram are assumed to lie along a single supply curve. The thirty-four years studied by Mr. Cochrane are divided into five periods, during each of which an index of output per worker on farms was fairly constant and showed no trend. This is taken to indicate that there were only minor technical changes in each period, and that the supply curve was, therefore, nearly stable. By relating an index of 'responsible prices' (i.e. prices prevailing during the planning period which, as we have seen, would be very difficult to identify) to an index of aggregate output Mr. Cochrane found that for four of the periods the regression line was almost vertical, and that each such line was to the right of its predecessors. This seems to indicate that the supply curve for food was almost perfectly inelastic, and moved to the right in a series of jumps, as in Fig. 2. In the period 1937–42 the time series shows increasing output; it is suggested that each point on this line is really on its own supply schedule, which marched to the right as technical advances which had been made in the slump were brought into general use during the boom. In support of this it is shown that the index of output per worker showed a marked upward trend during the period.

[1] W. W. Cochrane, 'Farm Price Gyrations—An Aggregative Hypothesis', *J.F.E.*, 1947.

Although this investigation concerned only food, there is reason to believe that supply conditions for agricultural output as a whole are very similar. We find that farm output is fairly stable around a rising trend, although farm prices are very volatile. Fig. 3 shows this very clearly for the United States 1919 to 1947; the check to the upward drift of production in the 1930's can be attributed in part to A.A.A. restrictions, and in part to droughts. The chart suggests that there may be some relationship

U.S.A. Farm Prices and Production 1919–47

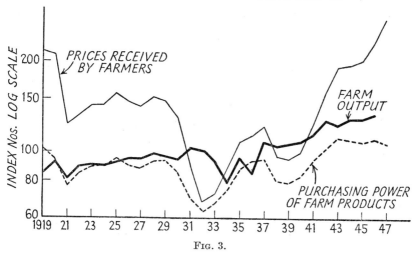

FIG. 3.

Sources: 'Index of Farm Output', U.S. Dept. of Agriculture, *Agricultural Statistics, 1946*, p. 561; ibid. *1947*, p. 533. (1935–9 = 100.)

'Index of Prices Received by Farmers', ibid. *1946*, p. 552; ibid. *1947*, p. 525. (Aug. 1909–July 1914 = 100.)

'Index of Prices Paid by Farmers for Commodities used in Family Maintenance', ibid. *1946*, p. 551; ibid. *1947*, p. 524. (1910–14 = 100.)

between output and the purchasing power of farm products;[1] if there is a causal relationship here it seems that the response of output to changes in the value of farm products may at times be so lagged that movements of the two indices are in opposite directions for appreciable periods, as for example between 1930 and 1934.

League of Nations investigations indicate that insensitiveness of agricultural output to price-changes is a fairly general feature of farm production; it is not peculiar to the United States.[2]

[1] An index of the purchasing power of farm products has been calculated by dividing the index of prices received by farmers by the index of prices paid by farmers for commodities used in family maintenance. The latter index was used to deflate the price-index because it is analogous to the cost-of-living index which is used in converting money incomes to real incomes. It is not thought that the use of different base periods falsifies the general picture presented in the chart.

[2] Cf. League of Nations, *Economic Stability in the Post War World*, charts on pp. 76 and 85.

In peasant farming a fall in price may often lead to an increase in output.[1] A full discussion of this phenomenon would require a lengthy examination of the motives behind family farming, but the main point is that a peasant may attempt to counteract a fall in income by working harder and increasing the output of his holding, with the result that prices fall again. Because this feature of some kinds of farming has been mentioned to the present writer so frequently by students working in other fields, more space will be given to it than may be merited by its intrinsic importance.

There are probably numerous individual cases of perverse reactions to price-changes, and for a single producer without alternative occupation working in a highly competitive industry this behaviour may be rational. However, few crops are produced exclusively under these conditions, and there will usually be some producers who can react to a fall in the price of X by switching to the production of Y. We have already noted that the important consideration is the relative price of a commodity, and it is unlikely that a fall in this will lead to increased output, taking all producers together.

Nevertheless, it may well be that the supply curve for some products in particular markets is perverse over part of its length. For instance, high prices and incomes in the food-producing countries may lead to increased home consumption, which may reduce exports even though production has increased. There is also a possibility that a general rise in agricultural incomes will divert part of the exports of one agricultural country to other agricultural countries which, in the new conditions, can afford to buy farm products which they do not produce. Food producers are important consumers of their own output, and changes in their reserve demand may not be negligible. Processes of this kind are, presumably, in the minds of those who hold that the post-1945 food shortages in western Europe are partly due to a shift of the terms of trade in favour of agriculture; it is important that they should be distinguished from the cases in which a rise in price leads to an actual fall in total output. Furthermore, we have seen that relative prices are the important factor, and a rise in the price of cereals, for instance, may not increase the supply of cereals for sale if meat prices have undergone a greater rise, since farmers may then feed cereals to livestock or turn some corn-land over to grass. The complexity of the problem may be seen in the following figures from the Argentine. Wheat exports and acreage fell sharply during the war, but the cattle population increased. Wholesale prices of farm products rose, and total agricultural production and food production both increased; this rise in output is the more striking when we notice the recent activities of the Argentine government export

[1] Cf. J. W. F. Rowe, *Markets and Men*, p. 129, on native producers of rubber in Malaya.

monopoly, whose aim has been to discourage agriculture and to promote industrialization.[1]

Agricultural Statistics, Argentine

	Pre-war	1947	1948
Wheat Exports[1]	100	70	65
Wheat Area[2] (million hectares) . .	6·8	4·7	4·9[6]
Cattle[3] (million)	33	41	n.a.
Wholesale prices, Farm products[4] . .	86	161	190 (July)
Agricultural Production[5] . . .	100	102 (46–7)	112 (47–8)
,, ,, (Food)[5] . .	100	101 (46–7)	115 (47–8)

Sources: [1] F.A.O. *World Food Appraisal as of April 1949*, p. 24. Pre-war = 1935–9; [2] F.A.O. *Yearbook of Food and Agricultural Statistics, 1948*, vol. i, 'Production', p. 2. Pre-war = 1934–8; [3] As ([2]), p. 77. Pre-war = 1937; [4] U.N. *Monthly Bulletin of Statistics*, Aug. 1949, p. 173. Includes Forest Products. Pre-war = 1938. (1937 = 100); [5] As ([2]), p. 213. Pre-war = 1935–9; [6] ibid. 1949, p. 32 (unofficial figure).

In view of the general rise in food prices since 1939 the index numbers for food production given in the following table provide little evidence to support an assumption that the total supply curve for food is backward sloping. (Figures for Europe and Asia are not included because of the effects of war.)

Indices of Food Production
(Pre-war = 100)

Country	1946–7	1947–8	Country	1946–7	1947–8
Canada . .	121	116	Uruguay .	94	87
Cuba . .	158	150	Algeria . .	87	86
Mexico . .	131	139	Egypt . .	115	114
U.S.A. . .	138	134	Madagascar .	102	95
Argentine .	101	115	Fr. Morocco .	82	88
Brazil . .	114	115	S. Africa .	104	109
Chile . .	124	121	Australia .	89	108
Peru . .	113	118	N. Zealand .	107	110

Source: F.A.O. *Yearbook of Food and Agricultural Statistics, 1948*, vol. i, 'Production', p. 213.

However, it is still possible that at some level of prices supply reactions are perverse when we consider farm output as a whole. There is general agreement among those who work in this field that statistical supply analysis is in a very embryonic state, and there are good reasons for expecting it to remain so.[2] The most obvious requirements of the *ceteris paribus* clause rarely hold, and adjustments to index numbers do not show us what would have happened had other things remained unchanged. Not only are there movements along curves, but there are shifts of whole schedules; it is often found that in 'follow up' work in a given market at

[1] See N. A. D. Macrae, 'Argentina's Post-War Experiments. I', *The Banker*, Apr. 1949.
[2] See J. M. Cassels and W. Malenbaum, 'Doubts about Statistical Supply Analysis', *J.F.E.*, 1938.

a later date, results are obtained which differ from those obtained in the original investigation, and if a very long period is analysed a change in a complete schedule may have to be postulated.[1] Also, it is impossible to derive a supply schedule extending beyond the range of past prices.

In so far as it is meaningful to speak of a Marshallian supply schedule for particular products, one is tempted to guess that it is of the general shape of the curve shown in Fig. 1. It probably slopes upward to the right in the normal manner, and is more elastic in the middle than at the ends. The supply schedule for farm output as a whole is probably very inelastic, and it shows a marked tendency to shift bodily to the right as a result of technical progress and capital accumulation.

IV

The statistical derivation of demand schedules is, at first sight, a little more convincing than an attempt to construct supply schedules, because, for consumption goods, the response to price changes is not likely to be subject to such long time-lags that a *ceteris paribus* clause is obviously out of place. But the derivation of a long-period demand curve is subject to all the doubts which surround the long-period supply curve.[2]

One could begin to approach the problem by using the same market data relating to prices and quantities as were used in statistical supply analysis, but in this case it would be assumed that the demand curve remained fixed and that it could be traced by fluctuations in supply. But even in a theoretical discussion it is rarely assumed that the quantity coming to market in any period is the only determinant of price in that period, and it is clear that the following factors, at least, must be taken into account:[3]

(a) The value of money—i.e. the inverse of the general price-level.

(b) Money incomes of consumers.

(c) The distribution of income.

(d) Prices of substitutes and complements.

(e) Consumers' tastes.

(f) Expectations of future prices.

Changes in tastes and expectations are not measurable, and if these are important in a period under review the analysis may break down; it is also difficult to include changes in the distribution of income in the analysis.[4]

---

[1] Murray and Cohen, loc. cit., find that before 1914 wheat acreage in the United Kingdom varied with prices two years previously; after 1918 a one-year lag gave the best fit.

[2] H. Schultz, *The Theory and Measurement of Demand*, is the classical work in this field.

[3] Cf. Murray and Cornea, loc. cit.

[4] Mr. A. Loveday has pointed out to me that if a change in tastes is not autonomous, but is associated with some other measurable change such as a shift from manual to non-manual labour, it might be possible to allow for it.

Here we can only attempt a short summary of findings. The late Professor H. Schultz, concentrating on the wholesaler–dealer–farmer demand schedule because consumers rarely buy farm products in an unchanged form, found that, with the possible exceptions of buckwheat and rye, demand was inelastic for the ten commodities studied; and this can be said in spite of there being a large margin of error. Some of the elasticities remained remarkably constant over a very long period.[1]

There is little evidence that, for the whole market in any commodity, demand reactions are perverse, as in the well-known Giffen case.[2] Though for some groups of consumers the income effect of a change in price may outweigh the substitution effect it is unlikely that this will be so for all buyers in a market.[3] The Giffen cases will usually be outweighed by the normal ones, and the net result will probably be a normally inclined market demand schedule.

It is true that Dr. W. Bauer, using family budgets, found that the demand for rye, black bread, and potatoes fell as income increased in Germany; so did the demand for mutton in the lower-income groups, and for pigmeat and minced meat in the higher-income groups.[4] This conclusion, however, refers to income elasticity of demand which must not be confused with the income effects of a change in price; at some levels of income a similar result might be obtained for some manufactured goods such as cheap cars.

Of first-rate importance is the distinction between the final consumers' demand and the derived demand facing the farmer. The farm price of a product is usually only a part of its price to consumers, and many of the costs added in distribution are very inflexible: for example, wages and costing margins[5] are fairly rigid. Fig. 4 shows the relative stability of the costs of distribution of a market basket of farm-produced foods containing quantities equivalent to the 1935–9 annual average purchases per family of three consumers over the period 1916–46 compared with the instability of their farm value. Spectacular economic changes such as the aftermath of war or a major depression were associated with appreciable changes in the margin, but in more normal periods one is impressed with its stability. In every year between 1919 and 1942 the farm value was less than half the retail price, and in 1932 the farm value was less than one-third of the price to the consumer.

The increasing stability of the price of 'wheat' as it passes from farmer to baker to consumer in the form of bread is illustrated in Fig. 5.

[1] Op. cit., p. 556.   [2] Marshall, *Principles*, p. 132.
[3] Cf. J. R. Hicks, *Value and Capital*, pp. 34–5. Professor H. Schultz felt justified in assuming that, when dealing with a large market, the demand curve would be negatively inclined (op. cit., p. 52).   [4] Murray and Cornea, loc. cit.
[5] In the sense used by Mr. P. W. S. Andrews, *Manufacturing Business*, p. 157.

U.S.A. Farm Values and Marketing Margins of Food, 1916–46

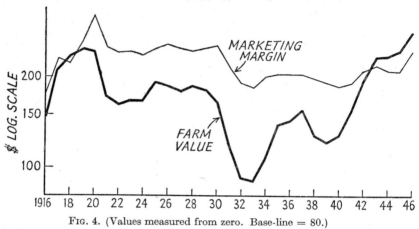

FIG. 4. (Values measured from zero. Base-line = 80.)

Sources: U.S. Dept. of Agriculture, *Agricultural Statistics, 1946,* p. 576; ibid. *1947,* p. 545.

U.S.A. Fluctuations in the Prices of Wheat, Flour, and Bread, 1931–41

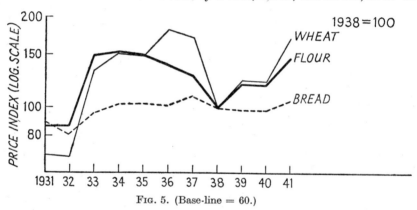

FIG. 5. (Base-line = 60.)

Sources: U.S. Dept. of Agriculture, *Agricultural Statistics, 1942,* pp. 9, 29, 30.

It seems, therefore, that there are some grounds for the hypothesis that the price paid by consumers equals the price received by farmers plus a fairly stable sum. It follows that the elasticity of demand facing the farmer is lower than the final consumers' elasticity of demand,[1] and this is espe-

---

[1] The formal proof of this is as follows:

Let Consumers' price = p; Quantity demanded = q; Merchants' margin = k (a constant)
then

$$\text{Consumers' elasticity of demand} = p/q . dq/dp$$
$$\text{Merchants' ,, ,, ,, } = (p-k)/q . dq/dp$$

because $d(p-k) = dp$.

This is less than consumers' elasticity of demand by $k/q . dq/dp$.

Cf. G. J. Stigler, 'Social Welfare and Differential Prices', *J.F.E.,* 1938.

cially true if the farm product is an industrial raw material such as cotton, wool, or rubber. A given percentage reduction in the farm price of a raw material will cause a much smaller percentage reduction in the price of the finished product, although the percentage increase in the volume sold will, in the simplest case where a single raw material is worked up, be the same for the finished product and the raw material.

This tendency for demand to become more inelastic as it is passed back to the producer may be counteracted if manufacturers and distributors can substitute the farm product for other factors of production. For example, when farm prices are low, it may pay to use raw materials more 'wastefully', and less may be spent on expensive methods of food preservation. It seems probable, however, that a very large reduction in farm prices would be required at any given time for these substitutions to become significant. Although Figs. 4 and 5 are based on United States data, it seems reasonable to suppose that the kind of model they suggest is applicable to a much wider geographical area, and the view that the demand schedule facing the farmer is price inelastic for most products appears to be warranted by the evidence contained in Professor H. Schultz's findings, and by theoretical deductions from our generalization about the manner in which prices paid by consumers are constructed.

V

Although there is little reason to suppose that the supply and demand curves for agricultural products are perversely inclined, the significant sections of both schedules may be inelastic. Fluctuations in effective demand can be pictured as movements of an inelastic demand schedule across an inelastic supply schedule, and cyclical adjustments may therefore be expected to operate through prices rather than through quantities.[1] That this is so is supported by an examination of Fig. 3 (p. 181). Figs. 6 and 7 show that this stability of output combined with fluctuating prices has produced an income for farmers which has been more unstable than the income produced by the relatively stable prices and fluctuating output of the remainder of the economy.

It has been suggested by some writers[2] that variations in farm incomes and the effective demand of farmers may be causally related to the trade cycle, and there is evidence that the downturn in agriculture preceded the crash of 1929. As our graphs show, in the United States the curve of farm income levelled off in 1925, and in Canada there was a sharp downturn

[1] See also F. C. Mills, *Price–Quantity Interactions in Business Cycles*, especially charts on pp. 46 and 47 showing cyclical changes in price and output for several different groups of commodities.

[2] e.g. Lord Beveridge, *Full Employment in a Free Society*, p. 303.

in farm incomes between 1928 and 1929.[1] The upturn in 1932–3 seems to
have been sharper and to have occurred earlier for farmers than for the
remainder of the economy; the graphs also indicate that the cyclical swings
in farm incomes are more violent than the fluctuations in other incomes.

Canada. Farm and Other Incomes, 1926–40

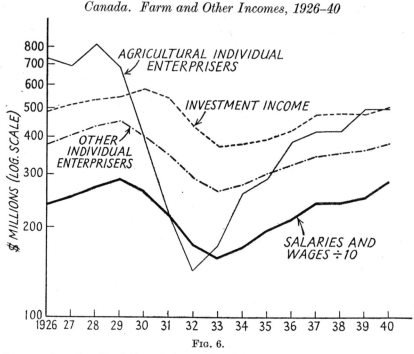

FIG. 6.

Sources: *Canadian Royal Commission on Dominion Provincial Relations*, Appendix 4,
p. 53; Dominion–Provincial Conference, Jan. 1941; *National Income 1937–40* (N.B.
Salaries and Wages to 1/10-scale for comparison.)

The need for caution in using these figures is very obvious; turning-
points are notoriously difficult to place from statistical data, and it would
be foolish to divert attention from the great fluctuations in industrial
investment if we are seeking causes of the cycle.[2]

VI

We pass now to a consideration of the efficiency of the price-system in
securing the kind of output that consumers desire. We shall consider
whether there is reason to suppose that the demands of consumers are con-

---

[1] Cf. League of Nations, *Economic Stability in the Post War World*. The charts on p. 85
confirm the view that for some products of major importance the downturn occurred about
1925, although the willingness of speculators to accumulate stocks at prevailing prices
retarded the decline for a few years.

[2] Cf. W. Arthur Lewis, *Economic Survey 1919–39*, p. 46. See G. Haberler, *Prosperity and
Depression*, chap. 7, for a discussion of agriculture and the business cycle.

U.S.A. Farm and Non-Farm Incomes, 1917–47

FIG. 7.

Sources: U.S. Dept. of Agriculture, *Agricultural Statistics, 1942*, p. 663 for 1917–29 estimates.

Statistical Abstract of the United States, 1948, p. 276, for revised estimates, 1929–47.

Note: The pre-1929 and post-1929 estimates are not comparable. For the years 1929 to 1947 Farm Income has been subtracted from National Income to give Non-Farm Income. Non-Farm Income is shown to 1/10-scale to facilitate comparison.

veyed back to farmers without distortion. More precisely we have to ask whether, in the equilibrium position towards which farmers may be expected to move, a movement of a unit of resources from the production of one farm product to another, or from agriculture to some other occupation, would provide a collection of goods which consumers would value more highly than the collection of goods which is actually produced. Alternatively we can ask if there is reason to believe that consumers would be willing to compensate the producers at any stage in the productive process (in its widest sense) for making some change in the size or composition of their output. Naturally, a precise answer to questions of this kind cannot be expected, but some tentative investigations of them have been made.

One approach to this problem draws heavily upon the work of Mrs. Robinson and Professor Chamberlin.[1] It has already been pointed out that most farm produce passes through the hands of dealers and processors on its way to the consumer. Farmers and consumers are many; dealers and processors are relatively few in any given market. From this general picture of the market structure the buying and selling policies of the middlemen, who are assumed to act in the Chamberlin manner, are deduced. Merchants are faced with a rising farm supply curve (because agriculture is assumed to be an increasing-costs industry) and a falling consumers' demand curve, and this is true of each individual merchant. Purchases and sales are assumed to be adjusted to the point where marginal revenue equals marginal cost, and prices of merchants' services are higher and output lower than the social optimum of welfare economics.

There is some evidence of monopsonistic action on the part of dealers; sales by auction are not free from restrictive practices through prior agreement. Professor W. H. Nicholls cites the case of the 'Big Four' meat packing firms in the United States who maintained an almost constant ratio between their purchases in five terminal markets for several years;[2] and from Canada comes evidence of similar practices affecting several commodities.[3] There is also evidence that a market structure favourable to monopolistic activities is becoming more common with the growth of chains of retail stores with centralized buying departments.[4] Even where there is no evidence of a nation-wide monopoly, localized monopoly power may still cause distortions.

The relative stability of distributors' margins which we have noticed in Section IV also suggests monopolistic action by middlemen; at least they appear to have a conscious price-policy, and this is a concept which is alien to the very formal theory of perfect competition developed by some of Marshall's successors. But the marginal analysis of monopoly does not lead us to expect a stable margin between buying and selling prices for

---

[1] W. H. Nicholls, *Imperfect Competition within Agricultural Industries*, is an example of very thorough analysis on these lines.

[2] Op. cit., p. 4.

[3] Cf. Canadian Royal Commission on Price Spreads, *Report* (Ottawa 1935): 'There was uncontradicted evidence given to us by a former official of Canada Packers, Ltd., that in Toronto it was the usual practice for this firm to arrange with Swifts, before the market opened, as to the prices to be paid for purchases of live stock. Also, the manager of the Western Stock Growers' Association, one of the largest ranchers in Alberta, gave evidence that if a packers' buyer gave an offer for cattle on the ranch, it would not be raised by any other packer-buyer either on the ranch or in the stock yards.' (p. 162.) The *Report* gives other examples of large-scale concerns facing the farmer in industries such as Fertilizers, Flour Milling, Tobacco, Fruit and Vegetable Canning, and Butter. The *Memorandum of Reservations*, pp. 276 ff., should also be noted.

[4] Cf. A. C. Hoffman, 'Changing Organization of Agricultural Markets', *J.F.E.*, 1940.

longer than a planning period, unless the demand and supply schedules are both stable, or unless shifts occur in some systematic fashion. When we observe a margin which appears to be fairly constant over periods of several years, except in very disturbed times such as 1916 to 1921, and 1930 to 1934, we are led to doubt the usefulness of marginal analysis in this problem. If this stability is explained by suggesting that entrepreneurs move towards a point of equilibrium determined by very long-run supply and demand schedules we should expect their buying and selling prices to remain as stable as their margin, but this is clearly not the case.

However we may account for the margin we are faced with the problem of deciding whether there are grounds for believing that it is too large. An excessive margin might not result in any distributor earning abnormally high profits; there might be too many firms in the distributive trades, none of which was large enough to obtain all the economies of scale.[1] But a reduction in the number of dealers might open the way for collusive action to raise the margin. It might be suggested that the number of wholesalers could be limited by a licensing system and their margins by decree; but wholesaling, like all other business, is risky, and it clearly contains an element of speculation, so that unless the community is prepared to bear a part of the risk it is difficult to suggest any method of payment for the services of middlemen other than freedom to fix buying and selling prices.

Mr. Andrews, it may be noted, suggests that wholesalers will only obtain a margin which represents the value of their services to the parties from whom they buy and sell, because, if the margin is greater than this, these parties will be attracted to wholesaling.[2] The parties referred to are manufacturers and retailers, and we have already seen that some large retailers are entering the wholesale trade in farm products; it does not follow that the farm-to-retail price-spread must be reduced by this process. Farmers and consumers could only make a direct attack on excessive margins by co-operative action; there is little reason to suppose that co-operative associations of producers or consumers would not indulge in restrictive practices, unless there were a joint association, and this would simply present a problem in administered prices. We can only conclude that the present methods of distribution may be unsatisfactory in so far as the same services might be performed at a lower cost, but there appears to be no readily available scheme whose superiority is very obvious.

[1] The concept of excess capacity is very vague when we are considering differentiated products, and the services of dealers in farm products are usually differentiated spatially. There may also be differences in the services they perform. This line of thought suggests that a distributor's margin, which is constant in money terms, may be a payment for varying quantities of services at different times. Thus, there is a sense in which the farm-to-retail margin shown in Fig. 4 may be less constant than it appears.

[2] *Manufacturing Business,* p. 179.

Another kind of distortion of consumers' demands has been noticed in the United States cotton market,[1] and it may occur in markets for other products. Small dealers often lack either the facilities or skill to perform grading operations, and they may even be ignorant of the price differences ruling in the terminal markets. Thus the farmer may be paid an average price for his crop as if it were a homogeneous commodity, though prices paid by spinners indicate that, at best, each grade is only a partial substitute for other grades. The farmer may therefore find it most profitable to produce maximum bulk instead of maximum value to the consumer. In cases of this kind there seem to be good reasons for establishing producers' marketing co-operatives which can provide grading facilities, and which are up to date in their knowledge of prices ruling in the terminal markets. Alternatively, public grading stations might be set up in local markets. It should be noted that provision for grading small lots in local markets is not a costless operation—it is one of the services for which dealers are paid—and it is possible that a given output is secured with a smaller expenditure of resources under the present 'inefficient' system than would be the case were some suggested improvements put into operation.

VII

The next question to be considered concerns the allocation of resources between agriculture and the remainder of the economy. This is a problem which has aroused more interest in the United States and in the primary producing countries than in Britain, where it is often taken for granted that the expansion of agriculture will assist in the solution of our balance of payments problem[2] as well as insure a part of our food supply against war or a slump in our export markets.

Much of the discussion has developed around the thesis that the proportion of the total labour force engaged in agriculture is much larger than is economically justified.[3] By this is meant, apparently, that there is evidence that the marginal private and social net product of labour in agriculture is lower than in other sectors of the economy; if this is so, it follows that a movement of labour from agriculture to some other employment in which its marginal product is higher would increase the real

---

[1] Cf. B. Youngblood, 'Analysis of the Relation of Quality to Price of Cotton', and A. B. Cox, 'Relation of Price and Quality of Cotton', *J.F.E.*, 1929, pp. 525 and 542 respectively.

[2] Cf. Cmd. 7072 (Mar. 1947), *Post War Contribution of British Agriculture to the Saving of Foreign Exchange*, and the *Agriculture Act, 1947*. For an interesting examination of the problem see C. H. Blagburn, 'Import-Replacement by British Agriculture', *E.J.*, March 1950, and E. A. G. Robinson and R. L. Harris, 'The Use of Home Resources to Save Imports', ibid.

[3] Many of the subsequent arguments in this section have been suggested by Professor T. W. Schultz's book, *Agriculture in an Unstable Economy*, and by its critics.

national income and raise incomes per head for those remaining on farms.

Two quotations will serve as a starting-point for the discussion. Dr. Kuznets, referring to the United States, writes: 'In agriculture, income per employed is half that in all industries combined.'[1] Mr. Colin Clark, after examining the statistics for several countries, says: 'It may be deduced that the situation is fairly stable when the agricultural worker is receiving something between a third and a half of the average income of secondary and tertiary producers.'[2] If we can assume that, in a competitive industry, such as agriculture, the wage will be approximately equal to the value of the marginal product of family labour or hired labour, and that in other sectors of the economy the wage will not be greater than the value of the marginal product, it follows that the ratio between marginal productivities will be at least as great as the ratio between wages. The marginal productivity of labour in agriculture must therefore be only about a half of its marginal productivity in industry. Hence a movement of labour from agriculture to other sectors would increase the national product and raise farm income per head.

This view has been adversely criticized on several grounds.

To begin with, it has been pointed out that the theory of perfect competition does not support the view that either wage rates or earnings in different occupations will tend to equality; the theory is satisfied when the net advantages of labour are equal. It is true that in taking non-measurable psychic satisfactions into account we remove the possibility of getting statistical evidence as to whether an existing situation could be improved, but the argument does draw attention to the possibility that labour remains in agriculture because it wishes to remain there, and the rest of the community may be compensated through having better terms of trade with agriculture than would otherwise be the case.

It has also been suggested that the difference between earnings in agriculture and earnings elsewhere is probably less serious than the available statistics show. Firstly, it is argued, the alternatives open to an agricultural worker between the wars were not 'employment in agriculture' as against 'employment elsewhere'. He could either have been a member of the agricultural labour force, in which case he would probably have been employed, or he could have been a member of the industrial labour force, in which case he would have run a high risk of unemployment. If we make the very favourable assumption that a newcomer to the factory labour force would have had the same chance of employment as an established factory worker, it seems reasonable to compare the average earnings of the

[1] S. Kuznets, *National Income. A Summary of Findings*, p. 7.
[2] Colin Clark, *The Economics of 1960*, p. 37.

farm labour force with the average earnings of the non-farm labour force. Because of the lower rate of unemployment in agriculture, farm incomes compare much more favourably on this basis.[1]

When payments in kind to farm workers are taken into account the gap is even less formidable; and when it is pointed out that the comparisons are often based on wage statistics for the more highly paid industrial employments because they are most accessible, there is a suspicion that further investigation might lead us to doubt whether there is any discrepancy to be explained.[2]

It must be borne in mind that much of the data used in this discussion relates to slump conditions in the inter-war years, and, as Lord Keynes pointed out, the classical theory of the distribution of resources is only fully applicable in conditions of full employment.[3] There is no doubt that, given a positive marginal productivity of labour in agriculture, the real national income is increased by the employment on farms of labour which would otherwise be unemployed, though the distribution of that income may be such that total farm income is lower than it would be were some farmers unemployed. This last possibility arises from the belief that the price elasticity of demand for farm products is less than unity. These considerations cast doubts on the wisdom of a policy of encouraging labour to leave farms during periods of agricultural depression which coincide with periods of heavy unemployment elsewhere. Those who remained in farm employment would be better off as a result of the migration, but it is highly probable that the rest of the community would be worse off, and it is impossible to make even a crude estimate of the balance of advantage that would result from applying the compensation principle of the welfare economists.

There was, however, a large net migration of labour from farms between the wars. This seems to prove that, in the minds of those who alone were qualified to estimate the net advantages of membership of one labour force or the other, the verdict went against agriculture, and this equilibrating movement can be used as evidence of the existence of a disequilibrium. Even in theoretical analysis the passage from one position of equilibrium to another is assumed to take time, but we usually postulate only a single initial disturbance and rule out the possibility of additional disturbances during the transition period by inserting a *ceteris paribus* clause. In the real world 'other things' rarely, if ever, remain unchanged for very long,

[1] Cf. C. Kaysen and J. H. Lorie, 'A Note on Professor Schultz's Analysis of the Long Run Agricultural Problem', *Review of Economics and Statistics*, Nov. 1948. Also T. W. Schultz, 'A Comment', in the same issue.

[2] Cf. Kaysen and Lorie, loc. cit. Also J. S. Davis, 'American Agriculture: Schultz' Analysis and Policy Proposals', *Review of Economic Statistics*, May 1947. Also T. W. Schultz, 'A Note . . .' in the same issue.

[3] *General Theory*, p. 378.

and we have to picture a modern economy as moving towards equilibrium positions which change before they are reached, so that we never find an equilibrium position existing in fact. This, of course, does not imply that equilibrium analysis is uninformative, but it does suggest that the mere persistence of a migration of labour over a long period of time is not in itself a ground for criticism of the economic system which produces it.

The question of whether such a movement of labour should be stimulated or left to take its natural course then arises. Returning to a more static type of analysis, we can say that anything which hastens the transition from one equilibrium position to another is economically desirable, provided that the action taken to stimulate the change does not alter the second position of equilibrium.[1] It is almost impossible to conceive of such a policy being implemented without the use of some resources. Thus a movement which set out from position 1 and which would have proceeded to position 2, may be deflected to position 2a, and we are left with the difficult problem of deciding in any given case whether it is desirable that position 2a should be reached more quickly than position 2. In practice, broad decisions of policy may not be difficult because positions 2 and 2a may be very similar and both of them very different from position 1, but the details of the action to be taken may pose the problem of deciding between positions 2a, 2b, ... 2n.

There are two considerations which make the discussion in the preceding paragraph of small practical importance. Firstly it seems that agricultural prices, and hence agricultural incomes, may be very closely dependent on industrial activity. Thus differences in income between agriculture and the rest of the economy are especially marked during depressions. Secondly, net migration from farms was reduced and in some parts of the world reversed during the slump. Given that these statements are generally true, it follows that a high level of employment in the non-agricultural sectors would make the need for a policy to accelerate migration from farms less apparent than in the 1930's. The gap, if any, between farm and non-farm incomes would be narrowed because effective demand for farm products would be maintained, and the existence of alternative employment would act as a spur to migration from agriculture.

Migration from primary industries, such as agriculture, to secondary and tertiary industries is, of course, a normal feature of economic progress. That the price system has provided incentives to these transfers is to be listed among its virtues, and given a high level of non-farm employment the transition may not be accompanied by serious agricultural distress.

[1] Cf. A. C. Pigou, *Economics of Welfare*, p. 169: 'If we suppose ourselves starting from a position of equilibrium and imagine *any* relative variation of demand to occur as between two occupations, until the appropriate transfer of productive resources has taken place the national dividend must fall below its maximum.'

Farm labour was not alone in its misfortunes between the wars; in Britain, for example, coalminers were probably held in the mines because of lack of alternative employments. Within the advanced countries the problem of transference appears to be surmountable if some measure of success is achieved with full employment policies, but the situation may continue to be serious in backward countries where national boundaries constitute an obstacle to labour migration from agriculture to industry unless international movements of goods are very freely permitted.[1]

We turn now to a view which, if true, suggests a more serious maldistribution of resources than that outlined above, because the distortion is likely to prove more permanent. The argument, though referred to in much of the literature, does not appear to have been very fully developed.

Industries are envisaged as lying along a scale of degrees of monopoly.[2] At one end is agriculture, perfectly competitive; at the other end are the highly monopolized industries, such as iron and steel. The monopolized industries through their price and output policy restrict their own employment of factors, and their labour force also tends to be highly organized into trade unions in order to exploit a monopolistic position. Thus the supply of factors of production seeking employment in the competitive sectors of the economy is increased, and their price reduced, without a corresponding reduction in the price of factors which succeed in finding a place in the monopolized sectors. The competitive sectors of the economy become a refuge for units of resources excluded from employment elsewhere; of these competitive sectors agriculture is one of the largest, and of the resources affected labour is probably the most important.

It seems to follow that to break up monopolies of all kinds would both increase the national income (by permitting factors to move out of agriculture where their marginal productivity is low into industries where their marginal productivity is higher) and bring about a more equal distribution of income. Both of these results would be generally accepted as desirable. But even if 'trust busting' produced a more equal distribution of income it would not necessarily raise the real income per head of any part of the population if the real national income were reduced because economies of scale were lost. And if the wholesale dissolution of monopolies is ruled out on these grounds, 'trade union busting' would not necessarily lead to desirable results if it resulted in each large employer being faced

[1] Here it is of interest to quote the Fourth Annual Report of the International Bank for Reconstruction and Development (1948–9): 'Perhaps the most striking single lesson which the Bank has learned in the course of its operations is how limited is the capacity of the under-developed countries to absorb capital quickly for really productive purposes', p. 8. The reasons given include: low level of education and health, administrative inefficiency, limited domestic resources and technical knowledge.

[2] Cf. J. K. Galbraith, 'Supply and Price Adjustment in Agriculture', *J.F.E.*, 1939.

with a rising supply curve of labour instead of a supply curve which was perfectly elastic at the negotiated wage; Fig. 8 illustrates the point. Given an employer's demand curve for labour, DD, and a competitive supply schedule of labour, LL, with a corresponding marginal wage cost schedule MM, employment will be OA at the wage AP. If now a trade union succeeds in negotiating a wage OT at which the employer can get as much or as little labour as he wishes, employment will increase to OC and the

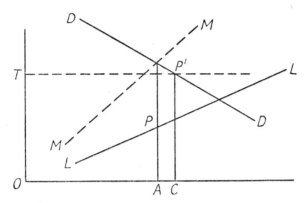

Fig. 8. (DD is a schedule of marginal value productivity of labour.)

wage will rise from AP to CP'. Thus, there may be an advantage to farmers in facing two sets of monopolies instead of one.

A modified form of 'trust busting' might, however, appear to offer a solution. Instead of breaking a monopoly into innumerable businesses which might act competitively but which would lose the economies of scale, an attempt might be made to reduce the degree of monopoly by breaking each monopolistic concern into a few businesses, each of which would be large enough to achieve all the economies of scale[1] open to the original monopoly, although the demand schedule for each new firm's product would be more elastic than the demand schedule for the product of the monopoly. A ban on the 'closed shop' might be enforced at the same time to reduce the amount of labour thrust on to farms.[2] Thus there would be less scope for the exploitation of agriculture in a monopolistic sense.

The outcome of such a policy might be to substitute a group of oligopolists for a monopolist, and these might engage in competition through selling costs rather than through price reductions. In at least one case in the United States this seems actually to have happened. When the Tobacco

[1] If economies of scale become less easy to achieve when a very large scale has already been reached, it should be possible to do this with very big concerns. Cf. P. W. S. Andrews, *Manufacturing Business*, p. 136.
[2] The political difficulties of these policies are ignored here.

Trust was dissolved in 1911 three separate concerns were formed, advertising expenditure soared, and selling organizations were duplicated.[1] As
Professor Nicholls points out, the possibility of reducing costs and prices
may often provide a motive for monopolistic combination.

Thus, two apparently promising approaches to a solution of the problem
of whether the existing distribution of resources might be improved fail us.
This is an indication of the immense amount of theoretical and empirical
work which still remains to be done rather than a reason for despairing
of economic analysis.

VIII

The 'problem of agriculture' is very largely bound up with economic
progress; one of the principal stands in the history of the Industrial
Revolution is the freeing of resources from the land for use elsewhere. We
therefore pass to a short section on relative rates of growth in different
sectors of the economy.

Here Professor Schultz suggests an approach which appears to be promising.[2] The theoretical argument is, in outline, as follows: given that the
existing distribution of resources is at an optimum (which implies that
there is no involuntary unemployment), and that there is a secular growth
of the national product due to the accumulation of capital and technical
progress, it may be concluded that, in order to maintain an optimum
distribution of resources, industries should expand at rates determined by
the income elasticity of demand for their product. That is, expansion
should be such that the composition of the increment in output will be
that which consumers will wish to buy with the increment in income.

Family-budget studies indicate that the income elasticity of demand for
many farm products is much lower than the income elasticity of demand
for the products of secondary and tertiary industries.[3] Thus, unless the
rate of expansion of output of secondary and tertiary industries is much
greater than the rate of expansion of agricultural output, the terms of
trade will tend to move against agriculture. In this case there would be
some incentive towards automatic readjustment, because farm labour
would tend to seek employment elsewhere. But there may be a demand
from agriculture for assistance, and if aid takes the form of diverting some
government investment into farming while consumers are still trying to
bid factors of production away from the land, the process of adjustment
will be prolonged, because both the previous excess of resources devoted

---

[1] Example quoted by W. H. Nicholls, op. cit., pp. 64–6.

[2] T. W. Schultz, *Agriculture in an Unstable Economy*, pp. 113 et seq.

[3] Professor Schultz, loc. cit., suggests that industries be classified according to the income
elasticity of demand for their products.

to farming and the increment due to State policy will have to be attracted away from agriculture through the operation of the price-mechanism.

If we consider a single advanced country in which there is an upward secular trend in farm output, it may appear unlikely that tertiary production will expand at a sufficiently large multiple of this rate to maintain a balance. One may, therefore, be tempted to argue that programmes of agricultural expansion are a step in the wrong direction. But many important farm prices are affected by world trade, and the industrialization of backward areas may produce an increase in output of manufactures which will tend to turn the terms of trade in favour of agriculture; successful employment policies will also make for a high level of manufacturing output, and a sustained demand for farm products. Mr. Colin Clark, writing in 1941, ventured to predict that by 1960 'the terms of trade for primary produce will improve by as much as 90% from the average level of 1925-34'.[1] Few of us have the courage to make explicit predictions of this kind, but some prediction about the future terms of trade is implicit in any programme for expanding any part of the economy. In the nineteenth century private investors were required to make forecasts of this nature for a multitude of small-scale enterprises. Now that governments make themselves responsible for the direction of so much economic activity and usually intervene on a very large scale, it may be more important that these implied predictions should be made explicit.

IX

Having outlined some of the chief economic problems of agriculture we turn now to some of the attempts which have been made to solve them. Frequently in the past it seems to have been thought that the monopolization of farming was an appropriate counterweight to the monopolization of other industries, and there were attempts both by governments and by private groups to apply this kind of remedy. To most economists the only satisfactory justification for the creation of a monopoly is a belief that the fullest economies of scale cannot be obtained by any other form of organization,[2] but in the inter-war years, before Keynsian proposals for maintaining effective demand had become an accepted part of government policy, the problem of agricultural instability was often tackled as a salvage operation designed to raise the incomes of a depressed section of the community. Because of this, price-maintenance through restriction of output was openly accepted as the chief aim of policy, and economies of scale were not even desired. Given that the demand for farm products is

[1] Colin Clark, *Economics of 1960*, p. 52.
[2] Cf. Marshall, *Principles*, Bk. V, ch. xiv, sec. 5. Also D. A. E. Harkness, *Proceedings of the International Conference of Agricultural Economists*, Fourth Conference, 1936, pp. 39 ff.

inelastic against price, restriction of output is, of course, a method of increasing farm revenues from their sale.

But the more spectacular restriction schemes failed for a variety of reasons.[1] For example, a bumper crop could flood storage capacity; all producers could not be brought within the scope of the schemes, so that those who restricted their output were often merely providing non-participating foreigners with a larger share of the market; technical progress caused an unmanageable increase in supplies, and so on.

Greater success, where success means supporting farm incomes, appears to have been obtained by national restriction schemes in the importing countries. In Britain, for example, various parts of the industry were turned into legal monopolies run by committees of producers, and outside disruption was avoided by the use of such protective devices as import quotas and tariffs. An estimation of the wider effects of these policies is a very complex task. Presumably they did something to relieve rural distress in Britain, but it is possible that the natural protection which transport costs gave to British agriculture was an important reason why the agricultural depression in Britain was less severe than it was in other parts of the world. If British farm incomes were raised as a result of the restrictions they can be said to have helped to maintain the effective demand of home producers, but it seems that this could only be at the expense of the incomes and effective demand of farmers in the exporting countries whose produce was kept off the British market—unless, like the Danish bacon producers, they could combine to exploit their quota. And if the policies were effective in raising farm incomes they must have depressed the real incomes of the urban unemployed by preventing food prices from falling farther than they actually did fall. All this is an illustration of the general difficulty of analysing the goodness or badness of attempts to redistribute income in periods of general unemployment.

In the exporting countries the problem was much more serious, and an attempt to evaluate the results of the policies adopted is much more complex. In the United States, for example, government agencies were set up which guaranteed a minimum price for some important crops, restricted their acreage, and undertook the storage of surpluses.[2] It is doubtful whether acreage restrictions were effective in controlling output because the permitted acreage may have been cultivated more intensively, and the land which ceased to grow say, wheat, was often turned over to the production of a close substitute for wheat—e.g. a fodder crop of some kind. And though the agencies raised prices when they were buying they de-

---

[1] J. W. F. Rowe, op. cit., has provided the most readable brief account of these schemes.
[2] For a more adequate discussion of United States policies see G. S. Shepherd, *Agricultural Price Policy*.

pressed them when they were selling, so that it is not certain whether farm incomes over the whole period were raised or depressed. Writing of these schemes Professor J. S. Davis says that the picture of unrelieved gloom between the wars is false, and that the two real depressions were preceded and followed by reasonably prosperous years for people on farms. Later in the same article he writes: 'I know of no commodity in the inter-war period in which protracted persistence of abnormally heavy supplies and really depressed prices was not due primarily to government policies restricting its flow, holding down its absorption, and stimulating its production.'[1] Coming from the head of the Food Research Institute this criticism carries a good deal of weight, though we should note that opinions are not unanimous.

Turning to recent proposals for maintaining stability of farm incomes, we find that the League of Nations has recommended the creation of Buffer Stocks whose governors would enter the market as buyers or sellers when prices reached certain minima or maxima which could be varied from time to time. Thus the range of prices would be narrowed, as fluctuations in the price of gold are narrowed under the gold standard. At first sight the proposal looks promising, but some doubts as to its efficacy have been expressed. When one considers the costs of storage over periods of years, the danger that at some point an agency may run out of stocks or run out of cash, and the difficulty of arranging international finance for the scheme, it is seen that there are many problems in addition to the difficulty of reconciling the views of producers and consumers on price policy.[2]

It might be thought that a farmer could hedge his price by selling his crops forward in the futures markets, where these exist, and thus use a 'buffer stock scheme' which is already operated by private enterprise. There appears to be one overwhelming objection to this, apart from the fact that few farmers have contact with a futures market, or could offer a minimum parcel if they did.[3] The trader who sells forward is usually selling a commodity which he already possesses, but the farmer would be selling something which he hoped to possess at a later date. In the event of a bad harvest the spot price might rise above the price at which he had sold his futures, and the farmer would find himself with a small crop which he was committed to sell at a 'normal' price; in addition to this he would run the risk of having to buy at a high spot price in order to fulfil his

---

[1] J. S. Davis, 'American Agriculture: Schultz' Analysis and Policy Proposals', *Review of Economic Statistics*, May 1947, p. 87.

[2] I am indebted to Mr. R. S. Porter of Nuffield College for several discussions of his thesis on Buffer Stocks. For a more adequate discussion see his article in *Oxford Economic Papers*, Vol. 2, No. 1, 1950

[3] They could combine to offer minimum parcels. See J. C. Clendenin, 'Federal Crop Insurance in Operation', *Wheat Studies* (Stanford), March 1942.

futures contract. Thus a farmer could only hedge with safety the price of a quantity equal to his most pessimistic crop forecast. There is no way of removing the risk of price fluctuations from everybody's shoulders; it can either be shared between farmers and private speculators, or it can be borne by the community through devices such as buffer-stock agencies. There may, of course, be very good reasons for sharing the risks by these or other means.

Even if there are serious difficulties in removing price uncertainty, it seems that uncertainties about yield should prove amenable to an insurance solution. The risks are largely fortuitous, and the standard yield could be adjusted to allow for secular changes. Several schemes have been tried, but none so far with financial success.[1] The chief reasons for failure were as follows.

To underwrite the *value* of a crop is to accept a risk both on yield and on price. With cyclical price movements of great magnitude claims are almost inevitable at some stage in the downswing, but there is no compensating increase in premiums when prices are rising. It seems that no agency has ever felt able to charge premiums sufficiently high to cover this risk.

The alternative is to underwrite the *physical yield* of a crop, and this was attempted in the United States Federal Crop Insurance Act of 1938, which confined the cover to the yield of wheat. The actuarial basis was the preceding ten years' average yield on the individual farm and either 50 or 75 per cent. of this could be insured, though in practice the 50 per cent. cover was rarely used. Premiums and claims were payable in wheat or its current cash equivalent so that price movements were not among the risks covered, and lack of normal care disqualified claimants from benefit. The principal object of the scheme was to ensure that farmers at least recovered their working capital each year.

The difficulties encountered were bound up with adverse selection of risks and administrative costs. In the early years insurance benefits acted as a subsidy to marginal land, and, though in the course of time the practice of planting wheat in unsuitable soil would pull down the ten-year average for a farm, the practice led to losses at first. Other causes of loss were found in the practice of farmers who only insured their crop in years when they expected a poor yield, and in this these farmers were helped by late season insurance which enabled them to decide whether or not to insure after seeding conditions and even germination were known. Thus, the scheme was burdened with a high proportion of bad risks at the start; it was also found that premiums which were loaded to cover administrative

---

[1] On crop insurance see F. Arcoleo, 'Crop Insurance', *International Review of Agriculture*, Part II (Agricultural Economics and Sociology), 1940. Also J. C. Clendenin, loc. cit.

costs were usually too high to be attractive. In addition to these difficulties it is suspected that it is often the farmer who is financially insecure who prefers to bear the risks of yield himself. The scheme has been continued on an experimental basis since 1948, but enough has been said to show that a self-supporting method of insurance is very difficult to devise in this field.

. . . .

The limitations of this essay are shown by the topics which have not been mentioned, as well as by the sketchy treatment of those which have received some attention. Among the neglected subjects are included the supply of capital to the industry (farming seems to suffer from the Macmillan gap); the supply and utilization of special skills and abilities (managerial ability without capital behind it has few opportunities on farms); the question of tenant right which is still a possible barrier to improvement in some parts of the world; and the problems of family and subsistence farming. We have seen that there are many respects in which the operation of the price mechanism in agriculture is unsatisfactory, but we have also seen that the remedies are not without their own drawbacks. The one fairly clear conclusion that emerges is that agricultural problems are closely connected with those encountered in other parts of the economy and cannot be treated satisfactorily in isolation.

VI

THE RESPONSE OF LABOUR TO ECONOMIC INCENTIVES

(i) *The Results of Empirical Studies 1936–9*

By HERBERT W. ROBINSON

1. Introduction

ADJUSTMENT of the amounts of labour in different occupations and areas in order to correct disequilibria presents, perhaps, the most difficult of all the problems of optimum economic change. Labour is a unique factor of production, completely unlike raw materials, machinery, and buildings. Disregarding for the moment international migration, the total population, and therefore the total number of potential workers, cannot be changed rapidly; changes in birth and death rates are governed by complex economic, social, and physiological factors, and, even when they occur, produce results only after the lapse of many years. It is true that the proportion of the population willing to work for remuneration may change more rapidly, but usually such changes occur only under extreme economic or social pressures like depression or war. Disequilibria in the distribution of a factor such as a raw material can be ameliorated both by redistribution of available supplies and by adjustments in the total production of such raw material. And even though buildings cannot be moved from one area to another (though this is occasionally done over short distances in the United States), at least it is possible to concentrate new construction in those areas requiring buildings. But correction of dis-equilibria in the labour market is much more exclusively a matter of redistributing the existing labour force industrially, geographically, or both. Furthermore, a human being has, at any given time, a set of parti-cular abilities, certain attitudes towards his environment, including resistance to change, and, more important, is part of a family and a local community. He requires living accommodation and a host of ancillary services wherever he is located. While his ability to learn may make him, within limits, a flexible factor of production, his other characteristics make his response to economic stimuli a complex and unpredictable phenome-non, particularly when a change of occupation or area is involved. Finally, labour is at the same time the consumer, and, whenever the worker's income or location is changed, so, to some extent, is the structure of demand. A comprehensive empirical study of the working of the price (or wage) mechanism in the case of the labour market would, therefore, have very wide ramifications.

The studies made at the Oxford University Institute of Statistics by a group of research workers[1] in the years 1936–9 were complementary to work already done by numerous other workers in the same or allied fields (see the Bibliography given on p. 243). The group concentrated on only a few of the problems connected with the labour market; namely, those pertaining to migration of labour between areas and industries as a means of reducing unemployment in Great Britain. The economic waste and human misery caused by the high level of unemployment in the thirties, and its concentration in the 'depressed areas', were, of course, responsible for this emphasis. Moreover, Oxford was itself a rapidly growing industrial city and presented unusual opportunities for studying, at first hand, the movements of workers from depressed areas, and even the case-histories of individual migrants themselves. Apart from chapters contributed to the *Survey of Social Services in the Oxford District*, the results of the work were published in a series of articles in the *Oxford Economic Papers* and the *Sociological Review*. Three of the articles, by Makower, Marschak, and Robinson, entitled 'Studies in Mobility of Labour', described efforts aimed at developing methods of measuring both spatial and industrial 'mobility' of labour, and at relating variations in mobility to economic factors such as the state of trade, the type of unemployment, sex, age, skill, and so forth. Another three articles, by Daniel, gave the results of a more intense study of individual migrants to Oxford, made with the object of ascertaining the psychological factors influencing spatial migration and the demographic effects of migration on the losing and gaining areas. The studies as a whole were intended to throw light on the problems of depressed areas and industries, the duration of adjustments in the labour market, and, if possible, to help assess the importance of administrative measures bearing on training and transfer of labour.

The present chapter is a summary of the three 'Studies in Mobility of Labour' and their findings, supplemented by some of the conclusions reached by Daniel. It consists of three sections: first, a brief description of the material used; second, a description of the various statistical concepts and measurements evolved; and, finally, the findings of the statistical calculations and tests applied. Since it is only a summary the reader is referred to the original articles for more detailed explanations of the sources, limitations, and manipulations of the data, the assumptions underlying the methods used, and the proofs of statistical formulae.

[1] The group consisted of E. Ackroyd, G. H. Daniel, H. Makower, J. Marschak, and H. W. Robinson, assisted by S. Moos. Dr. J. Marschak, then Director of the Oxford University Institute of Statistics, was responsible for the overall direction and co-ordination of the studies.

2. The Material Used

The value of the studies lies very largely in the fact that extreme care was taken to collect data from all possible sources—local (i.e. Oxford) and national, private and official—and that it was standardized and refined as far as the ingenuity of the research workers and the reliability of the data would allow. And since similar measurements and techniques were applied to data obtained from several independent sources, it was possible to check and re-check the validity of the conclusions reached, and assess the precision of the statistical coefficients derived. The material used is described briefly below.

Migration into Oxford

Material A: In July 1936, by permission of the Ministry of Labour, an examination was made of all the unemployment insurance books exchanged at the Oxford Employment Exchange at the annual countrywide exchange of books. Particulars were taken of any 'foreigner (i.e. a worker who had first entered the insurance system in a place other than Oxford) including the place where the worker had entered insurance (office of origin), sex, age, and the industries to which he was attached in July 1935 and in July 1936. Out of a total insured population in Oxford of 32,202, there were 11,055 such 'foreigners' who must have migrated to Oxford, either directly or by way of other areas in Great Britain, between 1921, when the insurance system started, and 1936.

Material B: In order to obtain data on half-yearly migration into Oxford during the period July 1933 to June 1937 an examination was made of the 'Claims Register' in the Oxford Employment Exchange. When an immigrant first applies for unemployment benefits in a city a collection of insurance documents, called his 'claim unit', must be transferred from the office where he last registered as unemployed to the new office; the Claims Register contains records of all such claim units transferred. A 50 per cent. sample was taken for each half-year, and particulars noted as to the office at which the immigrant had last claimed unemployment benefits. Since, considering the whole period, the geographical distribution by counties of the sample of transferred claim units was similar to that of the 'foreigners' obtained in Material A (the correlation coefficient was 0·86), it was regarded as a satisfactory sample of immigrants into Oxford from each county in Great Britain. In using the material, however, it was borne in mind that transferred claim units excluded those of immigrants who had no occasion to claim unemployment benefits, and that the sampling factor therefore depended upon the rate of unemployment among immigrants in the particular half-year concerned. The total number in the sample was 4,677, indicating that claim units transferred in the period totalled 9,354.

Material C: In November 1937 Daniel made a sample of all the claim units on file in the Oxford Employment Exchange and found 6,460 belonging to 'foreigners'. Since, in July 1937, the total number of 'foreigners' was 11,860, it was evident that only about 55 per cent. of all the insured immigrants coming to Oxford had been recorded in the Claims Register and, therefore, in Material B above. Furthermore, it showed that much less than 70 per cent. of the migrants who had become unemployed in Oxford between July 1933 and June 1937 had remained there until the end of that period. A claim unit gives the office of origin and up-to-date information, dating back to five years before the claimant first sought benefit or assistance, about his unemployment and industrial history. It also includes data on age, date of marriage, date of birth of the claimant's wife, and date and place of birth of his dependants. It is possible to reconstruct from the claim unit the incidence and length of the claimant's spells of unemployment, location and occupational nature of such spells, and his movements within the country. Daniel took three samples: (a) 390 claim units representing one in every 24 men who first entered insurance in Oxford and had remained in Oxford (Oxford Natives), (b) 600 claim units representing one in every two men who first entered insurance in Wales but had lodged claims in Oxford (Oxford Welshmen), and (c) 450 claim units representing one in every 1,200 men who first entered insurance in Wales and were still in the areas covered by three Welsh Employment Exchanges[1] visited by Daniel (Welsh Natives). In addition, Daniel personally interviewed 60 'Oxford Welshmen', selected at random, to collect information relating to changes in the migrants' economic and housing conditions, and changes in their interests and use of leisure. Moreover, he inquired into their difficulties in adjusting themselves to life in their new home, their attitude to Oxford and Oxford people, and their views on family limitation and marriage.

Spatial Migration in Great Britain

Material D: From the Registrar-General's estimates of local 'resident' populations in each county at 30 June each year, annual estimates were made of the net migration to or from each county in Great Britain from 1923 to 1936.[2] They measured the gross inflow of persons of both sexes and all ages into any county *minus* the gross outflow of all persons from that county to all other areas, i.e. the net balance resulting from move-

[1] The three offices were Ammanford, Ferndale, and Maesteg. Claim units were selected from these offices in proportions of 1:4:4 to correspond to the geographical distribution of the offices of origin of the Oxford Welshmen.

[2] For the method of calculation see *Oxford Economic Papers*, No. 2, pp. 71–2.

ments both within the national area and between Great Britain and other countries. The figures were then corrected for international migration in order to obtain annual estimates of internal migration alone.

Material E: In July 1937 the Ministry of Labour made a 2 per cent. sample of all unemployment books exchanged in Great Britain. For each book the office of origin and the office at which the book was exchanged in July 1937 were recorded. The Ministry had already published[1] an analysis of the sample giving simultaneously the Division of origin and the Division in which the books were exchanged. They also generously supplied the group with an analysis by separate counties which enabled us to obtain, for any two counties A and B, the net movements by July 1937 of A-men to B and of B-men to A, and, by subtraction, the net flow between the two counties.

Inter-Industrial Migration in Great Britain

Material F: Statistics are published regularly by the Ministry of Labour relating to transfers from and to the coal-mining industry for each other industry; these made it possible to obtain statistics of net transfers of coal-miners (i.e. the number entering a new industry *less* the number returning from that industry to coal-mining).

Material G: The annual statistics of persons insured against unemployment in each industry were used to calculate a measure of the movement from any individual industry to all the others. For any period this measure was simply the number of insured in the industry at the beginning of the period multiplied by the difference between the percentage growth of industry as a whole and the percentage growth in the industry concerned; i.e. the movement between industries would be regarded as zero if every industry expanded by the same percentage. The measure gives the *net redistribution* of workers among industries, taking account of the effects of recruitment, retirement, death, and migration between industries. In order to reduce the amount of statistical work, the 105 industries into which the Ministry of Labour places insured workers were arranged in order of percentage increase from 1927 to 1937 and a stratified sample of 24 industries selected for analysis.

3. Basic Concepts and Definitions

The basic concept of the studies is *mobility*. It is assumed that though some individuals may move between occupations and between areas for purely fortuitous reasons, human beings in the mass make such movements in order to improve their economic position; and the 'mobility' of a given group of workers, however the group may be defined, can thus

---

[1] *Ministry of Labour Gazette*, Aug. and Sept. 1938.

be conceived of as the proportion of their number who actually migrate in response to a given economic stimulus, operating during a given period of time. Other things being equal, the economic stimulus is obviously dependent upon the size of the occupation or area to which the group is attracted (since there are obviously more chances for a single individual to obtain employment in a large occupation or area than in a small one), and upon the difference in the well-being or prosperity of the workers as a whole in the receiving occupation or area. The 'other things' which are assumed equal are, of course, distance of movement involved, difficulty of assimilation into the particular occupation or area, and any other factors which determine the discomfort and cost of making the change.

Coefficient of Mobility

If a is the population (working or total) of an occupation or area A, b the population of an occupation or area B, and M_{ab} the number of persons moving from A to B, we can say that

$$\frac{M_{ab}}{a} = \lambda_{ab} f(b, V_{ab}), \tag{1}$$

where λ_{ab} is defined as the *coefficient of mobility of the population of A with respect to B* and f is some function of the size b and V_{ab}, the relative prosperity of the occupation or area B to that of A. Of course, we might go farther and say that

$$\lambda_{ab} = \lambda_a \phi(\alpha_b, \beta_b, \gamma_b, \&c.), \tag{2}$$

where λ_a is the fundamental *coefficient of mobility* of the population of A with respect to any occupation or area, and ϕ is some function of α_b, β_b, &c., the various deterrent factors such as distance, difficulty of economic assimilation, characterizing B. Accordingly, equation (1) may be written

$$\frac{M_{ab}}{a} = \lambda_a . \phi(\alpha_b, \beta_b, \&c.) . f(b, V_{ab}). \tag{3}$$

If, therefore, for many occupations and areas such as B, we had sufficient quantitative data regarding M_{ab} and the remaining variables, as well as definite knowledge of the forms of the functions ϕ and f, we could determine statistically the fundamental 'coefficient of mobility' λ_a of the population A.

In practice the data limited the practical possibilities, and we were never able to estimate λ_a. But by various statistical processes it was possible to find λ_{ab} and even to ascertain approximately the part some of the deterrent factors α, β, &c., played in determining it. It was necessary, of course, to take account of the fact that movement of labour in response to a given economic stimulus does not, in general, occur instantaneously

P

but over a period of time, so that the migration in a given period is a function of the economic stimuli in each of several preceding periods.

It should be noted that the above general formulae could be applied to gross movements from depressed to prosperous areas as well as from prosperous to depressed areas. In such cases, however, f is a decreasing function of V_{ab} and, of course, the coefficients of mobility apply to different populations. Net migration between two areas could obviously be related also to the same variables by the use of yet another function. Further-more, the formulae could be used to consider indirect as well as direct movements. If we were considering, for example, the number of A-men moving to B we could apply the formulae to all the possible movements of A-men, including all those movements via other areas C, D, E, &c., which result in A-men's eventual arrival in B; i.e. movements such as $A \to B, A \to C \to B, A \to D \to B$, and $A \to C \to D \to B, A \to C \to D \to E \to B$. Finally, M_{ab} could be defined in many ways so long as the independent variables a, b, V_{ab}, &c., were chosen to correspond. Thus M_{ab} could repre-sent movement of men, women, total population, insured workers, non-insured workers; it could even represent the 'net redistribution of workers' measured in Material G. In all cases, however, the coefficient of mobility would refer to the particular population considered; great care had there-fore to be taken when comparing the various resulting coefficients with each other. It was clear, however, that formula (3) was readily adaptable to all the available data, so long as it was cautiously applied.

Perhaps the most important simplification in the above basic concept and formula is the assumption that movements between two areas or occupations can be considered in isolation; that, if M is the total migration from a losing area, that part of M which moves to B (M_{ab}) depends on conditions in A and B only. Actually, any worker in a depressed area has the choice of moving to any one of many less depressed areas scattered all over the country, and movements from A to B therefore depend also on the proximity of other prosperous areas to A. To take account of such considerations, however, would be a monumental statistical task and they were accordingly neglected throughout the Oxford studies. For this reason alone it was clear that, however successful the results, there would always remain considerable unexplained residuals whenever our less complex formulae were fitted to the data.

Measurement of Prosperity

A difficult choice was involved in deciding on an index of V_{ab}, the dif-ference in prosperity between areas. Some research workers in the United States had attempted to measure the 'plane of living' by combining number of income-tax returns, telephones and radios, wage rates, income per head, retail sales per head, and proportion of the population on public relief, into one index. A rough attempt to construct a prosperity index had been made by the *Marketing Survey of the United Kingdom*, where family incomes, distributed into three broad groups, were combined with other factors such as unemployment, overcrowding, telephone subscribers, and owners of private cars. In our case an easily available index of prosperity, which the material indicated was relevant to migration, was the proportion of insured workers in employment, statistics of which were published in great detail by the Ministry of Labour. This index neglected payments made to the unemployed; it also neglected differences in wage rates as between different industries and areas. However, it was possible to test the suitability of the employment rate by comparing it, for areas known to have been subject to considerable migration, with calculated indices of 'expected earnings' (average earnings per insured person), and 'expected receipts' (average income, in both wages and unemployment relief, per insured person).[1] The results, shown in Table 1, indicate that, on the whole, the employment rate alone was at least as relevant to decisions to move as either of the other indices, if not more so.

TABLE 1

Migration 1935–6 and 'Indices of Prosperity' 1935

(The last three columns refer to insured population only)

	Net movement to (−) or from (+) other parts of Great Britain per 1,000 pop.	Employment rate	'Expected earnings'	'Expected receipts'
		(Great Britain = 100)		
London and Home Counties	+9·1	113	114	102
Staffs., Warwick, Worcester, Leicester, Northants .	+3·0	109	111	103
Yorks. (West Riding), Notts., Derby	−1·9	97·5	96	98
Lancashire . . .	−2·5	85·5	72	88
Northumberland, Durham .	−12·3	83	95	107
Lanarkshire, Renfrew, Dumbarton, Mid- and West-Lothian. . . .	−3·5	80	94	99
Glamorgan, Monmouth .	−15·7	77·5	82	110

If V_{ab} were measured simply by the difference in the employment percentages in the two areas (or, what amounts to the same thing, the

---

[1] See *Oxford Economic Papers*, No. 1, p. 90 and Appendix I, p. 120, for details of these calculations.

difference between the unemployment percentages) it would be implied that, other things being equal, workers would move equally between two areas whether the rates of unemployment were 35 and 30 per cent. or 10 and 5 per cent. Empirical studies, however, indicated that the level of unemployment in the receiving area was also important, i.e. that workers were not only interested in the absolute difference in the chances of being employed but also on the chance of employment itself in the receiving area. They could see little incentive to move, for example, if they felt that, after migration, it was very likely that they would remain unemployed. Some students of the subject had also made the point that, since there is always a certain level of unemployment even in the most prosperous areas, the chance of finding employment falls off even more rapidly than the unemployment percentage rises. These considerations suggested the use of a formula such as $V_{ab} = (u_a - u_b)/u_b^\rho$, where u_a and u_b are the unemployment percentages in A and B respectively and ρ is some constant.[1] Empirical tests seemed to indicate that, if ρ was put equal to 1, the effect of u_b was approximately fully accounted for. In most of the statistical work it was therefore assumed that $V_{ab} = (u_a - u_b)/u_b$.

In order to simplify the statistical calculations further, f was assumed to be a linear function of the product $b.V_{ab}$, and equation (1) therefore became

$$M_{ab} = \lambda_{ab}.\frac{(u_a - u_b)}{u_b}.ab. \tag{4}$$

The expression $\{(u_a - u_b)/u_b\}ab$ was called the *attraction* or *incentive to move* between A and B. The *uncorrected coefficient of mobility* λ_{ab} (uncorrected in the sense that it was affected by distance and many other factors) was thus the migration per unit of attraction. Use of this basic formula greatly simplified many of the statistical problems. For instance, it implied that the coefficient of mobility for net migration from A to B was simply the sum of the two coefficients of mobility for the gross migrations from A to B and from B to A.

Because the actual scale of migration in Great Britain in the periods considered was so small it was decided, throughout the studies, to measure migration on an annual basis and to measure populations in thousands. *Thus the uncorrected coefficient of mobility was defined as the number of persons moving per year, from an area with 1,000 population to an area with 1,000 population, when the unemployment rate in the former area is 100 per cent. higher than that in the latter.*

Duration of Adjustment

In a perfect labour market one would expect to find always a uniform level of prosperity in all areas and all industries. Immobility of labour

[1] See Appendix I, *Oxford Economic Papers*, No. 2, p. 95.

would show itself in inequality of workers' prosperity and inequality of unemployment rates. We might, therefore, conceive of *excess unemployment* in an area or occupation as the amount by which unemployment in the area would be reduced if workers in the whole country were redistributed in such a way as to equalize unemployment rates everywhere. By dividing this excess unemployment by the actual number of unemployed moving annually from the area we could obtain a measure of the *duration of adjustment*, or, the number of years required, if there were no fundamental changes in the general economic situation, to equalize unemployment rates. The reciprocal of the duration of adjustment is a measure of the *speed of adjustment*. Statistically, two assumptions were required in making such measurements; first, that the proportion of migrants from A who were unemployed before moving was s, and second, that the proportion of all migrants who did not succeed in obtaining employment after arriving in B was k. The 'excess unemployment' f_a in A is then

$$f_a = s \cdot \frac{ab(u_a - u_b)}{a(k - u_a) + b(s - u_b)}, \tag{5}$$

and the rate, or speed, of adjustment is M_{ab}/f_a while the duration of adjustment is f_a/M_{ab}, or $s \cdot u_b/\lambda_{ab}\{a(k - u_a) + b(s - u_b)\}$. The two proportions k and s may, of course, have any value between 0 and 1. It is interesting to note that when $k = s = 1$, i.e. when all migrants from A are unemployed and all remain unemployed after arriving in B, then

$$f_a = ab(u_a - u_b)/(E_a + E_b),$$

where E_a and E_b are the numbers employed in A and in B. And in this case the duration of adjustment is

$$\frac{f_a}{M_{ab}} = \frac{u_b}{\lambda_{ab}(E_a + E_b)}. \tag{6}$$

In other words, the concept of the duration of adjustment in this case is related in a simple manner to the concept of the coefficient of mobility defined in (4) above.

4. The Findings

The purpose of the studies was to reduce mobility of labour to a measurable quantity in order to discover, on a scientific basis, the variations in the response of labour to economic incentives at different times, at different places, in different industries, and among different people. A very rough analysis of the Registrar-General's estimates of the populations of the individual counties of Great Britain showed that, excluding international migration, the total net gains by migration of gaining counties in the ten years 1926–35 was, on the average, nearly $\frac{1}{2}$ per cent. of the total population per annum. And nearly half of this was 'long-distance' migration between the eight large divisions into which the Ministry of Labour divides the country. But migration was twice as large before the slump of 1931 as after, despite the fact that, after that year, the need for adjustment by migration became greater. We wanted to go behind these overall statistics to get an idea of *how much* the response of labour to economic incentives was different in the two periods, and to get quantitative estimates of the part played by the different factors such as age, sex, distance, and industrial composition of depressed areas in determining mobility. The value of the results obtained from the application of the statistical techniques described above lies, therefore, not in the causal relationships revealed, for it must be acknowledged that many of these are perfectly obvious *a priori*, but in the fact that such relationships are measured quantitatively.

The Oxford Material

Material A gave the geographical distribution of 9,663 immigrants who had come to Oxford between 1921 and 1936, while Material B gave it for 4,677 immigrants who had arrived in the period 1933 to 1937. Although the correlation between the two distributions was 0·86, the counties farther away from Oxford accounted for a larger proportion of the migrants in the latter period.

Influence of prosperity and depression on mobility. Using Material B, for each one of the Ministry of Labour divisions the migration in each of the seven twelve-month periods beginning each July and January (between July 1933 and June 1937) was combined with a weighted average of the attraction in the same twelve-month period and the preceding six months,[1] to yield measures of the coefficient of mobility uncorrected for distance or other factors. The results are plotted on a logarithmic scale on Graph 1. It is clear that the coefficient of mobility rose rapidly in the years 1933–7 as the country became more prosperous. For Great Britain as a whole, by July 1937 the coefficient was more than three times as great as it had been in July 1933. This indicated that, with a *given* discrepancy in economic conditions (as measured for instance by attraction) there was much less long-distance migration in depressed than in prosperous times, as indeed one would expect, if only because, in depression, more workers are subject to long-period unemployment, their resources become exhausted, and fewer are able to bear the costs of moving. Graph 1 also shows that the coefficient of mobility is definitely higher for those divisions nearer to Oxford than for those far away.

---

[1] This amounted to using a 'distributed lag' with weights of 2:1 (see p. 220).

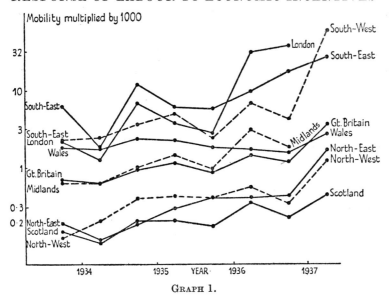

GRAPH 1.

Influence of Distance on Mobility. In order to examine further the influence of distance on mobility, Material A, which is more exhaustive and reliable than Material B, was used. Since this material represented those workers who had come to Oxford during the years 1921–36 and were still present in 1936, it was necessary, in calculating the mobility coefficients for each county, to weight the attraction in each year by a 'survival rate' calculated from the chances of re-emigrating from Oxford, dying, or retiring from insurance in each year.[1] Average county mobilities for 1921–36 were thus obtained which could be directly compared with county mobilities calculated from Material B. It was clear, from the average mobility coefficient for Great Britain, that the mobility of the British insured population was remarkably low; if unemployment in an area with 1,000 insured was twice as great as in an area with 1 million insured, the size of the coefficient indicated that only about 3 persons per annum would have actually migrated to the large, more prosperous area.

Table 2 shows that uncorrected mobility, calculated from Material A, varied greatly between counties. The relation between distance and mobility for each county is shown on the scatter diagram (Graph 2) measuring (on a double logarithmic scale) the uncorrected mobility of the county population in 1921–36 against the average distance of the county from Oxford.[2] A similar diagram based on Material B[3] (not reproduced here) showed great similarity. In both diagrams the scatter was not great and

[1] For more details see Appendix III, *Oxford Economic Papers*, No. 1, p. 121.
[2] For the method of calculating these average distances see Appendix IV, ibid. p. 122.
[3] See ibid. p. 104.

TABLE 2

Mobilities for Divisions and Counties with respect to Oxford

| From | Weighted distance from Oxford (miles) | No. of immigrants in Oxford in July 1936 | Mobilities 1921–36 | | | | | |
| | | | Uncorrected for distance* | | | Corrected for distance | | |
			Men	Women	Total	Men	Women	Total
SOUTH-EAST:								
Home Counties	81	1,504	9·6	4·0	6·3.	83	10	21
Rest of SE. .	63	669	24·9	6·9	20·4	196	14	123
Bedford	48	199	‖	‖	‖	‖	‖	‖
Bucks.	27	259	633·6	178·9	542·9	570	63	430
Cambs.	80	23	19·5	11·0	17·2	166	27	123
Norfolk	141	39	2·8	0·6	2·2	75	4	49
Suffolk	132	75	7·8	0·8	6·2	185	5	123
Sussex	109	74	24·5	28·7	25·6	393	12	341
Berks.†	25	937	248·1	42·4	202·1	191	13	133
SOUTH-WEST:‡	67	2,302	20·4	6·1	17·1	120	11	85
Cornwall	233	25	2·0	0·9	1·8	157	15	115
Devon	171	62	3·4	1·9	3·0	137	18	101
Dorset	110	24	5·8	2·4	5·2	94	10	70
Gloucester	58	328	6·2	3·5	7·0	36	5	26
Hants .	67	232	8·8	3·3	7·7	52	6	38
Somerset	82	108	10·8	6·2	9·6	96	16	72
Wilts. .	29	586	221·4	37·9	187·3	231	15	171
MIDLANDS:	70	910	3·6	1·1	2·9	23	2	16
Derby	106	37	0·9	0·5	0·8	14	2	11
Hereford	74	20	10·2	11·8	10·6	71	25	65
Leicester	77	64	5·6	1·3	3·9	44	3	26
Northants. .	49	89	10·5	1·4	7·6	32	1	20
Notts.	101	71	2·1	0·4	1·6	29	2	19
Shropshire .	107	32	3·1	3·4	3·2	48	14	41
Staffs.	86	157	1·6	0·3	1·3	16	1	10
Warwick	56	369	11·0	3·8	8·7	45	5	30
Worcester .	64	69	5·5	1·5	4·1	29	2	19
NORTH-EAST:	214	637	1·0	0·3	0·8	64	4	44
Durham	256	218	0·9	0·5	0·9	88	10	67
Lincs.	124	61	2·6	2·3	2·5	54	12	44
Northumberland .	258	111	1·3	0·4	1·2	125	8	90
Yorks. N.R.	225	32	0·8	0·6	0·8	59	10	46
„ W.R.	154	191	0·8	0·4	0·6	40	4	29
„ E.R.	187	25	0·8	0·1	0·7	26	1	16
NORTH-WEST:	171	516	0·9	0·3	0·7	38	3	24
Cheshire	132	57	1·0	0·2	0·8	23	1	15
Cumberland.	262	31	1·3	0·4	1·1	128	7	88
Lancs.	165	424	0·9	0·3	0·7	34	2	21
Westmorland	230	4	8·8	7·2	8·3	658	113	504
WALES:	117	1,195	3·5	1·3	3·3	66	6	51
Carmarthen .	145	38	2·3	1·5	2·3	67	10	54
Denbigh	130	12	1·0	..	0·9	24	..	18
Glamorgan .	116	862	3·9	1·5	3·7	62	7	56
Monmouth .	96	214	3·4	1·1	3·2	42	4	33
Pembroke .	195	34	5·6	4·4	5·5	300	52	238
Rest of Wales	178	35	1·8	0·7	1·4	79	7	52
SCOTLAND:	387	158	0·4	0·2	0·4	92	7	61
Great Britain‡† .	..	7,891	3·3	0·9	2·7	..	..	..
N. Ireland .	..	16	..	..	..	..	..	..
Oxfordshire§	..	1,756	..	..	..	..	..	..
TOTAL†§ .	..	9,663	..	..	..	..	..	..

* Multiplied by 1,000.   † Without Abingdon.   ‡ Without Oxfordshire.   § Without Woodstock.
‖ The unemployment rate of Bedford was lower than that of Oxford.

the correlation coefficients were 0·82 and 0·72 respectively (the 1 per cent. significance level is about 0·37). This indicated that the variations in mobility as between different counties could, to a considerable extent, be accounted for by differences in distance from Oxford.

In order to measure the influence of distance it was assumed that μ_{ab}

TABLE 3

Relation between Mobility (uncorrected) and Distance

Migration	Data used	Unemployment	No. of counties	Correl. coeff. between log. mobility and log. distance	'Spatial friction' Mean (arith.)	'Spatial friction' Limits (70% prob.)
A. Number of 'foreigners' exchanging unemployment books in Oxford in July 1936.	Men	Average for 1921–36 weighted according to estimated 'survival' rates of migrants, i.e. allowing for re-emigration, retirement, and death.	44	0·82	2·06	±0·23
	Women		40	0·69	1·78	±0·30
	Men and women		44	0·80	2·03	±0·25
B. Number of new 'foreigners' claiming for unemployment benefit in Oxford during the period:	Men and women					
July–June 1933/4		12 months' lag	14*	0·82	1·69	±0·36
Jan.–Dec. 1934		,,		0·84	1·66	±0·34
July–June 1934/5		,,		0·86	1·58	±0·29
Jan.–Dec. 1935		,,		0·89	1·60	±0·26
July–June 1935/6		,,		0·88	1·75	±0·30
Jan.–Dec. 1936		,,		0·89	1·79	±0·29
July–June 1936/7		,,		0·81	1·72	±0·13
1933–7		6 months' lag	43	0·72	1·62	±0·26

* Only those counties who sent more than ten migrants in *each* twelve months' period are included in this calculation.

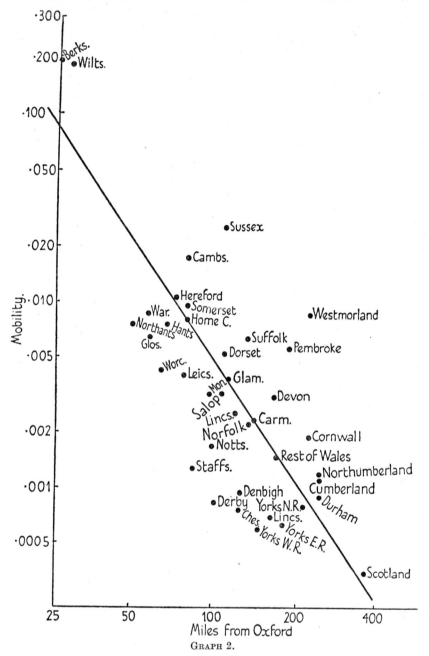

GRAPH 2.

was the mobility corrected for distance only. Then, on the lines of equation (2), and in the light of the clear linear relationship apparent in
Graph 2, it was assumed that

$$\lambda_{ab} = \mu_{ab} . D^{-\nu} - \epsilon_{ab},\tag{7}$$

where the distance of the county from Oxford is D, ν is a constant, and the influence of the remaining deterrent factors was accounted for by a residual ϵ_{ab}. The slope of the line in the scatter diagram, being identical with ν, can thus be used to measure the influence of distance alone on migration.

Regression equations were accordingly fitted to the various sets of data with the results shown in Table 3. The slope varied, according to the material used, between $-1\cdot6\pm0\cdot3$ and $-2\cdot1\pm0\cdot2$ (using 70 per cent. probability limits). An increase in distance by 1 per cent., other things being equal, thus reduced migration by from $1\frac{1}{4}$ to $2\frac{1}{4}$ per cent. in all cases considered. This coefficient was given the name *spatial friction*. The values of spatial friction, shown in Table 3, and the range of its probable variation, suggest that it did not vary significantly as between different types of labour, or as between different years if the years are not too far apart.

The coefficient μ tells us the average number of persons who would move to an area with 1,000 insured from an area with 1,000 insured *over a distance of one mile*, if the relative difference between the unemployment rates is 100 per cent. On the basis of the empirically calculated value of spatial friction, the values of μ, the 'mobilities corrected for distance', are given for each county on the right-hand side of Table 2. They show, of course, much less variation than the uncorrected mobilities. However, elimination of distance still leaves considerable variations in mobility, from 658×10^{-3} for Westmorland to 14×10^{-3} for Derbyshire, variations which must be due to factors other than distance.

Excess Unemployment and the Duration of Adjustment. Using formulae (5) and (6) it was calculated that, on the assumption that all migrants were unemployed and remained unemployed after migration to Oxford, the net number of unemployed who would have had to move from the rest of Great Britain into Oxford in July 1936 to bring Oxford's unemployment rate up to the average rate in Great Britain, was 1,500. The actual net migration into Oxford in the year 1936–7 was only about 1,000. At this rate, therefore, the duration of adjustment was about eighteen months. Thus, despite the very low mobility of the British population revealed by the Oxford material, the fact that Oxford was a relatively small city meant that only a short time would have been required for the flow of migrants from all over Great Britain to bring the Oxford unemployment rate up to the country average. However, the fact that one year later (in 1937–8) the duration of adjustment was still fourteen months is an indication that the assumption that no migrants obtain employment is incorrect. On the assumption that migrants continued to obtain employment at the same rate as in 1937–8, the duration of adjustment would have been about five years.

Male and Female Mobility. Comparison of the mobility of men with that of women is difficult, because it must first be decided what constitutes the 'incentive to move' for women. If only the female unemployment rates are used for calculating incentives for female migrants, it appears that mobility is on the whole very much greater for women than for men.[1] However, common sense indicates that women are influenced much more by family earnings than by their own personal earnings, and that total unemployment rates, for men and women, are more relevant for women's migration. Using total unemployment rates, mobility of women was found to be only just over one-quarter of the mobility of men, as is shown clearly in Table 2. Although the influence of distance, or spatial friction, was not significantly higher for women, their average mobility was many times lower.

Chronic Unemployment and Mobility. The same unemployment rate may mean different economic situations according to the proportion of the unemployed who are chronically unemployed. The depressed areas contained a high proportion of workers who had been unemployed for over a year. In London and the south, on the other hand, a high percentage were out of work for less than three months. A comparison was accordingly made of the extent of long-, medium-, and short-term unemployment experienced before migration by Welsh migrants to Oxford and the distribution of such types of unemployment among all Welsh workers.[2] This showed that the chronically unemployed, i.e. those unemployed for over a year, were about half as mobile as those unemployed for shorter periods.

Time-lags in Migration. In all the calculations above, a weighted average of the attraction in the same period as that in which the migration occurred and the attraction in a 12-month period starting 6 months earlier (with weights 2:1) was used. Application of such a time-lag was decided upon only after successive correlations of mobility with distance, using in such correlations all the possible combinations of attractions in successive 12-month periods preceding the actual migration. Maximum correlations were found for a zero lag and for a 6-months' lag, indicating that the lag between the occurrence of a discrepancy in prosperity and the resulting migration is very short—probably not more than 6 months in most cases. Accordingly, the distributed lag described above was selected as most appropriate for these studies.

Industrial Structure and Mobility. Since it was evident that the same counties displayed high or low mobility whatever material was used,

---

[1] See Table 5, *Oxford Economic Papers*, No. 1, p. 108.
[2] Using Material C and a special divisional analysis of unemployment kindly lent by the Ministry of Labour. For the actual statistics see ibid. pp. 109–11.

an attempt was made to look more closely into the variations in mobility, as shown in Table 2, to discover additional factors affecting mobility. It was decided to test how far industrial structure was an important factor—for migration into Oxford had taken place very largely on account of the expanding motor industry located there (Pressed Steel and Morris Motors). Table 4 below shows the industrial structure of Oxford in 1936 and the

TABLE 4

Oxford's Insured Industries

Industry	Foreigners		Non-foreigners		All insured	Foreigners as per cent. of all insured
	Number	per cent.	Number	per cent.		
Motor	4,882	44·3	5,571	26·4	10,453	46·7
Building: skilled	618	5·5	1,487	7·0	2,105	29·3
„ unskilled	887	8·0	887	4·2	1,774	50·0
„ all	1,505	13·5	2,374	11·2	3,879	39·2
Distributive: men	1,135	10·3	2,546	12·0	3,681	30·8
„ women	376	3·4	2,069	9·8	2,445	15·4
„ all	1,511	13·7	4,615	21·8	6,126	24·7
Omnibus service	298	2·7	232	1·1	530	56·2
Others	2,859	25·8	8,355	39·5	11,214	25·5
Total	11,055	100·0	21,147	100·0	32,202	34·4

Reproduced from *The Economics and Government of a Changing Area*. These figures include people who went to Oxford after having been retired from H.M. Forces.

proportions of 'foreigners' in each important industry. No less than 44·3 per cent. of all foreigners were in the motor industry. The next step was to find, for each of the twelve counties with the highest and the twelve counties with the lowest mobilities, the percentages of all occupied persons occupied in certain selected industries. The results, based on the 1931 census, are shown in Table 5 (which also shows the ratio of occupied men to occupied women).

Certain features of the table were immediately apparent. The group of twelve counties with highest mobility (Group I) had a lower proportion of textile workers than the group of twelve counties with lowest mobility (Group II). This suggested that both male and female labour in the textile industry was not easily transferable into the motor industry. Furthermore, the table showed that mobile counties had a larger proportion of agricultural workers than immobile ones. The difference between the mean proportions occupied in a given industry in the two groups was tested for significance (where the figure in the last line of Table 5 is numerically smaller than the figure in the line above it the difference is significant). It was found that mobility was significantly lower when there were high proportions occupied in the metal industry (males), textiles (males and

TABLE 5

Industrial Structure of Twenty-four Counties showing Percentages of Males (M.) or Females (F.) engaged in Selected Industries. (Census, 1931.)

The counties are arranged in order of their corrected mobility.

County / Industry	Total M.	Metal Motor M.	Engineering Not elect. M.	Engineering Elect. M.	Textiles M.	Textiles F.	Clothing M.	Clothing F.	Agriculture M.	Building M.	Mining M.	Personal service M.	Personal service F.	Commerce and Finance M.	Commerce and Finance F.	Transport and communication M.	Transport and communication F.	Public admin. M.	Public admin. F.	Ratio F/M %
I. High Mobility																				
Bucks	10	6	1	1	·	1	2	4	12	10	·	9	45	13	12	7	1	10	7	35
Sussex	6	2	1	1	·	·	1	3	13	13	·	13	58	20	15	8	1	9	5	53
Pembroke	4	1	·	·	·	·	1	4	31	6	1	4	48	13	15	9	·	10	10	31
Wilts	18	6	1	1	1	4	1	7	19	8	2	7	45	11	14	7	·	15	9	29
Berks	7	2	2	2	1	·	1	6	12	7	1	12	47	17	15	8	1	11	7	42
Suffolk	9	2	5	·	·	3	2	8	16	7	·	8	47	15	16	6	·	9	8	35
Cambs	4	1	1	1	·	1	2	4	26	9	·	6	45	15	13	7	·	8	7	39
Cornwall	6	1	2	·	1	2	1	4	26	8	1	6	52	14	19	9	·	10	8	34
Devon	9	1	1	1	·	2	1	6	17	10	8	8	51	15	18	8	·	17	7	38
Cumberland	9	1	1	1	2	7	1	5	19	5	1	4	38	13	16	10	1	7	8	36
Northumberland	14	1	3	·	·	1	1	4	6	5	19	4	39	16	24	10	1	7	8	37
Somerset	6	2	2	1	1	3	4	14	20	9	25	8	45	15	13	8	·	7	6	45
II. Low Mobility																				
Monmouth	14	1	1	·	11	30	1	3	5	3	39	3	41	11	23	11	1	6	14	21
Yorks, W.R.	16	2	4	7	11	30	1	12	4	5	18	3	41	14	13	8	1	6	6	45
Gloucester	10	3	3	1	13	32	2	10	1	8	4	4	35	18	16	12	1	8	7	45
Lancs	14	2	5	2	·	·	3	10	9	6	6	4	18	16	15	11	·	7	6	55
Northants	7	2	2	1	4	9	28	50	12	6	2	6	22	12	10	7	·	7	5	44
Worcester	27	1	2	2	7	30	2	9	13	7	2	5	27	13	13	7	·	6	6	46
Notts	8	2	3	1	·	2	2	10	16	6	26	4	21	14	13	8	1	6	8	44
Yorks, E.R.	13	1	2	1	6	17	1	4	13	7	1	4	41	19	19	18	1	7	6	41
Cheshire	4	2	5	2	·	·	3	9	8	6	27	5	31	19	16	13	·	7	8	48
Denbigh	27	1	·	·	1	5	1	3	15	6	15	6	18	13	15	6	1	7	9	30
Stafford	14	4	3	2	7	29	1	7	6	5	29	3	26	11	13	7	·	5	6	45
Derby	14	4	3	1	7	29	1	5	6	5	29	3	26	11	13	8	1	5	7	33
Mean: Group I	8	2	3	1	1	2	2	6	17	8	5	8	47	15	16	8	1	10	8	38
Mean: Group II	13	2	3	2	4	13	4	11	8	6	14	4	29	14	15	10	1	6	7	41
Difference II–I	5·0	0·2	0·2	0·8	3·7	11·1	2·4	5·2	-9·4	-2·5	8·8	-3·3	-17·4	-0·6	-0·9	1·4	0·2	-3·5	-0·4	3·6
Signif. diff. (5% level)	4·5	1·4	1·8	1·0	2·1	6·3	3·3	6·4	5·3	1·5	8·8	0·7	6·7	2·2	2·7	2·6	0·3	1·7	1·5	6·4

females), and mining, and significantly higher when there were high proportions occupied in agriculture (males), personal service (males and females), building and public administration (males). Proportions in the distributive trades, in the motor industry, and in engineering did not seem very significant. Variations in the mobility corrected for distance were thus found to be in part explained by differences in industrial structure. Conclusive results, however, cannot be obtained, because proportions in the various industries in each county are only averages of the varying proportions in the individual, sometimes highly specialized, towns and districts. Furthermore, there may be spurious correlation; for instance, mining counties are often less agricultural than others and it is, accordingly, not certain whether mining or agriculture is the more important factor affecting mobility.

In order to probe a little deeper into the influence of occupation on mobility an analysis on exactly the same lines was repeated for individual cities which either had displayed exceptionally high or low mobility, or were known to be specialized on the motor industry. This analysis showed that proportions in the textile industry seemed to be clearly associated with low mobility, a possible explanation being the specific kind of skill required in the textile industry. Only a weak correlation seemed to exist between the proportion in the motor industry and high mobility. This unexpected result, and the lack of any apparent correlation with the engineering industry, seemed to be a consequence of the fact that the motor industry was largely built on processes not requiring any particular special skill.

Some Personal Factors affecting Mobility. Since Daniel's investigations, using mainly Material C, were much more detailed, and related to a sample of persons whose individual histories were known, rather than to large statistical populations, his results threw more light on some of the special personal, economic, social, and political factors at work which could not be taken into account in the more general studies. His interesting observations on the effects of labour migration on fertility have been published in the *Sociological Review*[1] and will not be discussed here. However, it is useful to consider those findings which throw light on the conclusions reached in the general studies above.

In studying the response of persons of different ages to the incentive to move, Daniel measured the coefficient of mobility as defined in (4) for Welshmen aged 16–64 divided into ten-year age groups. He found that, putting mobility among persons 16–24 equal to 100, mobility was only 27 at ages 25–34, rose steadily to 73 at ages 45–54, and then dropped to 50 at ages 55–64. He attributed the high mobility of the young adults to fewer

[1] 'Labour Migration and Fertility', *Sociological Review*, vol. xxxi, No. 4, Oct. 1939.

personal attachments, and the detrimental effects of mechanization and the Seniority Rule on prospects of juvenile employment in the South Wales coal-mines.

From data regarding spells of unemployment, marital condition and size of family he obtained several important results. Younger migrants were unemployed for considerably less time before moving than were older migrants. Married men moved more (compared with single men) at ages 16–24 and 45–64 than at the middle ages 25–44. Single men made about 27 movements per hundred years of recorded history compared with only 17 movements made by married men and also moved fairly uniformly throughout their life until they passed the age of 45, when their movements fell off markedly. Daniel concluded that married people moved less between 25 and 45 because the number of young dependants tends to be largest in these years. He also noticed that men with large families moved less rapidly than men with small families and attributed this to the fact that, though the prospects of employment and the possible earnings were the same for both, an unemployed man with many dependants received larger payments from unemployment assistance, insurance benefits, and other sources. He could not, therefore, improve his economic position by migration so much as could a man with a small family. Furthermore, large families found the high cost of moving, difficulty of securing suitable accommodation, and more numerous personal ties to the community, very formidable obstacles to migration.

In studying the changing age composition of migrants over the period 1928–37, Daniel concluded that there was a tendency for the younger and more active members of families to be the first to move as new opportunities arose after the depression. Furthermore, a 'pioneer' often, through personal contacts, induced a large movement of workers of all ages and types from the same community. Thus 18 per cent. of all the Welshmen in his sample had moved to Oxford from Pontycymmer, a small mining-village near Maesteg. He attributed the increase in the proportion of older married men in later years to the beneficial effects of the Household Removal and Family Removal Schemes introduced in 1934 and 1935, under which a migrant received financial assistance in moving his family and belongings to a new city. He also noticed the stimulating effect on juvenile migration after 1934 of the special grants, training centres, and hostel accommodation provided under the Industrial Transference Scheme. Coefficients of mobility showed that, whereas in 1931–2 juvenile mobility was only 64 per cent. of adult mobility, it had risen relatively throughout the period and, in 1935–6, reached 173 per cent. of adult mobility.

Daniel's study of individual employment histories[1] indicated that 'delay'

---

[1] See 'Some Factors Affecting the Movement of Labour', *Oxford Economic Papers*, No. 3.

in moving into a job, as measured by the length of the spell of unemployment, was greatest if the worker had both to change his occupation and migrate at the same time. In interviews he discovered that there was considerable reluctance to change occupation; some coal-miners complained of the hardship they underwent in adjusting to their new work even though they eventually found it lighter than coal-mining. The hardships were greatest for older men and those long unemployed. Furthermore, the change in occupation often involved the sacrifice of status and earnings since many skilled men had to accept unskilled occupations. Skilled men even tended to remain in the depressed area, seeking less skilled work in their own industry in the hope of eventually regaining their old jobs, rather than to move to unskilled work elsewhere.

He found that delay was very short for the few men who migrated in depression years, but that, in 1933-5, when prospects of employment in Oxford appear to have been greatest, many men who had been unemployed for long periods were included among the migrants. The immense surplus of labour in the coalfields—by 1932, 37 per cent. of the insured population of South Wales was unemployed and 34 per cent. of the unemployed had been without work for over a year—meant that prospects of employment there were almost nil. The movement of the older, longer-term unemployed therefore depended almost exclusively on the employment opportunities elsewhere, and on the gradual recognition of the fact that the only hope of regaining employment lay in migration. Response to improvement in employment possibilities in Oxford seemed to be almost instantaneous. He also found that once a man had made his first migration his delay in moving again was much reduced.

Among the interesting sidelights on the individual problems involved in migration, Daniel noted that married people without children are particularly mobile because, while the ties holding back such a family are weakest, the possibilities of its finding suitable accommodation in a new area are greatest. Furthermore, when the wife's pregnancy preceded marriage, as was the case for 50 per cent. of the newly married Oxford Welshmen, an additional stimulus to migration existed. A vivid illustration of the difference in economic incentives for men with and without dependants is the fact that weekly pay-packets in Oxford averaged 58s. for single men and 53s. for married men, yet single men had only to pay the same amount—25s. per week—for board and lodging as in Wales, while married men had to rent houses in Oxford at an average rental of 17s. in Oxford compared with only 10s. 6d. in Wales. An unemployed single Welshman moving to Oxford increased his money income on the average from 15s. a week to about 45s. a week, a gain of 30s. a week, while the average married man with, say, four children, increased his

Q

money income only from 42s. 6d. a week to 45s.–50s. a week. Thus, married men enjoyed a negligible improvement in their economic position, particularly since they had received many additional unemployment and depressed-area benefits in Wales, including free school milk and meals for their children, absence of expenses connected with employment such as bus fares, and any small sums obtained from odd jobs. Finally, he found that assimilation into a new community is much easier for young single, or newly married, persons than for members of large families who tend to keep alive in each other the old ways of life; thus while 10 out of 15 married Welshmen expressed a preference to return to their old job in Wales, only 12 out of 45 single migrants wished to return, and 9 of these had married Welsh girls after migration to Oxford.

The National Material

Since the national statistics only permitted analysis of movements between one county, or one industry, and the rest of Great Britain, it was not possible to investigate the effects of type of unemployment, age, or individual area on mobility. Influences of distance also could not be measured. However, by considering movements in all directions in all parts of the country it was possible to obtain results of more general application because the characteristics measured were those of the population as a whole.

Long- and Short- Distance Migration 1923–36. In order to obtain some measure of the total amount of migration within the national area, the *net gains and losses* of all counties obtained from Material D were summed without regard to sign for each year from 1923 to 1936. These figures were then adjusted for international migration and halved in order to obtain the *total net movements* between counties.[1] *Total net 'long-distance' movements* were next estimated by taking half the sum of the net movements between the eight Ministry of Labour divisions. By subtraction, estimates of the *total net 'short-distance' movements* within the divisions were derived. The results, both in absolute figures and as percentages of the whole population, are shown in Table 6.

Disregarding movements in 1924–5, which are influenced by the Wembley Exhibition, about half the average yearly movement (which was about 0·39 per cent. of the whole population) was in the form of 'long-distance' movement. Furthermore, the average annual number of inter-county movements sank by one-third after the depression to 0·31 per cent. of the population in 1931–6. While 'short-distance' movements fell only slightly from 0·19 to 0·15 per cent. after the depression, the much more sensitive 'long-distance' movements were halved (0·26 to 0·13 per cent.). Variation

---

[1] For the reasoning behind these calculations see *Oxford Economic Papers*, No. 2, p. 74.

from minimum to maximum was also much higher (515 per cent.) for long-distance movements than for short-distance movements (335 per cent.).

TABLE 6

'Long-distance' and 'Short-distance' Movements, 1923–36*

Year (1 July–30 June)	Total net movements between counties	Total net movements between Divisions	Total net movements between counties but within Divisions	% of population of Great Britain			Total of relative unemployment discrepancies (without regard to sign)	
	(1)	(2)	(3)	(1)	(2)	(3)	(1) Counties	(2) Divisions
	(000)	(000)	(000)					
1923–4	92	63	29	0·21	0·15	0·07	..	1·32
1924–5	15	0·3	15	0·04	0·00	0·03	..	2·43
1925–6	113	64	49	0·26	0·15	0·11	..	2·82
1926–7	187	67	120	0·43	0·15	0·27	..	2·88
1927–8	296	163	133	0·67	0·37	0·30	17·75	3·10
1928–9	147	76	71	0·33	0·17	0·16	14·67	2·89
1929–30	243	143	100	0·55	0·32	0·23	14·48	2·99
1930–1	224	183	41	0·50	0·41	0·09	13·85	2·64
1931–2	106	32	74	0·24	0·07	0·17	13·64	2·44
1932–3	137	54	83	0·30	0·12	0·19	14·55	2·72
1933–4	157	55	102	0·35	0·12	0·22	17·72	3·28
1934–5	136	65	71	0·30	0·14	0·16	19·48	3·49
1935–6	159	82	77	0·35	0·18	0·17	22·80	3·77
Average 1925–31	202	116	86	0·46	0·26	0·19	15·19	2·89
„ 1931–6	139	58	81	0·31	0·12	0·18	17·64	3·14
„ 1925–36	173	89	84	0·39	0·20	0·19	16·55	3·00

* All figures are corrected for international migration.

In order to compare these net movements with the incentive to move as conceived on p. 212, the relative unemployment was calculated for each county in each year; in all cases the absolute difference in unemployment rates was divided by the unemployment rate in the *gaining* area whether that area was the particular county (or division) or the rest of Great Britain. In each year the relative unemployment discrepancies were totalled for all counties (or all divisions). This total was equivalent to the percentage mean deviation of unemployment rates from their weighted average, the weights being the numbers insured in each county.[1] It would be expected that the total amount of migration in the country (in per cent. of the total population) would respond to changes in this index. Although Table 6 shows no close correspondence between total migration and dispersion of unemployment rates measured in this manner, the general movements do agree with a lag of 6 to 18 months. The striking fall in migration in 1928–9 is not accounted for by unemployment dispersion,

[1] See *Oxford Economic Papers*, No. 2, p. 81.

but perhaps results from the high level of prosperity which prevailed throughout the country in that year.

For each individual county, percentage gains and losses by migration were plotted against relative unemployment in that county for every year from 1927 to 1936; the resulting graphs showed considerable overall correspondence even though year-to-year fluctuations showed no strict relation. Similar graphs for divisions (reproduced on p. 84 of *Oxford Economic Papers*, No. 2) showed evidence of some correlation, particularly for London, the south-east, the north-east, the north-west, and Wales where the economic forces of prosperity or depression seem to have been sufficiently strong to outweigh disturbing factors. The best correlation was obtained by associating migration from 1 July to 30 June with attraction in the 12-month period starting 6 months earlier; i.e. the lag was most probably 6 months and it was unlikely that it exceeded 18 months. That the lag was somewhat longer than that found in the Oxford material was probably due to a lag in recording changes in local populations in the Registrar-General's enumerations.

Mobility in Great Britain. Still using Material D, the correspondence between percentage migration and relative unemployment was examined, not for given areas over a series of years, but for all areas in a given period. Accordingly, two scatter diagrams were prepared measuring these two variables on the two axes and representing each county by one point. One scatter diagram related to the average of the pre-depression period 1927–31 and the other to the average of the post-depression period 1931–6. Since the basic formula (4) implied the existence of a linear relationship, straight lines were fitted to the points by the method of least squares. The equations obtained were

$$1927\text{–}31 \quad -\frac{M}{a} = 0\cdot000212\,\frac{(u_a-u_b)}{u_b}\,.\,b.-3\cdot1,$$

$$1931\text{–}6 \quad -\frac{M}{a} = 0\cdot000185\,\frac{(u_a-u_b)}{u_b}\,.\,b.-0\cdot6.$$

The correlation coefficients were $-0\cdot78$ and $-0\cdot82$ respectively for the two periods; both were highly significant. Deviations of the individual counties from the lines were probably due in part to the variations in the geographical relationship of each county to the various prosperous and depressed areas in Great Britain, i.e. to the influence of distance. The constant terms in the equations might be indicative of a *threshold of incentive*, or a minimum level of relative unemployment which had to be exceeded before migration would start. In fact, however, the existence of such a threshold was not clearly established since neither constant term was significant. The equations also seemed to indicate that mobility of the British population fell slightly after the depression, but here again the change in the coefficient was not statistically significant.

The same technique was applied, first to a group of ten counties selected on account of the close relation exhibited in their case between migration and attraction, and second to the eight Ministry of Labour divisions. The two scatter diagrams are shown in graph 3 and graph 4 respectively.

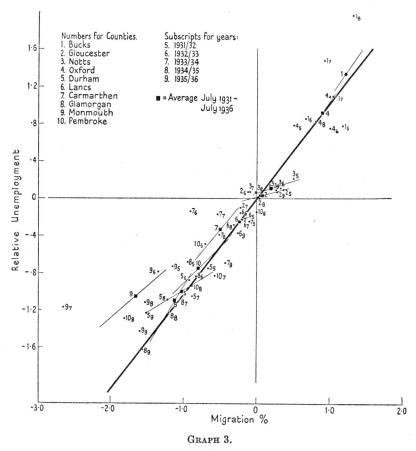

GRAPH 3.

Whereas for the counties the general tendency seemed to be for migration to respond to even the slightest incentive to move, for the divisions a fairly definite threshold of incentive seemed to exist. Since inter-divisional movements are long-distance movements, it would appear that an initial incentive of about 20 per cent. relative unemployment is necessary to start long-distance migration.

County Coefficients of Mobility. Table 7 gives, for each county, the coefficient of mobility, first for the period 1927–31 and second for the period 1931–6. Since migration and population are all in terms of total

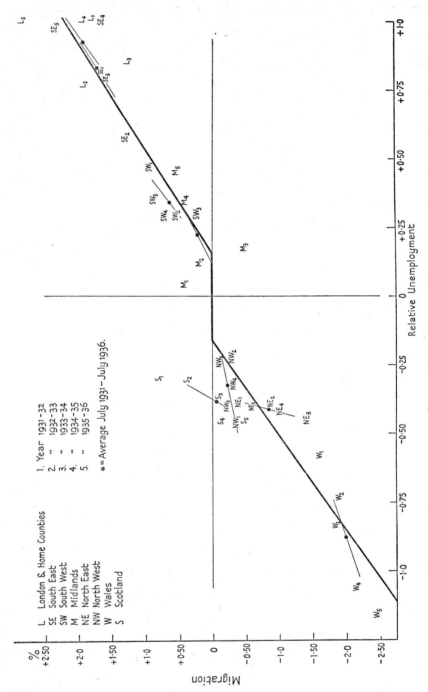

GRAPH 4.

TABLE 7

Average Annual Mobility by Counties*

	1927–31			1931–6	
	Average annual migration as % of county population	Average annual mobility		Average annual migration as % of county population	Average annual mobility
GAINING COUNTIES			**GAINING COUNTIES**		
SE. London and H.C.	+1·04	0·24	SE. London and H.C.	+0·66	0·17
Bedford	+0·51	0·07	Bedford	+2·04	0·23
Bucks.	+1·68	0·16	Bucks.	+1·23	0·22
Cambridge	+0·94	0·19	Cambridge	+0·50	0·10
Sussex	+0·84	0·11	Sussex	+1·41	0·24
SW. Berks.	+0·50	0·10	SW. Berks.	+0·46	0·14
Devon	+0·53	0·35	Devon	+0·21	0·14
Dorset	+0·83	0·24	Dorset	+0·69	0·35
Hants	+0·64	0·27	Gloucester	+0·07	0·45
Somerset	+0·06	0·03	Hants	+0·47	0·29
Oxon.	+1·82	0·32	Somerset	+0·08	0·04
			Oxon.	+0·90	0·22
M. Leicester	+0·14	0·04	M. Leicester	+0·30	·0·11
Northants	+0·06	0·03	Northants	+0·23	0·13
Notts.	+0·90	1·00	Notts.	+0·21	0·40
Warwick	+0·70	0·38	Warwick	+0·31	0·11
			Worcester	+0·59	14·87
NW. Westmorland	+0·92	0·25	NE. Yorks., E.R.	+0·16	1·47
NEGATIVE MOBILITY			**NEGATIVE MOBILITY**		
SW. Gloucester	+0·21	..	NW. Cheshire	+0·56	..
M. Worcester	+0·47	..	W. Rest of Wales	+0·05	..
NE. Yorks., N.R.	+0·25	..	Scotland	+0·03	..
Yorks., E.R.	+0·24	..			
LOSING COUNTIES			**LOSING COUNTIES**		
M. Shropshire	−0·41	5·76	SW. Cornwall	−0·08	0·15
Stafford	−0·84	0·79	M. Shropshire	−0·49	2·72
NE. Durham	−1·81	0·41	Stafford	−0·14	0·32
Northumberland	−1·10	0·41	NE. Durham	−1·04	0·24
Yorks., W.R.	−0·20	0·26	Northumberland	−0·23	0·12
NW. Cheshire	−0·03	0·04	Yorks., N.R.	−0·23	0·08
Cumberland	−1·36	0·78	Yorks., W.R.	−0·25	0·40
Lancs.	−0·62	0·50	NW. Cumberland	−0·63	0·23
W. Carmarthen	−0·80	0·18	Lancs.	−0·23	0·20
Denbigh	−0·74	4·06	W. Carmarthen	−0·50	0·38
Glamorgan	−2·05	0·39	Denbigh	−0·14	0·07
Monmouth	−2·44	0·50	Glamorgan	−1·11	0·25
Pembroke	−1·22	0·49	Monmouth	−1·34	0·32
Rest of Wales	−0·57	0·43	Pembroke	−0·79	0·28
Scotland	−0·62	1·07			
NEGATIVE MOBILITY			**NEGATIVE MOBILITY**		
SE. Norfolk	−0·39	..	SE. Norfolk	−0·13	..
Suffolk	−0·66	..	Suffolk	−0·13	..
SW. Cornwall	−0·24	..	SW. Wilts.	−0·29	..
Wilts.	−0·82	..	M. Derby	−0·05	..
M. Derby	−0·62	..	Hereford	−0·41	..
Hereford	−0·91	..	NE. Lincs.	−0·03	..
NE. Lincs.	−0·15	..	NW. Westmorland	−0·20	..
Average for Great Britain	..	0·21			0·19

* Mobilities are multiplied by a thousand.

population, these measures can be envisaged as indices of the mobility of families, on the assumption that each thousand insured migrants have attached to them a certain standard group of non-insured persons.

The above mobility coefficients are not directly comparable with the mobilities obtained for insured persons which are shown in Table 2.[1] In order to test the agreement, the coefficients obtained for Oxfordshire (0.32×10^{-3} in 1927–31 and 0.22×10^{-3} in 1936) were compared with the coefficient obtained for Great Britain in the period 1921–36 (2.7×10^{-3}) from the Oxford material. Correcting the latter by the ratio of insured to total population in Great Britain yielded a value of 0.7×10^{-3}. Thus, the mobility coefficient between the rest of Great Britain and Oxfordshire, though smaller, was of the same order of magnitude as that between the rest of Great Britain and Oxford City. Both sets of material thus indicated the same level of mobility of the British population.

The Rate of Adjustment. In a final analysis of Material D the country was divided into gaining divisions and losing divisions and the 'rate of adjustment' as defined on p. 213 calculated on two different assumptions, first, that k, the proportion of migrants remaining unemployed after migration, equals, and, second, that $k = 0$. It was assumed in both cases that all migrants were unemployed before moving, i.e. $s = 1$.[2] The results for the losing divisions as a whole were:

Percentage rate of adjustment per annum

	$k = 1$	$k = 0$
1925–31 . .	17·4	6·7
1931–6 . .	3·1	1·6

Thus, after the depression, the rate of adjustment was between one-fourth and one-sixth of the rate before the depression. Taking $k = 1$ it would have taken, in 1931–6, about 32 years of migration at the actual level to equalize unemployment rates, compared with only six in 1925–31. Taking $k = 0$, the duration of adjustment would have been 62 years and 15 years respectively. How far these rates differ from those in a small, rapidly gaining area is apparent from the fact that, for $k = 1$, the duration of adjustment was only 14–18 months in 1936–8 for Oxford City compared with 32 years in 1931–6 for the losing divisions of Great Britain. It should be noted that the reason for the great difference revealed in the rate of adjustment before and after the depression is not that the response of labour to economic incentives as measured by the mobility coefficient was any the less after the depression, but rather that the duration of adjustment depends also upon the unemployment rate in the country,

---

[1] The coefficient based on total populations gives results r times that based on the insured populations alone, where r is the ratio of insured persons to total population both among migrants and non-migrants.

[2] For a fuller description of the method used, and rates of adjustment for individual divisions under various assumptions regarding k, see *Oxford Economic Papers*, No. 2, pp. 92–3 and 96–7.

which was, of course, much higher in 1931–6 (see equation (6)). In other words, a severe depression of the type which existed in Great Britain after 1931 demanded, not the continuation of labour mobility on the same level as before the depression, but a four- to six-fold increase in mobility if the equalization of prosperity all over the country was to continue at the same speed.

Effects of Indirect Migration. Using Material E, relating to migration of insured workers, an attempt was made to measure mobilities taking account of both direct and indirect migration. It is shown in Appendix I of *Oxford Economic Papers*, No. 4, that serious statistical difficulties arise in calculating all coefficients of mobility in the most general case (direct and indirect movements; migration from prosperous to depressed areas and vice versa) for the seven Ministry of Labour divisions; this would

TABLE 8

Average Annual Mobilities* (uncorrected for distance)

Males aged 21–64

Mobility coefficient (order of prosperity L., M., SW., NE., NW., W., Sc.)	Average annual mobility × 10³: 1921–37	
	Taking account of indirect movements	*Assuming direct movements only*
M. → L.	7·577	7·577
SW. → M.	3·415	3·415
SW. → L.	18·309	18·310
NE. → SW.	2·218	2·218
NE. → M.	4·553	4·553
NE. → L.	2·182	2·187
NW. → NE.	226·800	226·800
NW. → SW.	2·234	2·239
NW. → M.	4·422	4·423
NW. → L.	1·820	1·826
W. → NW.	3·281	3·281
W. → NE.	2·947	2·951
W. → SW.	4·848	4·850
W. → M.	3·090	3·090
W. → L.	1·873	1·881
Sc. → W.†	· ·	· ·
Sc. → NW.	13·880	13·900
Sc. → NE.	71·570	71·610
Sc. → SW.	1·500	1·508
Sc. → M.	1·510	1·510
Sc. → L.	1·351	1·355

* On the assumption that no movements occur from prosperous areas to depressed areas.

† The mobility is negative. People moved from Scotland to Wales, although Wales was more depressed than Scotland.

normally require the solution of forty-two simultaneous equations. Therefore, the number of simultaneous equations was considerably reduced by neglecting altogether any movements from prosperous to depressed areas. The results of the calculations are given in Table 8.

Distance was obviously again a major factor in reducing mobility. It is interesting to observe that, for Sc → NE. and Sc → NW. the two mobility coefficients were 71·6 and 13·9 respectively, despite the fact that the distances of these divisions from Scotland are not very different. The discrepancy was probably due to the greater similarity of the industrial structure of the north-east to that of Scotland. Since the mobilities were of the same order of magnitude as those found in the study of the Oxford material, it may perhaps be concluded that the various calculations of mobility into Oxford were fairly typical of mobility of the insured in Great Britain as a whole. Furthermore, since the inclusion of indirect movements makes such insignificant differences to the mobility coefficients, it is clear that the errors arising from neglect of this factor in the earlier calculations were not serious.

Inter-Industrial Mobility. Since Material E also provided an analysis giving simultaneously county of origin and the county in which the books were exchanged in 1937, it was decided to select two areas on the basis of (a) heavy migration, and (b) concentration on relatively few industries, in order to make a second, more concentrated investigation into inter-industrial mobility. The two areas selected were Northumberland–Durham and Glamorgan–Monmouth. No less than 30 and 17 per cent. respectively of the books issued in these two areas were found elsewhere in 1937, and 51 and 53 per cent. respectively of the occupied populations of the two areas were in the mining and metal industries in 1931. It was hoped that, by having two such widely separated areas, comparison of the results might check the validity of the analysis.

As a first step, mobilities uncorrected for distance were calculated for men aged 16–64 for movements between each of the two areas and each county in Great Britain for the period 1925–37.[1] The correlation of log mobility with log distance was −0·52 for Northumberland–Durham, which is highly significant. That for Glamorgan–Monmouth was −0·32, which, because it is only just significant, indicated that factors other than distance were more important in determining the mobility of the population of this area. The spatial frictions defined on p. 219 were 1·46 and 1·21 respectively, somewhat lower than the level obtained with the Oxford Material (1·6 to 2·1). This indicated that the effect of distance was somewhat less for migrants from these areas than for migrants in Great Britain generally.

---

[1] For details of the method by which the 'attractions' and 'survival rates' appropriate to the data were calculated, see *Oxford Economic Papers*, No. 4, pp. 43–4 and Appendix II.

TABLE 9

Mobilities of (a) Northumberland and Durham Men aged 16–64, and (b) Glamorgan and Monmouthshire Men aged 16–64, with respect to each County in Great Britain, 1925–37

Counties	Migration estimates (a)	Migration estimates (b)	Uncorrected for distance* (a)	Uncorrected for distance* (b)	Corrected for distance† (a)	Corrected for distance† (b)
SOUTH-EAST:						
London and Home counties	32,150	29,750	1·36	1·75	4·32	0·81
Bedford	1,850	1,800	2·08	2·54	4·95	0·91
Bucks.	1,850	2,400	2·23	3·61	5·45	1·12
Cambs.	200	150	1·87	2·23	4·27	1·03
Norfolk	550	150	4·45	4·15	10·18	2·68
Suffolk	450	100	5·75	2·16	21·87	1·27
Sussex	1,250	1,050	0·68	1·25	2·75	0·62
Berks.	250	800	2·11	2·73	6·48	0·67
SOUTH-WEST:						
Cornwall	150	650	3·79	19·79	20·89	5·84
Devon	650	2,200	1·69	8·14	7·34	1·51
Dorset	150	650	0·50	2·66	2·09	0·54
Gloucester	450	2,750	1·00	11·84	2·80	1·51
Hants.	1,550	2,400	1·88	2·00	7·04	0·53
Oxon.	450	1,300	0·06	2·39	0·18	0·59
Somerset	250	2,850	0·39	11·03	1·46	1·10
Wilts.	50	550	0·07	4·44	0·26	0·76
MIDLANDS:						
Derby	850	350	1·31	0·38	3·57	0·14
Leicester	950	800	0·84	0·74	1·44	0·24
Northants.	150	400	0·95	0·74	2·09	0·27
Notts.	1,100	350	1·76	1·75	2·39	0·69
Shropshire	200	500	8·43	5·03	14·55	1·09
Staffs.	550	1,750	46·98	39·12	130·60	10·90
Warwick	3,850	7,150	1·17	2·67	2·29	0·66
Worcester	350	950	0·88	3·92	2·29	0·61
Hereford	‡	750	‡	19·87	‡	1·99
NORTH-EAST						
Lincs.	850	700	6·09	8·56	7·00	4·43
Yorks.	16,050	1,850	75·70	7·86	58·75	3·92
Durham	..	500	..	198·36	..	143·08
Northumberland	..	350	..	4·75	..	3·79
NORTH-WEST:						
Cheshire	350	350	5·62	10·82	6·45	3·20
Lancs.	2,900	1,500	6·32	9·36	6·04	4·02
Westmorland	150	‡	14·99	‡	4·53	‡
Cumberland	650	‡	251·75	‡	99·30	‡
WALES:						
Denbigh	‡	150	‡	21·99	‡	5·79
Carmarthen	‡	1,500	‡	569·35	‡	49·36
Glamorgan	‡	..	‡	..	‡	..
Monmouth	‡	..	‡	..	‡	..
Pembroke	‡	250	‡	513·32	‡	87·58
Rest of Wales	‡	2,100	‡	4,702·28	‡	802·43
SCOTLAND	2,400	800	15·17	6·81	13·55	6·76

(a) Figures refer to Northumberland and Durham.
(b) Figures refer to Glamorgan and Monmouthshire.

* Multiplied by 1,000.

† Using 1·46 for (a) and 1·21 for (b) as the power of distance ν in the formula $\mu = \dfrac{Mu_b D^\nu}{(u_a - u_b)ab}$.

‡ In these cases the mobility was negative or else the area (a) or (b) was less depressed than the county.

The individual uncorrected mobilities, and the mobilities corrected for distance using the coefficients of spatial friction 1·46 and 1·21, are both given in Table 9. In order to test the effect of industrial structure on the corrected mobilities Table 10 was prepared, setting out for each of the

TABLE 10

Mobility and Industrial Structure, 1925–37

County	Mobility corrected for distance (a) Northumberland–Durham	Mobility corrected for distance (b) Glamorgan–Monmouth	Mining metal	Textiles, dress-making	Agriculture, fishing	Bricks, pottery, chemicals	Light manufactures	Commerce, finance, distr. trades	Local services
Northumberland	..	3·79 }	51·4	0·9	3·7	2·7	4·0	21·6	15·7
Durham	..	143·08 }	53·2	0·9	2·9	0·8	3·7	24·5	14·0
Glamorgan	* *	.. }	43·4	2·7	4·2	9·1	6·8	17·3	16·5
Monmouth		10·90	31·0	3·3	16·9	0·8	5·4	24·2	18·4
Staffs.	130·60		32·0	10·9	6·1	2·7	6·3	23·7	18·3
Cumberland	99·30	3·92	9·7	2·2	28·1	1·0	9·1	23·2	20·7
Yorks	58·75	1·27	18·0	1·4	26·0	0·3	5·2	24·3	24·8
Suffolk	21·88	5·84	20·0	1·4	26·0	2·2	4·9	22·6	22·9
Cornwall	20·89	1·09	26·6	4·6	11·9	0·6	9·5	27·0	18·5
Shropshire	14·56	6·76	6·3	6·0	29·1	1·0	9·4	24·1	24·5
Scotland	13·55	2·68	10·7	2·1	16·5	1·0	6·6	26·4	36·7
Norfolk	10·19	1·51	12·4	1·3	7·5	1·3	5·4	27·7	44·7
Devon	7·35	0·53	6·5	1·4	13·2	1·4	8·2	32·7	38·8
Hants	7·05	0·62	35·4	8·4	5·7	1·7	6·1	22·8	18·1
Sussex	2·75	0·69	42·8	2·4	3·0	0·5	9·0	21·4	19·7
Notts	2·40	0·66	9·3	28·5	11·8	3·7	8·3	20·7	20·9
Warwick	2·30	0·27	7·0	1·8	18·8	0·7	6·3	24·0	38·4
Northants.	2·09	0·54	31·2	5·5	12·2	3·6	5·9	20·3	21·3
Dorset	1·87	0·61	11·9	4·9	19·1	1·5	9·9	25·6	27·1
Worcester	0·61	1·10	31·2	1·8	18·8	3·6	6·3	24·0	38·4
Somerset	1·47	0·24	11·9	5·5	19·1	2·2	9·9	20·3	21·3
Leicester	1·45	0·76	20·0	24·4	7·0	1·5	7·0	25·6	27·1
Wilts.	0·27	0·76	18·4	2·1	18·9	0·4	8·3	20·7	18·7
Oxon.	0·18	0·59	14·9	2·5	16·8	0·4	8·2	26·3	30·9
I. Average for 5 counties with highest mobility			32·4	8·0	8·2	3·8	6·5	22·4	18·7
II. Average for 5 counties with lowest mobility			19·7	9·9	13·9	1·8	7·8	22·2	24·7
Difference (I−II)			12·7	−1·9	−5·7	2·0	−1·3	0·2	−6·0
Significant difference (5 per cent. level)			11·7	6·3	7·3	1·6	1·7	5·6	7·4

* Net inflow of migrants into area (a) or (b)

ten counties in respect of which the Northumberland–Durham men had the highest mobility and the ten counties for which these men had the lowest mobilities, the corrected mobilities for both areas. These were compared with the proportion of occupied males in seven industry groups.[1] On the whole the figures suggested that mobility tended to be high when the percentage engaged in the mining-metal group was high. To test whether the proportions in the various industry groups had a significant effect on mobility, the difference between the average proportions in the five counties with the highest, and the five counties with the lowest, mobilities were calculated for each industry group and tested for significance (where the last line of Table 10 exceeds the line above the difference is significant). The one clearly significant difference was in the mining-metal group, suggesting that workers from predominantly mining-metal areas move more easily the more the industrial structure of the receiving county approximates to that of the losing area. There is also a significant difference for bricks, pottery, and chemicals. Other near-significant differences such as that for agriculture and fishing seem to indicate negative effects of these groups on mobility, but it is more likely that proportions in these occupations merely reflect the larger proportions in the attractive industries.

As a further check on these conclusions regarding inter-industrial mobility, Material F was used to calculate the coefficients of mobility for coal-miners moving into other industries in pre-depression and post-depression years. The results are given in Table 11. It may be observed that, here again, the mobilities are roughly of the same order of magnitude as the mobilities uncorrected for distance obtained from the Oxford material. The high mobility for building and public works contracting has little importance because coal-miners given relief-employment in this industry for even a few weeks were counted thereafter as members of this industry. Clearly, coal-miners moved most easily into other mining industries— for obvious reasons. They also moved easily into brick- and tile-making and into the metal industries, thus confirming the conclusions based on Material E. Mobility of coal-miners with respect to commerce and finance, paper-making, and the clothing trades was, as might be expected, low.

Using Material G—net redistribution[2] of labour in the two periods 1927–31 and 1931–7 for a sample of twenty-four industries—it was possible to measure the mobility of the whole insured population between industries. Using A and B to represent industries instead of areas, the concept of

---

[1] For a detailed list of industries included in each of the seven groups see *Oxford Economic Papers*, No. 4, p. 47.

[2] For the definition of 'net redistribution' see p. 208. It is simply $a(g_a - g_b)$, where g_a = percentage growth in industry A and g_b = percentage growth in the rest of industry B in a given period.

TABLE 11

Mobility of Coal-Miners

Industry* into which coal-miners moved	Mobility† (using net transfers)	
	1927–31	1931–5
Building and public works contracting .	28·8	60·5
Transport and communications, fishing, &c. .	7·0	1·8
Metal and metal goods manufacture . .	2·2	4·3
Engineering, engineers' iron and steel foundry	2·0	1·9
Explosives, chemicals, coke ovens, &c. .	3·6	2·8
Brick, tile, &c., making	7·1	9·0
Mining (other than coal-mining) . . .	10·7	18·4
Hotel and laundry services . . .	4·0	2·4
Construction and repairs of vehicles . .	1·5	0·6
Food, drink, and tobacco	0·5	0·4
Textile industries	4·5	1·5
Shipbuilding	−2·5	−0·2
Rubber and leather trades	3·5	0·5
Sawmilling, furniture, and woodworking .	0·8	1·0
Paper-making, printing, &c. . . .	0·1	0·1
Clothing trades (including boots and shoes) .	0·4	0·3
Commerce and finance	0·1	0·1
Other industries and services . . .	2·0	2·3
Total	5·1	4·6

* Classification used by the Ministry of Labour.   † Multiplied by 1,000.

attraction defined on p. 212 was used to measure the attraction between an industry A and the rest of industry B. The *coefficient of readjustment* (as distinct from the coefficient of mobility) was then defined as *the net redistribution of workers between one industry and the rest of industry per unit of attraction.*

In order to measure how closely net redistribution was related with attraction, the values of the two variables were plotted on two scatter diagrams, one for 1927–31 and one for 1931–7.[1] Only the scatter diagram for 1931–7 is reproduced here (Graph 5). Correlation coefficients for the two periods were 0·58 and 0·53 respectively, both highly significant.[2] The fact that the correlation was not perfect suggests that there are important differences in the ease of redistribution of workers between different

[1] Both variables were divided by the number insured in the industry in order to avoid spurious correlation.

[2] Since redistribution of insured workers 16–64 is composed of (a) juvenile entrants (16–18) into insurance, (b) adult entrants (18–64) into insurance, (c) insured workers transferring from one industry to another, (d) retirements from insurance, and (e) deaths of insured, correlations were tried between attraction and juvenile entrants, adult entrants, and the rest, separately. The correlation coefficients were 0·40, 0·19, and 0·30 respectively. Only that for juvenile entrants was significant, indicating that juveniles find differences in the nature of industries less of an obstacle to entry than do others—which, of course, is only to be expected.

industries. That it was lower than the correlation obtained in the spatial analysis based on Material A may be due to the fact that, in the latter case, the areas considered were fairly large and industrial peculiarities tended to cancel out.

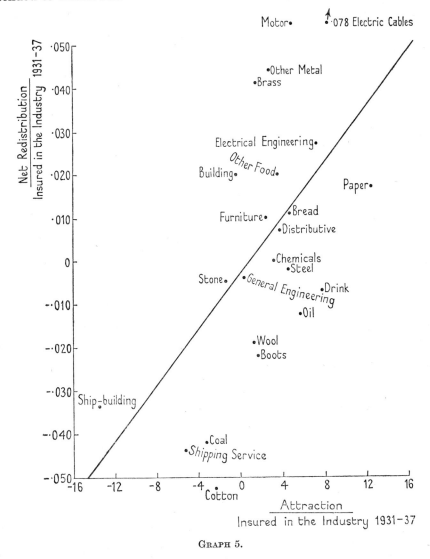

GRAPH 5.

The equations of the lines fitted to the two scatter diagrams were

$$1927\text{–}31 \quad - R = 0\cdot0027 \frac{(u_a - u_b)}{u_b} \,.\, b - 0\cdot0095,$$

$$1931\text{–}7 \quad - R = 0\cdot0032 \frac{(u_a - u_b)}{u_b} \,.\, b - 0\cdot0033,$$

where R is the net distribution of workers divided by the insured in the industry. In contrast to the results for spatial mobility, the average coefficient of readjustment was slightly higher for the post-depression period than for the pre-depression period. This would indicate that workers moved somewhat more freely between industries after the depression, but once again the difference is not statistically significant.

TABLE 12

Coefficients of Readjustment for a Sample of Industries

Industry	Coefficients of Readjustment*	
	1927–31	1931–7
General engineering	321·4†	n
Boots, shoes, &c.	24·3†	n
Coal-mining	22·8†	14·1†
Cotton	19·7†	30·6†
Woollen and worsted	16·1†	n
Building	13·1†	n†
Stone quarrying and mining . . .	7·4	3·9†
Distributive trades	5·7	1·6
Furniture making, &c.	5·6	4·0
Steel melting, iron puddling, &c. . .	5·6†	0·3†
Electric cable, apparatus, &c. . . .	4·8	7·4
Metal industry (not separately specified) .	4·0	12·8
Shipbuilding and ship repairing . . .	3·6†	2·8†
Electrical engineering	2·6	3·5
Other food	1·7	4·8
Paper and paper board	1·7	1·2
Motor vehicles, cycles, &c.	1·3	9·7
Printing, publishing, &c.	1·0	n
Chemicals	n	0·1
Oil, glue, soap, &c.	n	n
Brass, copper, zinc, &c.	n	23·8
Bread, biscuits, &c.	n	2·1
Shipping service	n†	9·0
Drink	n	n

* Multiplied by 1,000.   † Industries depressed relatively to all industry.
n = negative coefficients.

Individual coefficients of readjustment are given in Table 12. Among industries which should have contracted, shipping-services and ship-building had low coefficients, while coal-mining, cotton, and wool had high ones. The expanding motor industry had a rather low coefficient in the period 1927–31 but subsequently rose to third place among gaining industries. It should be borne in mind that the coefficients are dependent in part on the geographical distribution of the particular industry and reflect the spatial movements involved in redistribution between industries.

Components of Industrial Readjustment. Finally, in order to examine the part played by juveniles in the redistribution of the labour
force, an analysis was made, using all available sources, of the components
of changes in the number of insured males in a sample of industries. The
results, expressed as percentages of the labour force in 1927, are given in
Table 13. In some industries there was evidence of a high turnover of

TABLE 13

*The Components of Changes in Numbers of Insured Males for a Sample
of Industries (Annual Average 1927–31)*

(All figures are expressed as percentages)

Industry	Increase in insured males (16–64)	Juvenile new entrants (16–18)	New entrants (18–64)	Trans-ferences, retire-ments, and deaths	Trans-ferences
*Coal-mining	−2·53	+2·61	+0·12	−5·26	−1·63
Chemicals	+1·25	+2·47	+0·65	−1·88	+1·75
Oil, glue, soap, &c. . . .	−0·43	+2·35	+0·61	−3·88	−0·25
*Steel melting, iron puddling, &c. .	−2·55	+2·04	+0·21	−2·56	+1·07
Brass, copper, zinc, &c. . .	−0·83	+1·20	+0·26	−2·28	+1·35
*General engineering . . .	−0·33	+3·93	+0·55	−4·81	−1·18
Electrical engineering . . .	+4·43	+5·12	+0·92	−1·62	+2·01
Motor vehicles, cycles, &c. . .	+2·23	+4·47	+0·86	−3·10	+0·53
*Shipbuilding and ship repairing .	−1·55	+2·67	+0·36	−4·58	−0·95
Electric cable, apparatus, &c. .	+5·53	+6·65	+0·98	−2·10	+1·53
*Cotton	−1·43	+3·62	+0·16	−5·20	−1·57
Bread, biscuits, &c. . . .	+0·70	+4·71	+0·88	−4·89	−1·26
Other food	+2·58	+2·68	+1·69	−1·79	+1·83
*Building	+1·53	+2·75	+1·42	−2·64	+0·98
Distributive trades . . .	+5·28	+8·46	+1·99	−5·17	−1·56
*Shipping service . . .	+3·85	+2·72	+2·19	−1·05	+2·58
Printing, publishing, &c. . .	+3·23	+5·39	+0·82	−2·99	+0·64
*Woollen and worsted . .	−0·23	+3·64	+0·23	−4·09	−0·46
*Boots, shoes, &c. . . .	−0·38	+4·25	+0·61	−5·23	−1·60
Stone	+3·13	+1·90	+2·14	−0·91	+2·72
Other metal	+2·60	+5·44	+0·53	−3·37	+0·26
Furniture	+5·33	+7·76	+0·82	−3·26	+0·37
Drink	+0·38	+2·15	+0·60	−2·37	+1·26
Paper	+3·45	+2·39	+0·38	−0·67	+4·30
Total	+1·8	+4·28	+1·11	−3·63	0

* Industries depressed relatively to all industry.

labour; thus, in the case of the distributive, cotton, and engineering
industries, there was both a large inflow of juveniles and a large outflow
of older men. As regards transferences between industries, in those expanding industries where the *outflow* was large relatively to the net increase
in insured (e.g. the distributive trades) it is probable that a large proportion

5211   R

of the transferees was youths—possibly discharged on becoming eligible for adult wage rates. Although there was an obvious correlation between juvenile new entrants, adult new entrants, transferees, and the pull to-wards or away from each industry, the juvenile new entrants entered declining industries on a disturbingly large scale. Thus, while transference out of coal-mining was very high (4 per cent. per annum), juveniles continued to enter at a rate sufficient to increase the industry by over $2\frac{1}{2}$ per cent. per annum. The failure of depressed industries to contract more rapidly was due as much to the difficulty of damping down the inflow of juvenile workers as to the difficulty of transferring older workers out of the industry.

On the basis of the findings of the empirical studies certain practical steps were suggested which might help to increase the mobility of labour and thus reduce unemployment in Great Britain.

1. The possibility of placing industries in the depressed areas should, of course, be considered. Statistics could be published giving the occupation, skill, and age of workers in each part of the country for the guidance of new enterprises. But the drawbacks of changing the location of industries should be carefully borne in mind: the prosperity of an industry depends on many other factors besides the supply of labour—for instance, on easy access to raw materials and to markets.

2. The policy of facilitating the movement of labour to those places and industries where it is needed should be actively pursued. It has been seen that distance is a powerful force acting against the redistribution of labour. To reduce the friction arising from this source a system of free or cheap railway journeys for people in search of work might be introduced.

3. The fact that labour does respond, though slowly, to differences between the unemployment rates as between areas and industries suggests that local and industrial unemployment rates, as well as statistics of labour turnover, should be given much greater publicity at the Labour Exchanges; the redistribution of labour towards the prosperous areas and industries might thereby be speeded up.

4. Frictions against movement between industries are considerable and, in a modern dynamic economy where the industrial structure requires great elasticity, they are grave obstacles to progress. They depend fundamentally on differences in skill and on degrees of similarity between industries and occupations. These frictions can be reduced from two ends. Workers can be trained in new operations or new occupations when shortages occur, and operations in industry as a whole can be rendered less skilled and more standardized by the further application of machinery and division of labour.

5. Finally, we should point out that there are many other sociological and economic factors which cause the mobility of labour to be so low. These require, in the first place, very careful analysis. At each stage of spatial migration—the decision to work in a new environment among strange people; the business of moving one's home and family; the task of settling down (perhaps to a new occupation) with new workmates, new employers, and even new conditions of work; and finally the process of making fresh contacts for the pursuit of social and intellectual activities— there are very grave difficulties. New social and economic institutions which would moderate or remove these difficulties are clearly essential for any really satisfactory policy of increasing the mobility of labour.

BIBLIOGRAPHY

A. *The Oxford Studies*

1. E. ACKROYD and J. MARSCHAK, 'The Economics and Government of a Changing Area', chap. iii, *Survey of Social Services in the Oxford District*. Barnett House. 1938.
2. J. MARSCHAK, 'Industrial Immigration', ibid.
3. H. MAKOWER, J. MARSCHAK, and H. W. ROBINSON, 'Studies in Mobility of Labour':
   'A Tentative Statistical Measure', *Oxford Economic Papers*, No. 1. 'Analysis for Great Britain, Part I', ibid. No. 2. 'Analysis for Great Britain, Part II', ibid. No. 4.
4. G. H. DANIEL, Some Factors affecting the Movement of Labour', ibid. No. 3.
   'Labour Migration and Age Composition', *The Sociological Review*, vol. xxxi, No. 3.
   'Labour Migration and Fertility', ibid. No. 4.

B. *Other Publications*

5. E. G. RAVENSTEIN: 'The Laws of Migration', *Journal of the Royal Statistical Society*, 1885 and 1889.
6. A. REDFORD, *Labour Migration in England 1800–1850*. 1926.
7. H. JEROME, *Migration and Business Cycles*. New York. 1926.
8. 'Migration and Economic Opportunity', *Report of the Study of Population Redistribution*. Philadelphia. 1936.
9. B. THOMAS, 'Analysis of Migration into London and the South East and other Divisions', *Economica*. 1934 and 1937.
10. —, 'Labour Mobility in the South Wales and Monmouthshire Coal Mining Industry 1920–30', *Economic Journal*. 1931.
11. —, 'Use of the Census for Measuring Population Movements', *Private Paper*. 1937.
12. J. JEWKES and H. CAMPION, 'Mobility of Labour in the Cotton Industry', *Economic Journal*. 1938.
13. R. S. WALSHAW, 'The Time-lag in Migration Movements', *Sociological Review*, 1938.
14. *Evidence submitted to the Royal Commission on the Geographical Distribution of the Population*. H.M.S.O. 1938.
15. *Report on the Location of Industry in Great Britain*. P.E.P. 1939.
16. *Men Without Work*. Pilgrim Trust. Cambridge. 1938.

17. A. D. K. Owen, 'The Social Consequences of Industrial Transference', *Sociological Review*. 1937.
18. H. W. Singer, *Pilgrim Trust Unemployment Enquiry*, Interim Papers. 1937.
19. A. B. Hill, 'Internal Migration and its Effects upon the Death Rates with Special Reference to the County of Essex', *Medical Research Council Special Report Series*, No. 95. 1925.
20. *Planning*. P.E.P. 1936.
21. Results of numerous special statistical inquiries conducted by the Ministry of Labour are given in the Ministry's *Gazette*, *Annual Report* and occasional special CMD publications.

Extensive additional bibliographies are given in:

22. D. S. Thomas, 'Research Memorandum on Migration Differentials', *Social Science Research Council*. Bulletin 43. New York. 1938.
23. —, 'Research Memorandum on Internal Migration in the Depression', ibid. Bulletin 30. 1937.

(ii) *The Experience and Lessons of the Past Ten Years*

By HERBERT W. ROBINSON

1. Introduction

IF the results of the pre-war study of the labour market are to acquire any practical significance for the future, it will be necessary to supplement them with an examination of the experience of the vital ten years since 1939. Accordingly, in this section, we shall re-appraise the broad conclusions of the Oxford studies; then we shall examine the history of British labour policy during the war and post-war years, with the object of throwing into relief the main problems encountered and the lessons taught. However, fully realizing the complexity of the social, political, and economic problems confronting the nation to-day, and the difficulty of prescribing labour and location-of-industry policies which are both economically sound and politically feasible, the author will not venture to propose policy changes.

2. Significant Results of the Oxford Studies

Re-examination of the Oxford studies leads us to separate the results into two groups. One may be regarded as merely expressing in quantitative terms the effects on mobility of certain characteristics of human beings which have always been obvious *a priori*. The second is far more valuable because it indicates the nature and the extent of the response of labour to economic incentives in pre-war days, and in so doing throws light on the fundamental psychology of British labour at that time—a psychology which, perhaps, remains basically unchanged even to-day.

In the first category the most obvious conclusion was the decline in mobility with age. It goes without saying that as most men grow older they become less adaptable. Moreover, the longer they remain in one community or one industry, the stronger become the ties holding them to that community or industry. Mobility is affected both from the side of the willingness to change and from the side of the ability to adjust. Similarly, the retarding effect of married status and number of dependants was to be expected, since the attachment of dependants reduces the willingness and ability to move geographically, quite apart from the fact that it is also a corollary of advancing age. The adverse influence on mobility of prolonged unemployment perhaps indicated in some degree a reduced ability to adjust after a long period of stagnation, but more likely reflected merely age, marital condition, and the exhaustion of the funds with which to finance movement. Perhaps even the low mobility of females was to be expected since women, because their wage rates are usually low, almost always have to remain with their parents and husbands; their immobility therefore largely reflected the adverse effects on male mobility of age and marital condition. Likewise, the difficulty of moving workers between industries is obvious: not only are workers naturally disinclined to cast away skills which have been arduously, and perhaps expensively, acquired, but they find the acquisition of new ones both tedious and difficult. Furthermore, workers in an expanding industry naturally oppose any down-grading of their jobs in order to make it easier for transferees to enter the industry, and trade unions may insist on the satisfaction of strict requirements before admitting new members. The chief value of the studies lay in the measurements made of *how much* such factors as these influenced mobility.

Considered as a whole the studies showed that the British labour force did respond to economic incentives by moving away from depressed areas and industries into prosperous areas and industries, and in so doing tended to equalize unemployment rates everywhere. In due course, unless the major economic factors had changed, migration would have brought about an equilibrium, even though it could not itself have increased materially the average prosperity of the whole country. The process of adjustment was proceeding, however, only at a slow rate, and throughout the studies one is left with the impression that the response to incentives was very weak. Perhaps the most easily comprehended measurement is the 'duration of adjustment', the length of time required at the current rate of migration to equalize unemployment rates throughout the country. Of course, this measure depended on the assumptions made regarding the proportion of migrants who had been unemployed and the proportion who obtained employment after migration (s and k). The most realistic assumptions were probably that nearly all migrants were unemployed at the time of migration ($s = 1$) and that only some of them obtained employment after migration ($k < 1$). In such a case we saw, on p. 232, that, before the depression, it would have taken between 6 and 15 years to reach an equilibrium. And after the depression it would have taken between 30 and 60 years; so long, in fact, that one might almost assess migration after the depression as insignificant in terms of what was required. Though inter-industrial mobility was greater than spatial mobility, it would still have taken up to 20 years after 1931 for inter-industrial transference alone to equalize industrial unemployment rates. Likewise, the deterrent effect of distance was remarkably powerful; using the measurements of 'spatial friction' given on p. 217, it appears that, if the distance involved in movement between two areas of given relative prosperity increased from, say, 30 to 300 miles, the number of migrants would fall to about one-eightieth of its former level.

Even more revealing was the fact that, in order to fit the facts, migration between any two areas had to be assumed proportional to the relative difference in unemployment rates. It can easily be shown that, if the 'duration of adjustment' is to be the same in depression as in prosperity, formula (4) should have been not $M_{ab} = \lambda_{ab} \cdot \dfrac{(u_a - u_b)}{u_b} \cdot ab$, but rather

$$M_{ab} = \lambda_{ab} \cdot \frac{(u_a - u_b)}{(K_{ab} - U_{ab})} \cdot ab, \tag{7}$$

where K_{ab} is a constant and U_{ab} is the total number of persons unemployed in the two areas A and B. Now, if we assume that the migrant would obtain the same wage rate whether employed in A or B, and that the unemployment rate represents the proportion of time the average worker spends out of work, the absolute discrepancy in unemployment rates $(u_a - u_b)$ is proportional to the increase in expected earnings to be obtained by moving from A to B. According to formula (7), for a given incentive— as measured by such an expected increase in earnings—migration should have *increased* with an increase in the general level of unemployment. And this is logical, because, when unemployment is high, a given absolute increase in expected earnings would represent a greater *percentage* increase in earnings. Perfectly rational workers would tend to move according to such a formula. In practice, workers tended to move according to formula (4), which implied that, for a given incentive, migration *decreased* with an increase in the general level of unemployment, and therefore greatly extended the period of time required to equalize unemployment rates in a severe depression.

Any explanation of this phenomenon in psychological terms must, of course, be very tentative. However, several factors might have operated. First, for most workers migration meant taking a chance that an equally skilled job would not be available in the new area, and therefore that expected earnings might even be lower than in the depressed area. Second, being already established in a depressed area where rents and some other costs were low, migration might involve higher living expenses and less comfortable accommodation. Third, the existence of unemployment insurance, public assistance, and other benefits, made the difference in expected receipts after migration much smaller than mere differences in employment rates would indicate. Thus, if receipts while unemployed were 50 per cent. of earnings while employed, the increase in total receipts to be obtained by moving from an area with 20 per cent. unemployment to an area with 5 per cent. unemployment would not be 19 per cent. but only $8\frac{1}{2}$ per cent. Finally, the individual potential migrant probably considered his chances of employment inferior to those of the natives of the more prosperous area, and was therefore extremely sensitive to the rate of unemployment in that area. If one can combine all these considerations into a general statement, the average worker in a depressed area before the war was unwilling to spend the effort and money involved in migration, and perhaps suffer hardships in a strange community, for the sake of improving his expected receipts only slightly. And the higher the unemployment rate in the more prosperous area, the less attractive did the chance of improvement appear, and the more certain and secure by contrast seemed life in his own depressed area. Add to these factors the psychological difficulties of moving to a new area with strange people, accents, customs, and surroundings, the reserved nature of the average modern Britisher and his strong attachment to family and home-town, and it is understandable that the response to incentives was not only weak but also, in the depression, inhibited.

Looking back on these studies one is almost tempted to believe that the British nation, which had always been distinguished by its pioneering spirit, suffered some dampening of this spirit in the twentieth century. Relatively few, at any rate, seemed willing to stake the chance of a loss for the chance of a gain involved in migration in search of work after the First World War. Perhaps much of the explanation lies in the unprecedented upheavals of the war, the sheer magnitude of the great depression, and the enormous pools of unemployment which developed in certain areas and industries. But some probably lies also in the rapid development of a 'Social Security' system in this century which, while it avoided untold misery, also blunted the spur of threatened need and poverty. This is not to say by any means that there had been any loss of self-respect or that all workers did not value very highly the satisfaction of earning a living,

For it was always stressed that unemployment benefits and assistance were not 'doles' but the maturity of insurances, as it were, which had already been paid for by past contributions and taxes, and were for the express purpose of carrying the worker over a period of unemployment. Unfortunately, many expected, with a blind faith, that whatever readjustment was needed would occur in their immediate environment and that none was needed in themselves. Already the feeling was present that 'the government ought to do something about it', which meant, in its most extreme form, that a job at the old trade in the same area, perhaps even in the same firm, should somehow be engineered by the State. In other words, the average worker wanted and looked for security, and preferred it, even if it meant a low standard of living in a depressed area, to a venture into the outer economic environment where uncertainty was inevitable and economic improvement problematical.

3. Experience during the War Years

The outbreak of war brought the problems of mobility of labour sharply into focus. The armed forces had to be built up and equipped with all the weapons of modern war as rapidly as possible. Thus, while a substantial part of the man-power of the nation was being siphoned off for military training, normal civilian requirements of goods and services were being supplemented by vast service requirements of munitions and supplies, causing the man-power needs of industry to expand. A major re-deployment of man-power was therefore demanded; the young men (and, to a lesser extent, the young women) had to leave their jobs and enter the armed forces; the unoccupied men, and the much larger body of unoccupied women and housewives, had to return to, or enter for the first time, the various branches of industry. Furthermore, since the exodus to the forces exceeded the number of new workers becoming available, those branches producing the less essential goods and services had to contract sharply in order to allow the required expansion in those producing the munitions and supplies of war. An equilibrium would only be achieved when the fully equipped armed forces reached such a size that, in order to maintain them in their war operations, the whole available civil population was fully occupied in producing their supplies and sustaining the economy on the lowest level of comfort which could be tolerated. Such re-deployment required that many millions of workers who would not be needed for the armed forces would nevertheless have to leave their less essential jobs and take completely new ones in the expanding industries, often in quite different localities from those in which they had been working.

During the first nine months of the war, recruitment of men for the armed forces was determined by the speed at which the arms and equipment they were to use could be produced. But while this could be accomplished as speedily as desired by use of the National Service Acts, the recruitment of labour for key industries depended almost entirely upon normal economic forces, supplemented by exhortation and appeals to patriotism, and proved extremely lethargic. As Mr. Churchill says in *The Gathering Storm*: 'the sense of extreme urgency was lacking. There was a "twilight" mood in the ranks of labour and of those who directed production as well as in the military operations.' In commenting on a special survey of employment in the engineering, motor, and aircraft group of industries, which had been given huge orders, often on a 'cost-plus' basis, and could afford to offer high wages, he said in a note to the Cabinet, dated 4 May 1940:

'This Report suggests that in this fundamental group, at any rate, we have hardly begun to organize man-power for the production of munitions.

In (previous papers) it was estimated that a very large expansion, amounting to 71·5 per cent. of the number engaged in the metal industry, would be needed in the first year of war. Actually the engineering, motor, and aircraft group, which covers three-fifths of the metal industry and which is discussed in this survey, has only expanded by 11·1 per cent. (122,000) between June, 1939, and April 1940. This is less than one-sixth of the expansion stated to be required. Without any Government intervention, by the mere improvement of trade, the number increased as quickly as this in the year 1936/37.

Although 350,000 boys leave school each year, there is an increase of only 25,000 in the number of males under twenty-one employed in this group. Moreover, the proportion of women and young persons has only increased from 26·6 per cent. to 27·6 per cent. In the engineering, motor, and aircraft group, we now have only one woman for every twelve men. During the last war the ratio of women to men in the metal industries increased from one woman for every ten men to one woman for every three men. In the first year of the last war, July, 1914, to July, 1915, the new workers drafted into the metal industries amounted to 20 per cent. of those already there. In the group under survey which may fairly be taken as typical of the whole metal industry, only 11 per cent. have been added in the last ten months.'

Although to a large extent this poor performance was due to the inevitable difficulties of enlarging productive capacity rapidly and of finding the skilled men for key jobs, the labour force had, in fact, once more displayed its low mobility, even in the face of a national emergency. The inadequacy of labour movement may be gauged from the fact that, despite the net recruitment of 1·8 million persons into the armed forces by mid-1940, the number of unemployed had fallen by only 50 per cent. and was still 645,000, or $3\frac{1}{2}$ per cent. of the labour force. It was only in the midst of the obviously disastrous Battle of France that it was realized that the normal incentives to labour, even when combined with special ones growing out of the war, such as the schedule of reserved occupations, were inadequate to achieve the required speed of re-deployment. Accordingly, on 22 May, an Act of Parliament was passed giving the government practically unlimited powers over the life and liberty of the people. The Minister of Labour was empowered to direct anyone to perform any service required, subject only to a fair-wages clause. Labour supply committees were to be set up in important centres. A Production Council was formed and a Director of Labour Supply appointed. It finally proved necessary, in order to obtain the desired distribution of labour between industries and areas, to develop, under these powers, a whole armoury of labour controls—Regulation 58 A (I), which provided for direction of a person to any job in any area; Restriction on Engagement Orders, which restricted the rights of employers to engage workers; Essential Work Orders, which limited both the freedom of employers in 'scheduled' essential undertakings to discharge workers and the freedom of workers in these undertakings to leave their employment; Registration for Employment Orders under which men and women, especially those possessing urgently needed skills, had to register particulars about themselves and thus become liable for direction into essential work. By the end of the war these controls applied to all men and women aged 18 to 50 and, in theory at least, every person was finally, under the broad supervision of the Ministry of Labour, working in that particular job in that particular area in which he or she could contribute the maximum to the war effort.

Alongside these drastic measures widespread adjustments became necessary in the normal standards and practices applied in the factories and workshops. Agreements were made between the employers and the trade unions for existing rules, regulations, and customs to be relaxed, so that alternative classes of workers, including women, might be employed on jobs hitherto performed by skilled men; industrial processes were 'broken down' to enable the maximum utilization of up-graded workers and persons trained in a narrow range of skilled operations. Schemes of payment by results were put into operation. That these changes were not made easily is demonstrated by the fact that it was not until 1943 that they were fully introduced into the shipbuilding industry, and in most cases it was expressly stated that they were 'for the period of the war only'.

The magnitude of the vast movements of labour which finally occurred is shown in Table 1. Even this table does not convey a complete picture of the tremendous movements of persons involved during the war years. At the peak of war mobilization there were almost one million men aged 65 and over and women aged 60 and over in industrial employment; about 400,000 of these would normally have been in retirement. About half a million men, aged 14–64, and $2\frac{1}{2}$ million married and single women, aged 14–59, not normally employed in industry, entered industrial employment or the services. No less than 900,000 women with household responsibilities took up part-time employment. The total available man-power at

TABLE 1

Changes in the Working Population and its Distribution among Industries* 1939–48

(Men aged 14–64 and women aged 14–59)

All numbers in thousands.

	June 1939	Max. or min. 1939–45		June 1947		
					% Inc. or dec.	
	Number	Number	% Inc. or dec.	Number	Max. or min. to 1947	1939–47
Working Population	19,750	22,281	+13	20,357	−8	+3
Males	14,656	15,222	+4	14,618	−4	..
Females	5,094	7,253	+42	5,739	−20	+13
Armed Forces and Auxiliary Services	480	5,090	+960	1,292	−75	+168
Males	480	4,653	+870	1,228	−73	+157
Females	..	467	..	64	−86	..
Civil Employment	18,000	16,416	−9	18,650	14	+3
Males	13,163	10,133	−23	13,047	+30	−1
Females	4,837	6,769	+40	5,603	−17	+16
Agriculture and fishing	950	1,048	+11	1,080	+3	+14
Mining and quarrying	873	799	−8	829	+4	−5
Metals, engineering, vehicles, and ship-building	2,812	4,659	+65	3,485	−25	+23
Chemicals, explosives, paints, oils, &c.	294	618	+110	356	−42	+20
Textiles	1,002	634	−37	783	+24	−22
Clothing, boots, and shoes	752	455	−39	629	+32	−17
Food, drink, and tobacco	654	518	−20	609	+17	−7
Cement, bricks, pottery, glass, &c.	265	159	−40	253	+59	−4
Leather, wood, paper, &c.	859	536	−37	768	−42	−10
Other manufactures	177	123	−30	218	+78	+24
Building and civil engineering	1,310	623	−53	1,344	+117	+2
Gas, water, and electricity supply	242	193	−20	266	+38	+10
Transport and shipping	1,233	1,146	−7	1,417	+27	+15
Distributive trades	2,887	1,927	−33	2,319	+20	−20
Commerce, banking, insurance, and finance	413	264	−36	347	+31	−16
National and local government, civil defence, fire service, and police	1,465	2,112	+44	2,173	+3	+49
Miscellaneous	1,812	1,331	−26	1,774	+33	−2
Registered unemployed and ex-members of H.M. Forces not yet in employment	1,270	74	−94	415	+460	−67
Males	1,013	54	−95	343	+540	−66
Females	257	20	−95	72	+260	−72

* Two part-time workers are counted as one full-time worker.

its peak (counting two part-time workers as one full-time worker) had been increased by 13 per cent. of its 1939 level; and since unemployment, which had been 1·27 million in 1939, was almost eliminated, the man-power actually being used in industry or the forces increased by one-sixth, from 18½ million in 1939 to no less than 21½ million at the climax of the war effort. All this was additional to the inflow of juveniles at the rate of over 600,000 per annum and a corresponding loss through death and retirement.

Besides this mass influx of persons into industry, most of whom had to learn their jobs *ab initio* with a minimum of training, the net expansion of the armed forces was 4½ million persons and, of course, many more actually passed through; there was, therefore, a tremendous turnover of individuals in industry. Finally, there were the violent changes in the distribution of man-power between industries; the metals and engineering industry expanded by 1·85 million or 65 per cent., chemicals by 0·32 million or 110 per cent., and national and local government, civil defence, fire service, and police by 0·55 million or 44 per cent. Undoubtedly many millions of workers moved from the contracting industries, chief among which were the distributive trades (down by nearly 1 million), textiles and clothing (down by 0·7 million), and building and civil engineering (down by 0·7 million), into these expanding industries.

The revolutionary changes in the factories and workshops may be gauged by the increase in the proportion of women, from 2·7 women per ten workers in industry in 1939 to 3·9 women per ten workers at the peak of female mobilization. In the engineering industry, traditionally a skilled industry, the number increased from 1·0 to 3·5 women per ten workers.

As a rough approximation we can estimate that over 10 million persons, or 55 per cent. of the pre-war working population, had to learn new jobs in industry or the services during the war years. And the new jobs in a substantial proportion of cases were quite complex; personnel in the armed forces were highly mechanized and equipped with the most complex electrical and mechanical devices, and those in the workshops and ordnance factories had to produce these same devices to exacting standards. Even unskilled volunteer female labour had to learn the intricacies of coupon-clipping in a shop or the clerical routine of an office. The British population thus displayed, in the most convincing way, that it was physically capable of learning new jobs remarkably quickly. Given the willingness of the firm to design its production line according to the capacities of the available labour, to train new workers of all ages, and to grade up semi-skilled workers to perform more skilled work while breaking down skilled operations into a number of less skilled ones, and given the willingness of trade unions to co-operate wholeheartedly in achieving these ends, the physical barriers to mobility of labour between industries proved surmountable. As regards spatial mobility, those who found themselves in the armed forces were stationed in all parts of the country, and civilians moved from one town to another much more freely as part of the process of building up the war industries and manning the new factories, often locating themselves far away from the large industrial centres. Millions of younger persons found themselves much more independent of family and home-town and to that extent much more mobile than ever before. At no other time had so many individuals seen so much of the country, observed the variations in economic standards and conditions of life between localities, and learned to understand the ways of life of communities in other parts than their own. One indication of the extent of the movement is the fact that the number of passenger-miles on the railways increased from 19,000 million in 1938 to over 35,000 million in 1945. By the end of the war the nation had achieved levels of inter-industrial and spatial mobility sufficient to meet those called for by the depths of any depression.

To sum up the experience of the war years: it is apparent that, given all the characteristics of British labour and industry in 1939–40, the mobility of labour proved remarkably low even under the stress of war and the stimulus of unsurpassed patriotic zeal, and in order to achieve redistribution of man-power at an adequate speed, a complete system of governmental labour recruitment and direction finally became necessary; but a clear demonstration was given of the physical possibilities of moving labour between industries and areas, and of transforming the structure of the economy, on a scale far transcending any readjustments which could conceivably be required in time of peace. In other words, while labour showed it possessed the physical mobility, it also showed it did not possess the willingness, in the environment in which it found itself, to use this ability. The economic incentives required to achieve the needed degree of movement were outside the realms of possibility, and so the incentives of threats and penalties had to be applied as the prime means of securing labour, retaining it in essential work, and transferring it from job to job. No less than 8·6 million workers were at one time covered by the Essential Work Orders, 11·8 million applications were made during the war to National Service Officers for permission to leave, discharge, or transfer, and half a million appeals were made against the National Service Officers' decisions; in addition untold numbers (statistics have not been published) were directed to essential work.

4. The Post-War Labour Market
Britain's Changed Economic Position

At this point we may profitably consider, in very general terms, what are the characteristics of Great Britain's world economic environment following the tremendous upheavals of the war, and the problems these characteristics raise for the British economy. First and foremost, it has now become clear that, while the war disrupted the economic life of the entire world, industrial capacity, particularly in the metals and engineering industry, was being created at a much faster rate than it was being destroyed in almost every country. At the close of hostilities, therefore, given the willingness of the United States to divert some of its wealth to making good the more serious destruction in certain fields and certain countries, most nations could expect, after their agriculture had revived, standards of living equal to or even surpassing the most prosperous pre-war years—provided their productive resources could be adapted to peace-time needs and kept fully employed. This has two important implications. In the first place it means that, after a period of re-stocking and heavy investment to rebuild consumers' inventories and change over the productive apparatus from a war basis to a peace basis, there will have to be extensive readjustments to meet quite different long-term requirements. Secondly, all the vagaries and caprices of consumer demand when standards of living are high will come into play once major investment needs have been satisfied; and these will require increased flexibility in the productive apparatus, perhaps even exceeding that attained before the war.

In addition to these inevitable consequences of the war-time distortion of economic systems there have, however, been international changes of great magnitude: the development of industrial capacity in many overseas countries due to shortage of supplies from their traditional suppliers; the redistribution of the world's wealth, resulting in higher standards of living in under-developed areas and reduced willingness to export food and raw materials; and, above all, the general psychology resulting from the 1930's and the war years which has led to controls of various kinds, economic nationalism, and schemes for artificially improving the terms of trade or for insulating the economy from adverse external changes. To Great Britain, whose position has been seriously influenced also by the liquidation of a substantial part of her overseas investments and the growth of a very heavy external debt, these latter changes mean even more than to other countries; for her whole economy was built on international exchange of a special character, based largely on conditions which existed before the First World War. Another important factor is the tremendous impetus given to scientific research during the war years, which has led to new products, new methods of production, and, probably in many instances, altogether new cost relationships between different products, between different countries, and even between different areas in the same country. These effects will probably need several years to work themselves out and to influence the possibilities of international trade. It took twenty years after the First World War to find the delicate balance between the British economy and the world economy. That balance has now been disturbed, and no one can see clearly just what shifts in the structure of the British economy a new balance will demand.

There are other factors too. Britain's population will soon be declining, and average age is already rapidly rising; with a falling working population considerable reductions will at times become necessary in certain industries and areas, perhaps on a scale far exceeding those which occurred in the depression. Her natural resources, after over one and a half centuries of exploitation, are becoming ever more difficult to work. All in all, the prospects are for a much greater level of uncertainty than at any other time in her history, both in the home economy and in her overseas trade. Furthermore, because of the change in her debt position, she will be much more violently affected by any future external developments. All this is quite separate from the added complications of the strained political relations which have developed between the great powers and superimposed other internal and external economic problems.

The inevitable conclusions to be drawn from these facts is that, if the standard of living is to be safeguarded, the British economy must, more than at any other time, be extremely flexible and adaptable, ready to switch available man-power, facilities, and resources promptly between industries in response to changes in internal or external conditions. Yet, on the other side of the balance sheet, the war had assisted in providing the very flexibility required. In 1945 productive capacity as a whole was far in excess of the labour available to man it and, except for a few bottlenecks, there was no difficulty in finding the capacity to meet demand, however that demand might be composed. Moreover, as explained above, the nation's man-power had been shuttled between industries on an enormous scale during the war and, by and large, experienced man-power existed for even the most rapidly expanding industries—labour, physically at least, was extremely mobile both industrially and spatially. The potential flexibility of the economy was thus very much greater than before the war.

The Choice between Political Philosophies

With the end of the war, however, the country also faced, at the 1945 General Election, the difficult problem of choosing between two basic political philosophies. On one side were the proponents of *laissez-faire* who believed in restoring, as far as practicable, the operation of free markets and competitive enterprise which had characterized a large part of the British economy before the war. On the other were the various Left-Wing elements all believing, in varying degrees, in State ownership and control of the factors of production as a means of abolishing the possibility of large-scale unemployment and raising the standard of living of the working classes. The implications of the two philosophies were numerous, and extended into every aspect of social and economic life. Here we shall examine briefly their implications for the labour market from a strictly economic point of view, ignoring the political pressures and prejudices which in practice undoubtedly cause divergences from ideal objectives.

In an ideal system of *laissez-faire*, labour would be perfectly mobile, willing to move between occupations and areas as soon as the slightest differences in unemployment and wage rates showed themselves. It would be willing to learn new tasks irrespective of the degree of skill involved, willing to co-operate with production-management in diluting skilled labour and in breaking down skilled operations, willing to accept payment by results, willing to adjust hours of work and to see particular wage rates vary according to the value set upon the work by a free market. And the employer would be willing to adjust wage scales according to the need to attract or repel workers, and willing to adapt his equipment and production techniques to the fluctuations of the market. Indeed, at the present stage of technical development, one could imagine that, when standards of living had reached extremely high levels, mechanization of labour would have proceeded to the point where no worker, except for a class of highly trained production-planning engineers, assisted by expert tool-makers, performed more than a single specialized operation on the production line. Transference to a new industry would, for most workers, involve perhaps only a week's training on a new machine. This is not to say that wages would be depressed, for it is conceivable that although there would be only a narrow range of individual wage rates, there would yet be a very high level of output per head, the composition of which would be promptly adjusted to the tastes and fancies of the mass of the population; a very high standard of living would thus be achieved. The State, in such an economy, would have a minor role and, apart from that amount of social security necessary to protect or assist the needy, its economic function would be to ensure maximum competition by anti-monopoly laws, and to speed up economic change by reducing frictions and uncertainties. In respect of the labour market, the State would analyse economic developments in areas and industries and disseminate information regarding opportunities of better employment for workers and better supply of labour for employers; it would try to aid workers actually on the move between areas and industries by assisting with training and travel, by providing temporary living accommodation, and by engaging in similar purely 'lubricating' activities.

The advocates of a socialist economy believed that, under capitalism, it was impossible to prevent periodic widespread unemployment; the economy must be planned. The State should fix fair prices, wage rates, hours, &c., ensure full employment at all times by planning current production and investment, and rely upon the flow of juvenile new entrants to provide any necessary redistribution of labour among industries. If additional mobility were required, some advocated the offer of economic inducements to enter under-manned industries, while others would have directed individuals into specific jobs in the national interest. No very clear position was taken on the question of migration of labour, the implication being that production programmes would, as far as possible, be planned on the basis of the existing geographical distribution of labour.

The basic economic question of location of industry was not the subject of much controversy, since the Commission on the Distribution of the Industrial Population had been unanimous in condemning the free play of economic forces which had produced the depressed areas and the great industrial conurbations such as London and Birmingham; its members had only differed in their recommendations over the form, functions, and powers of a proposed new body which would deal with the social and economic problems associated with the subject. The result had been the creation of the Ministry of Town and Country Planning and the universal acceptance of the idea of considerable government control over location of industry and town and country planning.

In fact, however, there was still an important field of questions over which the two opposing sides might differ. Any general governmental control and supervision over town-planning, amenities, housing, travelling facilities, &c., hardly interferes with the location of industry since, if uniform, it merely, as it were, creates additional costs of development common to all areas. Both sides agreed with government prohibition of development in particular areas for strategic reasons. But how far should the government, through the new Ministry, actually plan the location of all replacement and of all new capacity, and in particular, how far should it direct it to those areas in which unemployment threatens?

Under *laissez-faire* the entrepreneur takes into account labour supply, existing facilities, raw-material supply, fuel and power supply, transportation, and proximity of markets in locating his plant; indeed only by his so doing can the economy achieve maximum economic efficiency. Those who advocate planning stress the waste involved in building houses and ancillary services, and in moving populations, when redistribution is on any large scale. They also explain that, by using market prices, and existing demand, the entrepreneur is assuming continued depressed consumer demand in the depressed area, while, if there were full employment, his decision might be different. Furthermore, local rates and taxes increase with unemployment and become powerful repellants to industry. And finally, may not the businessman base his decisions on very imperfect expectations? Free enterprisers say, however, that arguments about waste are untenable since rents and wages, and perhaps other costs, will fall in the depressed area and rise in the prosperous area, thus improving the attraction of the depressed area to suitable industries and restoring an equilibrium; that the government should properly use exchequer funds to remove excess local taxes due to abnormal unemployment; that, if assisted to work properly by government, industry and labour, the markets and the free-enterprise system look after all economic aspects of the problem automatically. Even if the planners grant the validity of these arguments, they often say that any slight economic loss is well worth while if the psychological and sociological hardships involved in enforced migration of the unemployed and their families can be avoided. However, although the political parties may thus have differed substantially over location-of-industry policy, this issue was clearly subsidiary to the central one of whether a predominantly planned or a predominantly free-enterprise economy was to be the long-run objective of the nation.

The result of the election was, of course, the triumph of the Labour Party. This was not surprising. The nation had experienced violent shocks during and after the First World War; it had experienced the miseries of a great depression which had necessitated extensive and most unpleasant readjustments; it had just emerged from a Second World War, during which the lives of nearly every citizen had been seriously disrupted. We have already observed, in studying the response of labour to incentives after the depression, signs of a strong preference for security and stability. Was the decision of the electorate possibly a projection of this same preference, enhanced by war-time tribulations, into the political field? Many workers felt there could be no security in *laissez-faire* and preferred continuation of government control even if, as the opposition claimed, economic efficiency would be lower. With guaranteed employment at agreed rates of pay, a lower but constant standard of living would be preferable to a higher average standard marred by periodic depressions and the misery of large-scale unemployment. And who could prove that in fact, if full employment was made permanent, and incomes more evenly distributed, even inefficient central planning would not yield higher average returns for the worker than free enterprise and the markets? It is somewhat ironic that, at the beginning of a period when the country would need the utmost flexibility, the majority of the population plumped for stability at any price for the individual worker.

Events following the election seem to show that, for the average trade-union member (there are about 9 million members), the victory was considered to imply the opportunity to enjoy shorter hours of work, security in the job, better working conditions, strict trade-union controls, including safeguards on qualifications and entry of new workers, and progressively higher wages in all industries simultaneously. I do not believe more than a few workers believed any large-scale direction of labour would be involved in the type of socialist planning envisaged. Most, probably, expected job-tenure such as characterized the nineteenth century when the population and the economy were growing rapidly; in those days, even though cyclical movements caused temporary unemployment of up to 10 per cent. in depressions, a man could serve his seven years' apprenticeship and know that, over the years, there would be a steady demand for his specialized services in a growing occupation, probably with good prospects of promotion to foreman if he were conscientious and above average ability. Few really understood the fact that, in a country with a stationary or declining population, subject to all the new forces of the post-war world, it is extremely likely that some industries will suddenly prove permanently overgrown, and that considerable reductions in size will be needed, involving extreme flexibility both of the labour force and of the productive apparatus.

The 1947 Man-power Crisis

We shall now examine, again in the most general terms, the course of events following the election. The actual changes in employment and industrial distribution up to mid-1947 are shown in Table 1. Compared with the war years, almost all the males 14–64 and about two-thirds of the females 14–59 who had been drawn into employment by the war left the labour force. This resulted in a male working population about the same as before the war, and a female working population 13 per cent., or 580,000, greater than in 1939. Since the armed forces were over 800,000 higher than pre-war, but unemployment 855,000 less than pre-war, total civil employment was about 3 per cent. greater than before the war. The metals and engineering industries, though down 25 per cent. from their peak, remained 23 per cent. greater than pre-war, no doubt as a result of the great world demand for capital equipment. Agriculture and fishing, due to the world food situation, expanded beyond their war-time peak to 14 per cent. above pre-war levels. Consumer-goods industries generally remained smaller, with textiles and clothing, the distributive trades and commerce, &c., some 20 per cent. below, and food, drink and tobacco, leather, wood, paper, &c., some 10 per cent. below, the 1939 levels. Chemicals, oils and paints, and 'other manufactures' were 20–25 per cent. greater than before the war, reflecting technical developments during the war and investment demand. Finally, owing to the increased emphasis on government controls, the total numbers in national and local government increased still further to reach 50 per cent., or 700,000, above pre-war levels. The number unemployed or demobilized and in process of absorption into the economy was down by 67 per cent., or 855,000. At 415,000 they were only 2·2 per cent. of the total available labour force; considering the whole country there were conditions of super-full employment.

In order to discover as far as possible what mobility of labour had been required to bring about these post-war changes, it is necessary to consider the facts of the economic situation in the years 1945–7 and the policies followed by the government. In the first place, there was no shortage of productive capacity as a whole; for, if the peak labour forces in all industries are added together—a rough indication of the size of the industrial capacity in total—we obtain a total of 21 million, compared with a total working population (including armed forces and unemployed) at the end of the war of 20·4 million and an actual working civilian labour force of 16·4 million. And after two years, though 3·8 million persons had been released from the forces, the actual civilian working population was still only 18·7 million persons. If the numbers absorbed in government service are excluded, the actual civilian working population in June 1947 totalled only 16·5 million compared with total peak forces in non-government work of 18·9 million. Nor was there any shortage of effective demand. Inside the country there were the enormous deferred demands of consumers and industry, made effective by great liquid balances and artificially restricted prices; and to home demand was added an infinitely large external demand for investment and restocking, made effective by large sterling balances, British contributions to UNRRA, and the policy of maximizing exports. There was a sellers' market both at home and abroad. It was quite clear that the limiting factor on production would be available labour.

The method used by the government to control the structure of production was, in the first stages, simply to restrict the flow of available materials, fuel and power, construction, and imported equipment to each industry according to the volume of production deemed desirable, and to continue, on a limited scale (mainly in respect of persons liable to be called up for military service), the application of the Control of Engagements and Essential Work Orders. Since the numbers employed on production for civilian consumption at home had fallen from 4·6 million at mid-1939 to only 2·4 million at mid-1945, such control of the labour market through control of other factors of production was extremely powerful in preventing unwanted increases in any direction. But there remained the problem of procuring an increased supply of labour in those fields where a rapid expansion of output was desired. At first the government seems to have had some confidence that, by restriction of employment opportunities in other sectors, sufficient economic incentives would develop to attract labour into the favoured industries. It was an avowed aim of government policy to effect redistribution of man-power as far as possible on a voluntary basis and to narrow the field of compulsion to the strictest limits; accordingly, by the middle of 1947, the scope of the Ministry of Labour's controls over labour and management was almost whittled away. Whatever chances of retaining them had disappeared when the fuel and power crisis of February 1947 caused unemployment to rise to over 2 million and rendered the retention of controls anomalous. Reliance was placed on appeals to women to enter or return to industry and to men and women to stay on at their work instead of retiring, on recruitment of foreign workers, on publicity campaigns in areas where labour was urgently needed, and on special efforts to recruit men for coal-mining and other under-manned industries.

The position into which the government had worked itself was, however, an impossible one. As is shown later, the economic indicators had been deliberately disconnected; in resorting to appeals, the government confessed they were inadequate. Yet it still left the flows of labour to be largely determined by them. Such a situation clearly could not last.

Before discussing the next phase in the post-war labour market, however, let us examine to what extent the working population had been required to change jobs and move from place to place. Considering first the change in the distribution of the labour force between industries as shown in Table 1, the most noteworthy feature is the fact that it was only in the case of agriculture and fishing, 'other manufactures', building and civil engineering, public utilities, transport and shipping, and government that the post-war labour force exceeded both the pre-war and war-time maxima; and in all those cases together the total increase over the past peak was 376,000. Thus, considering the fact that about 600,000 juveniles, the most adaptable of all workers, entered the labour force each year, hardly any adult in the labour force in June 1947 *need* have been in any occupation in which he or she had not worked either before or during the war. The net redistribution between industries which actually took place thus required little re-training of labour; even ex-members of the forces who changed their peace-time occupation probably learnt their new trade, or a closely allied skill, during their war-time service. However, in so far as the one and a half million persons who retired from the labour force were replaced from other industries, there may have been some genuine inter-industrial mobility in the pre-war sense; but this must have been small.

Table 2 shows the extent of changes in the distribution of the insured population among the regions of Great Britain between 1939 and 1947. These statistics show the effects of the government's deliberate policy of retaining munitions production and encouraging the growth of new industries in the 'Special Areas', now called the 'Development Areas'. This policy, which had already been laid down in May 1944 by the Coalition Government, was intensified by the end of 1945 through the control of the erection of new buildings and of the extension of old ones, and through the allocation of raw materials, fuel, and power. It is clear from a comparison of the changes in total insured workers in the depression period,

TABLE 2

Changes in the Distribution of the Insured Population among Regions

Area (pre-war classification)	Insured—July 1937 as % of July 1932	% Net redistribution 1932-7	Area (post-war classification)	Insured—July 1947 as % of July 1939 Men	Women	Men and women	% Net redistribution 1939-47 Men	Women	Men and women
Scotland	103	—4	Scotland	95	100	99	..	+2	+1
North	100	—7	Northern	97	146	105	+2	+38	+7
North-west	100	—7	North-west	94	99	95	—1	—9	—3
North-east	104	—3	E. and W. Ridings	95	99	96	..	—9	—2
			N. Midlands	97	101	98	+2	—7	..
Midlands	110	+3	Midlands	95	107	98	..	—1	..
			Eastern	98	125	104	+3	+17	+6
London and south-east	114	+7	London and south-east	90	99	93	—5	—9	—5
			Southern	101	139	109	+6	+31	+11
South-west	110	+3	South-western	98	127	104	+3	+19	+6
Wales	98	—9	Wales	94	177	105	—1	+69	+7
Great Britain	107	..	Great Britain	95	108	98	..	..	..

1932–7, with the changes in insured *males* between 1939 and 1947, that the pre-war spatial redistribution of the labour force was stopped and even reversed after the war: the northern region, which had declined by 7 per cent. in the five years 1932–7, actually increased by 2 per cent. between 1939 and 1947; and Wales, which had declined by 9 per cent., fell by only 1 per cent. There were also considerable changes resulting from the war-time evacuations from London and the south-east, and from the post-war Greater London Plan, which provided for decentralization of population and industry for strategic reasons; but these represented rather a redistribution of labour within the former, more prosperous, midlands, south-east, and south-west of the country. The full effects of the government's policy are seen most clearly in the changes in female insured population between 1939 and 1947: in the northern area, which had declined so rapidly before the war, the female insured population expanded by 38 per cent.; and in Wales, where it had declined even faster, the female insured population expanded by 69 per cent. The facts of the situation are best seen in the following table relating to the total labour force.

Unemployment Rates and Redistribution of the Total Labour Force 1939–47

	% Net redistribu- tion 1932–7	% Unemployment			% Net redistribu- tion 1939–47
		July 1937	Dec. 1946	Dec. 1947	
Scotland .	−4	14·5	5	3	+1
Northern .	−7	16·2	5	3	+7
North-western	−7	13·0	3	2	−3
Wales . .	−9	21·3	7½	5½	+7
Great Britain .	..	10·1	2½	2	..

Apart from the north-west region, which was only partially affected by the programmes for the Development Areas, we see clearly that, while the pre-war areas remained relatively depressed (in the midst of country-wide over-full employment) they actually gained workers relatively to the rest of the country. It is important, however, to note that the new employment opportunities were given mainly to the female populations of these areas. There was no real migration of labour into the areas.

While changes in the distribution of the insured population before the war reflected fairly faithfully the direction of geographical movements of the whole population, changes in the total insured population between 1939 and 1947 represent rather the changes in the proportion of the female population, aged 14–69, in insured employment within the various regions. For the whole population this proportion increased from 26 per cent. in 1937 to 29 per cent. in 1947; but this was due mainly to a very sharp increase inside the Development Areas which, before the war, had been much more dependent on industries employing men than were the more prosperous regions.

In order to examine changes in the geographical distribution of the population we have prepared Table 3, comparing the net redistribution in the eight-year period 1939–47 with that in the earlier eight-year period 1931–9.

TABLE 3

Changes in the Distribution of Population 1931–47 (in thousands)

Area	Popula-tion 1931	Popula-tion 1939	Popula-tion 1947	% Net redistribution		
				1931–9	1939–47	1931–47
United Kingdom Population (Figures in parenthesis = % Net Migration)						
England and Wales	39,952	41,460	43,050	+0·1 (+1·4)	+0·1 (+0·5)	+0·2 (+1·9)
Scotland	4,843	5,007	5,139	−0·3 (−0·7)	−1·1 (−1·0)	−1·4 (−1·7)
N. Ireland	1,243	1,295	1,350	+0·4 (−0·4)	+0·6 (−2·5)	+1·0 (−2·9)
United Kingdom	46,038	47,762	49,538	.. (+1·1)	.. (+0·3)	.. (+1·4)
England and Wales—Civilian Population*						
Northern	3,041	2,990	3,009	−4·9	−0·7	−5·7
North-western	6,185	6,199	6,223	−3·0	−0·9	−4·0
E. and W. Ridings	3,920	3,950	3,971	−2·5	−0·8	−3·3
N. Midland	2,958	3,077	3,210	+0·8	+3·0	+3·9
Midland	3,742	3,990	4,218	+3·4	+4·4	+8·1
Eastern	2,433	2,741	2,878	+9·5	+3·7	+13·7
London and south-eastern	10,329	10,757	10,499	+0·9	−3·7	−2·9
Greater London	8,204	8,375	8,090	−1·2	−4·7	−6·0
Rest of south-east	2,125	2,382	2,409	+9·1	−0·2	+8·8
Southern	2,135	2,339	2,433	+6·4	+2·7	+9·4
South-western	2,615	2,718	2,848	+0·7	+3·5	+4·4
Wales	2,594	2,486	2,501	−7·3	−0·7	−8·2
England and Wales	39,952	41,246	41,786	..	..	..

* Figures for 1931 include armed forces.

This table shows plainly that, despite the policy of bringing employ-ment to the Development Areas, the movement of population has con-tinued to be away from them. War-time developments and post-war government policy have, however, succeeded in greatly reducing the scale of the redistribution. Apart from Scotland, where outward movement between 1939 and 1947 exceeded that between 1931 and 1939, the net redistribution fell from an average of 5 per cent. for the three depressed areas covered by the northern, north-western, and Wales divisions to an average of only 0·8 per cent. By far the greater part of the net redistribu-tion away from these areas in the sixteen years was achieved during the first eight years, 1931–9. Within the more prosperous central and southern part of the country, there has been the considerable movement away from the Greater London area into the other regions remarked on earlier.

To summarize our conclusions regarding mobility of the British labour force after the war, hardly any real inter-industrial mobility was required to meet the needs of the immediate post-war structure of the economy, and government policy has automatically limited spatial mobility by using all available controls to locate industry wherever any surplus of labour appeared. The economy has been directed on the basis of an existing geographical distribution of population, and a 'public works' attitude has been taken in locating new capacity—placing it in those areas where female labour is most plentiful (which happen to be those where family incomes were lowest before the war due to the low proportion of females in employment). In considering this policy, one may well ask what has been the economic cost to the economy of locating industry primarily on the basis of available labour. Was it economically desirable, when in the midlands, for example, there was a shortage of female workers, indicated by an unemployment percentage of $\frac{1}{2}$ per cent., and in Wales there was female unemployment of 9 per cent., to provide new facilities in the less prosperous areas, to strive, by persuasion, to increase the proportion of the population in employment in the more prosperous area, and even to import foreign labour to meet local shortages? What would be the consequences of a serious fall in the demand for male labour in the basic industries in the Development Areas? Admittedly, family incomes might be sustained by the fact that there was now much greater scope for female employment, but would the men be satisfied if their wives and daughters were working while they were unemployed? Would they be more or less disposed to migrate with their families to a more prosperous area? Would it be government policy to build still more industries in depressed areas, to absorb unemployed male workers, regardless of economic cost? Or would it favour the migration of whole families although this would indicate that recent investment in Development Areas had been misdirected?

Re-introduction of Labour Controls[1]

The failure of government policy to achieve the necessary expansion of employment in the most important sectors of the economy had been admitted even while the controls on labour were being eliminated. A White Paper analysed the man-power position in January 1947 and called attention to the widespread shortage as well as to the serious under-manning of some important industries such as coal-mining, agriculture, tinplate and sheet steel, building materials, iron foundries, textiles, clothing, footwear, furniture, paper and printing, and laundries. It emphasized the need for expanding exports and increasing production. A White Paper of February 1947 further emphasized the importance of securing the correct distribution of the labour force, and pointed out that the existing distribution, by industries and by places, was not satisfactory. But the policy of progressively removing controls nevertheless continued.

[1] The reader should bear in mind that this chapter was written at the end of 1949.

On 6 August, however, the government finally took action to meet the obviously serious situation: the Prime Minister stated in the House of Commons that it would be necessary to ensure the direction of effort into channels where it would be most fruitful. It would be necessary to take some measure of control over the employment of labour, and a control over the engagement of labour would therefore be reimposed. But, since this would control only the movements of those falling out of work, it might be necessary to limit employment on less essential work. Further-more, in order to prevent workers remaining unemployed or taking unessential work, the use of powers of direction would be resumed to a limited extent. However, he was careful to add, this would not be a resumption of the general powers of direction but an essential supporting measure to enable the control of engagement to be exercised effectively. This speech was followed by a new Control of Engagement Order which channelled recruitment of labour (men aged 18 to 50, and women aged 18 to 40) through the Ministry of Labour as during the war, and by the resumption of the use of the power to direct persons seeking fresh employ-ment, including direction into work other than their 'normal' occupation, or to essential work in other districts provided 'suitable' accommodation was available. On paper at any rate, these supporting measures were much fiercer than those the Prime Minister's speech appeared to portend, especially when a new Registration for Employment Order on 11 Novem-ber 1947 gave power to the Minister of Labour to require men aged 18 to 50 and woman aged 18 to 40 to register particulars about themselves, presumably as a preliminary to direction. Thus, in the second half of 1947 the allocation of labour by a combination of dampened economic incentives with exhortation and publicity, which had clearly failed to work, was abandoned in favour of the compulsory system evolved during the war.

In practice, however, use of the new controls has been very cautious. Juveniles under the age of 18, the most mobile class of workers, may enter any occupation, as can women with children under 15 years old and most men and women discharged from the forces (Class A); and local offices of the Ministry of Labour may issue permits for workers to obtain work by their own efforts. The number of workers actually directed has been very small; between 6 October 1947 and the end of 1948 only 535 directions were issued, of which 506 were to prevent men leaving coal-mining or agri-culture under the old powers. Thus, the total working population actually decreased slightly between June 1947 and June 1948, and it was only because of a reduction in the size of the armed forces from 1·29 million to 0·85 million that a 2 per cent. increase in the total in civil employment was obtained. And the rise in the labour forces of some of the important under-manned sectors was: agriculture and fishing, 3·3 per cent.;

coal-mining, 1·2 per cent.; tinplate, 2·0 per cent.; textiles, 6·7 per cent.; clothing, −4·9 per cent.; and building and civil engineering, 2·3 per cent. The controls did not result in any marked improvement in the distribution of the labour force industrially.

There is a very distinct obstacle to use of the controls in that they have, as Mr. Harrod has pointed out, 'to be administered with some gentleness, equitably among claimants, often on the basis of prior usage . . . to secure mobility by coercion is not part of the order of the day'.[1] For, it is manifestly inequitable that it should be the freshly unemployed man who is directed to the area or industry to which labour will not go voluntarily, and to attempt to select individuals for direction from the total labour force (employed and unemployed) would be an impossible task, since it would dislocate existing production and arouse great resistance in the ranks of labour. In fact, it soon becomes clear that the average working man will, so long as he has the free vote, never endorse planning if it involves any appreciable direction of labour from job to job and from area to area, particularly if at the same time the industries and areas which are under-manned are in that condition just because they are unattractive economically, and, owing to other controls, cannot raise prices and offer higher wages. Thus the government is in the strange position of having planned economic incentives out of existence and of having set up in their place the powers to distribute the available labour according to plan, without being prepared, in practice, to employ those powers because of the adverse political effects of such action. Fortunately, since the general post-war economic situation has so far resulted in practically full employment, and has not involved any very radical changes in the structure of British industry, the existence of other means of control over production has meant that effects of deficiencies in the government's labour policy have been confined to lack of additional labour for certain under-manned sectors of the economy, and they have not had many far-reaching effects.

5. The Problems Ahead

It is essential to realize that Britain has been fortunate in several important respects. First, the country concentrated so heavily on war production that it has been possible, after the war, to achieve considerable flexibility merely by restricting the recovery of non-essential production. Second, the great increase in the number of females in employment during the war has lent additional flexibility to the labour force. Third, post-war demand at home and abroad, and the prostration of Germany and Japan, have been such as to ensure full employment and at the same time keep the traditional British industries—those such as coal-mining, iron and

[1] *Soundings*, Sept. 1949, p. 7.

steel production, shipbuilding and ship repairing, and tinplate manufacture, which were depressed before the war—more than fully occupied.
Fourth, sad as it is, the need for much larger armed forces and higher
levels of munitions production than before the war has intensified labour
shortages and spread post-war readjustments over a longer period. All
these, and other factors, have simplified the post-war labour problem and
narrowed it down to finding sufficient labour for certain under-manned
sectors.

The country now faces, however, an altogether new stage in its post-war
history. Germany and Japan are now in process of enlarging production
and export, while restocking and investment programmes all over the
world are now entering a declining phase. E.R.P. assistance from the
United States will now taper off, and it is necessary to achieve a balance
of payments by 1952 under much more difficult conditions than existed
before the war. The working population has already begun to decline:
the Ministry of Labour expects a fall of 550,000 between 1946 and
1951, 370,000 of which is due to the raising of the school-leaving age.
World-wide currency revaluation commenced with the devaluations of
September 1949, and there may be many repercussions before stable relationships are established. Thus, fundamental changes may have to be made
in the British economy in the not-too-distant future. Already, warning
signs have appeared in the shipbuilding industry. Is the government's
labour policy adequate to meet these and the longer-range problems mentioned earlier ?

Economic incentives in the labour market are largely inoperative. The
basic reason is that food prices and rents have been set at artificially
low levels and the working population is led to believe that it can enjoy
a standard of living higher than the nation can in fact sustain, even with
American aid. The only way the illusion can be maintained is to restrict
production and importation for the home market, relying on a strict
rationing system to equate supply and demand for items whose prices
are set artificially low, and on 'rationing by the purse' for items such as
clothing, *new* houses, amusements, and luxuries, which sell at high prices.
Furthermore, heavy investment and welfare programmes require very
high levels of taxation ; income tax is extremely high for marginal income
while indirect taxes weigh heavily on the very items whose distribution
is left to free markets. The result is an apparently high money-wage in
terms of rationed items and rent, which yields a substantial surplus even
after income tax and necessaries have been provided for ; weekly earnings
were 90 per cent. higher in October 1946 than before the war, compared with
a cost of living only 31 per cent. above pre-war. However, this surplus can
only be spent on very expensive goods and services or saved at artificially

low interest rates. Incentives for non-working members of families to join the labour force are therefore very weak and, since wages are not often linked to individual performance, there is more incentive for those in work to 'just get by' than to put forth maximum effort. Thus, because acquisition of the most desirable goods is largely divorced from effort, and the scale of effort required to obtain the less desirable goods is made so great, the effort put forth by the nation rests, not on economic incentives, but mainly on exhortation and agreed 'norms' of output.

Within this system there are few incentives for individual workers to enter under-manned industries or areas. Because of the government's policy of stabilizing wages so as not to aggravate the suppressed inflation, and the labour unions' conception of a 'fair' pattern of industrial wages, which means changes must be in all wages or none, it is rarely possible to raise wages to attract workers to an industry. Geographical movements are hampered by the idea that wages should be the same for the same work in all areas, and, perhaps more important, by the policy of creating employment in any area where surplus man-power appears. Furthermore, the existence of practically full employment has removed the impelling force of unemployment. And as newly unemployed persons now have greater reserves, receive higher rates of benefit than before the war, have many advantages deriving from the enlarged welfare programmes, are eligible for benefits for the maximum length of time, can buy rations at low prices and pay controlled rents, the stimulus of unemployment is now much less, even when it exists, than it was before the war. Finally, as we have already seen, the labour controls are, because of political considerations, used very sparingly. Under present conditions, therefore, the desire of the individual worker for stability and security, on which we have remarked earlier, seems to have been realized completely, but only at the expense of nearly all rational allocation of labour.

Above and beyond all this, we must ask whether, in fact, the whole structure of artificial prices, wages, and profits now ruling as a consequence of the complex structure of allocations, building permits, taxes, and hidden subsidies, could in any case produce economic incentives that would really point to economically desirable change; the answer is obviously that in the present state of affairs the full force of free consumer demand centres on those sectors not subject to control and usually points to the most undesirable economic change. The government is constantly having to plug leaks by additional taxes (e.g. the tax on betting) or more rigid controls (e.g. direction of street-traders in London to other employment). Symptomatic is the extent of gambling and entertainment of all kinds in an economy outwardly dedicated to 'austerity'. To sum up, such economic incentives as do exist are very weak, or, when strong, they are usually undesirable and promptly weakened by government intervention; the government is committed to the operation of an economy without normal economic incentives and markets—a form of planned economy. And a pertinent question is how the government, under these conditions, can decide that a particular industry is under-manned on any basis which satisfies the requirement that the real net economic contribution of an additional worker in that industry to the national income exceeds that of an additional worker in any other industry. I am inclined to believe that consumers' wants are largely ignored or distorted in making such decisions and that any basic economic coefficients which may be used in making them are subject to very great errors.

This system may work under the conditions which have ruled for the four years after the end of the war but can it work in the future? If any decline occurred in home and overseas demand for metals and engineering products, investment goods generally, and perhaps coal, and therefore reduction was required in the size of industries producing them, what would be the consequences? Following present policies, investment programmes would be initiated in those areas in which unemployment was threatened. But in what directions would such investment programmes be developed? Without meaningful economic indicators it would be extremely difficult to choose; one obvious possibility would be housing and public works to meet an assured demand at home. But if quite large investment programmes were required, how would they be financed? Could a serious fall in exports or rise in imports be avoided whatever the form of the investment chosen? And if not, how could imports be adjusted downwards in such a way as to avoid curtailing other production and creating even greater surpluses of labour? By cutting still further imports of food and consumption goods for the home market? And how would the labour market be organized under such conditions? Would not many workers choose to live on reserves and unemployment benefits at least for a considerable period? Would masses of workers be directed into new occupations at wage rates perhaps lower than they had received in their old occupation? And what of the capacity which has already been built up in the Development Areas to use female labour? Is it really economic? Can it continue to operate under future conditions without subsidies of one kind or another? Will the government not be in the position of throwing more and more resources into preventing the natural economic decline of such areas? How long will the savings in housing and public utilities in the more favoured areas, into which population would normally have migrated, continue to outweigh the economic cost of locating industry in Development Areas if housing and public-works programmes eventually become necessary in the latter areas themselves?

It is important that, in facing the difficult problems ahead, Britain should bear in mind certain hard economic facts. Man has always had to adapt himself to his changing environment or pay a heavy price, and this holds true for the British economy in the changing modern world. It can be planned on the basis of security and stability in the job for the individual worker; but this will involve more economic controls, hidden subsidies and levies, hidden differential exchange rates, and so on, all of which will cost something in terms of economic efficiency as well as administrative machinery. Furthermore, the standard of living will be made more uncertain, since fundamental economic adjustments to external forces will be postponed rather than expedited. Security in the job is undoubtedly a luxury, and like most luxuries has its own high price. The alternative is—at the expense of some sacrifice in the security and stability of the individual worker—to foster by all possible means the maximum mobility of labour and resources, in the hope that optimum adjustments to outside forces can be made so fast that normal technological progress will ensure a constantly rising standard of living for the whole nation, despite occasional set-backs when external conditions take too unfavourable a turn.

The issue should not be clouded by assuming that greater mobility and freer markets mean abandoning 'social security'. Almost no one to-day denies the social justice of assisting the destitute, the sick, and the maimed from State funds, providing National Health and Unemployment Insurance and Old-Age Pensions (so long as they do not require large State subventions), and operating many other so-called 'welfare' programmes. Many, I think, would favour extension of these programmes, as the standard of living rises, to cover an even larger proportion of man's elementary needs. Where differences of opinion arise is in deciding when and where such programmes begin to distort the working of the economic system to an extent such that economic cost exceeds social gain. And economic cost rises very rapidly when 'welfare' extends to protection of the individual against changing his occupation and place of work. Much depends, I believe, on the standard of living out of which the economic cost must be paid. The United States, with a very high standard of living, could afford to give up considerable wealth to assure its citizens a life sheltered from major economic upheavals and social hazards, and still not substantially distort the overall development of its economy. In countries less favoured the economic cost, being so large in relation to the national income, soon reaches levels that seriously imperil the efficient operation of the economy.

It is a remarkable fact, however, that it is in the United States that the workers and unions display extreme willingness to co-operate in maximizing productivity by all possible means, in accepting decisions of the market, and in moving freely between industries and areas. In Britain, where such flexibility is imperative if the standard of living is to be safeguarded, labour and government, in their zeal to shield the worker from negative incentives, seem to have succeeded in eliminating the positive ones also. The result is an economy of few incentives, and therefore of low mobility, with the danger that stern realities will be overlooked or ignored on the grounds of humanitarianism—just as if, for instance, out of concern for a convalescent, he were to be provided with a wheel-chair for the rest of his life in order that he might be spared the pain and effort of learning to walk on his injured limbs again. The fundamental problem is *how much* future national income the average man would willingly sacrifice for personal security and stability. Few realize even that such a sacrifice must be and is being made in Britain to-day; even fewer realize the exact extent of the sacrifices made to secure the welfare programmes and immobility of labour thus far established. Will the mass of the population ultimately comprehend the choice that has been made? And is allergy to economic risk-taking now so highly developed in the British nation that the choice, if comprehended, would be approved?

INDEX OF AUTHORS CITED

PRINTED IN
GREAT BRITAIN
AT THE
UNIVERSITY PRESS
OXFORD
BY
CHARLES BATEY
PRINTER
TO THE
UNIVERSITY